RYAN ELLETT AND KEVIN COFFEY

The Texas Rangers: Two Decades on Radio, Film, Television, and Stage

Ryan Ellett and Kevin Coffey

2014

The Texas Rangers:
Two Decades on Radio, Film, Television, and Stage
By Ryan Ellett and Kevin Coffey
© 2014, BearManor Media All Rights Reserved.
No part of this book may be reproduced in any form or by any means, electronic, mechanical, digital, photocopying or recording, except for the inclusion in a review, without permission in writing from the publisher.

Published in the USA by:
BearManor Media
P O Box 71426
Albany, Georgia 31708
www.bearmanormedia.com

ISBN: 978-1-59393-589-4
Printed in the United States of America
Book design by Robbie Adkins

Acknowledgements

Research on the history of the Texas Rangers was pioneered by country music historian Glenn White in the 1960s. This book incorporates his research which was never formally published. Beginning in the mid-1990s, Kevin Coffey sought to expand upon White's research, but there remained huge gaps in this neglected group's history when he and Ryan Ellett began collaborating in 2011. Ellett began researching the band's history independently, and it was through the good fortune of communications with Chuck Anderson, webmaster of the premier internet site www.b-westerns.com, that he and Coffey were introduced and began to work jointly on a Texas Rangers book.

Band members Herb Kratoska, William "Bill" Lorentz, and Gomer Cool all left first-hand accounts of their time with the band, Cool's being the most extensive. Steve Cool, son of Gomer Cool, and Ed and Jim Crawford, sons of Robert Crawford, added their memories of the Texas Rangers. Melody Waters, daughter of Ozie Waters who performed with the band in the early 1930s, added her memories.

This book would not have been possible without the rich archival material available on the Texas Rangers located at Iowa State University and the University of Missouri-Kansas City. Their special collections staffs, headed by Tanya Zanish-Belcher (Iowa State University) and Stuart Hinds (University of Missouri-Kansas City), were invaluable in enabling access to the historical material. Their patience during the perusal of thousands of pages of documents was admirable. Marva Felchlin and Karla Buhlman, similarly, were exceedingly helpful in providing information from Gene Autry's archival collection.

Glenn White also graciously allowed access to his groundbreaking research into the group and his archive of recordings. A number of others, notably Michael Feldt, Steve Muckala, Donnie Pitchford, Jeremy Prichard, Randy Riddle, and Karl Schadow, all contributed pictures, recordings, written sources, and general research suggestions through the course of this project. Martin Grams, Jr., provided specific information noted within the text.

Jack French, editor of *Radio Recall*, and Bob Burchett, editor of *The Old Radio Times*, both published small portions of themes covered in this book, and those articles aided in the clarification and enhancement of some findings presented herein. Some of the material was reviewed at the 6th Annual Great Plains Radio History Symposium, Kansas State University. Thanks to Dr. J. Steve Smethers, Associate Director for Graduate Studies and Research, organizer of the symposium, as well as attendees who made helpful comments about some of our conclusions. Some content was also presented at the 2011 Cincinnati Old-Time Radio and Nostalgia Convention where valuable feedback was received.

A few individuals indicated a preference not to be mentioned for their assistance, but our thanks is noted here. There are, surely, others who have contributed to this book who are not included here. Their omission is inadvertent, but their help is still greatly appreciated.

Introduction

Western cowboys entered the popular imagination in the late 19th century as the Golden Age of the West was coming to an end. The dime novel exploits of heroes such as Buffalo Bill and outlaws like Deadeye Dick thrilled millions of readers. The cowboy took on various roles, most often as a lone dispenser of justice and righter of wrongs, but sometimes as legitimate lawman. At other times, he was a detective and sometimes an Indian fighter. The popularity of Buffalo Bill Cody's Wild West shows in the late 1800s also put the cowboy in the role of entertainer, whether with rope tricks, fancy horse riding, or sharp shooting. In fact, the cowboys of popular fiction, ironically, seemed to do "everything except caring for cattle" as Jules Verne Allen noted in his 1933 volume *Cowboy Lore*, an account of his time working as a cowboy during the era's demise in the 1890s.[1] This observation was echoed by Douglas Green in his comprehensive review of the singing cowboy entertainment genre. He noted, "it is fascinating to reflect how few of these men are shown actually tending cattle."[2]

It is within the last of these roles, assumed by fictional cowboys as entertainer, that the singing cowboy evolved. The cowboy of popular culture is a nebulous figure, one that is difficult to define and categorize. All of the types of men mentioned above qualify as cowboys to the average man on the street, and all of them are based, at least nominally, on historical fact. The cowboy singer, as unrealistic as he may seem on the surface, can also claim roots in the authentic cowboy traditions as an heir to the singing tradition of the old-time cattle herders. While not nearly as strong a tradition when compared to the connection between spiritual music and the former slaves who were contemporaries of cowboys, and sometimes were cowboys themselves, the evidence suggests that singing was not uncommon among these Western laborers.

Charles Siringo wrote what is considered the first authentic cowboy biography, *Texas Cowboy*, 1885, about his years working

---
1 Allen, p. 4.
2 Green, p. 12.

the range during the 1870s and early 1880s. In it he mentions how they would handle restless steers with "melodious songs which kept them quieted." He indicated the singing was not a regular occurrence but only necessary when conditions were right to agitate the cattle.[1] Exactly what songs these men sang is unknown, but Charley Hester remembers singing "The Old Chisholm Trail," "When You're Throwed," and "Sam Bass" during his days as a cowboy in the 1870s.[2] The songs of the range were varied and far more than traditional western tunes, as illustrated by former cowboy Edgar Bronson's memory of a song contest with a drunken co-passenger on a lonely stagecoach. Bronson's repertoire included hymns such as "Shall We Gather at the River" and "A Charge to Keep I Have," as well as some "operatic airs and comic songs."[3] In addition to traditional trail tunes, hymns, popular arias, and gag tunes, historian Peter Stanfield finds references to folk and minstrel songs in the cowboy's library.[4]

While the authentic range cowboys disappeared by the end of the 19th century their popularity in Western stories only grew and became increasingly disassociated from the realities of the cowboy life. The continued interest in Western figures perhaps led inevitably to marketing of cowboy songs to the general public via a variety of song books for home performance. In the early years of the 20th century numerous such cowboy songbooks were published including "Songs of the Cowboy" (1908) by Jack Thorpe, "Songs of the Western Cowboy" (1909) by G. F. Will, and "Cowboy Songs and Other Frontier Ballads" (1910) by John Lomax. This same John Lomax would go on to make many famous field recordings during the Great Depression. Tin Pan Alley, always alert to a potential hit song, cranked out countless numbers written in a traditional cowboy style. The general public, with little knowledge of authentic and historical trail tunes, loved them and was not concerned that they were cranked out by struggling musicians in gritty New York City and not dust wranglers on horse back. Because so many of these early tunes were written in a traditional style and promoted as old-time tunes,

---

1 Siringo, p. 59, 81.
2 Hester, p. 18, 27, 76-77.
3 Bronson, p. 119-120.
4 Stanfield, p. 49-52.

with dubious author recognition, it quickly becomes difficult to tell which may have been authentic verses sung by cowboys and which are later nostalgic tributes to a by-gone era.

This rise of the popular cowboy at the turn of the century neatly overlaps the rise of the motion picture industry; indeed, these two iconic American symbols, cowboys and cinema, would each be very different today without the other. Jon Tuska in his massive history *The Filming of the West* identifies Western movies dating back to 1898, though the first with an actual story is the legendary *Great Train Robbery* (Edison Manufacturing Company, 1903). During the early 1900s the cowboy figure was a hit in silent motion pictures as well, the genre accounting for up to twenty percent of films by the end of the century's first decade.

Alongside their popularity in movies, the new record industry discovered there was good money to be made producing cowboy records. Ironically, according to Greene, the first traditional cowboy song was not released on record until 1919, all prior recordings having been newly penned tunes in what was considered a traditional style. This 1919 record featured the songs "Jesse James" and "The Dying Cowboy" performed by Bentley Ball.[1]

During the 1920s Western music, the broad umbrella under which cowboy songs were placed, was popularized on yet another new medium: radio. Green points out that songs of the West were lumped together with hillbilly (country), string bands, gospel and barbershop quartets and aired to rural audiences all over the country. The music mix was so popular that variety shows featuring performers across the genres sprang up in nearly every metropolitan area across the country. None are more legendary and well remembered than the *National Barn Dance*, broadcast on WLS out of Chicago beginning on April 19, 1924, and the *Grand Ole Opry*, debuting on Nashville's WSM on November 28, 1925. These programs would serve as training grounds for many singing cowboys; one of the most famous, Gene Autry, appeared on WLS' *National Barn Dance* in the early 1930s.

By the end of the 1920s, singing cowboys and western-themed groups were popping up all over. Records documenting radio's first decade are rare, so the vast majority of these groups have been lost to history. Carson Robison began singing cowboy songs over Kansas

---

1 Green, p. 17.

City's WDAF in 1922 and went on to a long songwriting, recording and performing career, much of it Western in focus. Based in New York City for much of his career, he also made several successful and influential trips to the United Kingdom. One of the earliest, most successful Western bands was the pioneering Otto Gray's Oklahoma Cowboys who got their start under the leadership of Billy McGinty. McGinty was a former Teddy Roosevelt Rough Rider and real Oklahoma cowboy, whose start on radio in Oklahoma served as a springboard to groundbreaking national touring and recording stardom. Jules Verne Allen was another early radio singer of cowboy tunes and a former real working cowboy. He also produced a volume on cowboy lore and left some of the best recordings of traditional cowboy tunes. Luther Ossenbrink, the "Arkansas Woodchopper," was on the air by 1928 over KMBC in Kansas City. The Ranch Boys were an attraction on Los Angeles' KHJ radio as early as 1929. A later incarnation, led by original member Jack Ross, became one of the most important of pre-World War Two western vocal groups after relocating to Chicago in 1934. Following quickly on the original Ranch Boys was the highly influential Beverly Hill Billies, a western-flavored vocal group that hit the L.A. airwaves (on KMPC) in the spring of 1930. They engendered something of a national trend with their immediate and phenomenal success. Although their trappings were more quasi-"mountain" than cowboy, their impact on western music was great and their success, coupled with the earlier precedent of the Oklahoma Cowboys, set the stage for much of what followed. In 1933, the biggest western group of them all, the Sons of the Pioneers, formed in Los Angeles where they got a start on KFWB. Such bands multiplied over the next decade and could be found on stations of every size in rural and urban markets.

It was into this exploding music field that Arthur Church ventured in the early 1930s. Owner of KMBC, Kansas City's CBS affiliate, Church had placed numerous Western-cowboy singers in front of his microphones. In 1932, he put together the Texas Rangers, a group made up entirely of staff musicians and owned by the station's parent Midland Broadcasting Company. KMBC's most prominent early group was the Massey Family, some of whose members also played in early versions of the Texas Rangers. Products of real ranch life in Texas and New Mexico, the Massey's image exploited that heritage while their music both embraced and transcended it. They incorporated jazz and pop music alongside the cowboy music and fiddle traditions passed down through their father and others. When the Massey's left for greener pastures in Chicago, Church positioned the Texas Rangers as the station's chief exponents of Western music.

The Rangers' membership experienced many changes over its long history, but the classic lineup from the mid-1930s to the early 1940s centered upon a vocal quartet whose roots extended back to their late 1920s college days and who originally performed at KMBC in a non-western role as the Midwesterners. The quartet was initially made up of Bob Crawford (baritone), Duane Swalley (lead tenor, replaced by Fran Mahaney in 1935), Rod May (2nd tenor), and Edward Cronenbold (bass). The quartet was accompanied by four musicians Gomer Cool (fiddle), Herb Kratoska (guitar and banjo), Paul Sells (accordion), and Clarence Hartman (bass).

Over more than two decades, from 1932 to the mid-1950s, the Texas Rangers made a mark in nearly every entertainment medium of the era, most prominently on radio. They were also in ten western films, commercial recordings, hundreds of transcription recordings for radio, and then television.

The popularity of singing cowboys and western groups peaked before World War II and went into steady decline afterwards. Country music, having shed the "hillbilly" moniker, was the new music of choice for the former Western audience. Nevertheless, there continued to be Western hits through the 1940s, most notably Roy Rogers and the aforementioned Sons of the Pioneers. Like many performers in the singing cowboy genre, the Texas Rangers never regained their pre-War fame as the 1940s wound down. Public interest had turned to other musical styles and the Sons of the Pioneers sufficed to entertain those still interested in Western and cowboy songs. There was a bit of a revival in the 1950s spurred by Walt Disney's *Davy Crockett* television series, but the *Crockett* sensation proved to be a fad, and the cowboy and Western scene fell back off the general public's radar.

Just as identifying the first singing cowboy is a dubious task, so is choosing the last of the singing cowboys. Historian and revivalist singing cowboy Douglas Green argues that Marty Robbins deserves that title with his Western songs and film singing roles that were prominent through the late 1950s and even endured into the 1960s. Robbins recognized that pure Western would not make a career, so he delved into other country and pop genres. Of course, Western and cowboy tunes never disappeared completely, but it has survived as a niche musical branch with a small but devoted following.

By Robbins' time the Texas Rangers had dispersed, each man going his own way, never to perform together again. Because the vast majority of the Rangers' music had been available only to radio stations and not to the record-buying public, the band quickly fell out of the public memory, and they have since been little more than a footnote in the history of Western music. For two decades the group entertained listeners across the country. They lifted fans' spirits through the Great Depression and World War II, then kept those spirits high during the early years of the post-war economic boom. The Texas Rangers left a far greater legacy, both purely musical and in relation to their importance as exponents of western music on radio and in film, than they have so far received. This is their story.

Table of Contents

Acknowledgements iii
Introduction. v
Chapter 1: Before the Texas Rangers, ... 1
Chapter 2: Enter: The Texas Rangers 11
Chapter 3: Expanding Into Drama. 39
Chapter 4: Kings of Kansas City Radio 61
Chapter 5: Hollywood. 87
Chapter 6: Sponsored Nationwide 125
Chapter 7: The Camel Caravan Tour 159
Chapter 8: The War Years and Beyond 181
Chapter 9: The Texas Rangers on Television. 207
Chapter 10: Fade Away. 231
Appendix A - Recording Sessions 1934 to 1953 253
Appendix B - *Life on the Red Horse Ranch*, Guide to
    Episodes 1-65 289
Appendix C - *Under Western Skies* Station List. 312
Appendix D - Filmography. 313
Appendix E - Early Radio Appearances. 322
Bibliography 324
About the Authors. 334

Chapter 1: Before the Texas Rangers

Radio is Born

Radio broadcasting, the medium by which the Texas Rangers would gain much of their fame, was still a relatively new commercial endeavor in 1932 when the band's first lineup was formed. The exploration of what would become radio technology stretched back to the late 1800s and included such scientific minds as Heinrich Hertz, Nicola Tesla, and William Crookes. It is Guglielmo Marconi, however, who is widely acknowledged as the father of radio. His wireless telegraphy research led to primitive transmissions in Morse code by 1895 and the formation of the Wireless Telegraph and Signal Company, Ltd. in 1897. Eleven years later in December, 1906, Reginald Fessenden made what Alfred Balk called the "first planned and announced transmission of music and speech," in a nod to claims for earlier, but unproven, voice broadcasts by other radio pioneers.

The first decade of the twentieth century witnessed a surge of interest in this new technology, which allowed individuals to communicate over increasingly long distances with little more than a homemade unit and some wire strung up in the air. Unfortunately, while the number of amateur radio users proliferated, oversight of the airwaves continued to be virtually nonexistent, leading to a Wild West environment in which radio operators broadcast over each other and blatantly interrupted and disrupted commercial communications.

Up until 1912 radio operators, whether professional or amateur, were not required to be licensed in any way before getting on the air. This changed with Congress' passage of the Radio Act of 1912 which created a licensing process by which individuals could prove their skill and receive a call sign along with the privilege to broadcast. Just two years later in 1914 the Amateur Radio Relay League (ARRL) was formed for amateur operators and it continues to be the largest such organization.

Though voice and music transmissions were possible by the 1910s, they were rare and Morse code continued to be the language of the medium. Stations resembling the music and talk outlets which predominate today were still years off. Nevertheless, it was into this primitive but burgeoning world of radio that Arthur Church, then a high school student in Lamoni, Iowa, found what would be his lifelong passion.

Arthur Church

The man ultimately responsible for bringing the Texas Rangers musical group into existence was Arthur Burdette Church, who was born with little fanfare in the tiny town of Lamoni, Iowa, on August 5, 1896. Lamoni's founding preceded Church's birth by only 17 years, having been platted in 1879. Joseph Smith III, son of the founder of the Latter Day Saints, or Mormons, built his home in Lamoni in 1881, and the town would come to have a strong Mormon influence including the religiously affiliated Graceland College. Arthur was the son of Charles F. Church who ran the Lamoni Gin-Seal Gardens, a business which sold ginseng and golden seal.

At the age of 17 or 18 Church discovered radio while enrolled in a senior high school physics course. In 1914 he built his first radio, described as "an old 'stone crusher' rotary spark gap," which he used for amateur radio operations. Using homemade equipment was the norm for amateur radio operators at the time; commercially built radio units would not appear on the market until after the end of World War I. For an antennae Church strung a wire from the gable of his family's barn to a pole in the nearby pasture. This primitive radio set, in his bedroom, was connected to "a maze of wires, condensers, and dials." Within a year, Church had made connections with other amateurs in the region and had begun selling radio parts while using his homemade rig to spread word of his business. Little did Arthur know at the time that he would make a life-long career of radio, a career which ultimately spanned across five decades.

Around 1915 Church was granted his first radio license, 9WU. Soon after, he began operating 9YO, Graceland College's station where he was a student, with two fellow amateurs. During the summer of that year Church enrolled in the Dodge's Institute of Wireless at Valparaiso, Indiana. Originally founded to train telegraphers, the school had added coursework on radio as the technology grew in popularity. His goal was to earn his First Grade, or Commercial operator's license, which he did a year later. His radio business continued even as he prepared for school.

Dodge Telegraph and Radio Institute.
Courtesy of Michael Feldt.

While informing his friend Ralph Batcher of his plans to attend Dodge's, he asked if Batcher could place an advertisement for him in the June issue of the *Hawkeye Bulletin*, a publication for Iowa amateur operators. Church had received the rights to sell a unit produced by the Mignon Wireless Corporation of Elmira, NY. Their new piece of equipment had set the long distance receiving record for the Lackawanna Railroad and was priced at $8. Mignon was founded just the year before, in 1914, and later became a part of Universal Radio Manufacturing Company. After his summer in Valparaiso, Church announced that he planned to attend the Iowa State College of Agricultural and Mechanic Arts (now Iowa State University) in Ames, Iowa, beginning in the fall of 1916.

Radio and World War I

Though a disaster for millions, the first World War proved to be a boon for the young radio industry. In the years leading up to the United States' entry in the war, developments in the field had slowed and become enmeshed in a tangle of complicated patent claims and lawsuits. Despite the passage of the Radio Act of 1912, which was meant to bring order to the airwaves, men such as Marconi, Lee De Forest, and Edwin Armstrong battled each other in court. Their ongoing legal skirmishes prevented basic advancements from being shared among competing interests and slowed the overall growth of radio's commercial prospects.

Recognizing the military potential of wireless communication, especially between naval ships and their land-based counterparts, President Woodrow Wilson gave the U.S. Navy authority over all commercial and amateur broadcasting stations with the exception of those under the supervision of the U.S. Army Signal Corp. Little concerned about patent wranglings, the Navy declared that all applicable technologies and inventions would be utilized to produce war goods. Holders of the various intellectual properties could apply for restitution after the war. From the resulting government contracts, industrial luminaries such as Western Electric, General Electric, and Westinghouse staked their place in what would be a post-war radio boom.

These high level government and industrial machinations were far from Church's quiet life, but the European conflict eventually reached him, even in Iowa. After a year of studies at Iowa State College, he left in 1917 to participate in the war effort by training draft eligible men in radio using his station in Lamoni in conjunction with both the government and Graceland College. The next year Church officially enlisted in the army on July 4, 1918, with the goal of working with radio. Not quite ready to forsake everything for the benefit of Uncle Sam, and before his enlistment became official, Arthur married Cicely Ida Case, the Tahitian-born daughter of missionaries for the Reorganized Church of Latter Day Saints.

On September 1, 1918, Major R. E. McGuillin assigned Church the rank of Sergeant in the Army Signal Corps at Fort Leavenworth, Kansas. There he designed a radio instruction course for non-commissioned officers. Four months later on January 1, 1919, Church was appointed Sergeant, First Class of the Signal Corps at Franklin Cantonments, Camp Meade, Maryland. With the Armistice signed on November 11, 1918, and World War I coming to an end, Church's time in the army proved to be short lived. He worked at Camp Meade's electrical and radio lab until, due to demobilization, he received his papers for honorable discharge. The papers were signed January 27, 1919, by Major William Perdee at Camp Dodge, Iowa.

Acclimating quickly to civilian life after his short stint in the army, Church got back into the radio business as soon as he could. During the winter of 1919-1920 he sold equipment as a licensed agent for Lee DeForest, one of biggest names in early wireless technology. Among his sales as DeForest's Midwestern representative was the first "factory-built radio telephone transmitter" intended for use at Nebraska Wesleyan University in Lincoln, Nebraska. At the same time, recognizing that radio might not provide a steady income for his young family, Church went back to school long enough to earn his teaching degree.

During 1920 Church was back in Lamoni operating 9YO at 1 kilowatt for Graceland College with a Technical and Training School class license. Dr. Frederick M. Smith, head of the Reorganized Church of Jesus Christ of Latter Day Saints, asked Church to come to Independence, MO, to build a station for the church. The result was station 9AXJ, a special amateur class station Church built as part of his newly founded Central Radio School. At the same time Ray Moler and Kenneth Krahl, later employees of Church's Kansas City station KMBC, were running 9AVK in Holden, MO. The two stations, 9YO and 9AVK, created a rudimentary "network," regularly sharing messages. The Central Radio Company placed an ad in the November, 1920, *Wireless Age* magazine describing itself as "the largest and best radio supply house in the central states. A complete stock of all leading makes assures prompt shipments. Exclusive central states agent for A. H. Grebe & Co." The same ad described the Central Radio School as "the best radio school in the central west. Modern, complete equipment. Special licensed radio station. Experienced instructors trained to teach. Low tuition rates and living expenses. Both radio-telegraph and radiophone courses. Our school only nine miles from Kansas City. Enroll any time. New classes formed first Monday of each month."

Beginning a radio school was a natural step for a radio enthusiast like Church, who had only recently received his education credentials. At the age of 23 Arthur relocated to Kansas City, Missouri, where he established the Central Radio Company alongside his Central Radio School at 575 Grand Avenue, Kansas City. 9ZH, Church's first commercial-grade transmitter, though he was still classified as holding a special amateur license, went on the air April 21, 1921. Thus, was born the station which would eventually become Kansas City's CBS radio outlet, KMBC.

Church's 9ZH was just one of countless stations going on the air in the post-War airwaves gold rush. Six months earlier KDKA (originally 8ZZ) in Pittsburgh, PA, had broadcast the November 2, 1920, presidential election results between Republican Warren G. Harding and his Democratic rival James M. Cox. While other stations, as opposed to individual operators, have been identified as the first radio station i.e., Detroit's 8MK (later WWJ), the University of Wisconsin's 9XM, and Charles Herrold's station in California, KDKA is now widely recognized as laying legitimate claim to the distinction.

A written account of the contents of Church's primitive broadcasts to Kansas City listeners has not survived, so now the broadcasts can be surmised based only on what other stations were airing. Religious services, sports accounts, and amateur music performances filled the few daily hours when the era's stations went on the air. The station also likely ran commercials for his radio school and store. Commercially manufactured radio units were still not the norm at the time; most listeners bought their own parts and used plans from a wireless magazine to construct their own.

After a period of experimental broadcasting, Church was finally authorized to air with the call letters WPE as of April 4, 1923. By this time Kansas City was being served by a number of stations, notably WHB and WDAF. The latter was owned and operated by the *Kansas City Star*, one of the city's major newspapers, and now the only one. WDAF was officially licensed as of May 16, 1922, but had been in operation prior to that, primarily airing local musical talent. In January of 1924, Arthur Church's call letters were changed from WPE to KFIX, but the station continued to operate as a limited commercial station, the classification assigned to it while still WPE.

Three and one half years later on June 29, 1927, the letters were changed, again, to KLDS to emphasize the Reformed Latter Day Saints Church's connection.

The radio industry was well on its way to becoming an immensely profitable enterprise in the United States. Business and technological barriers had been sufficiently passed so that on September 9, 1926, the National Broadcasting Company (NBC) was birthed out of a series of complicated corporate moves by such giants as AT&T, General Electric, and most prominently, the Radio Corporation of America (RCA). Though based out of distant New York, the new network impacted Arthur Church when rival WDAF signed on as Kansas City's NBC outlet, one of the network's 22 stations covering the Midwest and East coast. NBC's gala premier on November 15, 1926, included performances by no less than the New York Symphony, humorist Will Rogers, and dance band leader Vincent Lopez. Stations competing with NBC affiliates were put on notice that it would be an uphill struggle to match the network's star power. Rather than roll over for WDAF and its backers, NBC, and the *Kansas City Star*, Church and the staff of his young station rolled up their sleeves and worked even harder to build a profitable broadcasting business.

At this point in time, the station's programming still originated from primitive studios and a transmitter located at Stone Church in Independence, MO, just east of Kansas City. During these early years Church took on more than just the management tasks, which would consume most of his time after the station was more firmly established. He was never too proud to take on any task that needed done. In addition to handling many of the station's business matters, Church took an active hand in constructing the transmitter, worked as the program director, did some singing, and handled some operating tasks as well. Church even pitched in when needed for announcing duties, identifying himself simply as ABC.

Federal regulations increased so much in 1927 and 1928 that it became clear to those running KLDS that it could only continue as a commercial venture and not as a split amateur/commercial operation. To facilitate the transition, Church organized the Midland Broadcasting Company in June, 1927, and the group took over operation of the station from the KLDS Broadcasting Company. The new company requested the call letters KMBC on August 18,

OUR SCHEDULE

The Sears, Roebuck and Co., Farm and Home programs from Kansas City are presented through KMBC, the Midland Broadcast Central, operating on a frequency of 950 kilocycles (315.6 meters) by authority of the Federal Radio Commission. They are especially planned to be of helpful service and entertainment value to all friends of the World's Largest Store in the Kansas City territory. The schedule follows:

6:30– 7:00 A.M.—Early musical program. (Wednesday).

10:00–10:30 A.M.—Weather Forecast. Homemakers' program.

12:10– 1:00 P.M.—Dinnerbell program. Weather forecast; poultry and egg quotations; Journal-Post Town Crier; Producers Commission Association livestock comments; entertainment features.

1:00– 1:10 P.M.—U. S. Department of Agriculture feature or visiting speaker.

8:00– 8:30 P.M.—Allstate tire program. (Saturday).

8:30– 9:00 P.M.—Silvertone Little Theatre. (Saturday).

9:00–10:00 P.M.—National Radio Forum of C.B.S. (Saturday).

10:00–11:00 P.M.—Barn Dance and Variety. (Saturday).

Visit Our Studios. You are cordially invited to visit our Retail Department Store at 15th and Cleveland, to see our programs broadcast. Most of our friends visit the Bungalow Studio during our day-time programs and on Saturday nights between 6:30 and 7:00 or 7:30 and 8:00 when special features are presented for the visible audience, only. Visitors are also welcome at the Aladdin Hotel Studio of KMBC, 1211 Wyandotte St. KMBC is the Kansas City outlet of the Columbia Broadcasting System.

Our Farm Features. Daily at 1:00 o'clock, we broadcast up-to-the-minute farm facts from the United States Department of Agriculture or messages from farm leaders and "dirt farmers." We cooperate with constructive agricultural institutions.

Home Service. Our home advisor is a practical housewife and mother, presenting helpful and entertaining daily features for all homemakers. Doctors and other authorities are our guest speakers. Hear "George and Mary Gabby" each Tuesday morning and our home plays on Thursdays.

Boys and Girls. Every Saturday noon the Junior R.F.D. Club meets and thousands of KMBC boys and girls listen. Any boy or girl of 18 years of age or under may enroll and receive a membership button. Older folks enjoy this program too.

Entertainment. Our regular staff and visiting entertainers present a variety of songs and music of the type most popularly requested by our radio friends. Special dinnerbell programs include the Waterwitch half-hour on Mondays; mid-week barn dance on Wednesdays, Supertone musical instrument program on Thursdays and our farm implement and equipment program on Fridays, featuring "Doings of the Duffy's."

Write Us. Our programs are mainly improved by your comments and suggestions. Our artists broadcast to please you. We welcome your letters and cards.

Do you know that Sears, Roebuck and Co. pays the postage on every article listed in our new Spring and Summer Catalog that can be conveniently sent by parcel post? If you do not have our new General Catalog in your home, we will promptly mail one to you. Just write a card or letter to Dept. 144-A, Sears, Roebuck and Co., Kansas City, Mo. It will mean substantial savings to you.

Schedule from KMBC's days at the Aladdin Hotel.
Courtesy of Ryan Ellett.

1927, a reference to their company initials. The requested assignment was granted to the station for commercial use on September 16. The letters KLDS would continue to be used when the station was on the air for church use, which contractually could not exceed seven hours per week. Soon after, KMBC officials departed Independence and chose as their first broadcasting facility the top floor of Kansas City's Aladdin Hotel.

The Aladdin Hotel was new when KMBC set up offices on its sixteenth floor, having just opened its doors in 1925. The Italian Romanesque-styled building hosted marquee sports and Hollywood stars during its heyday, as well as mobsters and mistresses of local politicians. Now on the National Register of Historic Places, the Aladdin was remodeled in the early 21st century and continues to operate as an upscale hotel to this day.

The year 1928 would prove to be a momentous one for Arthur Church and KMBC in the long run. Early that year, the fledgling Columbia Broadcasting System (CBS) signed the upstart KMBC station to serve as its Kansas City outlet, the network's westernmost outpost. Founded just the year before, in 1927, the Columbia Phonograph Broadcasting System, Inc., was a marriage of two businesses which were facing very uncertain futures, the Columbia Phonograph Association and the United Independent Broadcasters Association. Despite the network's rocky prospects, Church may have sensed, even at this early time, that radio's future for the foreseeable future lay with the network concept, that his station would never have the resources to challenge WDAF and the talent it drew upon with its NBC affiliation.

The Midland Broadcasting Company was incorporated on October 27, 1928, and officially bought the station from the Reformed Latter Day Saints church for $36,750.40 on November 10. The bill of sale included the aerial towers located on the Stone Church in Independence, the contents of the radio studio, and all other equipment which made up the broadcasting station. On November 14, the state of Missouri granted the company's Articles of Incorporation. Upon the station's reorganization, Church became both vice-president and general manager. Around this same time William S. Paley purchased a 41% interest in CBS and family members bought enough additional stock to give them a majority interest in the network.

Building from the performing talent pool available in the city, and using the CBS network's coast-to-coast capabilities to reach new audiences, Arthur Church experimented with various entertainment acts. He was especially interested in country-western performers, searching for the right musical mix which would click with radio listeners. By 1932, just four years after KMBC's founding, Church's vision led to the creation of the Texas Rangers, a band which eventually would be considered the most successful of his stable of artists. They would thrive for more than two decades, entertaining listeners through the Great Depression, World War II, and the early post-war era into the 1950s.

Chapter 2:
Enter: The Texas Rangers

The Birth of Network Radio

While the nation slid into deep economic depression after the stock market crash of 1929, radio was one of the few industries that continued to be profitable and even thrive. Founded in 1926, just three years before the crash, the National Broadcasting Company reported a profit of over $2 million in 1930. The network's continued growth in the face of prolonged economic woes culminated with the opening of the 70-story RCA building, "a monument to the importance of radio in American life" according to its promoters, and centerpiece of Rockefeller Center. However, the good times were not restricted to NBC. Money poured into the industry at such a rate that the radio trade was responsible for $100 million in revenue by 1935; not bad for a commercial enterprise which was barely fifteen years old. Fully one-third of American households had at least one radio by 1932, and that number was growing rapidly, so in another fifteen years, nine out of ten homes would have at least one radio.

The growth of the major networks, NBC (both the Red and Blue Networks) and CBS, led to the consolidation of program origination, primarily in Chicago and New York. These metropolitan areas were blessed with the talent pools to sustain the extensive dramatic, comic, and musical productions necessary to fill air time, as well as the sizable business communities needed to provide financial sponsorship for the broadcasts.

Though the live entertainment of vaudeville had been in decline for some time, the 1930 closing of the Palace in New York, the pinnacle of the industry, ensured a plentiful supply of performers hungry for their next paycheck. The influx of stage talent with the collapse of vaudeville during the earliest years of the 1930s helped reverse the decline in listenership as the *Amos 'n' Andy* craze subsided in 1931. Theater headliners such as Eddie Cantor, Al Jolson, and Jack Benny all transitioned to the airwaves during the earliest years of the 1930s drawing huge numbers of listeners back to radio, though the performers themselves experienced varying degrees of sustained success in the medium.

Whether on stage or on the air, however, top talent had to be paid. While countless unemployed stood in the breadlines of Chicago and New York, the nation's largest companies budgeted millions of dollars to attach their product names to the emerging medium. Even in the tough economic climate of the early 1930s, businesses were willing to pay for the opportunity to sell their products over the air. In the words of eminent radio historian Jim Cox, "network radio proffered the ability to access the majority of the country with single announcements on the same day and, perceptually, in a more personal way."

With the great number of entertainers and businessmen in these two cities hungry to cash in on radio, most all of the top-rated radio shows during the beginning of the 1930s originated from one of the two. Chicago was home to the most famous program of all, *Amos 'n' Andy*, while *The Eddie Cantor Show*, *Rise of the Goldbergs*, *The Atwater Kent Hour*, and Rudy Vallee's *Fleischmann's Yeast Hour* all aired from New York.

Arthur Church, by the early 1930s in charge of day-to-day operations at Kansas City's KMBC, was not content to let these two cities solidify their hold on the broadcasting industry without a fight. While Church may or may not have thought that Kansas City could truly establish itself on equal footing with New York and Chicago in creating original material for the air, he was confident the city could be a player in the burgeoning industry. His station produced more original programming than most similar mid-size stations, which were content to run the network material, spin music records, and perhaps on occasion, turn over the microphone to some local singers.

Eschewing the network's full slate of offerings was a gamble for Church. Stations contracted with a network averaged just over $200,000 on income per year by 1935 compared to approximately $37,000 in revenue for independent stations. Audiences preferred network shows, and the money followed accordingly.

The risk on Church's part was two-fold, involving investments of cash and time. The cost of creating original radio material, which required writers, performers, sound men, and directors, could be significant. Quality talent cost good money, and smaller regional outlets such as KMBC could scarcely offer salaries comparable to those stations in the largest cities. Arthur Church was familiar with these financial dynamics, watching a number of home-grown stars such as Goodman Ace, Hugh Studebaker and Ted Malone eventually move on to network positions.

At the same time KMBC was investing substantial funds into its own original broadcasts, the station was investing its time, a precious commodity for any enterprise. Every broadcast hour of original material was one less hour available to air more network fare, thus running the risk of losing listeners interested in the nationally-known entertainers.

Much of the material developed in-house by KMBC had a rural focus to appeal to the large number of listeners beyond urban Kansas City's boundaries. In his insightful review of the most famous rural radio comedy of the time, *Lum & Abner*, Randal Hall notes that country-focused programming was proliferating on the airwaves during the early 1930s; Arthur Church and KMBC were certainly not forging a lonely new path in radio content. Even by 1932, at which time KMBC's *Happy Hollow* had been airing for three years, a *Variety* writer noted wearily of the program *The Real Folks of Thompkins Corners*, "This is another one of the long, long list of rural and country-town serials." *Happy Hollow* was one of KMBC's earliest original productions, a sketch comedy which highlighted rural tunes and humor. The series was on the air as early as June, 1929, and ran as a quarter-hour daily feature for seven years until 1936. It was carried over the CBS chain on various occasions, most notably between May 13, 1935, and October 9, 1936. One of the series' most popular characters was story-teller "Uncle Ezra" played by Everett Kemp, who portrayed the old bumpkin philosopher on different KMBC programs for close to two decades.

Though Kemp is not known to have worked on any Texas Rangers radio material, several other characters from KMBC's flagship show were played by individuals who would at some point be associated with the band. Ozie Waters, more widely remembered for his post-KMBC film work and records, and Eddie Edwards, one of the station's blackface comedians, were a popular duo on *Happy Hollow* and both performed with the Rangers between 1932 and 1935. Rube character Doug Butternut was played by Gomer Cool, one of the key members of the Texas Rangers. Several members of the Masseys, a musical family group, also had parts on the show.

Other early featured rural acts on KMBC would have long performing careers beyond Church's station. Among these was the "Arkansas Woodchopper," Luther Ossenbrink. The Ozark native was a singer, guitarist, and fiddler whose stay in Kansas City was short, perhaps not more than a year or two. Ossenbrink, often called "Arkie" for short, moved on to Chicago's WLS by 1930 where he was featured for many years on the station's *National Barn Dance* and was even voted one of the station's three most popular performers in 1938.

No less well-known were the Masseys, who also went by The Massey Family, The Musical Masseys, and most popularly, The Westerners. The group eventually included leader singer Louise Massey, her brothers Curt and Allen Massey, Louise's husband Milt Mabie, and Larry Wellington. They got their start playing small local events in the Hondo Valley of New Mexico in the 1920s, including broadcasts over a small local station which by 1932 had gone off the air. In 1928 they were persuaded by an agent with the Redpath Lyceum Bureau booking company to join the professional Chautauqua circuit. This lasted perhaps a year or two when, upon their father's advice, the band decided to get off the road and settle down with a radio station. Their first broadcasting work was with WIBW in Topeka, KS. Looking to expand his country offerings, KMBC's Arthur Church offered them staff positions, probably in 1929 and at the dawn of the Great Depression, the Masseys signed with KMBC.

While honing their broadcasting skills in Kansas City, the Masseys adopted first the name The Musical Masseys and later The Westerners (or more often Louise Massey & the Westerners), the latter moniker being the one by which they would be known until 1947 when they broke up. The Westerners departed KMBC by the end of 1933 (discussed in more detail below) and, like The Arkansas Woodchopper, landed on Chicago's WLS, a major station drawing rural listeners over the breadth of the Midwest and somewhat beyond. Radio, motion pictures and recordings cemented the Masseys as one of the most notable Western bands of the 1930s and 1940s. The long-term success of both the Westerners and the Arkansas

Woodchopper attest to Arthur Church's eye for spotting talented hillbilly acts.[1]

Birth of the Texas Rangers

"Hillbilly", Western music, and rural-flavored programming in general had been an important part of the mix at KMBC from at least the late '20s, when sometime in 1932 Arthur Church decided to put together a Western musical program which was dubbed the Texas Rangers. Although Gomer Cool, the last surviving Texas Ranger would maintain over 75 years later, that from the beginning Church had adopted the eight piece format, a singing quartet backed by four instrumentalists, that would characterize the group throughout its heyday, evidence strongly suggests that the first edition of the band consisted of only five performers.

This evidence includes Texas Rangers radio scripts dating from November, 1932, to January, 1933, the first of which, dated November 1, is the oldest extant piece of Texas Rangers documentation thus far uncovered and will be described in more detail later. These scripts range from that November 1 document through January 19, 1933. Twenty-eight exist, and they regularly reference five characters: Tex, Cookie, Old Timer, Al Massey, and Tenderfoot.

Also extant is a photograph of four clean-cut cowboys lounging around a prop campfire while a fifth man in black face and a cook's outfit looks on. Though undated in archival materials, the photo was located with documents from 1933-1934 and was used in the July, 1933, issue of *The Happy Hollow Bugle*, labeled with the same five names as those appearing in the 1932-33 programs listed above. Gomer Cool's later memory not withstanding, there is little doubt that the original KMBC Texas Rangers program featured only five performers and the classic octet lineup developed some months later.

The specific identities of the original five Rangers can be pinned down with relative confidence. Al, or Allen, Massey is named explicitly. He was well-established at the station as a member of the Musical Masseys and other staff groups, and had his own daily ten-minute spot

---

1 The Massey Family, like many country-western musicians of the era, are still awaiting a thorough and authoritative treatment by scholars of the genre. The background used in the chapter comes from Cusic, p. 41-43, Young & Nancy Young, p. 153, Wolff, p. 83-84, KMBC material, and www.hillbilly-music.com. Information about Luther "Arkansas Woodchopper" Ossenbrink comes from Porterfield, p. 39, and and www.hillbilly-music.com.

from 12:35 to 12:45 in the weeks preceding the debut of the Texas Rangers in November, 1932. Fiddler Gomer Cool confirmed that Massey played with the Rangers for a time early in their history.

"Tex" is unquestionably Tex Owens who spent much of the 1930s at KMBC performing both as a solo act and with the Texas Rangers. Owens was broadcasting at least by 1931 using the nickname "The Texas Ranger." That he was using this name before Church formed a larger group out of KMBC staff would contribute to later controversy, both among chroniclers of the band and within the band itself, over whether Owens was or was not technically a member of the band.

"Cookie" is almost certainly Eddie Edwards who also played a blackface character named George Washington White on various KMBC programs including *Happy Hollow*. Supporting this contention is the memory of Melody Waters, daughter of Ozie "the Ozark Rambler" Waters, who played with the Rangers between 1933 and 1934. She recalled Ozie talking about working with Edwards on *Happy Hollow*, a memory confirmed by KMBC documents. Similarly, Gomer Cool concurred that Edwards did perform with the Rangers at times. Most crucially, Edwards is among those listed on the recording contract for the Texas Rangers' 1935 *Life on the Red Horse Ranch* transcribed radio series, a program which featured the blackface character "Cookie." Before getting into radio, Missourian Eddie Edwards toured with the Fanchon and Marco vaudeville act and only later found his way to broadcasting via a Honolulu, Hawaii station. Edwards also had sound effects responsibilities for some station programming in addition to his acting and musical parts.[1]

The duo work of Edwards and Waters is sketchy and little known outside of a handful of documentary references and a very few reminisces of family and co-workers. A slim chance exists, however, that audio samples of their routines may yet surface. In early 1932, the pair made a series of about twenty recordings which were sold around the Kansas City metropolitan area, recordings which would provide considerable insight to this popular KMBC performing team but which are not known to survive.

The "Old Timer" character was popular KMBC personality Hugh Studebaker, although Gomer Cool would later suggest that he was portrayed by Bob Crawford. However, it seems clear through

---

1 Background on Ozie Waters provided by Melody Waters.

available evidence that Crawford, who as "Captain Bob" would later become the on-stage leader and the musical heart of the Rangers, did not join the group until later in 1933. At that time, Arthur Church brought in all four members of the station's Midwesterners Quartet, of which Crawford was a charter member.

The July, 1933, issue of KMBC's *Happy Hollow Bugle* reported that Studebaker had recently left the station for freelance work in Chicago, the center of Midwestern broadcasting. Like many of the station's employees, Studebaker had handled a variety of chores including writing, acting, and singing. The station's tribute to Studebaker mentioned his work in these different capacities including portraying the "Old Timer" with the Texas Rangers. One of his other most notable acting credits in Kansas City was that of the lead role of Jerry Powers on the KMBC-produced *Phenomenon*, a 1931-1932 serial which followed Powers on his time-traveling adventures. The series would later be revived for a 65-episode run on transcription records in 1937 with Frederick MacKaye assuming the part of Powers.

Studebaker also acted on the station's *Armchair Jaunts* program and was known as the Sanz-Man for some broadcasts. His writing credits included *Dream Boat*, another local production. As a musician, he served as organist for Ted Malone's *Between the Bookends*, a program of poetry readings that proved so popular that it was eventually broadcast on the CBS network for many years. Most pertinent in this study of the Texas Rangers was his long association with *Happy Hollow*, KMBC's flagship rural variety show on which Studebaker played the character Harry Checkervest. It is likely through his work on this program that he got to know the other musicians of the future Texas Rangers and became involved in the original version of the band as the Old-Timer.

"Tenderfoot" was the name used by Gomer Cool during his years with the band, so it seems natural to assume any appearance of the character involved Cool. Yet in a 1962 letter to historian Glenn White, Rangers guitarist Herb Kratoska would claim that the band's original fiddler was staff violinist Sam Leichter. Cool disputed this assertion, though he did recall that Leichter took his place for a while during an illness. Leichter would later briefly replace Cool again when the latter left the band for good in 1942. Since Kratoska was not among the original five performers on the program, and the surviving photo mentioned above appears to show Cool in the role of Tenderfoot, Cool's memory appears to be correct here.

The lineup of the Rangers seems to have remained static through their initial network run that ended in February, 1933 (see below for discussion of their early broadcast schedule), but things were far from static when they returned to their own regular broadcasts in May of that year. The May, 1933, issue of KMBC's listener publication *Happy Hollow Bugle* ran the photograph of the five original cast members described above and announced that Duke Wellington and Milt Mabie had recently joined the Texas Rangers, but not in time to be included in the photo. Duke Wellington was Larry Wellington, staff accordionist and a non-family member of the Massey group. He would leave the Masseys for Chicago a few months later. Bass player Milt Mabie was Louise Massey's husband and also played with the Musical Masseys. The following issue of the *Bugle* informed readers that Marion Fonville, a station announcer who also had two programs of his own, played Alabam with the group.

There would be further changes as spring gave way to summer, and it is clear that the "original" Texas Rangers, as founding member Gomer Cool thought of them, an octet with four singers and four instrumentalists, did not evolve until almost a year after the initial Texas Rangers broadcasts. Cool's insistence that these early versions of what would soon become the classic eight-man Rangers lineup were not *really* the Texas Rangers is unsupportable given all the other evidence to the contrary; nevertheless, it is very telling, attesting to the indelible impact that the octet had once it became firmly established in the fall of 1933.

Regardless of Cool's insistence many years after the fact, that such performers as Eddie Edwards, Allen and Dott Massey, Milt Mabie, Ozie Waters, and even longtime associate Tex Owens, who, after all, was later billed as the Original Texas Ranger, should not be recognized as official members of the Texas Rangers, there is no question they were featured on the show during 1932-33.

The Rangers debuted on CBS' coast-to-coast network beginning Tuesday November 1, 1932, with a 1:00 slot in the afternoon from their KMBC headquarters. It is possible that Ranger broadcasts in some form preceded this, but no evidence survives to indicate this was the case. Listeners at the time had a variety of programming options from which to choose, though musical performances still made up a considerable amount of prime-time broadcast time. Long-running and fondly remembered drama shows, such as *Vic and Sade*, *Little Orphan Annie*, and *Chandu the Magician*, were all beginning to leave their marks on the airwaves, but it was comedians who commanded the largest audiences in the era. Eddie Cantor, Jack Pearl, and Ed Wynn, former vaudevillians who made the transition to radio, held the top spots in the ratings during the 1932-33 season when the Texas Rangers made their debut. George Burns and Gracie Allen and Amos and Andy were already attracting large audiences, and still would be, eighteen years later in 1950 when the Rangers finally left the air for good. However, it was music, especially easy listening orchestras, who filled much air time. Vincent Lopez, Ben Bernie, Nelson Eddy, and Guy Lombardo personified the "potted palm" music of the day, while bands led by Cab Calloway, Don Redman, and Chick Webb lit up the radio for late night listeners. Interspersed between the big name bands were countless nameless sopranos, tenors, pianists, organists, banjo pickers, duos, trios, and quartets who filled endless hours of airtime.

The November 1, 1932, broadcast, the first known using the Texas Rangers name, was primarily a musical show with no dramatic sketches, a format Rangers programs would, for the most part, use throughout the band's existence. The debut opened with the strains of Tex Owens' signature tune, "Cattle Call." After the announcer's enthusiastic exclamation "The Texas Rangers!", the band launched into the show's theme song, "Get Along Little Dogies." The Old Timer, played by Studebaker, provided narration around the songs. He opened:

"Howdy, neighbor -- how-de-do, you-all! Now don't you-all bother to say 'howdy stranger,' because you're going to make yourselves acquainted with the Texas Rangers right now. Hey, boys . . . play some tunes that'll sort of show the folks we've been up to Kansas City selling some steer." This led to renditions of "Arkansas Traveler" and "Missouri Waltz." Tex Owens was introduced and he performed "Texas Ranger." The other songs on the broadcast included "Cowboy Yodel," "Wreck of the '97," "Friends Quarrel," and "Irish Washerwoman."

Only Studebaker as the Old Timer had a speaking part and he closed the broadcast with "And there you are, neighbor – that's about all there's time for. Seems to me those doggies had enough rest, so we'd better tighten up the cinches and get going. Much obliged for wrangling some grub for us. Guess we'll just set Tenderfoot [presumably Gomer Cool, though conceivably Sam Leichter] here on Long Ears and hit leather. But we'll be back soon, to say howdy neighbor."

Finally the unidentified station announcer intoned "The Texas Rangers will be back tomorrow at one o'clock Central Standard Time, shoving off from our Kansas City Studios." There was a final flourish of "Cattle Call" and lastly the solemn sign-off "This is the Columbia Broadcasting System."

CBS affiliates were under no obligation to carry the entire broadcast schedule of the network, so it is impossible to know just how many stations may have carried the Texas Rangers' program. A review of major metropolitan newspapers indicates it was not carried in Chicago, New York, or Los Angeles that day. The network's time on Chicago's WMAQ was used by Jane Addams in a talk about "The United Charities" while New York's WOR aired its own public service piece "Why a Food Budget?" Los Angeles' KHJ chose instead to carry *Carter's Birthday Party*. Interestingly, the Texas Rangers were not even carried over KMBC, their originating station. Instead, Church chose to run the Aunt Jemima musical program broadcast from New York.

This was not entirely unique; for a few years KMBC had been broadcasting programming over CBS which was not simultaneously carried over the Kansas City station. Most of these shows were musical in nature but spanned the breadth of genres, from Hawaiian songs to patter and songs with Ozie Waters and George Washington White, to the Old World routine of the Swiss Yodelers. The Songsmiths, Rhythmaires, and dance bands, such as the Plantation Grill Orchestra and the Terrace Cafe Orchestra, all aired to CBS from the KMBC studios while not being heard locally at the same time.

Los Angeles' KHJ did begin carrying the Texas Rangers show just a few weeks later, however, beginning Tuesday, November 29, at 11:00 in the morning, lining up with a 1:00 broadcast time from Kansas City. The Rangers' quarter-hour was preceded in L.A. by the Madison Ensemble at 10:30 and followed by *Musical Revue* at 11:15 that day. On Thursday they were followed by the American

Museum of Natural History. Their competition included *Words and Music* (KECA), *Magazine of the Air* (KFI), and *Carter's Birthday Party* (KNX). Los Angeles listeners had other western-themed acts to choose from throughout the day including the Texas Outlaws (KFWB), the Hollywood Hill Billies (KFI, KTM), Si and Elmer (KNX), and some unnamed Western artists (KECA). Soon after their debut on KHJ the station settled into carrying them twice a week on Tuesdays and Thursdays. These twice-weekly broadcasts were replaced in Los Angeles beginning January 10, 1933, by singer Adele Nelson. By the end of 1932, reportedly more than 5,000 letters were sent to KMBC studios from listeners between Kansas City and the West Coast approving of the Texas Rangers' broadcasts over CBS. For whatever reason, it appears that KMBC's network programming was sent only over CBS' western spur of stations, thus limiting the band's exposure in more populous eastern areas.

The Texas Rangers' program continued with a twice-per-week schedule through January and February, 1933, but was discontinued during March and April. However, the group made regular appearances on two other KMBC programs during this hiatus: *The Big Brother Club* (aired seven days a week) and *Happy Hollow* (aired Monday through Saturday). Thus, even without their own timeslot the evolving Texas Rangers had plenty of opportunities throughout the week to hone their skills and develop their own sound on the air.

Meanwhile, in addition to his duties with the Rangers, Tex Owens maintained a regular solo broadcasting itinerary with a fifteen-minute show Tuesday, Wednesday, Thursday, Friday, and Saturday mornings at 7:45. This was followed by a program under the sponsorship of Aladdin Lamps at 12:10 Mondays through Fridays for twenty minutes. Owens' broadcast was also carried over KMBC's experimental sister television outlet, W9XAL, during March and April. In later years members of the Texas Rangers would recall appearing on television during this era. While there is yet no documentary evidence to support these claims, it is possible that the Rangers may have performed with Owens on his shows, at least on occasion.

Owens' involvement with the Rangers would turn sour by the end of the 1930s, and the apparent mutual animosity that developed between him and the members of the Rangers continued to color Gomer Cool's memories of Owens even seven decades hence. The fall-out with Owens has tended to obscure his importance to the success of the early Rangers broadcasts. The Rangers would later come to resent Owens' presence and would strive to distance themselves from any suggestion that the "Original Texas Ranger" was actually a member of the group. Nevertheless, Owens was a hugely popular performer on KMBC and would remain so for the rest of the decade, and was clearly an integral part of the early Rangers broadcasts.

Born Doie Hensley Owens in Killeen, Texas in 1892, Owens tried his hand at a number of professions, including real ranch work, prior to embarking on his radio career. His sister Ruby became a popular performer, as well, as Texas Ruby and his daughter Laura Lee (who was for a time married to Rangers guitarist Herb Kratoska) would become a renowned western singer and yodeller. "Cattle Call," which Owens later claimed to have written while watching a snow storm through a window pane in Kansas City (it was set to the melody of an existing tune, "St. Paul Waltz") remains his greatest claim to fame.

After a two-month break without a self-named radio program, the Texas Rangers regained their own spot on the air in May, 1933. In addition to a twice-weekly evening show at 6:00 on Mondays and Wednesdays, the band earned a daily lunch-time twenty-minute broadcast which paired them most days (Thursdays they went on alone) with another KMBC musical act. On Mondays they played with Velma Massey, Wednesdays with Jerry Barrett, (who later enjoyed a career on the West Coast in Western music and films as Curt Barrett) Fridays with the Songssmiths, and Saturdays with the McCarty Girls. Fascinatingly, on Tuesdays they played with the Midwesterners Quartet, the foursome made up of Robert Crawford, Duane Swalley, Edward Cronenbold, and Rod May that would shortly form the heart of the classic Rangers lineup. While the four singers were long thought to have been founding members of the group-and Gomer Cool would maintain until his death that this was the case-these broadcasts, and other documentation, suggest that the vocal quartet had not yet been integrated into the still fluctuating Rangers personnel. The Midwesterners were given further air time with their own quarter-hour show on Tuesdays at 4:30 and then again with Ruth Royal on Wednesdays at 6:45 (later 5:45).

Beyond these radio appearances we know little of the band's activities from February, 1933, when their initial CBS run ended

The Midwesterners Quartet, early 1930s.
Courtesy of Ed Crawford.

The Midwesterners, for an unknown reason, standing around a WHB microphone, early 1930s.
Courtesy of Ed Crawford.

until July 13, 1933, when extant scripts and various written communications indicate an upswing in their work. The historical trail of surviving radio scripts picks up with the broadcast of July 13, 1933, on which five characters are again mentioned, but Tenderfoot is the only familiar one from the 1932 set of scripts. Any lingering ambiguity over Tenderfoot's identity is ended by a surviving November 14, 1933, script. Attached to the script was a memo which clearly identifies Gomer Cool as Tenderfoot. If Sam Leichter had at one time been the group's fiddler, as Herb Kratoska would later claim, he was apparently gone from KMBC by this time.

The other four characters in the July 13 script are Alabam, Marion, Bill, and Milt. Marion and Alabam are the only characters which can be identified for sure; they are both Marion Fonville, whose full name is mentioned in a Rangers radio program dated November 1, 1933. He was closely associated with the Rangers during 1933-35, including appearing on the group's initial Decca recording session in 1934 and playing a starring role in their syndicated series *Life on the Red Horse Ranch* the following year. Like Eddie Edwards above, Fonville is known to have done work with the Texas Rangers, both from Gomer Cool's recollections and because he appears on the cast contract for their 1935 syndicated series *Life on the Red Horse Ranch*. His full name is mentioned in a Rangers radio program dated November 1, 1933.

Born August 7, 1889, Fonville was a native of Tuskegee, Alabama, though he reportedly "receiv[ed] his education for the greater part in Missouri." KMBC's *Happy Hollow Bugle* mentions that his family moved to Mexico, MO, when he was eleven where his father, Col. W. D. Fonville, served as an early leader of the Missouri Military Academy.[1]

After finishing high school, Fonville enrolled at the University of Missouri, Columbia, with the intention of studying to become a mechanical engineer. After a short time there, he accepted a spot with Ralph Dunbar's performing company, thinking it would be a fun summer gig. Fonville enjoyed the work so much he did not bother returning to school and spent the next seven years performing as a singer, actor, pianist, and cornet player in a variety of vaudeville, lyceum, and stock productions. He entered the army during World

---

1 *Kansas City Journal-Post*, January 17, 1932, p. 5b. *Happy Hollow Bugle*, March, 1933, p. 7.

War I and saw action near war's end in the battle of the Argonne. Around 1926 or 1927 Fonville took his first known broadcasting job as chief announcer at KSOO in Sioux City, IA, then spent the next couple years announcing in the San Francisco area over KTAB, KPO, and finally KFRC, the city's CBS outlet.

On October 15, 1932, Fonville arrived at KMBC. Over the next few years he would take on various writing, announcing, and producing duties, including extensive work with the Texas Rangers. Fonville was credited in 1932 with writing the theme song for John Cameron Swayze, KMBC news commentator, who in the 1940s and 1950s, worked on network television news programs on NBC.

In addition to his straightforward duties as announcer on the Rangers program, Fonville portrayed Alabam. In all the surviving scripts between July 13, 1933, and November 13, 1933, Alabam is given the majority of the spoken lines and acts as the show's Master of Ceremonies, introducing the songs and initiating occasional banter with the other Texas Rangers.

Of the remaining two characters mentioned in the July 13 broadcast, the identity of Bill remains a mystery, while Milt, again, refers to Milt Mabie of the Massey Family. By early 1933 Milt was working as head of the KMBC Artists Bureau in addition to performing. His responsibilities as Bureau head included booking station talent to local banquets, shows, and fairs. "Bill" could be almost anyone, though almost certainly refers to a guitarist, since Mabie played bass and Cool the fiddle.

One candidate for this part was the station's Vance McCune, whose first name was William, though he did not generally go by that name professionally. McCune's most prominent role on KMBC was as Willie Botts, a black-faced character on *The Big Brother Club* program. He is noted to have displayed musical talent on the air.

Between September 15 and November 1, 1933, the CBS network scripts provide further evidence of the evolving personnel of the Rangers, as well as the first known references to several who would become long-time members. Alley Massey, a regular during the Rangers first incarnation in 1932-33 is mentioned again on September 15, and brother Dott Massey is mentioned on September 20. Although he had come to KMBC at the end of the 1920s with the rest of the Massey family, Dott had left Kansas City in the fall of 1932 to return to his home in New Mexico. Prior to that, he had had a number of responsibilities at KMBC including playing with the KMBC orchestra, a 12-piece group which featured classical music (he was an accomplished violinist and trumpeter, as well as a skilled vocalist). He had performed on *Happy Hollow* as Stanley Slipshod and then as Brick. He also took a job with the local Pla-Mor Orchestra and eventually became the band's leader. Unfortunately, as he recounted to western music historian Ken Griffis almost fifty years later, it was all too much, and he suffered a physical breakdown that necessitated his leave of absence from KMBC.

After recuperating in New Mexico, he re-joined the Massey Family in Kansas City in the summer of 1933 as they prepared to leave KMBC for WLS in Chicago. Indeed, a September 10, 1933, newspaper blurb from an El Paso, TX, newspaper describes him as already in WLS' employ, and neither he nor Allen appears in a Texas Rangers script again after that program of September 20. WLS' monthly publication *Stand By* confirmed this in 1935: "Dott came to Chicago and WLS with the act in September, 1933." Once in Chicago the band became The Westerners, "one of the most distinctive and popular acts in radio."[1]

The Masseys' involvement, particularly at this transitional period, surely explains why Herb Kratoska would later write to historian Glenn White that, "The original cast of the Texas Rangers…was the Massey Family and Tex Owens -- we formed our group to replace them when they flew the coup for Chicago."[2]

On September 25, 1933, Alabam mentions "Bob" for the first time. This is, of course, Bob Crawford, who would soon emerge as the Rangers' musical driving force. Although the Midwesterners Quartet, of which Crawford was a key member, would join the show around this time or soon after, there is some evidence to indicate that Crawford preceded the rest of the quartet on the Rangers broadcasts. A photo survives of a Tom Mix appearance on the station in September 1933, at which time he appeared with the Rangers. It shows Crawford alongside soon to depart members of the Massey family, including Allen Massey and accordionist Larry Wellington, but no sign of the remaining Midwesterners.

---

1 *Stand By!*, May 18, 1935. *Stand By!* was a weekly publication of Chicago station WLS.
2 Herb Kratoska letter to Glenn White, 1962.

Two days later on September 27, 1933, Alabam introduced the "new Ranger," Ozie. Thus Ozie Waters, a Missouri-born guitarist and singer, began a short stint with the band. Decades later Gomer Cool insisted that Waters was not a member of the Rangers, but he was unquestionably on the broadcasts during this time. It is likely his function was similar to that of Tex Owens, who was absent from the Texas Rangers broadcasts of this period, playing and singing alone without accompaniment of the rest of the group. Waters, who would enjoy a long performing career, was born Vernon Scott Waters on December 8, 1903, in Callaway County, MO, and thus shared geographic roots with many of the Rangers. After enlisting in the navy as a teenager he discovered radio and spent some time at KMBC in the early 1930s. Waters had a varied and successful career as a Western singer on radio, recordings, and in films after leaving KMBC. He would meet up again with his former bandmates in the late 1940s when all of them were in California. He would remain musically active until not long before his death in Colorado in 1979.

On October 18, 1933, three weeks after Ozie's debut, Arizona (guitar and banjo-playing Herbert Kratoska) got his first lines. Interestingly, his lines in the script were originally written for Waters but given to Arizona during a rewrite, as indicated by his name handwritten over the crossed-out Waters. Ozie continued to receive mentions and lines in subsequent scripts, so he had not left the band at that time as the lines substitution may have suggested. This October appearance for Kratoska aligns closely with the first surviving contract he signed with KMBC which was dated August 9, 1933. Kratoska recalled to Glenn White that his service at the station began in 1932, but he could easily have miscalculated the year when looking back 30 years later. He wrote, "I was staff guitarist of some 6 mos. Standing and tried out for the [group]. In fact, the group in tact were all staff members at that time."

Over the next few broadcasts three long-running characters are introduced in quick succession: Monte (played by accordionist Paul Sells) on October 24, Idaho (bassist Carl Hays) on October 25, and Tucson (bass singer Edward "Tookie" Cronenbold) on October 30. By mid-November, the group that Gomer Cool remembered as the true "original" Texas Rangers lineup was firmly established. A list labeled "Characters of Texas Rangers" attached to the script of November 14 lists Slim (Duane Swalley, tenor) and Dave (Rod May, 2nd tenor) in addition to Monte, Idaho, Arizona, Ozie, Bob, Tucson, and Tenderfoot (identified firmly as Gomer Cool by this time). Written under the list of names is the note "Give to Gomer Cool" indicating, perhaps, that he had assumed the job of writing continuity for the Texas Rangers broadcasts, a task which would be one of his primary responsibilities until leaving KMBC in 1942.

The vocal quartet at the heart of the Rangers from the fall of 1933 to the end of the 1940s formed and trained under Paul Craig at Church's alma mater, Graceland College. Tenor Duane Swalley (b. December 5, 1910) and second tenor Samuel Roderick "Rod" May (b. October 1, 1909) were both Iowa natives, while baritone Robert "Bob" Crawford (b. May 13, 1910) had been born in New Mexico before moving to Independence with his family in early childhood. The original fourth singer, British-born Arthur Oakley, rounded out the foursome but did not transition with the band to radio. Upon Oakley's departure, Crawford taught another friend, Edward "Tookie" Cronenbold (b. September 15, 1909), who was born and reared just outside of Kansas City, to sing bass, whereupon he joined the quartet. Arthur Church, an active member of the Reorganized Church of Jesus Christ of Latter Day Saints (RLDS, now known as Community of Christ), preferred hiring other RLDS members at his station if qualified individuals could be found. The Graceland College quartet fit the bill and eventually worked their way onto KMBC as full-time staff.

Graceland had two campuses, the main one in Lemoni, Iowa, the second outside of Kansas City in Independence. By the time the 1930 census was taken in April of that year, all the members of the quartet were living just outside of Independence in Blue Springs, Missouri. None are listed in that census as being employed at KMBC. Swalley, for example, was listed as a baker, while Crawford was listed with no occupation in the household of his parents. They may have been singing in some capacity on KMBC by this time and became full time employees in the coming months. As staff members, they performed under a number of names before being merged into the larger Texas Rangers band. In July, 1932, the foursome is identified as the Happy Hollow Barber Shop Quartet, regulars on the station's

The Happy Hollow Barbershop Quartette (l. to r. Swalley, May, Crawford, Cronenbold), ca. 1931.
Courtesy of Ryan Ellett.

Happy Hollow program. They would occasionally be referred to as the Lamp Post Four, and the Midwesterners, as well.

Of the instrumentalists that accompanied the quartet, little is known about bassist Carl Hays, who was a KMBC staffer and who gave way to the veteran Clarence Hartman (b. September 24, 1890 in Texas) a few months hence. Gomer Cool was an established musician, actor, and writer with KMBC before joining the Rangers. He was a regular on *Happy Hollow*, primarily as Doug Butternut and also half of the station's Danny and Doug singing duo, Danny being Ted Malone. Earlier in their time with the station the duo was known as Buddy and Ruddy. Cool was born April 20, 1908, in Nevada, Missouri, and joined KMBC in 1929. Though a capable violinist, singer, and actor, his ambitions lay in writing, and it was perhaps in that capacity he would have the greatest impact on the Texas Rangers over the next decade.

Accordionist Paul Sells was from Lima, Ohio, where he was born January 20, 1907. He was in Kansas City by 1930, working as a ballroom pianist, possibly at the Pla-Mor Ballroom. A surviving memo from January 19, 1933, indicates at that time he was leading the Pla-Mor Orchestra, a job he had inherited when Dott Massey left it a few months before. The Pla-Mor group had recently finished an engagement at The Tulsa Club, in Tulsa, Oklahoma, and the club's general manager wrote to inform Sells that he predicted the orchestra would "be one of the bright spots in the Musical World." The manager's premonition was accurate, though he surely did not envision Paul's place eventually being with an up-and-coming hillbilly group.

The Rangers youngest member, until the arrival of Fran Mahaney in 1935, was guitarist and banjoist Herb Kratoska, born in Bentley, Iowa, January 6, 1913. His family subsequently moved to Kansas and in 1930 were in Wichita. Herb's virtuosity on both guitar and banjo, and his flair for comedy, would prove one of the Rangers' most distinctive assets over the next decade and a half.

Perhaps the most obvious challenge to the reconstituted Texas Rangers was not maintaining the audience the program had built thus far, but rather, attaining some semblance of an 'authentic' Western sound. While all of the members had some familiarity with cowboy and hillbilly music and some had performed some variety of it (or something akin to it) on KMBC in the past, none of the eight had any particular affinity for or experience with Western music. The Quartet specialized in old pop chestnuts and religious music. Bassist Carl Hays' background is unknown, but Gomer Cool was a trained violinist and had never really done any Western fiddling. Paul Sells was a dance band pianist and Herb Kratoska was a string virtuoso with a taste and feel for jazz. Cool recalled in 2009 that when Church placed him with the Rangers, he immediately set to work learning old fiddle tunes that would fit the group's format and approach; it was almost all new to him. Similarly, he recalled that the Midwesterners Quartet had raided the station's library for any songs with even a hint of western, rural or folk flavor. The learning curve was steep, and there was a lot of woodshedding in the coming weeks and months. In addition, Cool and Crawford would both prove to be fine writers of songs in the romanticized and sophisticated style that had been popularized in recent years by writers like Billy Hill, who wrote the massive 1933 hit "The Last Roundup," and it would soon be elevated to an art form by Bob Nolan and Tim Spencer of the fledgling Sons of the Pioneers in California.

The Texas Rangers proved popular with listeners in Kansas City and beyond, and throughout 1933, the members appeared in a variety of combinations across the KMBC broadcasting schedule. While the Rangers had their own daily timeslot, they continued to be referenced in connection with ongoing series such as *Happy Hollow* (including Saturday night's *Happy Hollow Barn Dance*) and *The Big Brother Club*. Ozie Waters, frequently billed as the Ozark Rambler, and Tex Owens both had multiple solo programs every week.

Ozie Waters ca. 1931.
Courtesy of Ryan Ellett.

The *Happy Hollow Bugle* regaled readers with an account of a visit by the famous Tom Mix to the children's show *The Big Brother Club*, which opened with the following theme song:

The Big Brother Club is on the air,
Eee-i---eee---i--o
With shows and fun beyond compare,
Eee-i---eee---i--o
We drink Aines milk and so should you,
Morning, noon, and night; any time between will do;
The Big Brother Club is on the air.
Come on, gang, let's go!

Marion Fonville appears to have handled some announcing duties for the show and the Texas Rangers, "having donned their best cowboy outfits for the occasion," provided the musical entertainment. Though Gomer Cool very likely performed with the band at this point, he also was responsible for some behind-the-scenes duties as he was credited with "giving last minute instructions to the audience."

The Big Brother Club was a child-oriented feature aired daily from the KMBC studios. It was one of Church's first original productions, debuting in 1930. Though his staff attempted to sell the program to sponsors and networks to grow it beyond Kansas City, efforts fizzled, and the show left the air in 1935. Records from December 10 – 14, 1934, two years after the creation of the Texas Rangers, indicate *The Big Brother Club* had a strong following in Kansas City, in part possibly due to the Rangers' musical contributions. Broadcast in the early evening, a week-long survey taken between 5:30 and 5:45 demonstrated the program's strength.

Its weakest showing was Tuesday, December 11, the only day it commanded less than half the polled listeners with a 40% audience share. Still, this compared to 20% for the next nearest station. On Thursday and Friday of the same week it pulled 53% and 59% of listeners, respectively, and on Wednesday it earned an impressive 67% of the audience. Monday, the first day of the poll, recorded a whopping 92% audience share. Unfortunately there is no data by which to quantifiably measure the effect of the Texas Rangers on the *Big Brother Club*'s eye-catching numbers.

Some of the Rangers continued to play together in alternate combos on various KMBC programs. One of the most popular in the spring of 1934 was *A-G Musical Grocers*, a sketch which incorporated a number of advertised products including MJB Coffee, Aristos Flour, and Silver King Soap Powder. Gomer Cool wrote the scripts and was part of a harmony duo with Paul Henning. Paul Sells played Olaf, the grocery's meat cutter who played some accordion. Herb Kratoska was Elmer Jones, the store's stock boy, who also played humorous songs on the guitar.

On the Road

While radio was the central focus of the Texas Rangers, the band was also booked into theaters around the region, a practice common with KMBC musicians and many radio musicians in general during the era. While KMBC's artists worked on salary, many of the orchestras which aired from popular night clubs were not paid for their broadcasts. The air time was viewed as free publicity, so when playing in the same city for a few weeks bands would sometimes squeeze in radio appearances and even sometimes when they were on the road traveling from city to city.

The money involved in the personal appearances made by the Rangers and other KMBC staff groups was not substantial, but for a smaller station like KMBC any extra income – both for the station and for the performers – would have been welcome, especially as the Depression wore on. Ted Malone, in addition to having his own poetry program, *Between the Bookends*, also served as the station's program director. One of his tasks in this capacity was organizing these live bookings. In July, 1934, Malone negotiated with Oklahoma City's Standard Theatres Corporation for a multi-week booking. KMBC was requesting $600 for any four day stand (Thursday through Sunday) in late summer. Alternately, the Rangers' management offered to take $300 cash plus a 60-40 split of the concert gross, with the band receiving the larger portion. Standard Theatres, on the other hand, pushed for a 50-50 split, though they expressed some concern about other required costs. As negotiations moved forward, Malone had demanded a minimum of ten dollars per day on top of their base expenses, which with an eight-piece outfit, would not have been negligible. This concerned Standard management as Malone had not made clear exactly what the Ranger's expenses would be.

Nevertheless, they felt the group could do quite well in Oklahoma's medium-sized cities due to their radio exposure.

A letter from July 27, 1934, describes some details of the Texas Rangers' stage show. While they did not travel with their own scenery, they did require some for their concerts. Fran Heyser, KMBC's program manager, suggested to Paul Townsend of the Oklahoma City's Liberty Theatre, "a woods set with an open country back drop if possible." Also, they hoped for "a corral fence to be used back stage against the drop, extending into the wings on the left." Ideally it would "be about four feet high and practical, as they boys during some of the numbers will be sitting on it." Further, the Rangers would need "a lighted campfire – a practical tree stump that will be used during banjo solos and Tex Owens' solos." The Rangers had specific stage lighting requirements, too, and used small props, though these were carried by the band.

Not long after the Oklahoma trip, the boys stopped in Wichita, KS, for shows at the Miller Theatre. Exact payment terms are not known, though Miller management offered $450 for a three-day engagement (Sunday through Tuesday) while KMBC was holding out for $520. The difference was $70 for travel expenses between Kansas City and Wichita on top of the necessary $150 per day appearance fee. Malone urged a thorough review of the Rangers' offer since, "Wichita is home town of Rangers comedian Arizona [Herb Kratoska] he is well known on KFH so combination should be of added value to Wichita house."

These tours were sandwiched in between radio performances, some of which were still carried beyond Kansas City on CBS' western stations. *Variety* reviewed the Texas Rangers on July 3, 1934, and their daily (5:15 Central Time) sustaining show picked up by the network. The review was not an enthusiastic endorsement of the band, but positive nonetheless. The reviewer described it as "range songs, music and the wise cracks of the cow punchers around the chuck wagon and in camp," and noted "Dixie-accented" MC Marion Fonville leading the Rangers through their daily paces. The writer managed some faint praise for the group's "nice harmonizing [on] songs of the hills and plains."

Cowboy Radio

During these first two years of the Texas Rangers' existence their workload was primarily radio appearances, both locally on KMBC and nationally on the CBS network, and personal appearances around the region. As Church's new cowboy offering gained experience, confidence, and popularity, he surely could not help but keep a close eye on the competition both nearby and nationally. He likely cast a particularly keen glance up Chicago way, where WLS boasted not only the recently departed Masseys, but also the Prairie Ramblers. Chicago would also soon be the home of the Ranch Boys, who relocated to the city after gaining a foothold in Los Angeles. In Texas, the popular Light Crust Doughboys were riding high and had spawned two groundbreaking Western swing bands, Milton Brown and his Musical Brownies in 1932 and Bob Wills & his Texas Playboys the following year. On the west coast, the Beverly Hill Billies remained popular and influential despite ego clashes and internal strife, and on the other coast, Carson Robison and the quasi-hillbilly Rex Cole Mountaineers held sway. Western music, whether pop-flavored and romanticized or more authentic, was everywhere, and its popularity was set to explode.

With his extensive connections in industry and his ear to the ground, Arthur Church was surely well aware of this groundswell, and that knowledge may, indeed, have been the inspiration to develop an act like the Rangers for his own stable. Nor is it likely that Church was unaware of another WLS performer, Gene Autry, whose phenomenal success on film in the coming months would bring the popularity of Western music to new heights. Autry was an up-and-coming singer who had come to Chicago from Oklahoma. He had gone from strength to strength under the auspices of Brunswick's head of hillbilly and 'race' music Art Satherley, through exposure on WLS' *National Barn Dance*, and his own programs, especially following his massive 1932 hit, "That Silver Haired Daddy of Mine." An act which could capitalize on the same momentum and the growing taste for Western music, Autry's rise underscored what would be a valuable asset to the station, to say the least. Autry's popularity may explain why Church stuck with the format through the many personnel changes of 1932-33 and experimented with a variety of lineups, hoping to find one that might really click with listeners.

Unfortunately, it would be another Western group that coalesced around the same time the Rangers were fumbling toward a stable lineup and semblance of an identifiable sound, who would find national fame and acclaim and would set the standard for Western vocal groups for decades to come: the Sons of the Pioneers. The Rangers would emerge, in the greater scheme of things, not as also-rans, but more as a fascinating footnote. The Pioneers sound, epitomized by a painstakingly rehearsed vocal trio style and cushioned by the instrumental prowess of fiddler Hugh Farr and his guitar playing brother Karl, became the model for other groups that followed in their wake. These included the Riders of the Purple Sage, the Plainsmen, and others, so the Rangers became, despite wide exposure on a national scale, something of an acquired taste. The Rangers' emphasis on a quartet sound rather than the classic trio sound favored by the Sons of the Pioneers and those who followed them, and the fact that their sound, both vocally and instrumentally, was not based on any deeply ingrained feel either for the traditional cowboy and hillbilly repertoire, or for the more recent pop-tinged, Tin Pan Alley manifestation of these, set them apart from the start. The Texas Rangers would sound like no one else, and they adapted the Western repertoire to fit their strengths as much as they adapted to fit the style's characteristics.

The Texas Rangers remained fluid as Arthur Church, and the band itself, found their footing, a style of their own, firmed up on-air routines, and sought wider exposure. While they may not have possessed the intangible qualities that propelled Gene Autry and Sons of the Pioneers to the top, the Rangers were achieving modest regional success with their radio work and personal appearances. Church clearly believed they were capable of far more, so in the coming months he began to feel it was necessary to seek other manner of outlets to give the group's talents a showcase that might propel them to headliner status. Beginning in 1934, he and his Rangers would branch out via two new channels: serial drama and recording. Dramatic broadcasts would supplement and expand on their established song-and-patter broadcasts; recordings would open a more direct route to the music consumer. Fans, both nearby and far beyond the reach of KMBC, could purchase the Rangers' music directly, rather than remain dependent upon the whim of radio stations to air the band. These new directions would, in fact, contribute to much of the Texas Rangers' long-term success.

Chapter 3: Expanding into Drama

Western Adventures on the Air

Seeking performing opportunities beyond KMBC broadcasting and touring the immediate region, the Texas Rangers appeared in what are believed to be their first quasi-dramatic efforts in 1934. Western adventures stories, for decades a staple of dime store books and pulp magazines, and in more recent years of the silver screen, were beginning to gain a foothold on the airwaves. *Death Valley Days* was an early and long-running western anthology program, debuting in 1930 and running in a couple different formats until 1951. *Bobby Benson and the H-Bar-O Rangers* premiered in 1932 and *Lone Wolf Tribe*, focusing on Native American tribes, ran between 1932 and 1933. Of course, the most legendary radio cowboy of them all, the *Lone Ranger*, arrived on radio in 1933 and would go on to success in every entertainment medium. The trend could not have escaped Arthur Church's notice.

With his developing stable of Western performers and an ambitious young writer in Gomer Cool in their midst, it was perhaps inevitable that Church would seek to test the waters of the growing genre of western adventure programming with the Texas Rangers. Unfortunately, capable musicians do not automatically make capable actors, and the members of the Rangers were not actors; there is no indication any had professional or even amateur experience in any sort of theater production. Still, as Gomer Cool confirmed in 2011, and as is also indicated in historical sources like the *Happy Hollow Bugle*, several band members appeared in recurring roles on some of the station's dramatic programming and on the more lighthearted *Happy Hollow*. In KMBC's early days staffers did everything as needed, including acting, so it was not out of the ordinary for the Texas Rangers to be placed on a music show which included dramatic or comedic settings. As the surviving *Life On the Red Horse Ranch* transcriptions attest (the series is discussed below), some group members were far more comfortable in such roles than others, with Herb

Kratoska (a skilled comedian), Clarence Hartman (who replaced Carl Hays in 1934 and was arguably the most natural actor of the bunch), Bob Crawford and Cool himself proving the most adept.

Drama Songs

During the summer of 1934, KMBC aired a series of drama songs featuring the Rangers, a unique concept that likely was the idea of Arthur Church or Gomer Cool, who had also been writing the group's continuity since at least late 1933. The Rangers' various drama programs, which were always mixed with plenty of music, coincided with Cool's years with the band, and he is often explicitly identified as the author of surviving scripts and attributed with many others in KBMC correspondence. His membership may well have been the catalyst for the Rangers branching out beyond the standard musical format of most of the era's Western performers.

These drama songs took classic cowboy tunes such as "Sam Bass" and "Old Chisholm Trail" and fashioned them into quarter-hour stories. The scripts were each approximately ten pages long which, following the standard rule-of-thumb that one page equals one minute of air time, left five minutes for music. There was no title explicitly assigned to the surviving set of scripts for these broadcasts, and the term "drama songs" originates with staff at Iowa State University where the scripts are housed. Enough of the scripts are dated to conclude that they were broadcast roughly on a weekly basis, between May and August, 1934.

Though the Texas Rangers provided music for the dramas, it remains to be confirmed whether or not they acted in these shows. The scripts give only character names and leave no trace of the station staff members who took the parts, characteristic of most surviving KMBC scripts. This omission makes it difficult to determine exactly who was involved in which of the station's many original radio productions. Below is an overview of the Texas Rangers drama songs with storylines where available.

May 24, 1934. "Old Chisholm Trail"

June 7, 1934. "Little Joe the Wrangler" Joe, an abused orphan, goes out on the trail with Dave, Bob, and Jones. During a fierce storm Joe and his horse fall down a spot that has been washed out. Joe dies when his faithful steed lands on top of him.

June 13, 1934. "Jesse James" The story of Bob Ford who shoots down Jesse.

June 20, 1934. "The Gal I Left Behind Me" Lem heads out on the trail with fellow cowboys Jake and Hanson to herd cattle and fight off Indians. His job done, Lem returns home to his girl Emmy.

June 27, 1934. "Bury Me Out on the Prairie" Al shoots down Sam who insinuates his girl has been sleeping around. Al pays for the honor killing when he is chased down and shot by the law.

July 5, 1934. "Sour Wood Mountain" A bit of a departure in tone from the other broadcasts in the series, this hillbilly sketch focuses on two star-crossed lovers, Emmy and Zeb, from feuding clans.

July 10, 1934. "The Man on the Flying Trapeze" Elmer falls for Myra and only later learns she is the wife of Signor Bona Slang Diablo, the man on the flying trapeze. In a fit of jealous rage Elmer pummels Signor Diablo in their climactic confrontation.

July 26, 1934. "The Old Man's Story" Henry Jones shares with his friend, Joshua, the sad story of why he has never married. He had a girl once, but she doubts his fidelity and becomes so distraught in an argument one day that she becomes distracted and is run over by a runaway horse.

August 9, 1934. "Casey Jones" Casey tries to get the Cannonball Express to New Orleans on time, but a freight train has not pulled off the track as expected. The Cannonball Express is going full speed and cannot avoid disaster.

Undated. "The Dying Cowboy" Phil is new to the trail team. One day while helping a stranger out on the range he is shot down when his gun jams. It turns out he had earlier beaten that same stranger to the draw.

Undated. "Red River Valley" After working the western plains, Ned returns home to the city leaving behind Mary, his love. Ned finds he has fallen in love, not only with Mary, but with the western country itself and has no choice but to return to the Red River Valley.

Undated. "Sam Bass" Sam Bass is shot down while he and his gang hold up a train.

Undated. "Strawberry Roan" Jess, a stranger, arrives in town and promises to break Mr. Higgens' roan. Jess comes close, but even his formidable horse skills can't tame the strawberry roan.

Undated. "Utah Carl" Utah Carl and Lenora are in love. When the cattle begin to stampede, Carl manages to save Lenora but not himself.

Undated. "Wreck of the Number 9" Bill couldn't get his train over the mountain before the number nine arrived and he dies in the massive collision.

Undated. "Empty Cot in the Bunkhouse" Limpy dies in his cot after braving the cold to save a calf.

These song dramas faded quickly from the station's growing library of commercial intellectual property suggesting audience reaction was underwhelming. No evidence exists to suggest they were ever seriously considered for further use or rebroadcast. Numerous musical-drama series were proposed over the years, both for local airing on KMBC and for network use, but this concept was never revived or worked into new proposals. Even Gomer Cool, in pitching his many Texas Rangers-related ideas to KMBC management in the coming years, seems to have never considered breathing new commercial life into these scripts. Church and Cool may have quickly lost interest because they were turning their attention to a new dramatic production that would be significantly larger in scope than the drama songs.

The First Recording Sessions

Arthur Church's decision to get the Texas Rangers involved in dramatic radio and transcription recording was nearly simultaneous. The band's drama-songs aired throughout the summer of 1934, during which time the Rangers made their initial foray into the recording studio.

The first recordings by the Rangers which can be positively dated are two sides recorded in Chicago on August 27, 1934, for the fledgling Decca record label, which had recently been launched by former Brunswick Records executive Jack Kapp. The Texas Rangers were among the first Western/hillbilly artists recorded by the label; among the others were the Rangers' soon-to-be perennial rivals, the Sons of the Pioneers. Waxed that day were "Dude Ranch Party" Pt. 1 and 2 (C9353 and C9354). As the titles indicate, they were designed to present a continuous performance spread over two sides of a single 78 rpm record. It was an unusual recording and has the flavor more of an audition record than a commercial release. Indeed, 75 years later Gomer Cool believed it had been intended as the former and was surprised that Decca had released it as a commercial disc. Its commercial potential was certainly limited.

Reissued by the British Archive of Country Music in 2009 on a CD celebrating the Rangers' early years, the two sides provide the modern listener an idea of what the Texas Rangers' earliest broadcasts may have sounded like, a mixture of banter and classic old-timey tunes. Whatever his status as one of the Texas Rangers, Tex Owens participated in the August 27 session and the next day recorded four solo tracks: his signature "Cattle Call" (C9355), "Two Sweethearts" (C9356), "Rocking Alone in an Old Rocking Chair" (C9357), and "Pride of the Prairie" (C9358). His appearance on the "Dude Ranch" recording, and his conspicuous presence in *Life on the Red Horse Ranch* a few months down the line, underscores the ambiguity of Tex's membership in the band. He was clearly a "Texas Ranger" with the group in 1932, as discussed earlier, but may not have been part of the show at the time the classic octet lineup of the group coalesced in the final months of 1933. This may have been why the other Rangers seemed to regard him as something of an interloper, something that, as we shall see, would come to a head a few years down the line. Owens continued to have his own ambitions apart from the Rangers, but in the flurry of activity around the group in 1934-35, his fortunes appear to have been closely entwined with theirs.

Although the recordings have not been positively dated, the Rangers made their first recordings for the World Transcription Company around the same time as their initial trip into the studio for Decca. Eight sides have surfaced to date (four songs on each side of a single transcription disc), though others may have been recorded and pressed but not yet surfaced among modern collectors. Also, it is likely they were cut on the same trip to Chicago that produced "Dude Ranch Party." The World session included Tex Owens' signature "Cattle Call" (1057), as well as "Press Along to the Big Corral" (1058), "Bury Me Not on the Lone Prairie" (1059), "Texas Cowboy" (1060), "Popeye the Sailor Man" (1061) featuring Herb Kratoska and his "trick frog voice," "Lonesome Valley Sally" (1062), "They Cut Down the Old Pine Tree" (1063), and "New River Train" (1064).

If the Decca record sounded more like an audition recording than a commercial release, the World songs likely were essentially for audition purposes in more ways than one. They represent not only the first steps in an attempt to sell the Rangers nationally via recorded discs for radio syndication, but also were an audition for World. Church was getting a feel for World's capabilities and approach to see if they were the right company through which to pursue his ambitions for the group.

Church must have been satisfied with what he saw and heard from World, since his association with the company would continue through the end of the 1940s. This association would result in the recording and release of the Texas Rangers Library, a transcription series that would leave an impressive and musically impeccable legacy of over 600 recordings and would prove Church's most profitable venture in the history of the group.[1]

Church was less satisfied with the Decca record, which failed to establish the Rangers in the commercial market. He complained to Ted Malone and Marion Fonville several months later that he was very disappointed in "the relatively small record sales." He hoped that including more mentions of the recording in the regular Texas Rangers broadcasts might spur customer interest. There would be another recording session for Decca the following year amid the marathon recording sessions in Chicago to record *Life on the Red Horse Ranch*; however, the commercial recording career of the Rangers would continue to be disappointing despite later associations with Columbia and MGM Records.

Aside from the recording in Chicago, the focus of the Rangers remained radio and the group closed out 1934 with two weekly CBS appearances, Sunday evenings from 5:00 to 5:30, Eastern Time, and Monday evenings from 7:00 to 7:15, Eastern Time. The Monday program was billed *Night Time on the Trail*, a series title which would be used on and off for many years for various KMBC Western-themed programs and did not always feature the Texas Rangers. While they were frequently the band providing the show's musical numbers, the entertainment could vary, with the station's other bands offering their talents at different times. In addition to the Sunday and Monday CBS spots, the Texas Rangers were also heard locally on the Kansas City airwaves via KMBC every weekday at 12:30.

---

1 Ruppli.

The Texas Rangers Transcribed

Radio transcription series were a potentially lucrative source of income for the right talent, and Arthur Church was sure his Texas Rangers fit the bill. Freeman Gosden and Charles Correll had popularized the concept of radio transcription, the business of recording a program to rent or sell to interested stations, with their blockbuster *Amos 'n' Andy* show in the late 1920s. The recording process for transcription albums was different from commercial 78-rpms, so transcriptions sounded better than regular 78s when played over the air. Because 78-rpm records had short playing times and less-than-ideal sound quality, Western Electric devised a new recording system that used a 33 1/3 rpm format, which successfully resolved the problems with 78-rpms.

During the early 1930s several transcription companies sprang up offering new material to radio stations. *The Air Adventures of Jimmy Allen*, *Chandu, the Magician*, *Tarzan*, and *Cecil and Sally* were just a few series which achieved a considerable degree of popularity via various transcription services. By the middle of the decade four companies, the C. P. MacGregor Service, the RCA/NBC Thesaurus Library, the Standard Radio Library, and the World Broadcasting Service, had the most market share with their contracts with 350 stations nationwide.[1]

Correspondence shows that KMBC staff was auditioning Texas Rangers recordings to radio executives outside the Kansas City area by September, 1934. Very likely these auditions were created using the World numbers cut in Chicago. The audition programs are not known to have survived, so their content can only be surmised. Based, however, on later audition programs put together in the late 1930s and early 1940s, the show was probably a fifteen-minute set with three or four tunes interspersed by brief interludes of light banter by the band members, such as that evidenced on the "Dude Ranch Party" sides. George Halley, an orthodontist by training, was a KMBC representative based out of Chicago who was frequently referred to as "Dr. Halley." Halley spent most of the 1930s and 1940s working to sell KMBC's productions to sponsors, both at a regional and national level. In the fall of 1934 Halley wrote to Gomer Cool informing him

---
1 Millard, p. 173.

that two shows authored by Cool, *Kid Brother* and *Texas Rangers*, had been played for some unidentified Chicago radio sponsors. *Kid Brother* was a dramatic radio program while this Rangers audition was a musical program, perhaps consisting of some of the songs recorded earlier in the year. The potential sponsors were "very complimentary" of the content and the writing and assured Halley both programs offered "a great deal of human interest and audience appeal."

Nothing ultimately came of the audition for the Rangers, and there is no evidence to suggest that *Kid Brother* was sold to a sponsor. At least six scripts for *Kid Brother* were written, and the program was actively promoted by Church and his staff for two years until 1936. This communication between Cool and Halley is the first mention of Church's attempts to sell the Texas Rangers on record, a format which would prove far more successful for the band in the long run than their live radio shows. To enhance sales efforts for both *Kid Brother* and *Texas Rangers*, station executives created an advertising booklet for their salesmen in the field to share with potential advertisers. This sales book did note that the two CBS network series outlined earlier, *The Texas Rangers* and *Night Time on the Trail* were both available for sponsorship, and that they could also be used as a "transcription feature."

Life on the Red Horse Ranch

The exact origin of the Rangers' first transcribed series remains a mystery. Whose idea it was and when it was first proposed are not documented in any surviving material. Nevertheless, whether Texas Ranger fiddler Gomer Cool created the concept himself, or whether he was asked by Church or other KMBC officials to write a new set of musical-dramatic scripts, the project probably evolved late in 1934. The mechanics and feasibility of it all developed from the series of drama songs aired that summer, and from Church's testing of the waters, by recording for World in Chicago during the same period.

Conceptually, Church envisioned a program which could be recorded and then sold either to a single sponsor or to individual radio stations. With just a few parameters, showcasing the Texas Rangers' musical capabilities, and ensuring the works were clean and acceptable to a wide variety of sponsors (as all of Church's productions were), Gomer Cool set to work, and the resulting series was called

The Flying Horse Ranch. The original 26 scripts were not groundbreaking in any way; they told the story of a group of ranch hands on the mythical *Flying Horse Ranch*, who have to save their beloved ranch from nefarious schemers who would take control of it if given the chance. An engaging story was necessary to encourage listeners to return, but more important than the serial plotline, was the program's featuring plenty of music. Generally, the Texas Rangers performed three or four songs per fifteen-minute episode and also played the parts of the ranch hands.

To what extent staffers shopped the series to agencies or potential sponsors is unclear, but it remains a possibility that the idea was initiated by a sponsor. Perhaps it was someone who had seen potential in an expansion of the premise outlined in the five-plus minutes of "Dude Ranch Party, Pt. 1 – 2" and then approached KMBC with a program proposal. At any rate, in early 1935 the series was brought to the attention of advertising agency J. Stirling Getchell, Inc. by its Kansas City branch manager Karel Rickerson. Socony-Vacuum Oil Company of New York wanted to use the program to promote its White Eagle and Lubrite divisions. Getting the attention of such an up-and-coming ad company was a real coup for Church. Getchell's agency had earned its first major account just three years earlier in 1932 when they were given the chance to promote Chrysler's new Plymouth automobiles. After sales took off, other notable companies approached Getchell, including the then-second largest oil company Socony-Vacuum (later Mobiloil).[1]

Contracts between the Midland Broadcasting Company and J. Stirling Getchell, Inc. were signed on March 30 and Cool's *Flying Horse Ranch*, now renamed *Red Horse Ranch* (officially dubbed *Life on the Red Horse Ranch* but rarely referred to by the entire name) in honor of Socony's famous red horse logo, had the financial backing to get recorded. Thirteen KMBC employees were signed for the project: Gomer Cool, Doie Hensley (Tex) Owens, Duane Swalley, Edward Cronenbold, Roderick May, Robert Crawford, Ruth Barth, John Preston, Paul Sells, Herbert Kratoska (frequently referred to as "Herbie"), Eddie Edwards, Clarence Hartman and Marion Fonville (misspelled "Folville" on the contract and "Fondville" in a newspaper review).

---

1 Fox, p. 162-168

Life on the Red Horse Ranch cast photo.
Courtesy of Ryan Ellett.

Clarence Hartman, who had replaced Carl Hays in the Rangers' instrumental quartet sometime in the first half of 1934, was a very accomplished musician, having turned down a spot with the Kansas City Symphony to, instead, accept a staff position at KMBC. He was a member of the station's pared down orchestra along with Gomer Cool. Cool recalled him as a prodigiously talented musician who could play many instruments, though string bass, and occasionally jug or ocarina, was the only instrument he would feature with the Rangers. The oldest Ranger by almost two decades, Hartman was born in 1890. Thus, he was also two years older than Tex Owens. He was also the only Ranger beyond Owens who actually hailed from Texas. A long time resident of Ft. Worth, he was, at the time he signed his draft card during the First World War, working west of the city at the famed Crazy Water Hotel in the spa town of Mineral Wells. Mineral Wells was famous for producing the notorious Crazy Water Crystals, one of the most important sponsors of hillbilly and Western music on radio in the 1930s and '40s. However, just three years later in 1920, Hartman listed his occupation as physician!

The contract does not indicate which parts each cast member played, but except for a juvenile part added after the first 26 scripts were written and recorded, they can be surmised without much trouble. The characters the band members, and emcee and "leader" Marion Fonville, portrayed used the same names they had already developed for their earlier broadcasts and recordings. Robert Crawford played "Bob," and "Tex" was played by "Tex" Owens, the only two who used their real names. Gomer Cool was "Tenderfoot," Herbert Kratoska, "Arizona," and Paul Sells was "Montana" or "Monty," the same names these musicians had been using since joining the group. Edward Cronenbold played "Cheyenne," a nickname which would eventually be changed to "Tucson" and used for most of his tenure with the Texas Rangers. The unusual nickname "Tookie" may be a variation of his on-air name "Tucson" (or vice versa). Clarence Hartman was christened "Idaho," while Duane Swalley had the role of "Slim." "Dave," played by Rod May, was a nickname which lacked the western air of most of the others. Fonville was, as he had been for "Dude Ranch Party," "Alabam." Cool had made "Alabam" the romantic hero of the series. Eddie Edwards, one of KMBC's two resident blackface actors, played "Cookie," the slow-witted African American cook.

The remaining original cast of *Red Horse Ranch* had no further notable association with the Texas Rangers but deserve mention. Ruth Barth, who portrayed the serial's heroine, Ruth Carter, the daughter of ranch owner Sam Carter, was an unknown staffer at KMBC at the time but would perhaps become the most prominent alum of the show, aside from the Rangers themselves. In 1939, four years after *Red Horse Ranch* was recorded, Ruth married fellow KMBC employee Paul Henning, who later wrote for the highly rated radio comedies *Fibber McGee and Molly* and the *Burns & Allen Show* with George Burns and Gracie Allen. Even later during the 1960s, he created the popular television series *The Beverly Hillbillies* and was involved in the development of both *Green Acres* and *Petticoat Junction*.

John A. Preston played rancher Sam Carter, and worked for KMBC as early as May, 1932, when he appeared on the station's local series *Phenomenon* about a time-traveling hero. He is not to be confused with the western actor of the same name, whose given name was Andrew Jackson Rylee. Rylee, aka, John A. Preston, made a handful of western films in the mid-to-late 1930s including *Courage of the North* (1934) and *Timber Terrors* (1935). John A. Preston of KMBC was a veteran performer and came to KMBC after a fifty-one-year career as an actor and director on the theater stage. He claimed to have penned seventeen melodramas and performed or directed over 3,000 dramas during the course of his long career. In a memo written a few years later in consideration of a new set of *Red Horse Ranch* scripts, Gomer Cool indicated to Church that the character of Sam Carter could easily be written out of any new productions This contingency plan was necessary because Preston apparently left KMBC not long after *Life on the Red Horse Ranch* was completed.

The rival rancher and villain of *Life on the Red Horse Ranch* was played by Lou Marcell, a KMBC employee of several years standing at the time, who would go on to a long career in radio and in film after relocating to the West Coast. The St. Louis native is perhaps best known as the narrator in the opening sequence of the 1942 film classic *Casablanca*. The young actor who played the final character, Dewey Dawson, a boy who was added to the series after the writing and production of the first 26 episodes, remains unknown. He may well have been a Chicago-area child actor called in to cover the part with no further connection to Arthur Church or the Midland Broadcasting Company.

For Duane Swalley, *Life on the Red Horse Ranch* represented one of his last projects with the group. He left KMBC and the Rangers to follow his wife, who was a performer with Phil Spitalny's famous all-girl orchestra, which achieved a level of fame on radio, records, and film shorts during the 1930s and 1940s. The Swalleys moved to Chicago where Swalley found work at WLS with Red Foley and others. Swalley's replacement was the young tenor Francis Mahaney, who, at only 21, became the youngest Ranger. Marion Fonville, who had been connected with the Rangers since their inception in 1932, would also leave KMBC soon after the completion of *Red Horse Ranch*. Eddie Edwards, also part of the Rangers' broadcasts from the start, appears to have had no further involvement with them beyond the *Red Horse* recordings. Edwards continued on as a KMBC performer and sound effects man, eventually ending up in production by the late 1940s.

The *Red Horse Ranch* contract called for KMBC to produce and record no less than twenty-six episodes, each of which would have 90 seconds of space at the beginning and end for a commercial message.

The station had to cover all production costs but retained all rights to the show, allowing them to market it further when the partnership with Socony-Vacuum Oil ended. This initial order of 26 episodes was to be recorded by April 15, 1935, so they could then be sent out to anywhere within the territory being targeted by J. Stirling Getchell for Socony's Lubrite product. Getchell used *Red Horse Ranch* to promote the Lubrite Division centered on the St. Louis area and the White-Eagle Division which was headquartered in Kansas City.

The advertising agency was required to run at least two episodes per week, thus the initial 26 shows would fill a thirteen-week block, a common broadcasting schedule at the time. The contract indicates a full year's worth of episodes (104) was to be produced, though it appears that only sixty-five were written, all by Gomer Cool. All the scripts still survive, both of the series as *Flying Horse Ranch* and the revised *Life on the Red Horse Ranch*. Copies of 64 of the 65 episodes are extant and circulating among collectors of old-time radio broadcasts. Two additional undated scripts numbered 97 and 100 also exist, but no evidence survives to suggest that they were recorded or aired, though as detailed below, Cool and Church did discuss the possibility of a second *Red Horse Ranch* series.

Complete records of the show's run on various stations have not survived, so it's not clear how many stations actually ran the full 65-episode series. Notations on station materials hint that 39 episodes aired on WWJ, Detroit, and the full 65 on WHK, Cleveland.

The exact cost of the *Red Horse* recordings, unfortunately, is not easy to determine. There are no extant financial statements specifically for the recordings, but one general record from 1943 provides an idea. In 1936, just under $4,700 was spent on Texas Rangers transcriptions. There are

Life on the Red Horse Ranch transcription record. Courtesy of Randy Riddle.

few known Rangers recordings from 1936 itself, so it seems reasonable to conclude that this figure may include the 1935 World recording sessions as well, since they are not listed anywhere else on the financial document. With just a handful of other songs recorded during the mid-1930s, the majority of that cost can safely be attributed to the *Red Horse* library. Yet a separate reference to the series found among station memos pegs the per-episode cost as closer to $100 with World Broadcasting receiving about $15 of that. This would push the cost of the series much higher to approximately $6,500. Whether the lower or higher cost, or a number in between, *Life on the Red Horse Ranch* was a significant investment for Arthur Church and the Midland Broadcasting Company.

Recording on *Red Horse Ranch* began Tuesday, April 2, 1935, at the World Broadcasting studios in Chicago. The first 26 episodes were recorded over four days, with each actor earning fifty dollars per day for the work. World Broadcasting Systems was a major player in the burgeoning radio transcription market, recording both music and dramatic radio fare, and Church was wise to associate his product with the company.

While in Chicago, the Rangers also returned to Decca's recording studios, where they had waxed the unusual two-sided "Dude Ranch Party" the previous August. On April 6 they laid down eight tracks, a mix of already standard cowboy songs and love ballads, with a little bit of hokum fun thrown in: "Goin' Down to the Santa Fe," "Prairie Dreamboat," "Careless Love," "Let the Rest of the World Go By," "New River Train," "Lonesome Valley Sally," "The Big Corral," and "Trail to Mexico." Immediately following this, the group's four backing musicians waxed a further session under the name the Happy Hollow Hoodlums, a moniker by which they appeared on KMBC's *Happy Hollow*. They recorded three songs, "Down Home Rag," "Panama," and a promotional recording for the Julian Kohange Company, a shoe store. With the exception of the commercial, all ten sides that the Rangers, and Hoodlums, waxed that day were released commercially by Decca in the coming months. Sales were either not strong enough for Decca to consider further record releases by the group, or Church found something wanting in the group's relationship with the recording company and chose not to pursue any further commercial recording at this time.

The Texas Rangers were not the only radio cowboy band trying to cash in with some recordings. Decca had already recorded such groups as the Sons of the Pioneers, Stuart Hamblin's Covered Wagon Jubilee on the West Coast, and had signed the Chicago-based trio, The Ranch Boys, as well. The trio, originally from California, was led by Jack Ross who was joined by Joe "Curly" Bradley (later radio's Tom Mix) and Ken "Shorty" Carson. The Ranch Boys recorded multiple sessions at the Decca studios, both before and after the Texas Rangers.

Shows 27-65 of *Red Horse Ranch* appear to have been recorded over six days on a return trip to Chicago around the end of May (the exact dates are unknown, but the entertainment magazine *Variety* reported the Rangers' return to Kansas City in its June 5th issue). The shows may have been written after gauging the reaction to the first 26, since Cool added a juvenile role to the mix, played by an unknown child actor. Other cast and characters remained the same.

Red Horse Ranch was not the commercial breakthrough that Church hoped. It did reach a respectable number of radio markets, some of them the largest in the Midwest. It penetrated the large markets on WGN (Chicago), WWJ (Detroit, though some sources claim it ran on legendary station WXYZ), WHK (Cleveland) and WCCO (Minneapolis). Smaller markets included some in Illinois (WTAD, Quincy, WJBL, Decatur, WDZ, Tuscola, and WEBQ, Harrisburg), Iowa (WOC, Davenport, and WHO, Des Moines), Indiana (WFBM, Indianapolis, WKVB, Richmond, WHBU, Anderson, WBOW, Terre Haute, and WLBC, Muncie), Missouri (KMOX, St. Louis, and KFRU, Columbia), Colorado (KGIW, Alamosa, KLZ, Denver, KFXJ, Grand Junction, and KIDW, Lamar), South Dakota (KABN, Aberdeen, and KGFX, Pierre), Wyoming (KDFN, Casper, and KWYO, Sheridan), Kansas (KGNO, Dodge City, KFH, Wichita, and WIBW, Topeka), Montana (KGIR, Butte, KFBB, Great Falls, and KGCX, Wolf Point), Nebraska (KMMJ, Clay Center, KFOR, Lincoln, WOW, Omaha, and KGKY, Scottsbluff), and North Dakota (WDAY, Fargo, and KLPM, Minot).

A clipping from an unidentified trade newspaper, possibly *Billboard* or *Variety*, offers a rare assessment outside of KMBC and the Rangers, of *Life on the Red Horse Ranch*, which in Chicago was sponsored by Mrs. Wagner's Pies. The review was negative to say the least, and it's a credit to Arthur Church that such a critique was saved along with other program documentation. Curiously, the review, which also refers to Tex Owens as "Owen," to Fonville as "Fondville," and to John Preston as "Jed," names the Rangers' vocal group as the Midwesterner's Quartet, a moniker not often used by 1935 in reference to the quartet, which had long been integrated into the larger Texas Rangers outfit. The Midwesterners name is not referred to in station documentation after this point and it's not clear why KMBC publicity material for the transcribed series would not have referred to the band as the Texas Rangers, the brand name Church was making every attempt to publicize. The newspaper review also lists Fran Heyser, a long-time KMBC staffer who is not known to have had any creative input to the show, but who likely acted as a director, producer, or consultant of some sort. The radio reviewer does not pull any punches in describing the show for readers:

> 'Red Horse Ranch' combines the serial with music on the billbilly [sic] style by the Midwesterners.
>
> For the rest, there is a sketchy meaningless yarn sprinkled with such western plains local color as 'sho powerful glad to see you all,' ribs about a tenderfoot who turns out to be a hero by bulldogging a steer, even though the listening audience can't make much sense out of a sequence such as this, which after all, is strictly a visual experience. Much ado is made over the loss of a horse, which isn't likely to cause much palpitation among the hearts of what few women may be accidentally tuned in.
>
> It is a bad show from all angles, and the commercial plug is even worse. To top the general aura of poorness, there was an announcer who stumbled, stuttered and stammered.

Harsh as it is, even at the removal of almost 80 years, and with the rose-colored glasses of nostalgia over one's eyes, it is hard to argue with many of the points the reviewer makes. There is little that makes *Life on the Red Horse Ranch* stand out to aficianados of old-time radio. The ranch hands are, for the most part, indistinguishable from each other. Kratoska and Cool's characters are the most distinctive among the band members, and Kratoska and Hartman arguably the most skilled voice actors among them; and they are pretty much stock characters for western fare. With eight to nine members in the band, it would indeed be difficult to create unique personas for each in the very limited space available for character development. Sam Carter is the noble ranch owner, trying to scratch out an honest living in a tough business. Rose Carter, Sam's daughter, is a kind-hearted gal who wins the heart of all the boys. Cookie, the African American cook, displays buffoonery typical of many radio black-face characters of the time and is very similar to the Lightning character of *Amos 'n' Andy*. Unlike some other blackface characters of the period who were written and portrayed with some sympathetic qualities, however patronizing, Cookie is a character written, acted and regarded within the story by other characters with a palpable and bigoted disdain. Steve Bradford, the conniver trying to take ownership of the Red Horse Ranch during the first half of the serial, blends with countless such characters from western radio, television, and film. Given the format constraints, Cool, who would later spend many years as a radio and television writer, producer, and director with CBS, should probably not be judged to harshly for this early effort.

Ultimately, *Life on the Red Horse Ranch* was a showcase for the Texas Rangers as a musical group, with a flimsy story interspersed between tunes, and that is where its continued value lies. Not only does it feature the Rangers at their early musical peak, often performing songs that they did not record elsewhere, it also, significantly, showcases the wonderful and woefully under-recorded Tex Owens and the instrumental talents of the band's guitarist-banjoist Herb Kratoska, a musician whose virtuosity still impresses eight decades later.

After *Life on the Red Horse Ranch*

Though interest in *Red Horse Ranch* was limited to Midwestern stations and had ebbed by the summer of 1936, just over a year after its release, Church was satisfied enough with the results to have Cool look into the production of 65 new episodes, numbered 66 to 130. The primary concern in making new recordings involved music: could the new episodes be made using only public domain music? Cool's response was an unequivocal, "no." During the first 65 episodes the Texas Rangers had used 50 public domain songs, less than one per episode. Cool explained that some publishers affiliated with ASCAP, claimed copyrights on such cowboy classics as "Ridin' Old Paint," "Great Granddad," and "Old Chisholm Trail." However, Cool explained, it was the arrangements that were copyrighted and not the songs themselves, which were public domain. Thus, since the Rangers frequently made their own arrangements of these classic songs, technically more material within public domain could be accessed. Since Owens, Crawford, and Cool wrote original material which could be used, as did local songwriter Alvin Crocker, who placed several songs with the group, the available musical library did, in fact, make the project of creating 65 new episodes a possibility.

Secondly, Church wondered, how long would it take to have scripts revised and in shape for recording that Cool had already written? Cool insisted the revisions could be done in only two weeks, though three weeks would be better. He was also hesitant about Church's insistence that Sam Carter be written out of the series. Apparently, John Preston, who had played the part in the first 65 episodes, was unavailable, so Cool saw no reason that a new actor could not take over the part. In fact, a new voice could be "a great advantage." Recognizing that the series was not a top-of-the-line offering, Cool noted that if they took their time on the next group of recordings, he felt Church would "note a great improvement – in script, music, and production."

Church sat on Cool's responses for some time but ultimately chose to focus on renewed efforts to sell the existing *Red Horse* series rather than invest in a new set of episodes. This decision was reiterated in a year-end letter Cool sent to Church in which he reviewed KMBC programming that he felt had definite commercial possibilities, either at the local or national level. Among the prospects were four directly involving the Texas Rangers. The first was *Life on the Red Horse Ranch* which had only recently wound down its run as a circulating transcribed series. The second was a program called *Rough Riders*, which used the Texas Rangers' music in a Western serial format. Though never produced, staff did go so far as to create a program outline, some audition scripts, and possible names for the characters. Third, was the dramatized songs originally aired in 1934, an idea in which Church clearly had little interest since this is the only mention of these early Rangers broadcasts in company records aside from the original scripts. The final idea was *Night Time on the Trail*, a musical show with the Texas Rangers. *Night Time on the Trail*, which had enjoyed a run on CBS in late 1934, would get considerable attention over the next few years and eventually make its way back to the air after a CBS run in late 1934. One other program highlighted by Cool involved two of the Rangers, Herb Kratoska and Clarence Hartman. The two had created a show called *Captain Jack and His Jolly Crew* which consisted of musical novelties. At some point it had been tested on the air under the sponsorship of Malt-O-Meal.

The Texas Rangers ca. mid-1930s.
Courtesy of Ed Crawford.

Interest in *Life on the Red Horse Ranch* continued to trickle in from stations and potential sponsors over the ensuing years leading Cool to write an internal memo in 1939 to address the status of the series. It was, as the recordings suggest, and as Cool himself professed, not an action show. He even showed flashes of irritation to those within the company who continued to try and sell the series as such. The program was intended to spotlight the music of the Texas Rangers; sustained action was not doable when a quarter-hour broadcast featured four songs ("no more, no less"). In fact, to market the show as an action program was downright dishonest and sure to disappoint any buyer in a short period of time.

Outside of the nature of the show, Cool warned of the physical state of the then-four-year-old World pressings. KMBC actually had few quality records to share with potential buyers, with most of the best sounding examples residing in Chicago and New York. Listening to the copies on hand in Kansas City was "not [his] idea of how to get the show sold." He warned KMBC sales staff to "be pretty careful about what shows" they auditioned to potential clients since the sound quality for some of them could only be described as "pretty terrible."

There may have been other reasons for Cool's declining interest in *Red Horse Ranch* and his eventual downplaying of the sale ability of *Red Horse Ranch*, just a few short years after he authored and acted in it. By the end of the 1930s the Rangers had broadcast several different series on the CBS network and he was regularly pitching script ideas to networks and sponsors for new Rangers programs. He, doubtless, felt he had matured as a writer, and correspondence toward the end of his life makes it clear that he was far from proud of his early script work on *Red Horse Ranch*. In addition, by 1939, Church was looking into motion picture prospects for the group, and the last thing Cool or Church would have wanted was for any flaws evident in these early shows, whether in the quality of writing, or the performances, or the deteriorating condition of the recordings themselves, to leave a poor impression on possible financial suitors.

Upon the release of *Life on the Red Horse Ranch* in 1935, any hope that the increased exposure offered by the series would mean the Texas Rangers could now earn their keep in the relative comfort of the radio studio was short lived. They still had to get out on the road and perform live for fans in the region, as evidenced by a short tour in Wichita, KS. On September 15, 1936, they participated in a trio of concerts which were broadcast over Wichita's KFH. Despite their minor fame as radio stars, the band's booking was at a cleaning plant belonging to Lulling's City and Dry Cleaners, far from the bright lights of Chicago and Los Angeles, or even their own Kansas City. The "special occasion" which brought the Texas Rangers to the dry cleaning operation was a plant expansion, which the owners felt worthy of recognition.

Further burrs under Arthur Church's saddle were perceived infringements on the Texas Rangers name, a brand he felt it necessary to protect from use by other entertainers. They were not yet well enough established to lay unchallenged claim to the moniker. Despite all the attention he gave to creating new money-making opportunities for the group, Church was never too busy to overlook other acts which he felt may have been poaching, intentionally or not, on the growing reputation of his band. One such infringement caused a minor ruckus among KMBC staff in May, 1936. It had come to Church's attention that the legendary showman Billy Rose had appropriated the name for one of his acts, and Church quickly shared the offense with Ted Malone via memo. While in Texas helping the state celebrate its centennial, Rose had put together a musical organization that he billed as the Texas Rangers. Rose appears to have done more than appropriate the name. Internal memos seem to suggest that he might have turned down the KMBC Rangers for the job before using the name for his own group. KMBC's Ted Malone suggested planting a story in *Variety* "giving Billy Rose a dig because he would not buy an act that was too professional, and having finally found one that is louzy [sic] enough to fill the bill with him, he has hired it." Arthur Church, ever the professional, apparently declined to follow up on Malone's idea.

As 1936 wound down, rural music, including all its forms, was continuing to find ever larger audiences. Arthur Church and the Texas Rangers must have sensed that the time was right to make a splash with nationwide audiences, and *Red Horse Ranch* was not going to make that splash as envisioned. The *National Barn Dance* continued to boom out of Chicago, and the *Grand Ole Opry* was picking up steam over Nashville's WSM. In the Southwest, Western swing, a radio and dancehall hybrid of Western, hillbilly, jazz, blues and pop music epitomized by groups like Milton Brown & his Musical Brownies, Bob Wills & his Texas Playboys, and the Sons of the Pioneers, founded around the same time as the Texas Rangers, were gaining quite a following on the West Coast with numerous studio recordings and appearances in musical shorts and western features. Most crucially, Gene Autry, just two years earlier a rising radio and recording artist, had ignited the Singing Cowboy craze, and musical westerns were now one of most popular entertainments coming out of Hollywood. Autry was a major box office draw, and there was plenty of money to be made with Western music.

Chapter 4:
Kings of Kansas City Radio

Box K Ranch Boys and *Smilin' Valley Dude Ranch*

Radio in 1937 was a rapidly maturing industry with ever larger sums of money pouring into (or from) the pockets of networks, stations, advertisers, and performers; NBC was nearing annual revenue of over $41 million, six times that of nine years before. For modern-day fans of old-time radio programming, the year represents the beginning of a glorious golden age which would last into the postwar years. With Fascism and communism on the rise in Europe, H. V. Kaltenborn and Edward R. Murrow reported on world events to listeners. Homemakers kept house and raised children while following the daily exploits of their favorite heroines on such serials as *The Romance of Helen Trent* and *Ma Perkins*. School children thrilled to the adventures of *Little Orphan Annie*, *Jack Armstrong*, and the legendary *Shadow* after their school work was done. It was also a time when radio comedians who would dominate the medium until the 1950s were coming into their own. Programs such as *Lum 'n' Abner*, *Amos 'n' Andy*, and humorists George Burns and Gracie Allen were already developing devoted followings, while Fred Allen and Jack Benny were creating comedy personas which would be treasured for decades to come. Other performers, including Jim and Marian Jordan of *Fibber McGee & Molly*, Red Skelton, and Edgar Bergen with his wooden partner Charlie McCarthy, were attracting numerous listeners as well.

Despite the arrival of radio's heyday and the proliferation of top-notch comedy, drama, and music programs from Chicago and New York City, the homegrown Texas Rangers continued to exercise a strong hold on Kansas City listeners. The group had by now solidified its classic eight-man line-up: the vocal quartet of Bob Crawford (baritone), Rod May (second tenor), Ed Cronenbold (bass), and Fran Mahaney (tenor) and the instrumental backing group of Gomer Cool (fiddle), Paul Sells (Accordion), Clarence Hartman (bass), and Herb Kratoska (guitar). A survey from May 2, 1937, demonstrated their impressive air dominance in Kansas City against the competition. During their 30-minute Sunday morning timeslot between 9:00 and 9:30 they doubled the listeners of the next highest rated program. The singers attracted 47% of listeners for the first half of the program compared to WDAF's 23% with their radio news and WHB's 15% with *Music in the Air*. During the second fifteen minutes their ratings dipped to 34% which was still twice their closest competition, WHB's *Hits From Hollywood* (17%) and KXBY's *Breakfast Serenade* (17%). WDAF's *News of the Churches* and WREN's Larry Larson organ program each only claimed 8% of listeners.

The numbers were impressive enough to push KMBC staffers into developing a new broadcast vehicle for the Rangers, this time entitled *Smilin' Valley Dude Ranch*. On July 13, 1937, a half-hour audition, apparently broadcast live, was produced for Church's feedback. Unfortunately, he was interrupted during the audition by a long distance call and had to request a synopsis of the *Smilin' Valley* program concept.

Work on selling *Smilin' Valley* by Church and his sales team paid off in September, 1937, when Church signed a contract with N. W. Ayer & Son, Inc., advertising representative for the Kellogg Company. In September, 1937, the two parties agreed to a thirteen-week contract which called for 65, fifteen-minute episodes of a show to feature the Texas Rangers. Renamed *Box K Ranch Boys*, the daily feature debuted September 20 at 7:45 in the morning. N. W. Ayer & Son provided all the copy and continuity, while the Rangers provided the musical talent. The toll charge per week was $162 and the talent charge for the KMBC performers was $250 per week. The advertising company reserved the right to cancel the program with 30 days notice if the Texas Rangers became unavailable at some point and replacement talent acceptable to Ayer & Son could not be procured.

One month after the *Box K Ranch Boys* hit the airwaves a listener survey indicated Kellogg's investment in the Rangers was a wise one. Polled between October 25 and October 29, 1937, the *Box K Ranch Boys* program claimed 52% of Kansas City listeners versus 29% of listeners tuned in to the second place program *Musical Clock*. These number compared favorably to a similar survey completed in May,

The Texas Rangers as the Box K Ranch Boys For Kellogg's Rice Krispies. Courtesy of Ed Crawford.

1937, which showed the Rangers pulling in 35% of listeners in the 5:00 to 5:15 p.m. slot. They outdistanced WDAF's *Adventures of Dari Dan* (20%), the *Cocktail Hour* (19%), and Dixieland band music (13%).

The Rangers' domination of the Sunday morning time slot they had occupied for much of the year began attracting the attention of stations beyond Kansas City. The band received a letter on November 23, 1937, from Norman Thomas, president of WDOD in Chattanooga, TN. His letter was short and to the point:

> For some time we have been listening to your program on Sunday mornings from our station, and we are always interested in good talent.
> Possibly you have been at KMBC long enough that you would desire to make a change. If so, we would be glad to have you advise us along this line.
> Our idea was for your organization to play the same type of music you are now playing on the network, from our Radio Playhouse on the Noon-Day Show and on Saturday and Sunday nights.
> A reply either way will be appreciated.

It's a measure of how unique the Texas Rangers position at KMBC was – not a real band as much as such so much as a product – that the possibility that the Rangers were a KMBC creation and not an autonomous band that happened to be currently employed there appears not to have crossed Thomas' mind. Gomer Cool was quick to send a response for the band, indicating they were flattered by the offer but constrained by contracts which prevented them from leaving their positions at the time. With their Sunday morning network spot and a daily test spot as the *Box K Ranch Boys*, things were looking good for them. But 1938 was rapidly approaching and the Kellogg's show would very possibly be ending then. Thus, Cool indicated the band would "like to hear more of [the WDOD] proposition. What would the income be for the entire act of eight men? Would there be an opportunity for us to do other types of music on the station. . . I have been employed for several years here at KMBC as a dramatic writer – and wrote the 'Red Horse Ranch' transcription series which the Texas Rangers made for the Socony-Vacuum Company. Several of the boys have good comedy and dramatic talents. There [are] eight men in the act and all of them like to keep busy – if they find it worth while." Cool went on: "Needless to say, we'd like to live in your beautiful city and work in your organization. So if we find that the change is possible – and worth while – perhaps something can be done about it."

Were the Rangers actually interested in switching stations to a city with a population in 1940 of 128,000 compared to Kansas City's 400,000 residents that same year? Could WDOD really offer the network exposure and financial compensation that KMBC did? There's little evidence to even suggest any members of the Rangers had ever visited Chattanooga to determine whether it was a "beautiful city" or not, nor is it clear the extent to which Cool got input from his bandmates about the proposition. It's possible, too, despite the security that employment at KMBC offered, that at least some of the Rangers may have relished the idea of a job with a little more freedom and a less fully hands-on employer. Regardless, the fact that that both letters eventually found their way into the KMBC station archives suggests that perhaps the whole courtship was exploited by the Rangers to improve their own standing with the station.

However, if the Rangers seriously entertained the idea of using WDOD's interest as a bargaining tool with Church, they would have been negotiating from a weak position. Church owned the Texas

The Texas Rangers' quartet promotional still ca. 1938. Note the misspellings of Mahaney's and Cronenbold's names. Additionally, the picture features Duane Swalley labeled as "Fran Haney," so the still actually dates from years earlier. Courtesy of Jim Crawford.

Rangers name, so there was no chance they could build on that name recognition after making a move. While there was no questioning the singing and playing talent of the band members, they were not so skilled as to be irreplaceable, and both they and Church knew that. Further, despite appearing on CBS on Sunday mornings, the Texas Rangers had been unable to land a national sponsor for any of their broadcasts. *Life on the Red Horse Ranch* had sputtered after a year of circulation to Midwestern stations, and no one was convinced that Kellog's sponsorship of their weekday broadcast in Kansas City would be renewed after the initial terms of the contract were met. However good the group may have been, and however popular they might be in Kansas City and the surrounding region, their success remained modest and the matter of WDOD's interest was dropped. Church was behind them, and there was no need to look a gift horse in the mouth.

Meanwhile, the original *Smilin' Valley Dude Ranch* concept proposed in the summer of 1937, percolated another six months until January 13, 1938, when Cool wrote a note encouraging movement on the idea. George Halley, who promoted a lot of KMBC's transcribed series and worked for years selling the Texas Rangers, thought *Smilin' Valley* had merit and could find a buyer. By January, Cool had completed three complete scripts, numbered 1, 10, and 25, to give prospective sponsors an idea of where the show's storyline would go. The first two had even been recorded and were, at the time, in Halley's hands.

Brush Creek Follies

Church put off for the time being any decision about *Smilin' Valley Dude Ranch*, perhaps because his staff was working toward the debut of a new musical variety program. Named after a stream which meanders for ten miles through Kansas City, KMBC launched *Brush Creek Follies* in 1938 to cash in on the "barn dance" radio craze. Like the more widely known show on which it was modeled, *National Barn Dance* and *Grand Ole Opry*, *Brush Creek Follies* aired on Saturday nights and it would become a Kansas City institution for many years. Surprisingly little has been written about *Brush Creek Follies* considering it aired for fifteen years. Few recordings and scripts, or more pertinent in this case, cast/line-up listings and printed programs, appear to have survived. In the early 1950s the show remained on radio but also transitioned to television before coming to an end, purportedly due to labor difficulties, though changing tastes and habits certainly had something to do with its demise, as well. CBS aired portions of the broadcast each week to its network listeners, for a time making it one of the most widely listened to rural music shows on the air.

The Texas Rangers were not the focus of the weekly gala but band members, both with the full Rangers lineup and as individually featured performers, were the show's lynchpins. A sample program from January 8, 1938, one of the very earliest broadcasts, gives an idea of the performing acts found on a typical broadcast.

1. Theme "Put on Your Old Grey Bonnet" - Entire Company
2. Jackson County Stump Jumpers
3. Jenny Haskins
4. Winner of Contest
5. Colorado Pete
6. Glad Smith "Somebody Loves You"
7. Eddie Edwards
8. Manny Roy "Little Buckaroo"
9. Texas Rangers instrumental "Goofus"
10. Fran Mahaney "When Irish Eyes are Smilin'"
11. Herb Kratoska – banjo - "12th St. Rag"
12. Break – Square Dance
13. Jack Strucik
14. Girls' Trio
15. Little Joe
16. Winner of Contest
17. Jackson County Stump Jumpers
18. Tex Owens
19. Texas Rangers "Ain't Cha Comin Out Tonight?"
20. Job Negime
21. Herb Kratoska "Father Put the Cow Away"
22. Texas Rangers
23. Finale – Entire company

This set list indicates the Texas Rangers, or individual members of the group, were involved in 9 of 23 numbers, including the opening and closing, and their talents were clearly central to the *Follies'* early success. Over the next decade and a half, an endless array of singers, musicians, and performers graced the *Follies'* stage, originally at the Ivanhoe Temple, then later at Municipal Auditorium and Memorial Hall. Among KMBC's stable of artists who made recurring appearances were the Prairie Pioneers, Santa Fe Slim, Colorado Pete, and Hiram Higsby.

Looking Up on the Airwaves

Even with *Brush Creek Follies* up and running smoothly in the spring of 1938, Church continued to postpone any decision concerning *Smilin' Valley*, much to the chagrin of script writer Cool. However, an advantageous move for the Rangers on the CBS network pacified Cool for the time being. Beginning April 17, 1938, the Texas Rangers were moved from their Sunday morning time to an afternoon spot, originally from 5:00 to 5:30 and then in following weeks, due to daylight savings time, 4:00 to 4:30. Radio schedules confirm the band was heard from New York to Los Angeles in the new slot, which unquestionably offered a much larger potential listening audience than the Sunday morning time had, when comparatively few radios were turned on.

Publicity directors at CBS did their best to hype the move to the chain's stations with a notice sent out on April 9, 1938:

> "'Ride! Ride! Ride!' sing the Texas Rangers. And ride they do – into a new afternoon spot that will be welcomed by their thousands of listening friends on the Columbia network. Beginning April 17, the gay songs and music of the Texas Rangers, with Tex Owens, the Original Texas Ranger, will be heard on the Columbia coast-to-coast network.
>
> "The Texas Rangers and Tex Owens long have been ranking favorites. Their Sunday morning programs attracted so much favorable comment from thousands of Columbia listeners that theirs was the program selected to give new life and enjoyment to more listeners by placing the program on an afternoon schedule.
>
> "Playing more than twenty instruments the Texas Rangers offer western music in a tempo that adds new thrills to this always popular entertainment. Then the Rangers forget the west for a moment and tear into a bit of hot swing that leaves the 'alligators' clamoring for more. Tex Owens comes in with his 'Cattle Call' that is dear to the hearts of millions and the Rangers leave a sweetly solemn thought with a homey ballad and a familiar hymn appropriate to the day."

The move to Sunday afternoon must not have been noticed by many advertisers, as the broadcast continued unsponsored over the network. Behind the scenes, though, George Halley had been working his contacts and by June KMBC had a big fish on its line. On June 22 Halley informed Church that no less than the Blackett, Sample, Hummert agency had expressed interest in *Smilin' Valley Dude Ranch*, now referred to as *Smilin' Valley Ranch*.

The star of Blackett, Sample, Hummert was Frank Hummert, the highest paid advertising executive in radio by 1937. Along with his wife Anne, Frank Hummert virtually created the soap opera in the early 1930s, following a hunch that housewives would loyally follow daily installments of likable heroines. Hummert's theory paid off and Frank and Anne created long-running stalwarts such as *Just Plain Bill*, *Jack Armstrong*, *The Romance of Helen Trent*, *Ma Perkins*, and *Mr. Keen, Tracer of Lost Persons* and in the summer of 1938 they began seeking more information about *Smilin' Valley Ranch*. Blackett, Sample, Hummert requested an outline of an entire year's content based on a five-times-per-week schedule, to give clients an idea of the program's direction.

At the same time, another KMBC salesman, Harry Bingham, who had past success with the Corn Kix account, had interested a separate client in the show. With multiple advertisers interested in the program, Church urged quick action by Cool: *Smilin' Valley Ranch* "appears hot . . . this show is going to sell."

A meeting was scheduled with salesmen in early July and the disastrous results were shared with Church on July 8. Chick Allison, yet another KMBC salesman, apparently, had never heard of *Smilin' Valley Ranch* before he pitched it to the interested parties and "had no idea of what it was all about" according to Gomer Cool. On top of that, the recordings were not in good shape, a problem which would plague KMBC's efforts to sell *Life on the Red Horse Ranch* the next year. To top off the dismal sales meeting, Allison had no presentation of any kind worked up. He had apparently gone into the audition completely cold, with no knowledge of the show or any promotional material to present the potential sponsor.

It was clear that something was "drastically wrong," as Cool pointed out bluntly in a memo to Church. Church ran a tight organization; perhaps, Cool wondered, the salesmen were "not sold on or interested in" his shows.

"I do think," he continued, "it would be worth while for me to work with the salesmen-- tell them what I have in mind for the show-- get their frank reactions, before a show is auditioned. But perhaps that's out of line. According to our program director, about everything I've done in the past two years is out of line." Was it time for him to move on?, Cool pointedly hinted. Possibly this was not his first run-in with KMBC's sales staff.

Despite his frustration Cool was a team player who threw all his energy into the job at hand. His foremost responsibility was performing with the Rangers – and working to get *Smilin Valley Ranch* off the ground, as he detailed in his weekly report to Arthur Church. During the week of July 11 – 15, 1938, he explained, he appeared with the band on their 5:30 a.m. Show on Monday, Wednesday, and Friday. The Rangers took a break then regrouped at 10:30 for daily rehearsals. After another break they were back on the air for a daily 12:30 local broadcast. Cool was also squeezing in as many hours as possible on "a rush job" for the *Smilin Valley Ranch* audition script, for despite the poor initial sales pitch, interest in the concept remained. Cool had so much on his plate, in fact, that he missed Thursday's rehearsal. The absence caused some disgruntlement among the other band members and Cool subsequently felt the need to justify it in his report. "My feeling is that right now we must all give the 'audition' end of our jobs the first attention," he wrote, and hopefully the other boys would realize this, too. His other Ranger-related task that week was discussions and subsequent writing of the script for *Night Time on the Trail*, the band's Monday night program which was carried on CBS at 5:30 Central Time.

Beyond these assorted duties related to the Texas Rangers, Cool was involved in numerous other station programs. While most of the Rangers had other responsibilities beyond the band as well, they were generally music-related, while Cool's more frequently involved writing and producing. Among his productions was *The Joanne Taylor Show*, a daily program which aired from 8:15 to 9:15 in the morning. Debuting in 1932, and originally featuring Caroline Crockett Ellis as writer and the fictional character Joanne Taylor, *Joanne Taylor's Fashion Flashes* advertised the wares of local companies to great success. Bea Johnson took over the role of Joanne Taylor in 1936 when Montgomery Wards lured Ellis away to star in the transcribed series *The Travels of Mary Ward*. In addition to production duties, Cool had a few speaking lines in the program as well.

His week's schedule shows that much of Wednesday (July 13) and Thursday (July 14) were devoted to putting together the script and program details for a broadcast from Olathe, KS, for Farm Crop

Insurance. The show was carried over CBS at 1:45 on Friday (July 15). Now a major suburb of Kansas City with a population topping 125,000, in 1938 Olathe was a quiet rural outpost of less than 4,000, which seemed far removed from bustling Kansas City. The broadcast reportedly had many production problems that ate up more time than expected.

Several more hours that week were spent visiting the Helping Hand Farm to get material and ideas for a proposed KMBC series entitled *Adventures in Adversity*. The farm was connected with what is now called The Helping Hand of Goodwill Industries, which provided work and services to the area's needy. Workers at the farm grew food which was consumed by men, women, and children of the Helping Hand Institute.[1] Cool's goal was to have two scripts ready in the near future for a potential sponsor interested in building "good will" with the audience. Additional time was focused on one of the station's television programs for the week, which ended up being cancelled.

Fortunately, though *Smilin' Valley Dude Ranch* was never produced, a detailed audition script has survived and gives considerable insight to the proposed series, including the use of Rangers Clarence Hartman, Bob Crawford, and Herb Kratoska in acting roles. The announcer's introduction provides background not just on *Smilin' Valley*'s storyline but on Arthur Church and the performers cast in the program. Below is the beginning of audition's introduction:

> Gentlemen, you are about to hear three episodes from the new Arthur B. Church production, "Smilin' Valley Dude Ranch." Mr. Church has already introduced such well known national favorites as "Easy Aces", "Happy Hollow", "Between the Bookends", "Life on the Red Horse Ranch" and "Phenomenon". We feel certain that this program will prove equally successful. In the cast you will hear Johnny Green playing the part of our boy hero, Marty Green. Johnny is a typical loveable American boy who brings with him a wealth of professional experience in such programs as "Jimmy Allen", "Circus Adventures of Clyde Beatty" and many others. The part of Jim Sherwood, ranch foreman and companion of Marty Green, is portrayed by Woody Smith, veteran radio entertainer. Many Columbia network listeners will remember him as the big

---

1 Background on the Helping Hand Farm comes from the website of the Missouri-Kansas Goodwill Industries, http://www.mokangoodwill.org

Brother in the recent Big Brother Club series. Romantic interest in the role of Belle Williams is provided by Helen Grace Gardner, our feminine star of many KMBC productions.

Others in the cast are Clarence Hartman, a native of the Texas cattle country; Bob Crawford, who hails from the New Mexico plains; and Herb Kratoska as Loco, the jolly stable boy. And serving as a musical framework for our dramatic action we hear music by the Texas Rangers whose recording transcriptions

The post-war Texas Rangers lineup.
Courtesy of Jim Crawford.

on CBS broadcasts have made them popular coast to coast. Our show is written by Gomer Cool, author of numerous radio serials including the musical-dramatic western, "Life on the Red Horse Ranch". This thrilling western adventures story is a natural for unlimited merchandising. If you wish to tell your message to large responsive audiences of both children and grown-ups, it's the show for you. We present episodes one, ten, and twenty-five from the radio serial, "Smilin' Valley Dude Ranch".

Church, always on the lookout for profit-building promotional tie-ins for his programs, included several further selling points with this audition. First, the show's title, would incorporate the sponsor's name. Instead of the *Smilin' Valley Dude Ranch* it might be *Franklin's XX Dude Ranch* to use an imaginary company as an example. Each week's programs would include a contest, the winner of which would win a vacation to an actual dude ranch, all expenses paid, with transportation by TWA.

The Texas Rangers' multiple weekly broadcasts nationally over CBS and locally over KMBC remained the focus of their efforts. A surviving script from July 24, 1938, provides insight into the Rangers' Sunday afternoon (3:00 P.M. Central Time) broadcasts, which were carried unsponsored by CBS. It reveals that the basic structure of their show had not changed much since they debuted in 1932 indicating Arthur Church thought the idea was fundamentally sound, even if the Rangers had failed to pick up a national sponsor during that time.

> THEME   RIDE TEXAS RANGERS (FADE)
>
> ANNCR   Through our KMBC studios in Kansas City we invite you to join us for the songs of the Texas Rangers!
>
> THEME TO CONCLUSION
>
> ANNCR   In they ride again, those eight singing men of the West with music from the land of the tumble-week and sage-brush – music sung to the creak of the saddle and the rumble of cattle herds – the songs of the Texas Rangers!

The band then launched into "I Want to be a Cowboy's Sweetheart." Other numbers on the fifteen-minute show were "My True Love is Gone," "Dark Eyes," "I Left Her Standin' There,"

"Eleven More Months and Ten More Days," "Silver on the Sage," "Eyes of Texas," "Sweet By and By," and the closing theme "Ride Texas Rangers."

When the band's original master of ceremonies, Marion Fonville, left the outfit sometime in the mid-1930s after the production of the *Life on the Red Horse Ranch* transcription series, his role was eventually taken by Robert Crawford – or "Captain Bob." During these summer shows Crawford provided most, if not all, the dialog between musical numbers. Jimmy Coy is identified as the CBS announcer who introduced Crawford and the Texas Rangers.

The Texas Rangers made yet another bid for CBS' attention with a special audition program broadcast September 12, 1938. Originally called *Twilight on the Trail*, the show was finally aired as *Night Time on the Trail*. Unlike *Life on the Red Horse Ranch* and *Smilin' Valley Ranch*, the fifteen-minute program was primarily music, with bits of continuity connecting the tunes. The show opened:

EFFECTS   COYOTE HOWL

ANNOUNCER   Presenting – Night Time on the Trail!

THEME   COWBOY'S HEAVEN (SWELL.. THEN TO BACKGROUND FOR ANNCR)

ANNCR   We take you out along a western trail and invite you to an open campfire. There resting from a long day in the saddle are eight Rangers, bronzed by the prairie sun. As their horses graze nearby and a hungry coyote howls from the distant hills, they blend their voices in familiar songs of the west.

The boys then proceeded to sing such songs as "Ridin' Down the Canyon," "I'd Like to be in Texas," and "April Kisses."

The final version of the *Night Time on the Trail* script presents an interesting contrast to Cool's initial proposal, which opened with the announcer speaking in verse, a gimmick that echoed that used in a similar program, the syndicated *Pinto Pete & His Ranch Boys*. Wade Lane, the basso profundo and radio veteran in California, produced, wrote, and starred in this program, but later he was better known as Strollin' Tom. *Pinto Pete & His Ranch Boys* also featured the Rangers' now Chicago-based counterparts, The Ranch Boys.

The original opening lines of Cool's script, quite reminiscent of Lane's verse, instead were:

> ANNCR   Out on the plains where the sagebrush blooms,
> Where the sun is shining ever,
> The cowboy roams – a sorry man -
> For his day is gone forever.
> But let's wander back in memory's dream
> To the outposts that used to be,
> Where the badlands yield to the crystal stream
> As it wends its way to the sea.

The songs, though, were nearly the same, including "Sleepy Rio Grande," "I'd Like to be in Texas," "April Kisses," and "When the Bloom is on the Sage."

Night Time on the Trail was carried over the CBS network beginning in late summer, 1938, and the broadcast of Sunday, October 9, 1938, at 9:00 p.m. was used as a gauge of the show's popularity. Gomer Cool reported positive listener responses from coast-to-coast. One Los Angeles listener commented "Please let me congratulate you upon your presentation of the new program 'Night Time on the Trail' with the Texas Rangers . . . the program was quite unique and I enjoyed hearing a program so different after having heard other programs that were all very much alike. Yours for more programs like 'Night Time on the trail.'"

Another L. A. listener agreed, "Let me thank you for the cowboy music over your station at 7 PM Sunday known as Night Time on the Trail with the Texas Rangers. Real harmony. Unusual story. Let's have it every Sunday night."

On the other coast a Massachusetts listener was no less enthusiastic. She said "Last night . . . you gave us the Texas Rangers at 10 instead of a program otherwise planned. It was a joy to hear the Texas Rangers with their sweet songs especially my favorite 'The Last Roundup' and I hope they can come over the air to us very often at that time."

Urban Midwesterners wanted more, too. "Just to say," wrote a Detroit listener, "we enjoyed the Texas Rangers very much. It was the program following the Ford Sunday Evening Hour. Hope we get to hear them again."

Despite the positive notes of feedback, Church was not overly optimistic. Responding to Cool's memo he wrote, "Thanks for the above [listener notes]. I'll use it in another effort with CBS, but I've about exhausted my resources in trying to sell them on the idea of taking off one of their pets for ours." Nevertheless, *Night Time on the Trail* was picked up by CBS affiliates into the early weeks of 1939, proving it was finding at least a select audience.

In the meantime, the Rangers' adventure serial *Smilin' Valley Ranch* was going nowhere quickly, after a lot of promising interest just months before. KMBC attempted to record some episodes in October, 1938, with minimal success. Documents do not indicate if the recordings were made in Kansas City or back at the World Broadcasting studios in Chicago, where Church had recorded *Life on the Red Horse Ranch* in 1935 and *Phenomenon* in 1937. Regardless of the recording location, the results did not excite station management. Cool had rewritten the scripts upon request and a cast was pulled together, but after three hours of rehearsals both Cool and the executive in charge "agreed that the scripts were wrong and some of the cast wrong."

The scripts were rewritten yet again, though not to management's satisfaction. Casting of the lead character, Marty Green, was problematic, too. Months before, Woody Smith had been identified as the actor behind Jim Sherwood's voice, but he was definitely not "the right boy for the feature part." The one unidentified actor who best fit the role (possibly Johnny Green who was identified in the first audition summary) was decidedly too old for the part as it was now written. Somewhat despondent, a memo from another KMBC producer, Stu Eggleston, noted "it will take a lot of time and some expense ever to get this show right and I wonder if it wouldn't be better to forget it and try an entirely new western kid show. I cannot help but feel that this particular show best be discarded unless a brilliant writer can be found and an outstanding boy actor discovered."

Cool was not the only Ranger busy with other projects for the station. For example, Fran Mahaney had the chance to star in his own program, an audition of which was aired November 10, 1938, at 7:00 p.m. on KMBC, for a local audience. The try-out was for Perry Sargeant, a men's clothing store located at Tenth and Walnut, Kansas City. Introduced as "that Dapper Dan of Melody," Mahaney veered away from the Western standards popular with the Texas Rangers and used more American standards such as "Heart and Soul" from the musical *A Song is Born* and "Summertime" from George Gershwin's *Porgy and Bess*. Mahaney's show was a straight musical affair without the patter found in Texas Rangers' programming. He had no lines; all continuity was read by an unidentified announcer.

Tex Owens and the Texas Rangers

Throughout the 1930s, Tex Owens maintained a strong identity independent of the Texas Rangers despite his legitimate claim to be the "Original Texas Ranger." Unfortunately, his career has not yet been documented in great detail and the Arthur Church papers offer only clues as to his exact relationship over the years with the Texas Rangers and with Church himself. Two pieces of evidence, however, suggest that by 1938 he and the band were no longer playing together on any sort of regular basis and that the two acts' separation was not completely amicable. A schedule of his 1938 concerts, which was very heavy from April to October, the best months for road travel during pre-Interstate days, indicates live performances were an important part of his contribution to the station's bottom line, just as they were for the Rangers. The frequency of concerts would certainly have made it difficult for Owens to have any sort of regularly broadcast radio show, though certainly not impossible. Such a grueling schedule of concert dates and radio appearances would not have been out of the ordinary during the time for a regional artist like Owens.

Tex Owens 1938 Touring Schedule

February 4 – Trenton, MO
February 5 – Ararat Temple, Kansas City
February 9 – Butler, MO
February 15 – Harrisonville, MO
February 22 – Clinton, MO
March 8 – Clinton, MO
March 11 – Carrolton, MO
March 12 – Shell City, MO
March 15 – Olathe, KS
March 17 – Osawatomie, KS
March 18 – Trenton, MO
March 19 – Harrisonville, MO
March 21 – Irving, KS
March 22 – Herington, KS
March 25 – Chillicothe, MO
March 30 – Lawrence, KS
April 1 – Pleasant Hill, MO
April 3 – Warrensburg, MO
April 19 – Clinton, MO
April 20 – Fayette, MO
April 21 – Ottawa, KS
April 22 – Carrolton, MO
April 25 – Sedalia, MO
April 26 – Slater, MO
April 27 – Macon, MO or KS not clear
April 28 – Marceline, MO
April 29 – Iola, KS
May 3 – Osage City, KS
May 4 – Paola, KS
May 5 – Excelsior Springs, MO
May 9 – Brookfield, MO
May 10 – Marysville, KS
May 11 – Hiawatha, KS
May 12 – Marshall, MO
May 13 – Chillicothe, MO
May 16 – Moberly, MO
May 17 – Macon, MO or KS not clear
May 18 – Lawrence, KS
May 20 – Pleasant Hill, MO
May 22 – Warrensburg, MO
May 23 – Manhattan, KS
May 24 – Herington, KS
May 25 – Osawatomie, KS

May 26 – Junction City, KS
May 27 – Booneville, MO
May 30 – Brookfield, MO
June 1 – Windsor, MO
June 2 – Excelsior Springs, MO
June 9 – Lexington, MO
June 15 – Cameron, MO
June 16 – Booneville, MO
June 17 – Kirksville, MO
June 22 – Nevada, MO
June 23 & 24 Lamar, MO
June 27 – Lexington, MO
June 29 – Windsor, MO
July 1 – Brookfield, MO
July 2 – Urich, MO
July 4 – Moberly, MO
July 5 – Sedalia, MO
July 7 – Kirksville, MO
July 8 – Marshall, MO
July 9 – Chillicothe, MO
July 12 – Slater, MO
July 13 – Cameron, MO
July 15 – Clinton, MO
July 16 – Hamilton, MO or KS not clear
July 20 – Marceline, MO
July 23 – Pleasant Hill, MO
July 29 – Gallatin, MO
July 30 – Warrensburg, MO
August 30 – Stockton, MO or KS not clear
August 31 – Stockton, MO or KS not clear
September 3 – Independence, KS
September 8 – Alma, MO or KS not clear
September 12 – Rich Hill, MO
September 13 – Osceola, MO
September 14 – El Dorado Springs, MO
September 17 – Marysville, KS
September 21 – Brunswick, MO
September 22 – Salisbury, MO
September 23 – Savannah, MO

September 23 – Jubilesta, Municipal Auditorium, Kansas City, MO
September 24 – Pattonsburg, MO
September 27 – Warsaw, MO
September 28 – Sweet Springs, MO
September 30 – Excelsior Springs, MO
October 1 – Excelsior Springs, MO
October 2 – Appearance with Horace Heidt
October 6 – Savannah, MO
October 7 – Hickman Mills, MO
October 8 – El Dorado Springs, MO
October 11 – Versailles, MO
October 12 – Plattsburg, MO
October 15 – Humansville, MO
October 18 – Sedalia, MO
October 19 – Tipton, MO
October 20 – Archie, MO
October 21 – Gallatin, MO
October 22 – Tarkio, MO
October 31 – Show for Folgers Coffee
November 2 – Plattsburg, MO
November 6 – Pattonsburg, MO
November 9 – Stockton, MO or KS not clear
November 11 – Pleasanton, KS
November 18 – Maywood Church, exact location unknown
November 27 – Hill Billy Show, no further details
December 9 – Craig, MO
December 13 – Camdenton, MO
December 14 – Eldon, MO
December 16 – Rock Port, MO
December 27 – Bolivar, MO
December 28 – Buffalo, MO or KS not clear
December 29 – Norborne, MO
December 30 – Concordia, MO or KS not clear
December 31 – Gardner, KS

For these 117 shows and the countless miles which tied them together, Owens earned $2,575.27, or just over $22 per concert ($340 in 2010 dollars). Records do not indicate the touring costs racked up by Owens during the year, costs which likely were incurred by KMBC. Over the course of the year he was also credited with 29 appearances on *Brush Creek Follies* and 24 weeks of radio sponsored by Chicago's Aladdin Mantle Lamp Company. Owens rarely performed live on Saturdays that year, so likely his schedule was arranged to minimize conflicts with the *Brush Creek* broadcasts. For all this work "Tex" Owens pulled down $3,849.22, the equivalent of between $50,000 and $60,000 dollars in 2010, not bad for a hillbilly musician in Depression-era Kansas City.[1]

That some animosity may have lay behind the increasingly separate work load of Owens and the Rangers became clear in early 1939, when Clarence Hartman wrote a letter to Stu Eggleston of KMBC's management. "The Texas Rangers," Hartman complained to Eggleston on January 10, "are somewhat disappointed in learning that we are to share the honor to be bestowed on us on next Saturday's broadcast by the Governor of Texas, with someone whom we feel is entirely outside our group." Hartman was willing to concede that Owens may have had some "relation to the Rangers' group . . . in the past."

Gomer Cool, on the other hand, was unwilling to concede even that much when quizzed about Owens over seventy years later. He was emphatic that Owens *was not* a member of the Rangers though they did play together. Evidence suggests, however, that Owens had, indeed, been a key member of the original lineup in 1932-33. Yet his absence from the show when it finally coalesced into its classic format in the fall of 1933, when his boots appear to have temporarily been filled by the 'Colorado Ranger' Ozie Waters, may have contributed to his alienation from the octet that became the Rangers. Similarly, his return to prominent place in the show, and his major role in *Life on the Red Horse Ranch*, for example, might have contributed to the Rangers' resentment of him. By that time, they had established an identity and camaraderie as a group, and Owens truly was apart from that. Jim Crawford, son of Bob Crawford, admitted the band and Tex had their differences, and it may have simply been a clash of personalities rather than disagreements over specific artistic issues. His impression was that the band members felt Owens was pushy and

Tex Owens.
Courtesy of Ryan Ellett.

took some positions that created conflict when eight other musicians were expected to fall in line.

That being said, by the beginning of 1939 Hartman and the rest of the band were all of the opinion that, "for a long while . . . [Tex hadn't] added anything to [their] network broadcasts." A recent bone of contention had occurred on a broadcast just before Christmas, 1938, when Owens complained to others at the station that the Rangers were responsible for some mistakes he had made on the show. When confronted about the accusation, Owens was quick to apologize and acknowledge the band members had tried to help him with the number in question during rehearsals. That he and the Rangers were clearly not on the best of terms, is further suggested by a letter Hartman wrote Church that addressed Owens' exact standing of Tex Owens in the history of the Texas Rangers. "It is my understanding that Tex has made the statement that he was a part of the original Texas Ranger group," recounted Hartman, "but I learn from some of the old timers here in the station that he never, at any time, has been a member of the Texas Ranger group." Hartman was relying on hearsay here, and the motives, of and on which side of the fence his informants stood, is unclear.

Owens had, unquestionably, been an integral part of the original Texas Rangers radio show, but it might all boil down to a question of semantics. The early Rangers show was just that: a musical show, but not one that comprised of a specific band of that name, per se. As the show evolved in its early stages, there was a subtle shift in what "The Texas Rangers" signified: from a show with a loose group of entertainers–Fonville as the announcer and Old-Timer, Owens singing his songs, Edwards doing his blackface shtick as Cookie, etc.–to a clearly defined musical group who took the name of the show. And as time dimmed the memory of the original broadcasts, the group and the show became the same thing.

Church's reply does not provide any definite insight as to the standing of Tex Owens within the historical structure of the band. His handwritten response avoids the issue: "It is my feeling that the group has nothing to lose by having Tex included ... and even more important – [it] is valuable to KMBC." Clearly the issue of membership was a relative non-issue to Church, perhaps because the group was a business operation for him and not the close-knit family it had become to the men who had rehearsed, toured, and performed together so closely for several years. For the Rangers, the band was personal; for Church it was one of several money-making arms of his radio station, and individual claims to membership only concerned him insofar as these conflicts might affect their work.

The Rangers' arguments were to little avail and, as originally scheduled, Texas governor James Allred declared Owens and all

Texas Governor James Allred names the band honorary Texas Rangers. Courtesy of Jim Crawford.

Bob Crawford's certificate recognizing him as an honorary Texas Ranger. Courtesy of Jim Crawford.

eight of the Texas Rangers honorary members of the legendary law enforcement organization. Church may have chosen to avoid settling the matter in a firm manner at this time because evidence suggests Owens was instrumental in arranging for the commissions in the first place. Tradition passed down through the families of individual Rangers indicate that it was Owens' connections back in Texas that brought them the honorary recognition, which makes the Rangers' objections seem petty and short-sighted in retrospect. The Texas Rangers as a group may have reflected well on the state and organization that their name honored, but Owens was a native son, and reportedly also had some previous experience as an officer of the law, adding credence on several levels to the honor that the State of Texas was prepared to bestow upon the group. Arthur Church would naturally have wanted to avoid any decisions or statements that might have marred the event. Some of the other members felt it was publicity generated by the honor which helped them land their first movie roles with Gene Autry a few months later. Ironically, the visit was very likely the first time that the Rangers, apart from Hartman, had ever actually been in the state of Texas.

Tex Owens' son wrote to Arthur Church almost a decade after the honorary bestowment that relations between Owens and the Texas Rangers had certainly been raw in the past, and the hard feelings had not been assuaged by time. In 1948 the younger Owens alluded to conflicts between Owens, who at that time was living in Compton, CA, and the Texas Rangers: "… now about my daddy, Mr. Church. You know, and I know, that you never will have another personality like him, I don't know why you don't try to get him back. He did more for your station than anyone else, as a single I mean, and he's had so much tough luck, he was just getting the breaks when you let the Rangers push him around, and I know it and so does he, and he's a big man to be hurt by 8 little men that are too jealous to even help themselves."

Trail Blazers

Despite their personal differences, some of which lingered for years, the musicians were able to put them aside and carry on as professionals. By the end of November, 1938, nine months after CBS switched their Sunday spot from morning to afternoon, the Texas Rangers continued to dominate the competition in Kansas City. They racked up a 46% rating on the Sunday spot, with *Magic Key of RCA* coming in a distant second, reaching only 14% of listeners. The Red network's *Olympic Preview* attracted a 9.5% rating and Mutual's

Adult Educational Round Table a meager 5%. Their weekday spots, Mondays, Wednesdays, and Fridays, were no less impressive, though the competition was closer. NBC Red's *Musical Clock* reached 24.5% of listeners, just over half the number tuned into the Rangers, 46%.

An extant script from a January 8, 1939, broadcast gives us an idea of the Rangers' Sunday afternoon network format. It opened:

> THEME: RIDE TEXAS RANGERS (FADE)
>
> ANNCR: Through our KMBC studios in Kansas City, the Gateway to the West, we bring you the songs of the Texas Rangers and Tex Owens.
>
> THEME: (TO END)
>
> YELLS...AD LIBS
>
> 1. (INSTRUMENTAL INTRO) ROOTIN' TOOTIN' TWO GUN SHOOTIN' COW MAN
>
> ANNCR: (OVER MUSIC) Here they are – those ridin' singin' men of the west, with our favorite songs of the prairie trail – the Texas Rangers!

As had become customary since the departure of Marion Fonville, Bob Crawford provided most of the between-song commentary during the program rather than the announcer whose main job was to open and close the episodes. Songs from this broadcast included "Prairie Dreamboat," "The Mule Song," and "Never Say Goodbye."

More than three months after Eggleston had essentially nixed further work on *Smilin' Valley Ranch*, Cool accepted his challenge to create a new show premise for the Texas Rangers. His latest idea was *Trail Blazers*, which he summarized in a letter from February 22, 1939. Abandoning the serial format, *Trail Blazers* was to be a western anthology series focusing on "true stories of pioneers as told to us by their descendants." Gimmicks included using children or grandchildren of pioneers in a short interview segment, as well as accepting family stories submitted by listeners.

In response to Cools' request for a green light to put together an audition, Eggleston was enthusiastic. "I think you've got something here," he wrote. In addition to getting an audition ready, Cool was asked to compile a list of about six future story ideas to flesh out the concept. The timing for the project, however, proved to be less than ideal. At the same time, details for a West Coast relocation were being finalized and all eight members of the Texas Rangers would soon make the move from Kansas City to Los Angeles. This move, which for some of the band's members included uprooting families, was a top priority for each Ranger, and during much of the spring of 1939 attention to the development of new projects for the band slowed or came to a stop.

Trail Blazers would be just one of several Texas Rangers radio ideas which never moved past the conceptual phase. Despite Stu Eggleston's enthusiasm for the premise, the show was quietly shelved. No complete scripts survive, raising the question of whether or not Cool was ever able to finish the assignment. Neither is the program ever mentioned again by the Texas Rangers or KMBC executives, save for a single credit on Gomer Cool's professional biography written during that time period. Radio had been good to the Rangers for seven years and their ratings had consistently placed their broadcasts at the top of their various timeslots. But now everyone felt it was time to test other avenues: The big screen was calling.

Chapter 5: Hollywood

Colorado Sunset

In the spring of 1939 the Texas Rangers relocated to Hollywood and entered the movie business. Despite a few disappointments, the Rangers' talent and appeal, combined with the acumen and commitment of Arthur Church and his staff, had seen the group go from strength to strength. But this new venture opened up potential for far greater recognition and income. Although they were generally considered fodder for secondary features, i.e., "B movies" in the parlance of the day, with a similar meaning today, with top-billing only in smaller cities and the hinterlands, Western films were nevertheless big business. From Gene Autry's unlikely, but phenomenal, emergence as a star in 1935, singing cowboys had proliferated on screen and off. By one accounting, over 2,600 Western films were produced during the 1930s, 1940s, and 1950s, more than 85 per year or three new pictures every two weeks. While the genre would eventually boast of serious adult dramas such as *High Noon*, *Shane*, and *The Gunfighter*, during the pre-World War II years most were considered "B" fare and were geared primarily to young boys who idolized the likes of Tom Mix, Ken Maynard, and Buck Jones.

Neither Arthur Church, nor the Texas Rangers themselves, were under any illusions that they would become movie stars, but the singing cowboy craze had opened up lucrative possibilities for groups like the Rangers. While Autry had not been the first screen cowboy to sing, he was the first "Singing Cowboy" in a new genre that he had defined from the outset. Others came in his wake, with varying degrees of success, including Tex Ritter, Dick Foran, Fred Scott, and eventually an up-and-coming Roy Rogers, whose big break came when Autry walked out in a contract dispute in 1938. While the Texas Rangers were working on *Life on the Red Horse Ranch* in 1935, Autry was honing his acting skills in *In Old Santa Fe* and *Mystery Mountain*, a film and serial respectively, starring Ken Maynard, and then as the lead in the 12-part serial *Phantom Empire*. Prior to this, Autry had been a radio star at WLS in Chicago, and had steadily built his reputation as a recording artist after getting his initial break as a blue yodeler firmly in the mode of country music superstar Jimmie Rodgers. From his initial movie breakthrough in 1935, Autry's success had been phenomenal, and he was at the height of his fame by the time Arthur Church and the Rangers came calling.

One of the more significant by-products of the rise of the singing cowboys were the opportunities the films offered to other Western musical performers, particularly regionally prominent bands like the Texas Rangers. Again, Autry was a trendsetter. From the beginning, his films gave screen time to Western bands and singing groups. Most of the other singing cowboys followed suit, but Autry seemed particularly committed to the idea. While he occasionally used bands from the L.A.-area, like the Beverly Hill Billies, more often than not, he and his producers chose a band popular in a certain part of the country. This was in one sense simply astute business–using regionally popular bands, like the Light Crust Doughboys from Texas or the Tennessee Ramblers from North Carolina, would up the box office takings where those bands were popular–but that was far from the only reason the policy was pursued.

Autry liked the bands, too. In many cases, he hired groups he had encountered and been impressed by, or simply befriended, on his tours, and he seemed also to have liked to give up-and-comers the same kind of break he had been given. A number of groups had been featured in Autry films by 1939, and these appearances are historically significant today. They often afford fans and historians the only surviving footage of legendary Western musicians in action in their heydays or otherwise. These extra musical offerings were not de riguer in the Singing Cowboy westerns, but they were a common feature.

Among the groups that had taken fullest advantage of this in the coming years was the Texas Rangers' regular competition, the Los Angeles-based Sons of the Pioneers. They became established western movie favorites as early as 1936, with Autry and particularly with Charles Starrett, who though not a singer himself reflected the trend. Starrett's movies invariably featured Western bands or singers in support, as did those of other non-singers like Buck Jones and Johnny Mack Brown, who would later prove important in the Rangers' Hollywood years.

When the contract for the band to be featured in an upcoming Autry western was actually finalized is uncertain, as is when the decision was made to actually relocate the band to Hollywood for a considerable period beyond the few weeks' contracted work with Autry. It likely occurred sometime after February, when Cool was still working on the *Trail Blazers* audition, but well before May 19, when the band actually arrived in Hollywood.

Unfortunately, little survives in the Church files on the Rangers' move from Kansas City to Los Angeles. The move required no small investment on the part of Arthur Church, a man who did not spend money unless he felt there was a good chance of a healthy return. It is unclear whether Church or one of his representatives approached Autry, or Republic Studios, or if, in fact, Hollywood came calling. The group's sustained runs on CBS, and its reputation in the Midwest and beyond, would undeniably have piqued the interest of Republic as a sure-fire audience builder in the group's home territory. But it remains possible that this was a rare gamble by Church, who perhaps hoped, among other things, that a dramatic cross-country move and national exposure via film would reinvigorate a musical outfit whose greater prospects within the Kansas City region were limited. As successful as they may have been in and around Kansas City, there was little more for the Rangers to do there but cover the same ground. Cool might have been keen to think up new outlets for the band's talents, but in the end, it was just window dressing. If the Rangers were going to do anything more than sustain their popularity within KMBC's range, something new needed to be added to the mix.

It is reasonable to surmise that former KMBC writer Paul Henning, mentioned earlier, introduced former boss Arthur Church to the idea of giving the Texas Rangers a shot in film. Though not a film script writer himself, but as a writer for the popular radio comedy *Fibber McGee & Molly*, he could have had a number of Hollywood connections, both through the comedy team's 1937 film work in *This Way Please* and the program's relocation from Chicago to Los Angeles at the beginning of 1939. Correspondence from soon after the move confirms that Henning was an early contact of the band members in California.

The Texas Rangers were fortuitous in that their screen debut was with Gene Autry, affording them prestige and exposure they would not otherwise have enjoyed; however, it was ultimately neither the pleasure nor the calling card that the band and Church undoubtedly hoped it would be. Few of Autry's personal and business records survive from this era, and extant KMBC records offer no insight to the development of the professional relationship between Autry and the Rangers. So, we are left with what is on the screen and second-hand accounts of the experience. What is clear is that the Texas Rangers as a group were not fond of Gene Autry personally, though they had no problem working with him. Like their boss, Arthur Church, Autry was a hard-nosed businessman behind his screen and stage persona. His approach to work was very cut-and-dried, an attitude that Bob Crawford's son Jim Crawford said rubbed against the musical orientation of some band members. Whatever they, or the other band members, may have felt about Autry, two Rangers ended up working for him. Paul Sells would leave the Rangers in 1940 for a decade's work with Autry, and Clarence Hartman worked numerous recording sessions and other performances with Autry after World War II.

Production on Republic Pictures' *Colorado Sunset*, the Texas Rangers' first picture with the singer, was originally scheduled to begin on May 22, 1939, a date which was subsequently pushed back to May 31. In late May, 1939, the contracts were being written up for Church's signature after his agreement to waive the band's services for KMBC during the time necessary to film *Colorado Sunset*. In return, Church gained Republic's assurance that the band would be billed as the KMBC-CBS Texas Rangers, a name that both gave some free publicity to KMBC and emphasized the bands' experience performing over the national radio chain.

The group did some pre-recording of musical tracks during the final days of May before their first scheduled day of filming, May 31. As might be expected, the band members were excited about doing the film and were hopeful it might lead to many more opportunities in California, according to surviving correspondence from George Ferguson, who worked with the band through the Artists Bureau, Inc. One drawback with the film project, however, was that for the time being the Texas Rangers could not do any broadcasting, including their established weekly network show started in Kansas City. Restrictions were imposed by the Los Angeles Musicians' Union on new members or musicians transferring from other union locals. Perhaps, Ferguson wrote, some talented guests could be found to fill in for the Rangers until they could resume their radio show. Cool was disappointed by the turn of events, admitting in a letter to Church that losing the CBS spot "was quite a blow to us," and gloomily acknowledging, "Columbia can't do much for us now until our picture job is over." The limits to radio work imposed on the boys after their West Coast move seem to have caught them and Church off guard. Still, Cool thought overall things were looking up for the Texas Rangers.

A letter written by Cool at the end of May, 1939, reveals the band was not letting the loss of their network spot wreck their spirits. They were taking quickly to Southern California. The first Sunday after the cross-country relocation, for example, Cool went on a deep sea fishing boat and caught seven barracuda and several mackerel, which he described as "THE THRILL OF MY LIFE." The Rangers caught up with Ruth and Paul Henning, former KMBC employees, who were now making a name for themselves in Hollywood. The Cools attended a party at the Hennings and the Rangers reminisced about old times with Lew Marcelle, with whom they had worked on *Life on the Red Horse Ranch* a few years earlier. Marcelle and his wife had moved to California to pursue work with the movie studios, and he had enjoyed some success.

On another occasion, the Rangers attended a lawn party as the guests of honor at the ranch home of Smiley Burnette, with whom they became acquainted during the filming of *Colorado Sunset*. Several directors were there including Bill Eason, who also went by B. Reeves Eason and Breezy Easton, the latter used by Cool in his letters. Eason was director of dozens of shorts, films, and serials, especially westerns. Making a less than dramatic entrance, Eason and his wife appeared via a small cart pulled by "the laziest looking donkey." The Texas Rangers entertained party-goers with some tunes.

Cool found the experience of making *Colorado Sunset* different from what he had expected. Things were certainly less organized than he thought they would be. Even after several days of shooting at the end of May, the band still did not have a final script, though it had gone through several rewritings. The first four days, in fact, they had done nothing except "show up on the lot, sit around 'till noon, go out to dinner, and then go home." However, the fifth day, a Friday, found them recording for 11 ½ hours before kicking off for the day. They were used as accompaniment for every song, but they had not been given a chance for their own tune without Autry or Burnette and continued to push for one. All the boys had lines, though Cool admitted he was not sure they would all make the final cut, and they all got the chance to ride horses. Years later, when the film was edited to air on television, several of the Rangers' speaking parts were cut, and it would be many more years before the uncut film was released on video tape and later DVD.

It was a pleasant surprise for the band members to find that the production company had what Cool called a "democratic attitude" and was open to their suggestions, engaging in some back-and-forth regarding the numbers they played and other matters. Cool felt that Republic actually wanted them to be satisfied with the final picture, even though they were just background players. Cool also confessed to being a bit starstruck and excited to see such actors as Bruce Cabot, Jean Parker, and Phil Reagan around the studio lot, faces he and the others were used to seeing on the big screen.

Beginning June 1, 1939, the Rangers worked on location for at least four days, when all the riding and outdoor scenes were shot. They were long days: band members woke up at 4:00 a.m., were at work by 6:00 and did not knock off until dark. Cool also noted that the band had been warned to be wary of the stunt men hired to do the potentially dangerous riding scenes. They were known to "lay for the greenhorns who come in from the east," he wrote.

There were some problems regarding the band's representation, as well. George Ferguson had been involved in getting the Texas Rangers the Autry film booking, only to learn soon after that he was no longer representing the act. He had already lined up personal appearances in San Francisco and other parts of Northern California, and was hopeful that the issue of representation could be worked out with his agency. But he appears to have been superseded by the head of the CBS Artists Bureau, Murry Brophy. Brophy assured the band they could have a long and fruitful career working out of Hollywood once he got busy promoting them. In Brophy's opinion, *Colorado Sunset* was "VERY small fry," and he was eager to set up a "glorified audition" of the band for the heads of CBS, various ad agencies, and motion picture producers. Even the union difficulties could be ironed out, Brophy insisted. With work on Autry's film completed and a summer ahead of them with no immediate prospects, Brophy's plan

Texas Rangers with Smiley Burnette.
Courtesy of Steve Cool.

was to get the band into some theater bookings for the time being and then rustle up more work when "fall business opens up."

Half a continent away, Arthur Church still kept close tabs on the progress of his Los Angeles employees, even though Gomer Cool expressed frustration with the lack of communication between themselves and Church or any KMBC executives. While he might not have been communicating directly with the Rangers as much as Cool and the others would have hoped, he was continually involved in their day-to-day activities. Just as the Rangers were getting into the bulk of their work for *Colorado Sunset*, Church fired off a letter to Brophy concerning the contract the band had ultimately signed with Republic. Since Church's letters apparently have not survived, the exact nature of his concerns are not known, but in his reply, Brophy assured him that the contract the Rangers had signed was a standard freelance contract with the Screen Actors Guild. It called for three weeks work and guaranteed that they would receive $2,000, with no attached options. They were bound to Republic only for the one film.

It was necessary for the band to join the Screen Actors' Guild because of the strength of unions within the film industry. A sum of $238 was picked up by Republic. Each Ranger had to join individually;

the union would not allow the studio to hire them as a band, so each signed an individual contract with Republic. Slightly complicating the issue of pay was the four instrumentalists' membership in the musicians' union. These four, thus, were paid $66 per week and were paid a bonus above that amount to bring their full salary for film work in line with what the remaining members of the group were paid.

It's possible Church was distrustful of an agreement letter he had to sign with Republic releasing the men to work on the job. Nevertheless, the Artist Bureau's George Ferguson, who had worked so hard to secure the Autry film work for the Texas Rangers, assured Church that the release was only for Republic's protection and the Rangers continued to be under exclusive contract with KMBC. All the paperwork was an effort to avoid any post-release problems.

When *Colorado Sunset* was released on July 31st, the Texas Rangers were understandably thrilled to see themselves on the big screen. Bob Crawford was so excited that, much to the chagrin of his family, he would drag them all to watch the picture every time it was booked in a theater near their Burbank home. "Dad was just tickled to death," Jim Crawford recalled, "I never got so sick of one movie in my life!"

Johnny Mack Brown and *Under Western Skies*

By the summer of 1939 the Texas Rangers had wrapped up their work on Autry's picture and earned a new CBS radio network spot called *Under Western Skies* which starred Western film hero Johnny Mack Brown and female vocalists Leta Gayle and Ruth Halloway. The series was, like the bands' previous networks slots, unsponsored and hit a surprising number of snags while getting up and running, considering the Rangers' extensive radio experience. Charles Vanda, program director of CBS' Pacific Network, complained to KMBC's Karl Koeper in a July 15, 1939, letter that the network had to pay upfront for some unforeseen stand-by fees to the musicians' union, fees which, if Vanda had known about them from the beginning, would have made CBS "rather reluctant to make any commitment for this series."

To get the first broadcast up to the level desired by the network, CBS had paid $122 for extra rehearsals, a seemingly small sum but "a hell of a lot more" than Vanda had wanted to pay. To cut down expenses, Rangers accordion player Paul Sells composed all the vocal arrangements, which involved Halloway as well. Vanda admitted that they squeezed about three weeks worth of arranging out of Sells in one week for $125. This amount, compared to $41.67, which CBS had tried to pay Sells before the union stepped in and demanded the higher fee.

Despite the cost overruns, Vanda and CBS were willing to continue with the show because they had received considerable interest from potential sponsors. They were positive than within two months the show would be sold. Union Oil, in fact, was proving to be a very good prospect for a West Coast broadcast, which the network hoped might bring in $750 to $1,000 per episode.

Even though the Texas Rangers were back on network radio, Arthur Church was not happy. He wrote a scathing letter on July 29, 1939, accusing Artist Bureau general manager Murry Brophy of not keeping Church and KMBC brass in the loop on Rangers matters and even arranging projects for the band without Church's explicit consent. In a cool response Brophy assured Arthur that he would be "a good soldier" and "comply with your requests as outlined in this letter and either submit personally or have one of the men in the office submit all offers we secure for the TEXAS RANGERS before final commitments are made."

When accused of not providing any updates during the entire month of July, Brophy reminded Church of a telephone conversation they had just before Church left for the National Association of Broadcasters convention, which would take him out of town for several weeks to Atlantic City and New York. Since no business of any importance arose during that time, Brophy protested, he saw no reason to disturb Church on his trip. Brophy was also defensive about Church's criticism of the compensation he contracted with Universal for their second movie appearance, in Johnny Mack Brown's *Oklahoma Frontier*. Church questioned the $1,250 paid for five days of work during the summer of 1939, even though, Brophy pointed out, the Rangers had taken proportionately less with *Colorado Sunset*, on which they were paid $2,000 for three weeks of work shooting and recording.

Despite the bickering between KMBC and CBS management, *Under Western Skies* premiered in July, 1939, and aired through September 29 as a summer replacement series. A Friday afternoon broadcast slot in Los Angeles allowed for plum evening air times in Kansas City and even New York City. The trade magazine *Variety* gave *Under Western Skies* a positive plug in their July 12 issue, describing the Rangers as "a well-integrated unit ... far ahead of the usual cowboy giver-outers and showing evidence of discipline, rehearsal and musicianship ... the Rangers deliver a good grade of alfalfa." Brown, who played both himself and characters such as "Boss Wrangler," and the Texas Rangers were the only cast members to appear in all episodes. Singers Leta Gayle and Ruth Holloway appeared in separate broadcasts. Jerome Lawrence, prolific playwright and radio and television scriptwriter, is credited with penning the series, which opened with an announcer intoning that the program represented "the spirit, the color, and the romance of the west in a half hour of songs and stories by America's foremost singers of Western music."

The Texas Rangers on *Under Western Skies* with Johnny Mack Brown. Courtesy of Jim Crawford.

One KMBC promotional sheet credits Gomer Cool as a "writer" for *Under Western Skies*. Since this same sheet refers to Cool as the "author" of series such as *Red Horse Ranch* and *Night Time on the Trail*, series on which he is known to have been the lead writer, this possibly indicates that Cool had some input into the *Under Western Skies* scripts, even if Lawrence was credited as the primary writer. Ralph Scott served as producer of the short-lived series.[1] A station log of one *Under Western Skies* broadcast indicates a total of 67 CBS outlets picked up the program (see appendix C for complete list) from coast to coast.

Cool recalled that two other Kansas City transplants were associated with *Under Western Skies*. The first was Fred Shields, who appeared in some of the show's dramatic skits and reportedly worked as an announcer on one of KMBC's competitors before he relocated to the West Coast. The other was Johnny Boyland, who was credited with some writing duties on the program.

At the same time that *Under Western Skies* was hitting the airwaves, the Rangers had also started work on a second film with Johnny Mack Brown, their third overall since moving to California earlier in the year. Filming commenced some time in late July or early August, 1939. Arthur Church signed a contract with Universal for the band's work on the picture on August 18, 1939. The contract is retroactive to July 26, either indicating work on the film was already underway by that time, or that the contract also covered work on *Oklahoma Frontier*. Apparently, work on *Oklahoma Frontier* had already commenced without Church's explicit approval, hence Church's frustrations with Murphy Brophy. *Chip of the Flying U* also starred Bob Baker and Fuzzy Knight, both of whom had significant parts in *Oklahoma Frontier*. Unlike Brown, who did not sing, costar Baker was a singing cowboy who had several starring roles within the genre. The members of the Rangers felt as much warmth for Johnny Mack Brown as they had felt indifference for Autry during the filming of *Colorado Sunset*. Whether Brown's approach was less abrasive or whether their personalities just clicked more readily, they appreciated working with him and would back him in a number of films.

Oklahoma Frontier was eventually released in October, 1939. It is a measure of how inured the group had quickly become to the thrill

---

[1] In addition to KMBC archival material, some information on *Under Western Skies* comes from the Jerome Lawrence and Robert E. Lee Theatre Research Institute, The Ohio State University. Further details provided by www.worldcat.org.

The Texas Rangers with Johnny Mack Brown.
Courtesy of Ed Crawford.

of being in the movies, that it and subsequent movies with Brown and others, was not greeted with the same excitement that the release of *Colorado Sunset* had been. The novelty of appearing on the silver screen had faded a bit. Jaded, or not, by the three film appearances, the Rangers success in Hollywood to date had not secured much further work in the highly competitive film and radio industries on the Coast. They had been in Los Angeles six months, and though there had been both film and radio work, there was limited career value in further appearances in movies like *Under Western Skies*. Despite the upbeat reports from managers with the CBS Artist Bureau, further radio and live appearances were just a trickle.

Though most of Arthur Church's correspondence reflects the work of a hard-nosed businessman, an incident from this period shows a soft side that was not always visible in business dealings. In October, 1939, Rod May's sister-in-law came down with a life-threatening illness, and the doctors did not think she would survive. The Mays were unable to afford the flight from California to Kansas City, but Church forwarded them the cash needed to buy Mrs. May, Rod's wife, a ticket on TWA to visit her sister in the hospital. May's sister-in-law eventually recovered, and a relieved Rod May confided to Arthur Church that the help meant he had "more than just a boss but a very good friend."

On a lighter note, May had also taken up tennis after some other actors began calling him "Tubby" during the shooting of one of the films. It did not take long for him to actually gain an extra five pounds in the effort. During the autumn of 1939 Fran Mahaney, tenor with the band, and his wife welcomed their first child, a daughter, into the family, Melissa Anne Mahaney.

These personal joys in the families of May and Mahaney were tempered by the sobering cancellation of *Under Western Skies*, the Rangers' first network show since leaving Kansas City. "We were all sorry to lose our Radio Program," May lamented to Church, "but I guess it is just one of those things." His reaction is one of the few personal insights into the frustration all the members must have felt as yet another opportunity slipped away. Auditions at MGM, 20th Century Fox, and Paramount all garnered considerable enthusiasm, May assured Church, though actual assignments were not to be had.

Gomer Cool took a different perspective on the cancellation of *Under Western Skies*, however, and contrary to May's comments, he actually foresaw some advantages in the band's losing its sustained CBS program. Because of problems stemming from the rules involving traveling musicians and musicians transferring from other locals to the Los Angeles union, the Rangers could not apply for membership until they had been off the air for six months. Thinking they were much closer to getting their union cards, the extra delay was yet another disappointment for the boys. Up to that time, and including their months on CBS, the Rangers were classified as a traveling band, which came with various restrictions. To meet union requirements, they were not allowed to play outside Los Angeles for more than a week at a time, but they could still appear in person, perform at dances, make guest appearances on radio programs, and do recordings, including transcriptions.

Interestingly, just as Cool had lost his enthusiasm for *Life on the Red Horse Ranch* after its initial broadcasts, he was not keen on the just-completed *Under Western Skies* program, either. He was blunt with Church: It "was NOT a good show! Parts of it – the Rangers and the dramatic spot – were good. But the format as a whole was extreemly [sic] poor and certainly not up to agency network standards by any means." He actually felt liberated. Now, the Texas Rangers could audition for NBC, Mutual, and the large advertising agencies, which abounded in Southern California. He knew that if the band could only "present our ideas and our music" they'd get some big breaks. The faults of their prior radio work did not lie in the band's talents but in how they'd been presented to the public.

Seeking A New Direction

The autumn of 1939 was a time of momentous upheaval in Europe, and war became not only inevitable but a reality with the September 1 invasion of Poland by German troops. Half a world away in California, the Texas Rangers would have sat down for breakfast with the *L. A. Times*' blaring headline, "War Orders Given By Hitler." East Asia had been suffering under Japanese aggression since 1931, but with Germany's move into Poland, a truly global war had erupted; however, it would be more than two years before the United States entered the war against the Axis nations. The eight members of the Texas Rangers, all small town Midwesterners now resettled in sunny Southern California, were far more concerned about their immediate job prospects, or lack thereof. While Western leaders reflected on how Germany had, once again, put itself in position to drag the continent into brutal conflict, some of the Rangers reflected on their successes to this point, and how they might make the step to the next level of popularity.

The Rangers had been broadcast on a sustaining basis over the CBS network on and off since 1932, Gomer Cool reminded his boss, Arthur Church. How much longer should they stick with the same network which had never managed to sell them to a sponsor? Cool was troubled by a common question he heard when he tried to interest publications in pieces on the Rangers: "Why wasn't the act ever sold, after being on the air so long?" Because of his negative feelings regarding CBS' efforts on their behalf, Cool now suggested that it might be worth taking up the offer by station KFWB to broadcast from the Los Angeles station. Live auditions remained, in his opinion, the best way for the Rangers to promote themselves at this point.

One gem of an opportunity appeared to be a spot at Earl Carrolls' popular Los Angeles theater, into which their Los Angeles manager Harry Singer was prepared to help get them by the end of October,

1939. The boys seemed gung-ho on the gig, twice voicing interest in moving ahead with negotiations, as long as the booking did not prevent them from pursuing more lucrative jobs. However, it turned out that the Rangers were not unanimously in favor of playing at Carrolls. Two wrote to Church privately conveying their doubts about it. Herb Kratoska's misgivings were purely family related: he did not want to leave his new wife, Laura Lee Owens, Tex's daughter, alone at home every night. Bob Crawford's reservations were twofold. First, he did not think the Texas Rangers were, frankly, good enough for Carrolls' establishment. They were a hillbilly act and "ought to stick to it," and like Kratoska, he did not relish the idea of being out late performing every night. "If we go into Carrolls," Crawford declared, "nobody had better try to get me out of bed until noon the next day for radio or movies or anything else!"

The band did go for an audition, which did not go as smoothly as Singer hoped. Much of the blame, fairly or unfairly, was placed on Crawford. Unhappy with the arrangement of the microphones, he got angry with the audition stage manager and refused to announce the band's numbers. Though they went ahead without the announcements, he was still accused of ruining the first song. Singer was humiliated by the experience, and Cool felt it was unfair to the rest of the band for one member to "block the progress" of the Rangers.

About the same time the Texas Rangers were imploding for the Earl Carrolls audition, in October, 1939, there was a promising development on the radio front. Gene Autry was putting together a new radio program, and his close associate, Johnny Marvin, had approached the band about providing some backing music for the broadcasts. Marvin had a performing history dating to the early 1920s and by the end of the decades, was a very popular performer and prolific recording artist. He was a singer, played the ukulele, guitar, steel guitar, and violin. Johnny Marvin and his brother, Frankie, were Oklahoma boys who had made good in the big city, and took Autry under their wings when he landed in New York in the late '20s, hoping to land a recording contract. Marvin's career faded somewhat in the early Depression years, and when Autry reached major stardom in the mid-30s, he made sure that the Marvin brothers both had jobs in his organization. Marvin still performed and recorded occasionally, but for the most part he worked as songwriter and song finder for

Autry. Marvin made overtures to the Rangers about appearing on the new show, but he refused, for unknown reasons, to work through the group's manager, Harry Singer.

Pay was union scale, but, as Cool pointed out during negotiations, it would at least come close to covering the members' weekly salaries from KMBC. It would also provide the boys something to do besides endlessly rehearsing. A minor drawback to the deal, though one that would simmer as a source of irritation for the band, and especially Arthur Church, was that they would not receive any name recognition on the broadcasts.

That the band was now considering the Gene Autry show, instead of a gig with Earl Carrolls' theater, frustrated Cool. The Carrolls job would have actually paid more than the Autry program, and it would have let them perform as the Texas Rangers. The Autry show had been auditioned for sponsors by the end of October, 1939. Because the audition had been somewhat rushed through, a different backing band was used for it. However, Johnny Marvin sought to reassure the group that they would be Autry's musicians if Singer and Church ended up okaying their participation in the project.

Other intra-Ranger frustration revolved around the refusal by some band members to take part in a Salvation Army Benefit program over KNX on October 28, 1939. The band was invited to participate alongside other radio and film stars, but there were several negative reactions that perhaps indicated that at least a couple members overestimated their fame. One complained, "Well, they're throwing a big party for Jack Benny and some of the others up at Arrowhead before the program. If they don't want to do that for us, I don't see why we should do anything for them." Another added, "They'll just take us and shove us around and we don't have to take that stuff." Another, apparently forgetting the Rangers did not have a current assignment, asked "What'll WE get out of it?" Cool threw up his hands that "good publicity and a friendly contact with CBS" were, apparently, not enough incentive for the boys to give up a Saturday evening. Surely, none of them, honestly, put themselves on a par with the prominent Jack Benny, who, during the 1939-1940 radio season had the second highest rated show on the air and the highest rated show the next year.

In a personal letter to Church, Cool revealed his thoughts on the individual Texas Rangers with whom he'd been working for a few years. May was "the good boy of the act. Willing to work . . . [a] conscientious librarian." Mahaney was coming along. His vocal talents were still developing and his solos "have gone over as well in Hollywood (or better) as they did in Kansas City. . . when the show comes he gives 'em everything he's got." Cronenbold got high marks in Cool's book for apparently turning around some less-than-stellar work habits. After doing "an about-face," he was now "prompt at rehersals [sic], willing to work, and anxious to make a success of the act." Cool credited Clarence Hartman with having "done a great deal in pulling the Texas Rangers out of the hillbilly class," which should have opened more opportunities for the band. Sells, the accordionist, was recognized as a hard worker with arranging skills that had already been utilized in Hollywood. Cool noted Sells was "personally ambitious," however, and prophetically added that "so long as his efforts can be directed toward helping the act, he's very valuable." He may have sensed that there was a chance Sells would not be a Ranger much longer, and he would be proven correct. Herb Kratoska, just recently married, was a bit of a question mark in Cool's book. He wrote that "a man's attitude should not be judged during his first year of married life," so Cool was sure that Herbie would come through some recent rough patches "with colors flying."

His most pointed comments were aimed at Bob Crawford, indicating there may have been some distrust between the two bandmates. In Cool's words the quartet leader had "always been a troublemaker;" He was "spoiled and selfish" and not "personally ambitious." In Cool's opinion, Bob's commitment to the Rangers was limited to a desire to rehearse one or two hours a day and then "spend the rest of the time sitting around the house." Crawford's disagreements with band members (notably Clarence Hartman), emerged from his unwillingness to "follow the leader." Cool tempered his criticism by insisting that he had "always been on friendly terms with Bob" and that his opinion was "not colored by any personal differences." But his frustration was obvious.

It must have been Bob Crawford to whom Cool referred in closing the blunt letter: "When we came to Hollywood, we had a meeting, the eight of us, and agreed that we would leave no stone unturned in our efforts to make a success of the act. The majority of the boys still feel that way and are willing to work, night and day, at anything which promises to lead us in the right direction. But it is imperative that we defend ourselves against those who for personal reasons would hold us back."

The *Eb and Zeb* Discussions

One new opportunity presented itself not long after Cool wrote the letter quoted above, when the Rangers auditioned for a program featuring Eb and Zeb, a hillbilly duo whose radio appearances date back to at least 1932. Historians differ on the premier of the two characters. Some point to *The Al Pearce Show*, frequently called *Al Pearce and His Gang*, sometime between 1928 and 1932, while others refer to KFRC's *Blue Monday Jamboree* out of San Francisco in the late 1920s.[1] Pearce played Eb Peters and Bill Wright was Zeb Winterbottom, two rural bumpkins in a comic style that would be epitomized by the long-running *Lum 'n' Abner* series and was probably very similar to some of the humor used in the earlier KMBC program *Happy Hollow*.

The Rangers' manager Harry Singer approached Jack Partington, Pearce's personal manager, about the possibility of hiring the Texas Rangers for the program. Evidence indicates the negotiations went surprisingly quickly, and Pearce was enthusiastic in moving ahead with the project. The project was still hot into the New Year, as indicated by a letter from Harry Singer sent in early January, 1940, detailing plans to meet with Pearce to run over financial numbers. Everyone involved felt the project had such promise that a promotional record was made and immediately forwarded to an advertising firm for sale. The partnership and speed with which the deal was shaping up encouraged the band and they were excited to be a prominent component of the show.

Just as quickly as the new program took shape, however, it began to deteriorate. Pearce's radio show was unexpectedly canceled by his sponsor Dole Pineapple and, without wasting any time, he signed with Camel cigarettes. All negotiations related to his former show were suddenly put on hold.

[1] Tim Hollis' *Ain't That a Knee Slapper: Rural Comedy in the Twentieth Century* and John Dunning's *The Encyclopedia of Old-Time Radio* give slightly differing information on the earliest years of the duo's radio work.

The change came as a shock to Church and the Rangers, who thought they were on the verge of a new network broadcast. Even Pearce's closest associates, including his manager Partington, were not aware of the negotiations with Camel. The new contract did not allow Pearce to appear in any other radio show unless Camel or its mother company R. J. Reynolds agreed to sponsor it.

Unfortunately for the band, R. J. Reynolds was not interested, for the time being, either in *Eb and Zeb* or the Texas Rangers themselves, and the promising plans were shelved indefinitely. Sponsors found any number of reasons to pass on prospective radio shows, but in this case it seems likely that R. J. Reynolds refused to consider the new Pearce/Texas Rangers venture because they were informed it would cost $5,000 per week for sponsorship. The sum caught Arthur Church, who would have been involved in the negotiations, by surprise. Up to this point the price, including the talent, had been set at $3,500 in all the discussions in which he had been involved, and no one could determine at what point the cost had mysteriously risen over 40% to $5,000. Despite what must have been tremendous disappointment, Church's response was strikingly similar to that of Rod May's months before when *Under Western Skies* was canceled. Recalling the affair several months later in August, 1940, Church avoided placing blame and said simply that "the whole affair died a natural death."

1939 Wrap-Up

By the end of 1939, the Texas Rangers' first year on the West Coast, Church's financial investment in the band was far from paying off. A ten-month statement summarizing the band's income from May 15, 1939, to March 31, 1940, clearly showed the unit was not even close to breaking even. Its biggest payday had come from the work on Autry's *Colorado Sunset*, which netted them $2,000. The Johnny Mack Brown films, *Oklahoma Frontier* and *Chip of the Flying U*, each brought payment of $1,250. After their film income, the Rangers' next biggest money-maker was their radio transcriptions which earned an underwhelming $700. Along with a few live appearances, the Texas Rangers' income during this period was well under the $13,453 (with $1,140 of that for Harry Singer) in salaries and

Texas Rangers promotional still.
Courtesy of Steve Cool.

additional payments owed them. So far, the Texas Rangers had not proven to be financially successful since moving West.

Gomer Cool, writer of much of the Rangers' continuity and, with Bob Crawford, most of the original songs the group used, was the highest paid of the bunch at $1,928 for the seven months in California, while Clarence Hartman earned $1,638 and Paul Sells $1,536, his base income supplemented by his previously mentioned arranging duties. The others came in just under $1,500 apiece.

Though California had not led to riches, nor to their names in the marquee lights, and though Arthur Church had taken something of a financial bath in the process, nineteen thirty-nine was still an eventful and, despite the heavy operating loss the Rangers generated, successful year for eight hillbilly-cum-Western musicians and singers from Missouri trying to make it in times which were still economically challenging. While the Earl Carrolls Theater engagement had not panned out, and the Eb and Zeb radio program had failed to get off the ground, there were numerous highlights. They had managed a multi-week engagement on yet another CBS network show, *Under Western Skies* with Johnny Mack Brown, and most exciting of all, had notable musical roles in three motion pictures, one of them with a major star, the king of singing cowboys, Gene Autry. In addition, Autry's associates had approached the Texas Rangers about a sponsored network series, a project which looked in a very good position to move forward as 1940 dawned. Someone, probably Singer, took out a full-page ad touting the Rangers in *Variety* on December 27, 1939. It claimed the group was "RIDIN' HIGH...with the Nation-wide Radio Audience" and called the Rangers "ONE OF THE MOST VERSATILE MUSICAL-DRAMATIC ACTS IN RADIO." Singling out the individual group members, it christened Herbie Kratoska "Hollywood's new laugh sensation" and noted that all was "set to the smooth continuity of Gomer Cool." The Rangers were "rarin' to go, for an alert advertiser who will add the magic touch of exploitation and set himself for the Big Payoff."

Gene Autry's Melody Ranch

The Texas Rangers were still in an enviable position, so there was no excessive self-pity or doom-mongering when the Eb and Zeb radio opportunity fell through. The spot on Gene Autry's radio program, a project which had been in serious development since October, 1939, was still on the table thanks to sponsorship interest by Wrigley Gum. Philip K. Wrigley, head of the gum empire had taken note of Autry's popularity and approached Wrigley's advertising agency, the prominent J. Walter Thompson company, about creating a radio program for the Western star. Neither the work of Autry biographer, Holly George-Warren, nor KMBC archival material, offer any insight into how the Rangers, of all the bands which had worked with Autry, came to be chosen for the series. That they were already based in Hollywood would have been a factor, but regardless, with a whopping eight films to Autry's credit in 1939 alone and the clout to work with almost any band of his choosing, that the Texas Rangers were picked for Autry's first network radio series is a testament to their skill, versatility, and popularity.

Preliminary work on the show began on Sunday, December 31, 1939, when the Texas Rangers backed Autry up on a fifteen-minute preview, which was included as part of a larger broadcast called *Gateway to Hollywood*, and aired in the late afternoon. The broadcast's central skit was a reenactment of Gene Autry's meeting with Will Rogers in a train depot years before. Paul Rickenbacker, the J. Walter Thompson producer behind Autry's new upcoming program, had specifically requested the Rangers play for the special broadcast. This may have served as a sort of final audition for the band to ensure they were up to the job of backing Autry on the air.

The singing quartet of the Texas Rangers – Crawford, Mahaney, May, and Cronenbold – made a total of $50 each for the January 7, 1940, premier episode of *Gene Autry's Melody Ranch Radio Show*. As the boys had known would be the case, the singers made union scale, or $35, plus $15 for three hours of overtime work. The musicians on the show also received scale which, in their case, was $25 plus $12 for two hours of overtime. The four musicians of the Texas Rangers, Cool, Hartman, Kratoska, and Sells, were not included in the premier broadcast, only the vocal quartet.[1]

Agent Harry Singer's correspondence indicates that he knew the Rangers' instrumentalists would not be performing, at least initially. Significantly, Autry already had a stable of backing musicians, including fiddler Carl Cotner, steel guitarist Frankie Marvin, and guitarist Eddie Tudor, who provided the backing for Autry and for the Rangers quartet. Strangely enough, Carl Cotner was listed as the leader of the Texas Rangers on the December 31 script. Cotner, who had joined Autry in 1938 and would remain a close associate of Autry's, becoming his musical director until the end of Autry's performing career, was never a member of the Texas Rangers or employed by KMBC.

---

[1] Staff at the Gene Autry Museum refer to the program as *Gene Autry's Melody Ranch Radio Show* since there was no consistent and uniform name over the years. The announcer generally began each episode with "Welcome to Melody Ranch!" During its inaugural 1940 season scripts title it variously *Doublemint Gene Autry Show* and *Gene Autry Show Doublemint*. It was also referred to as *Wrigley's Gum Presents Gene Autry* among other related titles on different scripts.

CBS outlet KNX in Hollywood.
Courtesy of Ed Crawford.

Though Singer consented to the use of non-Rangers musicians, he did not think much of them after hearing the rehearsals. "They are only fair musicians, not to be compared with our boys," he wrote Church. "They could take them out any time and save that money as our outfit are finished in their work and can play rings around them at any style of music." He had no doubt that Autry and Rickenbacker would realize this soon enough. Accordion player Paul Sells' talent, however, was immediately recognized by the program's producers, and he was assigned arranging duties which, in turn, earned him a little extra in his paycheck. It would eventually earn him a permanent spot with Autry's organization, as well.

In the meantime, the Rangers, at least the vocal quartet, began the 26-week stint as the backing band on Gene Autry's *Melody Ranch* over CBS. Originally a quarter-hour program, the show aired Sundays and settled into a half-hour spot from 6:30 to 7:00 under the sponsorship of Wrigley's gum. Twenty-six episodes of *Gene Autry's Melody Ranch* were broadcast before the show went on its summer hiatus after July 14, 1940, but the Texas Rangers were heard on only 22. Whenever the program was done on the road away from its studio of origination, Hollywood's KNX, they did not perform. The first of these road dates was for the January 28, 1940, show which originated from Washington, DC, as part of the American Tribute to Music event. Three more episodes aired from Pittsburgh and New York on April 28, May 5, and May 12. Whether the Ranger musicians who were excluded from the December 31, 1939, audition ever made it on to *Melody Ranch* is not clear, but seems unlikely. Though the Texas Rangers are given credit on the program report page of the scripts, within the body of the script itself they are referred to as "quartet."

Gene Autry's Melody Ranch, a light dramatic skit interspersed with plenty of Autry's songs, proved more than satisfactory for Wrigley and the company. It never reached the top of the Hooper ratings charts, but during the 1955-1956 season, the show's last, it broke the top ten and tied at number seven with the long-running evening serial *One Man's Family*, Groucho Marx's quiz show *You Bet Your Life*, and *The Great Gildersleeve*, a program spun off fifteen years before in 1941 from the top-rated *Fibber McGee & Molly*. *Melody Ranch* also reached #14 (1952-53), #15 (1953-54), and #16 (1950-51). The Texas Rangers, however, were long gone before these prime years.

Much to the band's and Arthur Church's dismay, they were dismissed with little advance notice in the summer of 1940. Church wrote a scathing letter to Brophy on July 13 concerning the loss of the Autry program. It indicates that the Texas Rangers' management was pushing the J. Walter Thompson agency, in charge of Wrigley's radio advertising, for "some kind of recognition" which had eluded them during the first 26 broadcasts of *Melody Ranch*. So far, there had been no mention of the band's name throughout the entire series. If J. Walter Thompson did not see fit to grant the requested on-air recognition, then Church and Brophy asked for a 25% increase in financial compensation for the band's work, which they "certainly deserved." If neither of these demands was met, then Church could not guarantee to J. Walter Thompson that the Rangers would be available for a third 13-week contract.

Unfortunately for Church and his band, the prominent ad agency did not blink and released the band from their duties. They were replaced by the Jimmy Wakely Trio, a group from Oklahoma that Autry had befriended the previous year and advised to head west. After an initial shot at the Coast, they had returned to Oklahoma. Possibly Autry's preferred choice for backing vocal group in the first place, they were also protégés of Johnny Marvin, who took them under his wing when he was working out of Oklahoma City a couple of years earlier. They returned to California in the summer of 1940 to replace the Rangers, and *Melody Ranch* would serve as an early step toward major stardom for two of the trio's members, Wakely himself and Johnny Bond.

Church told a confidante after negotiations had proven futile that "we feel that we have done the right thing, and if we had the opportunity today to reconsider, our decisions would remain the same." Church and the band members had had their share of performing jobs at union scale wages. While such work brought in revenue to defray the salaries and other costs of the Rangers, it was not sufficient in the long run to make the band's cross-country relocation profitable, particularly if, as in the case of *Melody Ranch*, the job offered no name recognition to the group. They had to find more lucrative projects.

Could the Ed and Zeb project which looked so promising just a few months before be revived? In June, Bill Wright, Pearce's collaborator on the comedy duo, was hopeful something could be worked out with Pearce and Camel cigarettes even if Pearce himself was not involved. Their hopes were short-lived when both Pearce and Reynolds' advertising agency representative Dick Marvin each sent "a strongly negative reaction" to the idea.

Under New Management

Losing the Gene Autry program may have been the last straw for Church in regards to his professional dealings with Harry Singer. By July, 1940, he had made the decision to fire Singer and find another manager who could get better results. Writing to Clarence Hartman on July 13, Church informed the bass player that he would be taking over as the band's manager until a suitable replacement for Singer could be found. "Our reasons for terminating the agreement with Harry are entirely business reasons," Church assured Hartman. "We think a lot of him personally and are extremely sorry that the arrangement did not work out well for all concerned. We fully realize the sincere effort he put forth in the interests of all of us concerned."

The extent of Church's dissatisfaction with Singer's efforts, however, was reflected in his decision to continue paying Singer through August 17, the end of his current contractual period. Despite paying for Singers services, Church would not make use of them in any capacity during the last month of the contract. It was a rare time when Church paid out money expecting and demanding nothing in return. Hartman was authorized to tell the other Rangers of Singer's dismissal after the completion of the July 14, 1940, *Melody Ranch* broadcast, their last with the show. He was further authorized to make contacts on the group's behalf with Columbia Management, Inc. while a new manager was hired.

Even before the Rangers' final *Melody Ranch* broadcast, an audition for another program had been lined up, for a show called *A Day at Circle J*, written by Gomer Cool. The audition script, dated July 11, 1940, also featured Martha Mears and Lou Crosby alongside the Rangers. Mears was a Missouri-born singer who worked steadily in radio and film from the 1930s into the early 1950s. There is no indication she ever worked for Arthur Church at KMBC, but her Missouri background may have facilitated her connection with the Texas Rangers, with whom she would work on several projects during the 1940s. Lou Crosby was best known as the announcer for the popular *Lum 'n' Abner* radio show. The audition for *A Day at Circle J* opened with the song "Ridin' Down That Old Western Trail" then segued to an introduction supplied by an unidentified announcer.

> ANNOUNCER: Welcome to the West! Listen to a new western program ... "A Day at Circle J" ... starring <u>Martha Mears</u> and those hard-ridin', sweet-singin' sons of the Lone Star State ... The Texas Rangers! And here to howdy with you a bit before we raise the curtain on tonight's melody drama, is <u>our</u> foreman and <u>your</u> host ... Lou Crosby!
>
> RANGERS: (THEME ... UP TO FINISH)
>
> CROSBY: Thanks, Tom, and 'evenin', everyone, everywhere. Well, out here in the West, the sun has just gone down, but the sky is still all painted up with its last rays, and the hills over yonder have taken on a sort of purple haze that makes them look about twice as far away as they really are. It's the time of day that real Western folks just up and quit whatever they're doin' to sit around for a spell and cool down -- and may chin a bit about old times, or listen to a few favorite songs. Well, we kinda figured you might enjoy that, too, so we got the

gang together and worked up a little entertainment -- a couple of grand melodies and a story that represents the Western way of livin'.

With the Rangers taking acting roles alongside Mears and Crosby, the show featured the story of a ranch boss' daughter, Martha (played by Mears), who was coming to stay on the ranch for a while. None of the ranch hands are happy about the situation, not wanting to get recruited to babysit the young girl. Everyone's attitude changes, however, when she turns out to be a pretty young woman. On July 31, Church came to a verbal agreement with Robert Braun to act as the Texas Rangers' new California manager, effective August 1. Braun was taken on as staff at KMBC where he was designated a member of the station's program sales team with the expectation that the majority of his time would be focused on the Texas Rangers. He was also to undertake sales and promotion efforts of other acts as Church saw fit. Braun's weekly salary was initially $90 per week, $50 of which was straight salary while the other $40 was considered advances on expenses he would incur in the line of work. He was also eligible for bonuses ranging from 1% to 5% of Rangers income over $30,000 with percentages increasing as the income increased. His bonus would be a flat 5% on any California sales made on other KMBC properties.

Even after Braun's hiring, Clarence Hartman retained some of the responsibility placed upon him with Singer's departure. Though he reported to Braun, Hartman would remain the group's musical leader and the member authorized to finalize contracts with the American Federation of Musicians. Braun's responsibilities also did not encompass motion pictures, an outlet that remained under the guidance of Columbia Management. He was expected to cooperate and work with the agency but not answer to them. Karl Koerper, KMBC Vice-President and Program Director, was Braun's immediate superior. Church was not ready to place full faith in Braun until he had proven himself, so Church reserved the right of final approval to all contractual matters which Braun initiated outside of small one-time appearances.

In a separate note sent to Braun on August 2, 1940, the day after his employment contract was signed, Church confided that one of Braun's primary duties would be to instill some discipline and whip the boys back into tip-top shape. "Quite possibly they should be spending more time in practice," he suggested, developing "new arrangements, new ideas." Church continued with a slight dig at the band's former manager, "They should know you are their manager, and that you and I expect results. They may not have been pushed enough by their predecessor."

Nothing immediately came of the *Day at Circle J* audition effort, though it received a fair hearing by the advertising department at the Kellogg company. The recording was played for Kellogg on August 9, 1940, and one of the cereal company's ad men, Kenneth Grahm, assured Church's salesmen that he would "endeavor" to have the program previewed by some higher-ups. Beyond this small opening, the Texas Rangers settled for live engagements during the late summer months. Their show highlights during this time included the California State Fair in July and August and the Pomona County Fair in September. Recordings of the band's performances at the State Fair were made on July 30 and referenced for some time afterward in company correspondence. Playing for union scale, the band was paid $620. There is no evidence that the recordings were released in any form or that they became part of any of the Texas Rangers' broadcast series. Bob Braun indicated that station KNX's Russ Johnson had commissioned the recordings, possibly for promotional purposes.

Payment for the state fair concerts and recordings, seemingly a straight forward matter, turned into a muddle that was not resolved for several weeks. Part of the problem seems to have been that the agreement between Clarence Hartman, in his capacity as temporary manager of the group before Braun was hired, and KNX was not in writing and was never submitted to Church or Karl Koerper for any sort of review or approval. At the heart of the dispute was a twenty dollar difference between the amount KMBC officials believed had been agreed upon and the amount Columbia Management believed should be paid. The twenty dollars was credited to Paul Sells for some musical arrangements done for the recordings. When Hartman gave the complete bill for $620 to Columbia Management's Murry Brophy, Brophy informed Hartman that the recordings had been budgeted at $1,000, $600 of which was for talent. Brophy was non-committal about the extra $20 fee for Sells' work and vaguely told

Clarence that "he would look into the matter." In retrospect, it is difficult to understand how a $20 misunderstanding, an amount representing approximately three percent of the total talent budget for the state fair work, could have turned into such a contentious issue, requiring several weeks and input from multiple people to sort out.

Fallout from the Rangers' dismissal from *Melody Ranch* continued into late summer. Gomer Cool expressed concerns about the Rangers' situation to KMBC's Karl Koerper, who dealt with issues raised by Cool in an August 27, 1940, communication. Though neither Cool nor Karl had any wish to rehash the events behind the Rangers' removal from the radio series, events which had been reviewed repeatedly by all involved, Cool admitted it had "created problems within the Ranger organization." Most important of these was poor morale. Despite the reservations he raised in the fall of 1939 about whether the band should continue its long relationship with CBS, Cool insisted he "never lost faith in the value of the Texas Rangers or their ability to achieve success." He acknowledged that Paul Sells and Herbie Kratoska were evaluating their other artistic options and did "not intend to stay with the act if something doesn't happen." This was not the first time Cool had noted the possibility of their losing Sells, a talented musician and arranger, but it was the first hint of restlessness from Kratoska, whose superior skills as a guitarist and banjoist, not to mention comedian, would likely have been in high demand had he chosen to freelance. Kratoska's recent, and doomed, marriage to Laura Lee Owens, the daughter of Tex Owens, with whom the Rangers, or at least some members of the group, had an uneasy relationship, might have increased his frustration with the situation.

Communications between Karl Koerper and Arthur Church reveal that they were quite aware of the precarious situation involving these three Rangers. "Gomer was frank in saying that he would like to be taken out of the Rangers group," Koerper reported, and similarly Kratoska "wants very definitely to get out of the Rangers group." His recent marriage to Tex Owens' daughter, Laura Lee, was rocky and maybe getting back to Kansas City would help. Paul Sells, Koerper explained, was not so much against the Texas Rangers as he was for himself. "He is out to make all he can on the side, regardless of anyone's orders to the contrary." He considered himself the most important member of the band and had been carrying too much of the load for too long. Sells' presence was creating problems because he had no wish to socialize with the group, choosing to use his time to further professional contacts.

On the other hand, the band seemed cautiously enthusiastic about its new manager Bob Braun, who had been on the job just about a month. He was well-connected in Los Angeles and knew the ins and outs of L.A.'s music scene. Braun was a hands-off manager, however, at a time when the band could have used some outside discipline, a fact Church had addressed directly with Braun upon his hiring. Braun saw it differently, however, and in his opinion, the band members needed to work out their own personnel problems while he focused on landing them performing contracts. Whether this approach was appropriate for the Rangers' situation "remains to be seen," Cool concluded.

Another concern of Cool's was of a more personal nature: his writing aspirations, which had been utilized by KMBC and the Texas Rangers on and off for nearly a decade. Conversations with Koerper revealed that Cool was increasingly dissatisfied with his primary role as musician with almost no opportunities to develop his writing talent, which he saw as "a means of protecting [his] income," just as Sells was supplementing his income composing arrangements. While always an enthusiastic backer of the Texas Rangers in his correspondence, Cool admitted as early as August, 1940, that writing for radio was "the kind of future [he was] ambitious to achieve." Always careful never to assign blame for his lack of writing assignments to any individual at the station, he nevertheless indicated that KMBC was preventing him from pursuing leads. "Owing to the fact that my services as a writer have not been required by KMBC," he wondered, "what earthly harm can come of my submitting my material to agencies and other radio stations?"

Perhaps if the Texas Rangers had developed the commercial success hoped for by everyone in the band, Cool's attitude would have been different. The group was languishing, however, with only sporadic money-making jobs. Cool put it bluntly, "In prospect of this trip, I forsaw the gang plunging into the whirl out here – creating new shows, building new ideas, with the enthusiasm that such a wonderful opportunity as this should give. We could have, as a group, done so many things. The actual situation is too dismal to describe." Despite several disappointments, this is a curiously pessimistic appraisal in light of their film and radio achievements which were more impressive than any number of the era's hillbilly bands might have hoped to accomplish. Still, Cool's observations point to the prevailing malaise and frustration within the band rather than any outward success and seems accurate, as well, in light of a story related by Jim Crawford about those early days in California. Despite their regular KMBC salaries, money had become very, very tight at one point. Partly due to the work situation, and partly because jealous co-workers back in Kansas City sometimes delayed sending their paychecks, the Crawfords, the Mays, and the Cronenbolds, who all lived within a few blocks of each other, were all but out of food. Herb Kratosaka who was very frugal with his money, made a deal with his friends. He would buy food for the whole bunch if Crawford's wife, an accomplished cook, fixed the meals. She agreed and the musicians continued to practice on full stomachs.

Paul Sells Departs

There were questions during the fall of 1940 as to whether the Rangers were still a viable enterprise. In fact, Koerper and Cool talked bluntly about the group's disbanding and what needed to be done to avoid such a fate, perhaps the first such discussions to take place in the band's eight years of existence. If Church decided to break up the band, what would become of the members, all of whom were on the KMBC payroll as staff members, not solely as Texas Rangers musicians? These were questions and issues not easily answered, and they would be brought up numerous times in the coming years as the Rangers' fortunes fell and rose, and fell again. For his part, Cool claimed that the station did not owe him anything; he had received his fair salary since being hired. If the time came for him to leave KMBC, he would do so on good terms.

Paul Sells, too, had finally reached the end of his patience with the band, a situation that had become apparent to his fellow Rangers. In August, about the same time Gomer was writing separately to Church, Sells wrote to Program Manager Karl Koerper indicating he would be done with the Rangers if they had not been picked up for a sponsored coast-to-coast network program by October 1, 1940. This was a tall order based on the band's recent record of engagements; perhaps he knew it was unattainable.

"Don't misunderstand me," Sells told Koerper, this was not a personal decision. His dissatisfaction was with "the conditions surrounding the group." He continued, "There was a time when I was enthused about the possibilities of our group, but I must admit, I don't feel that way any longer. I have lost interest in what activities they have, and I have always felt that when a person loses interest in the group or persons he is working with, something should be done about it."

Conversations between Koerper, Braun, and band leader Clarence Hartman were in line with Sells' reasoning, though they did not take the same "business is business" attitude that Sells had adopted. Braun claimed he had been informed by members of the band that Sells had indicated on different occasions that he was not "interested in the welfare of the Texas Rangers as a group if said welfare in any way hampered his own progress." Sells would argue, with some amount of justification, that he had always met his contractual obligations, and that in a line of work as cutthroat as music, one had to take opportunities when they arose. His co-workers weren't quite so understanding; to them he was "a rather difficult chap."

Braun also laid some of the blame for Sells' dissatisfaction at the feet of his wife who was, Braun wrote, "not all that [was] desired of a lady." She did not get along especially well with the other band members' wives with the exception of Mrs. Herb Kratoska. She was accused of egging Sells on and encouraging him to leave the Rangers. And, frankly, though the income from the Autry radio program was not significant, the loss of $100 per week above and beyond the regular KMBC salary did not sit well with the couple.

An honest discussion on August 12, 1940, made clear the situation and convinced Braun that acceding to Sells' demand for release from his contract was in the best interest of Church, KMBC, and the Texas Rangers. Sells was absolutely unhappy with the state of the Rangers and disgusted by the lack of ambition among most of the players. True or not, in his opinion "the rest of the boys [were] satisfied to knock out a living wage and let it go at that." Sells was especially down on the singing quartet who, in his opinion, had no "inclination to rehearse individually or collectively."

Though they may not have approved of Sells' self-serving attitude toward Rangers' business, communications indicate the other seven were not overly concerned about his potential departure. Other than Kratoska, who was non-committal about what should be done with Sells, the band members were actually "in favor of a change" as far as his place in the group. Hartman was of the opinion that losing the accordion player and arranger would not "affect the commercial or musical value of the Rangers" but admitted it would mean extra work for everyone, as a new player would need to be broken in.

Motivation of his band mates aside, finances were a major irritant for Sells. The singers were receiving an extra $25 per week for living expenses, and Sells was insulted that he was not included in that deal. Losing the Autry show was especially frustrating because he had been given the opportunity to stay on as an individual musician separate from the rest of the Rangers who were dismissed. Sells claimed that he had been given verbal permission by KMBC management to accept other engagements so long as they did not interfere with his ability to carry out all responsibilities concerning the band. Yet he had not been given the okay to stay on *Melody Ranch* even though the band had no other ongoing commitments at the time. What he took as a breach of faith by station management gave Sells concern about the extent to which he'd really be allowed to take advantage of other offers which might further his musical career.

Herbie Krataska, a seven-year veteran with the group, was also making overtures about leaving the Texas Rangers, and these were not taken lightly. Braun was in agreement with others that Kratoska and his guitar skills were "definitely an asset to the Texas Rangers and his loss would be serious." Kratoska's dissatisfaction may have been compounded by his wife's unhappiness. Laura Lee Owens (later McBride) would go on to a long career as a country music singer, yodeler, and pioneering female disc jockey in both California and Texas. However, in pre-war Los Angeles, despite a very active Western band scene, she was having difficulty finding work, a problem she did not have while they were based in Kansas City.

In the midst of gloomy talks of losing band members, or disbanding the group altogether, a flicker of hope flared when Church heard a rumor that the Eb and Zeb project, which had surfaced in 1939 before sinking under Al Pearce's contractual obligations, might have new life. He had heard via Harry Singer, who, himself, had heard from Pearce's manager, Jack Partington, that the show was "in a position to go ahead." The broadcasts would include Pearce and had been given the green light by R. J. Reynolds. Excited at the prospect, Church asked Braun to look into it quickly.

In the meantime, disputes with Columbia Management concerning the California State Fair continued, and on August 20 Braun received a check for $600 to cover the Rangers' fee. Unaccounted for was the $20 due Sells for his arrangements, a fact argued over weeks before. Brophy, Columbia's representative, said "this price was to cover the entire deal." In addition, Columbia Management's bill for the engagement was 10% of the $600, a previously unmentioned commission that caused further irritation after the unsuccessful back-and-forth over Sells' unpaid arranging fee. After weeks of wrangling, Braun left further dealings regarding both the recovery of the missing twenty dollars and the Columbia commission to Church. Braun had been under the impression that Columbia Management was not entitled to any sort of commission, 10% or otherwise, for any job that was paid at union scale. He pointed out he had been hired after the recordings and really did not know all the details which might have been worked out beforehand. He suggested that Church's office "take up the matter of arrangement charges and commission." The suggestion seems to have been acceptable to Arthur Church back in Kansas City, as there is no surviving documentation that indicates Braun ever dealt again with issues surrounding the California State Fair recordings. Neither does the record indicate the extent to which Church and Kansas City staffers may have followed up on the issue.

Whereas the Rangers, owing to the objections of a couple of band members, had been unwilling to participate in the Salvation Army Benefit broadcast the year before, attitudes had changed by the early fall of 1940, and the group appeared in the Sixth Annual Police Show, a benefit performance at the Los Angeles Coliseum for which they were not paid. The bill boasted an all-star line-up including Earl Carroll, Bill Robinson, the Hall Johnson Choir, Mickey Rooney, a sketch featuring Penny Singleton and Arthur Lake, Blondie and Dagwood on radio and on the screen (programs and films based, in turn, on the *Blondie* cartoon strip), and Jack Benny and Rochester.

The show ran from 7:30 to 11:30, and the Rangers appeared briefly as a group, then returned to accompany Gene Autry on his spot.

By October, 1940, the Texas Rangers' fortunes were on the upswing. Despite the year having been a rather disjointed and disappointing one, their film work had continued. Early in the year, they had appeared in a musical short featuring the singer and dancer Armida, and at mid-year appeared in the Judy Canova vehicle *Scatterbrain*, and another Johnny Mack Brown feature, *Son Of Roaring Dan*. Another movie with Brown, *Ragtime Cowboy Joe*, followed at summer's end. They did not, however, have a nationally sponsored radio show. So Paul Sells departed quietly as he'd requested. KMBC brass had decided that to allow Sells to remain would have been "unfair to the remaining seven members of the group." Upon leaving, he signed an agreement which allowed the Midland Broadcasting Company, parent of KMBC, "unrestricted use" of his name and likeness "in advertising and publicizing the Texas Rangers," rights which he granted for 2 ½ years, until June 10, 1943. This ensured there would be no problems using existing advertising and publicity materials and, most importantly, recordings and musical arrangements in which he had some involvement. Not surprisingly, since he had been appearing on Gene Autry's recording sessions since March, 1940, and had become a crucial part of a newly emerging Autry band sound, Sells quickly joined the Autry organization. His accordion and arrangements became an integral part of Autry's sound on *Melody Ranch*, also in recordings, and much more. He was also busy in recording studios with other performers, including Tex Ritter, but remained with Autry until at least 1950.

Ultimately, Sells' leaving had minimal lasting impact on the band; little effort was made to retain his services, and little time was spent bemoaning his loss to the Texas Rangers. Church and the staff of Midland Broadcasting Company were making inroads with two potential sponsors, Old Gold Cigarettes and Kellogg, for a new Rangers radio program. Years before, the latter had successfully partnered with them on a Kansas City program. While Church himself was the point man in the Old Gold negotiations, Midland's Chicago representative, George Halley, took charge of the Kellogg discussions, which involved travel to their offices in Michigan.

Halley's first contact with the cereal company dated to the fall of 1939, a full year earlier. During the first half of 1940 he had auditioned the Rangers to the company, as well as another KMBC feature, *Across the Breakfast Table*. Uninterested in the latter show, Kellogg asked for more material by the Rangers, and in September Halley provided them with the audition disc *A Day at Circle J*, cut that summer. The audition discs were sent to Chet Foust at the J. Walter Thompson advertising company, which held the account for some of Kellogg's cereals. In addition, Halley sent along an audition of a children's western serial written by Gomer Cool, tentatively called *Thunder in the West*. Encouragingly, Foust was receptive to both auditions and asked for more detailed cost information concerning *Circle J*.

An October 11, 1940, meeting between Foust and Halley found the two at odds as to how to begin determining a price for the program. While Halley wanted a list of potential markets under consideration by Kellogg, from which he could then create a reasonable quote, Foust told him to do just the opposite. Kellogg's representative J. A. Briggs, Foust said, will want to know "what kind of price you can afford to make him before he can determine what markets he can use this medium in in comparison with what other known media costs will be for the market in question." As these discussions continued, while unbeknownst to Kellogg, negotiations with representatives from Lorillard's Old Gold cigarette brand concerning the same audition episodes were moving forward.

The Texas Rangers ca. 1940.
Courtesy of Ed Crawford.

Chapter 6: Sponsored Nationwide

A Day at Circle G Ranch, aka *The Old Gold Show*

Old Gold Cigarettes, manufactured by the P. Lorillard Company, was one of the largest products to sponsor the Texas Rangers. Prior to the show's debut, there were concerns among Church's staff that either CBS or P. Lorillard Co., or both, may not have been entirely forthcoming in providing all pertinent information about the deal. As early as September 25, 1940, there were conversations which raised red flags, especially for George Halley, who was negotiating out of Chicago. Halley had a discussion with CBS' Bob Somerville about the proposed series during which Somerville was "vague" in providing details requested by Halley. Separate talks with P. Lorillard Co. representative Blayne Butcher resulted in the cigarette maker disputing the prices Church had earlier quoted them for the cost of the show. The figures Halley was using were all wrong, insisted Butcher, who then claimed Arthur Church had earlier quoted $200 per week for the first 26 weeks and $300 per week for the second 26 weeks as the cost to the potential sponsor. Church's take on the situation has not been recorded, so it is impossible to know what price he actually quoted to Lorillard and CBS. The prices laid out in a preliminary contract written by the Midland Broadcasting Company were 1/7 to 1/4 higher than these quoted by Bob Sommerville, suggesting that he was trying to get the program at a considerable discount for CBS.

There was further confusion and mixed signals about the show's master of ceremonies. Singer Martha Mears, who had participated in the audition recording, was hired for the job, but Halley could not even get a straight answer from Somerville as to her fee. Church had authorized Halley to spend as much as $991 for the show's production costs including an M.C., presumably for a 13-week contract. Somerville claimed he could not remember the specific salary information, but the cost for singer Mears still kept the total price well below $991. This information suggests that Church had been asked to fork over the full amount by an agency representative without being given a detailed accounting of the project's price breakdowns.

During a conversation on September 27, 1940, Church clarified for Rangers' agent Bob Braun exactly where he stood on payment issues for the *Circle G* project.[1] Russ Johnson, who had earlier been involved in KNX's recording of the California State Fair concerts, was now somehow involved in the Old Gold negotiations. He was telling Braun that the best route was to sign a 26-week deal with no raise after the first 13 weeks. Church, however, insisted in no uncertain terms that he had spoken directly with Lorrilard's Blayne Butcher and that their agreement was for four, 13-week periods with raises upon each renewal. The first 13-weeks would net KMBC $891 per week, with a $50 increase for the first option, and then a hefty $250 increase for the third and fourth 13-week options. A flat fee for the first 26 weeks was unacceptable to Church.

Yet more confusion and miscommunication ensued when executives turned to assigning writing duties. Just a week before Lorrilard's advertising company, Lennen & Mitchell, hoped to debut the program on October 2, 1940, they had not even settled on a script writer! The agency was dickering over the cost of hiring a writer insisting they had only thirteen dollars left in the budget for the job. Lennen & Mitchell hoped to have an internal man write it in order to avoid paying Gomer Cool an extra fee for the work. Braun pointed out, however, that the union might insist on an outside writer, though that apparently proved not to be the case. Thomas (Tommy) Tomlinson, an employee of Lennen & Mitchell, ended up performing writing chores for the series. Tomlinson had at least one other notable radio credit to his name, a series called *I Was There*, an anthology program.

Lou Crosby was to work as the program's announcer, but wires got crossed, yet again. "I was told ... that Lou Crosby was to get a hundred" for the first set of broadcasts, Church informed Braun. Braun was astounded. "Well they tell me he is getting eleven fifty per broadcast," he informed his boss, nearly 50% more than Church's understood salary. To top it off, Braun, with obvious signs of disgust,

---

1 Originally titled *Life on Circle J Ranch*, when Lolliard cigarettes got involved for their Old Gold brand the title was altered to *Life on Circle G Ranch* to reflect the sponsor's initial. However, the series would continue to be referred to by both titles in private correspondence.

informed Church that even after the question of who would write the show had finally been cleared up, somehow Lennen & Mitchell had not bothered to allocate any money for sound effects. "What I actually think," Bob confided, "is that Arthur [Kemp, a Lennen & Mitchell agency executive] went over-board to sell the time, and made a very, very close deal." L & M was now scrambling to bring costs in line with what it had promised.

There were also some differences in programming opinion between CBS and Lennen & Mitchell executives. While the network was pushing the agency to buy the Texas Rangers for a series, an agency representative named Robson was pushing his company to buy "a big KNX production" called *I Was There*, the same show with which *Circle G* writer Tommy Tomlinson was involved. *I Was There* has been described by old time radio historian John Dunning as "dramatic first-person accounts of true human adventures." Premiering in 1935, *I Was There* was sponsored over the years by Hunt's Tomato Sauce, Mobil Oil, and Sea Island Sugar Cane. At the time of the *Circle G* negotiations, *I Was There* was in the middle of a healthy eleven-year run which lasted from 1935 to 1945. CBS, however, stuck strongly by the Rangers and pushed for *Circle G*.

Halley found CBS' sudden push for the Texas Rangers curious, as the network had never been such an advocate during the band's first eight years. The network executives may, in fact, have had little interest in the actual quality or content of either program; rather, their support may have reflected behind-the-scenes business maneuvering. George Halley suspected that Lennen & Mitchell may have been in a "shaky position" with P. Lorillard Co. due to disappointing results they had shown since winning the Old Gold account; Halley characterized L & M's results to date as "unusually poor." He further suggested that CBS may have been offering up the Texas Rangers to Lennen & Mitchell so that if the new program got low ratings, similar to the agency's previous efforts, and P. Lorillard Co. decided to drop Lennen & Mitchell as a result, CBS' more prestigious *I Was There* show would not be "tarred with the stick of failure," as Halley suggested, due to a connection with Lennen & Mitchell.

Whatever the network's motives, Halley and Church, nevertheless, wanted to make the best of this opportunity. "The boys are going to have to do a real audience getting job," Halley wrote, "and there are going to have to be some clever and bang up commercials." They would have two weekly quarter-hour spots versus five, half-hour spots for the competing cigarette companies, which put them at a serious disadvantage. Less time on the air gave them fewer opportunities to hook listeners and sell them on the sponsoring product.

Regardless of any reservations it may have had, the Midland Broadcasting Company entered into a contract with the P. Lorillard Company, Inc., on October 8, 1940. The tobacco company's Old Gold Cigarettes were to be advertised twice-weekly by the Rangers and Martha Mears on *A Day at Circle G*. The series originated live over the Columbia Pacific Network for thirteen weeks beginning October 9 and was recorded to be replayed over the Michigan State Network and up to nine stations in other markets. The transcribed episodes were required to be aired over a thirteen week span, which had to begin within four weeks of their original West Coast broadcast.

At $230 per week in compensation, the series was far from a windfall for Church. But, for both him and the Rangers, it was, crucially, a coveted *sponsored* series, and such projects had been frustratingly rare for the Rangers over the years. Lorillard agreed to pay up to $20 per week for each additional station over which they decided to sponsor the Old Gold Series; so, bigger money was a distinct possibility, though not guaranteed. Further, if Lorillard chose to renew the contract for a second thirteen-week base, weekly payments would rise to $280, while each additional station would remain at the $20 maximum.

The contract with P. Lorillard was not exclusive, though the Texas Rangers were prohibited from appearing in radio programs advertising cigarettes or any tobacco product. They were, however, free to appear on programs advertising non-tobacco products as long as the shows were not heard in the same markets as the Old Gold program. If the competing series were sustained, then the band could even be heard in the same market as their Old Gold sponsor so long as their series were not scheduled near to each other.

The *Circle G* theme song was written by Rich Hill, a member of the CBS Pacific Network's Continuity Department, and featured Martha Mears. In the end, the show aired over 31 stations outside of the Pacific Network, primarily in the Midwest (on their connection with the Michigan Radio Network), but with a notable number along the Eastern seaboard and a very few in the Southeast.

City	Station	Day	Times
Syracuse, NY	WSYR	Tues. & Thurs.	6:15 – 6:30 p.m.
Rochester, NY	WHAM	Tues. & Thurs.	6:15 – 6:30 p.m.
Buffalo, NY	WBEN	Tues. & Thurs.	6:30 – 6:45 p.m.
Pittsburgh, PA	KDKA	Tues. & Thurs.	6:15 – 6:30 p.m.
Baltimore, MD	WFBR	Tues. & Thurs.	6:15 – 6:30 p.m.
Kansas City, MO	KMBC	Tues. & Thurs.	6:15 – 6:30 p.m.
Detroit, MI	WXYZ	Tues. & Thurs.	6:45 – 7:00 p.m.
Battle Creek, MI	WELL	Tues. & Thurs.	6:45 – 7:00 p.m.
Jackson, MI	WIBM	Tues. & Thurs.	6:45 – 7:00 p.m.
Flint, MI	WFDF	Tues. & Thurs.	6:45 – 7:00 p.m.
Lansing, MI	WJIM	Tues. & Thurs.	6:45 – 7:00 p.m.
Bay City, MI	WBCM	Tues. & Thurs.	6:45 – 7:00 p.m.
Grand Rapids, MI	WOOD-WASH	Tues. & Thurs.	6:15 – 6:30 p.m.
St. Louis, MO	KMOX	Tues. & Thurs.	9:45 – 10:00 p.m.
Atlanta, GA	WSB	Tues. & Thurs.	6:15 – 6:30 p.m.
Richmond, VA	WRNL	Tues. & Thurs.	6:30 – 6:45 p.m.
Ft. Wayne, IN	WOWO	Tues. & Thurs.	8:45 – 9:00 p.m.
Jacksonville, FL	WJAX	Tues. & Thurs.	7:30 – 7:45 p.m.
Cleveland, OH	WTAM	Wed. & Fri.	6:00 – 6:15 p.m.
Minneapolis, MN	WCCO	Fri. & Sun.	6:45 – 7:00 p.m.
Des Moines, IA	WHO	Mon. & Thurs.	6:00 – 6:15 p.m.
Charlotte, NC	WBT	Tuesday	8:30 – 8:45 p.m.
		Saturday	8:15 – 8:30 p.m.
Norfolk, VA	WTAR	Mon. & Fri.	7:45 – 8:00 p.m.
Nashville, TN	WSN	Thurs. & Sat.	6:30 – 6:45 p.m.
Tampa-Lakeland, FL	WFLA-WLAK	Mon. & Fri.	6:30 – 6:45 p.m.
Orlando, FL	WDBO	Mon. & Wed.	7:00 – 7:15 p.m.
Denver, CO	KOA	Mon. & Thurs.	9:30 – 9:45 p.m.
Harrisburg, PA	WHP	Tues. & Thurs.	8:30 – 8:45 p.m.
Washington, D.C.	WRC	Tues & Sat.	7:30 – 7:45 p.m.
Omaha, NE	KOIL	Thurs. & Sat.	9:45 – 10:00 p.m.
Lincoln, NE	KFOR	Tues. & Thurs.	7:30 – 7:45 p.m.

Midland Broadcasting officials took a hands-on approach to the production of *A Day at Circle G Ranch*. Bob Braun reported that after the October 18 broadcast he approached producer Sam Pierce to complain that the commercial was "covering the Rangers feature musical and vocal selection." Pierce was responsive to Braun's appeal to "correct this situation" and made adjustments in following broadcasts. Braun justified his intervention to Church by saying that the band needed to be given every opportunity to be heard by the audience in a positive light. In his opinion, the Old Gold program was basically a "showcase" for the Texas Rangers, which could be used to sell future series, and hopefully, one of which would be carried on the full CBS network. For Church and Braun, *A Day at Circle G* was a stepping stone, a means to an end, rather than an end in itself.

In the midst of the excitement and stress of creating the new Old Gold program, the Rangers had to deal with the difficulties of incorporating new accordion player Joe Strand into the band to replace Paul Sells. Thirty-eight at the time, and older than everyone in the group save Clarence Hartman, Strand had immigrated to the States from Sweden. The younger brother of Manny Strand, a well-known bandleader and conductor, Joe Strand was a highly skilled musician and arranger, at home with everything from classical to hot jazz. He was, Gomer Cool remembered almost seventy years later, never particularly happy with his role as accordionist in a Western band, even one as accomplished as the Rangers, but he remained with the group until it began to disintegrate in the war years. Whatever he may have felt about dressing as a cowboy and playing Western and folk melodies, the gig with the Rangers was relatively high profile, with both radio and movie work to come. If surviving performances can be considered representative, Strand was given plenty of opportunities to shine in solo and group settings.

Sells had been playing with the group for seven years, however, and the Rangers' highly polished sound and the tightness that came from a half-dozen years without personnel changes, would not be easily maintained after the departure of Sells, the instrumental group's lynchpin, regardless of Strand's ability. On top of the rehearsals necessary at KNX for the Old Gold broadcasts, the group practiced an additional two to three hours every day at the house of Clarence Hartman. Besides his musical skills, Strand also did a Swedish dialect which Braun thought had the potential to drive some comedy sketches. He went so far as to discuss this with the Old Gold writer Tommy Tomlinson. This would have been the first known dialect comedy bits worked into Rangers material since Eddie Edwards' blackface stint as Cookie, which appears to have been phased out not long after *Life on the Red Horse Ranch* in 1935. If Strand's dialect was used, it never became a regular feature and was not referenced beyond that single report by Braun in October, 1940.

Besides honing their sound with Strand, Bob Braun was pushing the Rangers to sharpen the musical selections used on their broadcasts. The Rangers were given the freedom to choose their own repertoire on broadcasts, but at least one of their shows disappointed CBS management because the band failed to include any up-tempo songs; Braun informed them that "the consensus of opinion was that it lacked a bit of brightness." They were encouraged to add some special arrangements to their repertoire and pushed to write new material as well, songs which would be added to their small, but growing, recorded library.

Strangely, Arthur Church was "surprised" when he finally saw the *A Day at Circle G* title ascribed to the Old Gold program. Taken aback, he confessed to George Halley, his Chicago-area salesman, that this was not the title he thought was going to be used. In fact, he thought Old Gold had been sold on a totally different Texas Rangers series. Given what a hands-on executive Church usually was, that a decision of this sort could be made without his knowledge is baffling. Perhaps it indicates the extent to which decisions about the show were made in Lennen & Mitchell and Lorillard offices without input from Church's Midland Broadcasting Company.

Records indicate KMBC staff created the title *A Day at Circle G* (altered slightly from the prototype *A Day at Circle J* used on audition scripts). Church wondered if the Rangers might be able to get away with using the same title on a separate series in markets not blanketed by Old Gold. However, account representatives at the Lennen & Mitchell advertising agency and Lorillard Tobacco executives were keen enough on the title that Halley indicated it was unlikely that any of them would consent to such an arrangement, even on a test basis, in other markets not covered by the Old Gold deal. Similarly, since the Columbia Broadcasting System now controlled the *Circle J* title there was little likelihood that the name could be used on a Rangers program picked up by a competing network.

That it was never made explicitly clear to Church that Old Gold would be using the *Day at Circle G* proposal clearly irked him because he repeatedly brought the matter up to his men. Heretofore, discussions about the Old Gold series had simply referred to it as *The Texas Rangers*. Had he known Old Gold was purchasing the *Circle G* series, he would not have had other executives trying to sell the same program, *A Day at Circle J,* to other clients. This turn of events was especially problematic in that two potential sponsors, the makers of Horlicks Malted Milk and cereal-maker Kellogg's, were interested in the series.

Regardless of any interest Horlicks or Kellogg may have had in sponsoring the Texas Rangers, whether *A Day at Circle J* or some other series, Arthur Church's Los Angeles associate Murry Brophy was confident in the program's future in partnership with Old Gold. While perfectly willing to talk with ad men to find sponsors for other Texas Rangers series outside of the Old-Gold sponsored markets, Brophy felt good about the chances that Old Gold would decide to extend its sponsorship to a coast-to-coast broadcast, beyond CBS' Pacific stations, the Michigan Radio Network, and the handful of other subscribing stations. Such a development would preclude the Rangers' appearing on any other show which might create competition for their own *Circle G*. Therefore, Brophy advised that it might be wise at the time to hold off on discussions with other sponsors.

In November, 1940, just a few weeks after *Circle G* hit the airwaves, the Texas Rangers quartet, sans the backing musicians, was hired to do some soundtrack recording for Universal Studios, where they had worked with Johnny Mack Brown on several films earlier in the year. The session paid above union scale for a change, scale plus 20% in this case. Scale for the work was $100, and with the overage, the total payment came to $120. The work was completed on December 4, but it is unclear for which film this work was done. It might have been for one of Brown's films, but his features completed around this time feature Jimmy Wakely's Rough Riders, who were more than capable of doing their own soundtrack singing.

This side job did not distract Bob Braun from the task at hand, which was getting *A Day at Circle G* renewed by Old Gold, the Rangers' biggest commercial opportunity to date. The company would be making its decision in early December, 1940, as the original thirteen-week contract wound down. It was, of course, "necessary that the Texas Rangers contribute their share" in order to persuade Old Gold to continue to use the Rangers to advertise their product. Braun was dismayed to report to Church that he did not feel some of the boys were giving their absolute best. He would be meeting them very soon, however, to take care of this situation.

According to Braun, a primary reason for the inadequate performances was insufficient time available for the group to practice the

A Day at Circle G Ranch advertisement.
Courtesy Jim Crawford.

broadcasts' special arrangements, a problem he laid at the feet of the show's producers. The Rangers practiced several hours a day, but they had only been receiving the show's arrangements 48 hours ahead of air time, too late for them to be fully polished in rehearsal. To remedy this, Braun arranged with Lennen & Mitchell to get their okay to prepare ten or twelve arrangements of their own in advance which could then be used on upcoming programs.

Critical reception of the series was positive and *Variety's* reviewer, eschewing for the most part the patronizing air with which the weekly usually handled Western hillbilly shows, gave the Rangers' musical performances high marks. The review, as a whole, was far kinder than the trade press had been with earlier series featuring the Rangers, such as *Life on the Red Horse Ranch*:

> "Call it corn or what you will, this simple little piece of the cow country and its grizzled characters is listenable and relaxing. What makes it fall so easily on the ears is the soothing music of the Texas Rangers, given billing of 'America's foremost singers of Western songs' and living up to it to the hilt.
>
> As for the tales spun at Circle G ranch, they're true to formula and lighter in treatment than those coming off Gene Autry's 'Melody Ranch.' On this catching there was some banter about a rodeo contest with the cowhands of Triple T, but it's all incidental to the music.
>
> Singing group leads off with the theme, 'Two Cigarets in the Dark' backing up Martha Mears, also a pleasant little vocalizer. It's perfect harmonizing, not one voice rising in crescendo above the other and blended for soft, billowy effect. It carries a lull that goes well with carpet slippers and smoking jacket. Rendition of 'Call of the Canyon' was especially noteworthy in its subdued, restful passages."

There was more good news when the Erwin, Wasey & Co. advertising agency approached Rangers management on behalf of Horlicks, makers of a famous malted drink. They were interested in attaching the Horlicks name to the Texas Rangers in the industrial centers of Detroit, Chicago, and Cincinnati. Because of the contractual restrictions with *A Day at Circle G*, Church suggested the company try and interest Horlicks in the five-year-old *Life on the Red Horse Ranch* transcriptions. Admitting that the Rangers were a "more finished group" now than they were in 1935 when the transcriptions were originally recorded, Arthur Church liked the much cheaper price they could quote for *Red Horse* than they would be forced to quote for an original *Circle G*-style series which would involve brand new recordings.

Church told both Brophy and Halley that no amount lower than $1,600 for test copies could be given to potential buyers of a new

Circle J show. Including singer Martha Mears in any new program significantly upped the cost, yet in Church's opinion, a fresh production could not be successfully made without her. He also did not see any way they would be able to produce a quarter-hour transcription set for less than $500 per episode. This was partly due to Mears' fees, but also to union scale wages, which he called "terrific." While looking for a sponsor for a half-hour coast-to-coast version was an option, when Church ran the figures, he did not see how such a project could be produced at a lower cost than a fifteen-minute transcribed version. This $500 cost must have seemed nearly astronomical to Church, whose biggest production investment up to this point was a time-traveling series called *Phenomenon*, which was produced for approximately $140 per quarter-hour episode.

The biggest obstacle to selling *Life on the Red Horse Ranch*, aside from the production qualities discussed by Gomer Cool and Arthur Church in years past, involved ASCAP and the unions. Broadcasters were in the middle of a dispute with the composers' organization regarding music license fees; ASCAP was attempting to double the royalty fees paid to its members for broadcast use. Negotiations were not going well, and both NBC and CBS were contemplating banning the use of any ASCAP material on their programming. The *Red Horse* transcriptions, unfortunately, included a lot of material whose provenance was covered by ASCAP publishers; consequently, there was a real possibility the songs would not be usable after December 31, thus making the series unsalable for the time being.

The ASCAP situation was a major crisis in the industry, a significant byproduct of which was the formation of ASCAP's less highbrow rival BMI. But more immediately, the concerns about working within the rules of an often deliberately prickly musician's union remained troublesome for Rangers' projects. The exact details remain unclear, but at some point KMBC advanced the members of the Texas Rangers money for living expenses, in fact, "quite a lot" according to station correspondence. Church apparently felt that the group could reciprocate with some studio recording time. The Rangers, or the musician's union at least, felt otherwise, presumably demanding that union scale be paid and union rules followed for any recording done. In order to avoid a potentially damaging row with the powerful American Federation of Musicians (AFM) over the situation, which could adversely affect far more than just the Rangers but his entire operation, Church asked Halley to approach his Chicago contacts about the tenability of KMBC's position. Carefully he cautioned Halley to be discreet, as he would "rather keep KMBC out of any such discussion." He preferred that "the information should be kept on an abstract basis and not on a basis of a specific employer or a specific man or group of men."

Ultimately, all of the excitement and energy which went into developing *A Day at Circle G* for Old Gold cigarettes and similar auditions for Horlick's and others came too little. Old Gold did not renew after the first 13-week contract and the series disappeared quietly. As described above, despite a generally positive response and regardless of the quality of the show, there were several strikes against *Circle G* from the beginning. These involved maneuvering by the sponsor, the ad agency, and CBS, and the show's ultimate fate seems to have been out of the hands of Church, Braun, and the Texas Rangers themselves. Surviving correspondence suggests that no one involved saw any point in continuing the program in its present format or of renewing the Old Gold partnership with a different project.

Music Library

Perhaps the most significant development of late 1940 was the initial discussions about the creation of a Texas Rangers transcribed library. In mid-fall Church asked Braun to begin putting together a list of selections which could be used in such a library, which would subsequently be rented to subscribing stations. The work of creating such a list was passed on to Gomer Cool and Clarence Hartman, and by November 16 the job was finished. The list of tunes had been separated into those published by ASCAP, those published by BMI, and those in the public domain. A separate list of numbers, also divided into the same three groups, was created for the vocal quartet. Many of them were of a religious nature sung a capella and occasionally featured all eight members of the group singing. Columbia Records, which was one of several records companies contacted by Karl Koerper about a possible transcription library, was already expressing interest in doing the recordings. The Rangers' film agent, Murry Brophy, was also in favor of recording with Columbia.

The musical library idea gained momentum in December, 1940, when discussions with Kellogg heated up again, perhaps with a renewed sense of urgency now that *A Day at Circle G* was off the air, and the Old Gold account was gone. Early in the month George Halley formally submitted some prices to a Kellogg's manager for possible sponsorship of a show based on the original *Circle J* audition record. For 26 weeks of a once-a-week half hour program, Midland Broadcasting wanted $1,200 per week or $2,300 if the company preferred five, fifteen-minute programs. Both options would come with a 25% increase with every 26-week renewal. If Kellogg was willing to accept a non-exclusive arrangement, which would allow Midland to market the band to other sponsors while under contract to Kellogg at the same time, then their cost dipped to $900 and $1,700.

Sensing that the price might have been a bit high for Kellogg at that time, the following week Halley suggested the cereal maker consider a transcribed series created from the Texas Rangers' recorded selections. Despite the inevitable seasonal slow down as Christmas and New Year's approached, Halley prevailed upon engineers at World Broadcasting to put together a new audition record using songs the band had recorded at their studios over the years. This audition was mainly musical and did not have the storylines of such series as *Life on the Red Horse Ranch*, *Gene Autry's Melody Ranch*, and *A Day at Circle G*.

Despite the disappointment of losing the *Melody Ranch* gig at mid-year, 1940, the band's first full year in California had been a good one in many ways. It opened with a 26-week stint (22 episodes) on Autry's coast-to-coast *Melody Ranch*, and ended with the group's 13-week sponsored stint of their own, *A Day at Circle G*. On the big screen they had appeared in Judy Canova's *Scatterbrain* and several Johnny Mack Brown features.

On the other hand, the year was representative of much of the Rangers' long existence. Alongside a number of successes and promising developments, there were a number of disappointments that kept the group from firmly establishing themselves as a nationally-known marquee act that did not have to scratch and claw for its next assignment. The New Year was set to begin just as 1940 had–uncertain, with a promising prospect, but nothing firmly set. To bring that prospect to fruition the Rangers' management focused all their efforts on finalizing a Kellogg contract to get fresh income pumping into Midland Broadcasting's coffers.

1941

Nineteen forty-one began with behind-the-scenes discussion regarding the development of *A Day at Circle G*. A confidential memo circulated among Bob Braun in Los Angeles, George Halley in Chicago, and Arthur Church in Kansas City clarifying the role of writer Tommy Tomlinson in the development of *Circle G*, which had recently concluded its run. The memo queried whether Tomlinson had been given the program idea by Midland Broadcasting to develop into a full-fledged series or whether he might have actually come up with the ideas and concepts himself. If the idea for the *Circle G* format and style originated with Tomlinson, Church gave Braun the nod to make overtures about hiring him on at KMBC.

It's unclear whether Church was simply looking for an additional writer for his production staff or if, in fact, he had it in mind that Tomlinson might supersede Gomer Cool as the go-to man for Rangers ideas and scripts, a role that had belonged to Cool since 1933. Tomlinson's audition script had made a strong impression on all three, showed "marvelous promise," and should have been turned into "an exceedingly popular opus." Halley noted that the script hit the perfect note of "light comedy drama with plenty of romance" combined with "just enough, not too much, music by the Rangers and Mears to add piquancy to the whole period." Of course, Halley confessed, he had not been able to hear any of the series since it was not carried in Chicago or any station he could pick up there.

This was not to say, Halley clarified, that he thought Cool could no longer meet the writing demands of KMBC. His strengths, however, were not with material that involved romantic storylines or "light delicate situations with sparkling dialogue." Rather, George Halley felt Cool's true talent lie in writing quick-paced and action-packed children's programming, such as the audition program *Thunder in the West*, which Halley had been trying to sell for a while. Was this a fatal flaw in Cool's writing? Not necessarily, Halley readily admitted, noting that part of the problem was Cool had not had many chances to write dramatic scripts since 1935's *Life on the Red Horse Ranch*. These discussions went no further, however, and Tomlinson's name is not mentioned in any further correspondence. Either Church or Braun abandoned the idea of pursuing him, or he was not interested in working for Midland.

Though the Rangers were absent from the airwaves during the first months of 1941, discussions for new broadcast work were underway on multiple fronts. In Chicago, George Halley finally delivered a quote to Kellogg to use the Texas Rangers in a transcription series created from their musical recordings. Projected to run only in Texas, KMBC asked $475 a week for a 13-week commitment, $375 a week for a 26-week commitment, or $350 a week for a 39-week agreement. A firm reply was not forthcoming for a couple months.

At the same time on the West Coast, Arthur Church and Bob Braun met in early February with Arthur Kemp, Lennen & Mitchell executive. A few months earlier Braun had accused Kemp of skimping on the price quoted to Lorrilard to get the *Circle G* program on the air, which he felt had possibly resulted in an inferior series of broadcasts. Business was business, however, and Kemp had visited with officials from Horlick's Malted Milk and discussed using the Texas Rangers, Martha Mears, and Will Wright in a new program to advertise a Horlick's product.

The idea was more in-depth than the straight transcribed music series pitched to Kellogg. Kemp's idea for Horlick's was a "home spun" set of broadcasts revolving around actor Will Wright who would be cast as a sort of "old story teller" or "friendly philosopher." At the time Wright was just getting into radio and embarking on a film career as a character actor that would last to his death in 1962. Within two years he would be a busy actor on West Coast radio with numerous appearances on programs such as *Suspense*, *Jack Benny*, and *The Amos 'n' Andy Show*. He lasted on dramatic radio programming well into the 1950s as the genre began to give way to television. The new program would also reunite the Rangers and Martha Mears after their recently fizzled effort for Old Gold cigarettes.

The meeting with Kemp went so well that both Church and Braun left with the firm impression that, not only was Kemp singularly focused on selling the Rangers' prospect, but also that he planned to have all the performers in the recording studio within the week. In addition to the Horlick's project, Kemp requested price quotes from Midland for a 26-week Texas Rangers test run over CBS' California

The Texas Rangers on stage.
Courtesy of Jim Crawford.

network and a few alternate scenarios, quotes which Braun was quick to supply. Follow-up communications with Kemp confirmed he was entirely sold on the Rangers idea.

Alas, the Rangers, Church, and his team were to be disappointed by Kemp, yet again. Not only was the Rangers idea not the only one on which Kemp was focusing with Horlick's, he was actually proposing three or four ideas to the company, only one of which involved the Texas Rangers.

Braun repeatedly pressed KNX's Russ Johnson in the heady days following the meeting with Kemp to find out details about the recording session for the Horlick's audition. Johnson could only fend off Braun with vague replies before finally breaking down and admitting that multiple ideas had been submitted to Horlick's, only one of which was for the Texas Rangers; an audition was not imminent as Braun and Church had been led to believe. While it was completely understandable that Kemp might want to submit several ideas to a new potential client, on February 11, Kemp finally admitted to Braun that he did not plan to make a new audition recording. Instead, he was submitting a recording from the Old Gold *Circle G* program as an inexpensive way to showcase what a Texas Rangers series could sound like.

Soon after the receiving the news from Kemp, Braun relayed the information to Halley in Chicago. Braun maintained his professionalism but was clearly exasperated with the discrepancies between what he was being told by Kemp and what Kemp was actually doing. Submitting the *Circle G* recordings was not a problem, but it would have been nice to know this was the plan rather than get everyone geared up to create an original audition record. Kemp's evasive and misleading statements led Braun to confess, "There is some doubt in my mind if there will be much effort made on behalf of the Texas Rangers." He and Church had been upfront with Kemp that they were in discussions with Kellogg's about a potential sponsorship deal with the cereal giant, but Kemp had apparently not been entirely upfront with them. If the Kellogg deal was finalized, then the band would not be able to appear on other broadcasts under the Texas Rangers name, a contractual possibility which Braun had made clear to Kemp from the beginning and one which may have raised a red flag with him. That, along with Church's insistence that he was not willing to accept just any payment deals put on the table by CBS or potential sponsors including Horlick's, may have cooled Kemp on a Texas Rangers program. Braun bitterly complained that he based his assumptions on the fact that they were not willing to "sell the Texas Rangers down the river to make a time sale easier for Columbia." As they had demonstrated in negotiations with the *Melody Ranch* producers, Midland Broadcasting was not desperate and would not sign just any commercial contract that was offered.

Though Arthur Kemp's enthusiasm for selling the Rangers to Horlick's seemed to be quickly diminishing, Bob Braun was not ready to concede defeat on a possible partnership and strongly suggested that Arthur Church have George Halley bypass Kemp and get in touch with the company himself in light of some prior contacts. Church agreed and Braun encouraged Halley to make the trip to Horlick's offices as soon as possible; "speed is essential" he urged.

The Kellogg Transcription Series

While the finalization of a Horlick's deal may have increasingly been up in the air, after nearly a year of discussions the Midland Broadcasting management had signed a contract with the J. Walter Thompson Company on behalf of the Kellogg Company. Midland Broadcasting agreed to provide 200 selections from the band's transcription library by April 15, 1941, just one month from the signing for play on a number of Texas stations. Fifty of these songs were required to be delivered by March 31 and another 50 by April 7. To cut royalty costs, no material from ASCAP publishers was to be included, only BMI tunes or songs which Midland otherwise would guarantee free of any copyright infringement.

There were, as was expected, some conditions to the deal. KMBC was not allowed to sell the Texas Rangers either nationally or regionally to any company which manufactured "ready-to-eat or cooked cereals," nor could they approach any other advertisers or stations in Texas about separate deals. Midland was to receive $350 per week with the rates rising up to $475 per week if the contract was terminated before December 28, 1941. Kellogg reserved the right to play up to 90 minutes of Texas Rangers material each week in time slots of their choice though a daily 15-minute show was always the intent of all discussions.

While Church's executives continued to angle for new work for the Texas Rangers, in March, 1941, the band headed into the studio for a week of recording to meet the first deadline of the Kellogg contract. Work began the day after the Kellogg contract was finally signed. Between Monday, March 17, and Friday, March 21, the Rangers recorded 82 songs (on 16 sides, or 8 16-inch transcription discs). On Tuesday, March 25, and Wednesday, March 26, they laid down 45 more tracks on eight sides. The recordings were made in conjunction with World Productions, whose association with Church and the Rangers stretched back to the mid-30s. The sessions were held at World's Hollywood studios. After taking a few days off, the Texas Rangers returned to World for more recording. At six sessions between the 1st and April 8, they recorded 90 more songs.

Upon the conclusion of the April 3rd recording session, Bob Braun wrote to Arthur Church imploring him to contact Dana Merriman at BMI and put some pressure on him to clear some original songs written by Woody Smith, Gomer Cool, and Bob Crawford, all KMBC artists. Braun had sent along 21 compositions by Cool and Crawford for review, yet only six so far had been declared original and ready for recording. By the end of the following day, Friday, April 4th, the band would have recorded all the selections which had thus far been cleared. In order for Church's men to stay on schedule and finish the recordings sessions by Monday, April 7, the new songs needed to be cleared. The remaining clearances came through in time for the Rangers to finish recording on Tuesday, April 8, a delay of just one day. After wrapping up work on April 8, Braun and an exhausted group of musicians reported to Church that after recording 217 songs on 42 master records over 43 studio hours, the Texas Rangers transcription library as required by the negotiated terms with Kellogg was finished.

These two-hundred-plus recordings captured the Rangers in a wide variety of moods and styles, underscoring not only their versatility as a group but the breadth of their repertoire and individual talents. Beyond the most obvious song choices, cowboy or Western tunes, both traditional and modern, these early sessions featured numerous a capella hymns and American vocal classics, which often boasted the double-quartet, with all eight men singing. There were pop songs, novelties, instrumental features for Herbie Kratoska and Joe Strand,

and a healthy dose of excellent original songs from Crawford, Cool and others. Crawford and Fran Mahaney shared most of the solo vocal chores.

Church was sure his group was now poised to finally break into the mainstream. To build on their momentum KMBC staff put together a script for an audition record introducing the recently completed Texas Rangers transcription library. Touting their nine years of industry experience, the copy was careful to make clear they were "not just another cowboy, western, or hillbilly group." They were much more than simply a cowboy group, "a top-notch legitimate musical outfit, specializing in the type of selections most loved by the largest group of radio listeners – the family." The song list included a Gomer Cool-penned novelty tune, "Joseph De Renaldo," a vocal piece which utilized all eight Rangers' voices, "The Song of the Pioneers," and a classic hillbilly fiddle and vocal romp, "Old Dan Tucker." Herbie Kratoska, the group's increasingly accomplished plectrist, was featured on a stunning solo guitar version of Rimsky-Korsakov's "Flight of the Bumble Bee" and sweet singing Fran Mahaney soloed on "Believe Me If all Those Endearing Young Charms." The audition writer could not emphasize too much the variety of songs to be found in the rental library: "gospel hymns, both accompanied and unaccompanied ... old time barber shop favorites, comedy songs ... and a great variety of vocal combinations." Decades later in his 2009 assessment of the band's output Kevin Coffey acknowledged their diverse sources of inspiration when he noted the Rangers "adapted the Western repertoire to fit their strengths as much as they adapted to fit the style's characteristics."[1]

The Rangers barely had a chance to take a breath before they were scheduled to begin work on a new Johnny Mack Brown picture for Universal on April 19, 1941. Records refer to the film as *Fighting Fury*, clearly a working title since Brown did not have a film released by that name. The movie in question must either be *Law of the Range* or *Rawhide Rangers*, which were released on June 20, 1941, and July 18, 1941, respectively, and both of which featured the Texas Rangers. Little did Midland Broadcasting Company or the band realize at the time that, despite winning parts in eight films in the two years

---

1 From the liner notes of *The Texas Rangers, Vol. 1: The Early Years* released by the British Archive of Country Music in 2009.

since moving to California, these two Brown films would be the last motion pictures in which the Rangers would appear for six years.

That summer on June 16, 1941, Bob Braun signed a contract with the Music Corporation of America (or MCA, as it was better known) for the Rangers band to perform at the California State Fair for the third consecutive year and to record five fifteen-minute transcriptions to be used to publicize the fair. Despite the hassles surrounding payment for the 1941 State Fair recordings Church had no qualms about doing it again. The publicity records were to be completed within about ten weeks by August 25 at studios in Los Angeles. They were permitted one hour of paid rehearsal time for each quarter-hour promotional transcription. In return for the use of the Texas Rangers, KMBC received $1,050.

The deal also called for ten consecutive days of personal appearances at the state fair grounds in Sacramento, CA, between August 29 and September 7, 1941. Each day's work could not exceed four hours per rules laid out by Sacramento's American Federation of Musicians Local No. 12. The individual members were paid $10 per day for the performances, with any additional costs added on for transportation back and forth between Los Angeles and Sacramento. Payment for the live shows totaled $1,125 for Arthur Church's company, which, combined with the $1,050 from the recording sessions, made for a tidy sum at a time when the band did not have any other pending projects.

Back in Kansas City, Arthur Church and George Halley were beginning negotiations with representatives of Kellogg and the J. Walter Thompson company about altering the sponsorship contract then in place. Originally, Kellogg had agreed to the right to renew the contract for 52 weeks at $350 per week but now wanted to look at renewing in 13-week segments instead of having to commit for an entire year. This was a blow to Church, who was eager to lock in a long-term agreement for his band. They had had more than their share of 13-week renewable contracts that had all-too-frequently ended sooner rather than later. "Unsettled world conditions," explained J. A. Briggs of Kellogg, "make it imperative that Kellogg, with factories in Australia and England, keep their operation flexible to the maximum." Admittedly, Briggs was not exaggerating, with German U-boats taking a heavy toll on Allied shipping for over a year, the

German army pushing deep in the Soviet Union, and America's poor diplomatic relations with Japan deteriorating further, the prospect of the United States' entry into World War II was chilling to Kellogg. In addition to committing to only 13 weeks at a time, they also sought the right to cancel the program at the end of a 13-week cycle with only 30 days notice. This would put their radio advertising more in line with the cancellation policies of their other advertising outlets such as outdoor ads which required 60 days notice, spot announcements two weeks, and newspaper ads overnight.

Church certainly did not like dropping from a contractually guaranteed 52 weeks to only 13. The guaranteed income was an important issue, but not the only one. It would also become more difficult for KMBC to sell the Texas Rangers elsewhere not knowing exactly when the transcription library would be on the air in Texas. Increased flexibility for Kellogg resulted in decreased flexibility for Midland Broadcasting. Taking into account the uncertainties on the KMBC side, which would come with the reworked deal, Halley countered to Kellogg, would they be willing to ease the restrictions in place on selling the Rangers to stations outside the six Texas markets sponsored by Kellogg?

In the face of Church's misgivings, Halley encouraged him to approve the 13-week renewal cycle to maintain the positive relationship they had developed with Kellogg through the year. Kellogg gave every indication that they wished to continue the sponsorship into 1942 and beyond and were even looking at expanding into additional markets. The cereal company was in the driver's seat, according to Halley; "Frankly, I think we'll lose Kellogg entirely unless we do agree." Church relented on August 13, hoping that giving ground now would result in more advantageous terms down the road.

Ever the optimist, George Halley took the time to put together tentative price plans for various markets, should Kellogg be convinced to not only continue their Texas Rangers sponsorship, but actually expand their range in the coming months. The ultimate goal for Midland was to hit the $1,000 per week sponsorship level, which he felt was reasonable if Kellogg entered all their targeted metro areas. These areas included Kansas City, Omaha, Minneapolis, St. Louis, and Cincinnati on top of the current Texas cities. He recommended a fee of $910 for the first 26 weeks in all these markets, rising to $1,025 for the second 26 weeks, though perhaps reversing the amounts, charging the higher amount for the first 26 weeks instead, might serve as incentive to maintain the sponsorship for a full year. Halley also went ahead and quoted prices for lesser plans: Without Cincinnati the fee should drop to $835/$930 (first 26 weeks/second 26 weeks); without Cincinnati and St. Louis the fee should drop to $735/$810. For just Kansas City, Omaha, and the Texas area the fee would be $625/$675 and for just adding Kansas City they would raise the rate from $350 per week to $500/$525. For good measure, Halley pointed out to his boss that at comparable rates, KMBC could net $4,000 a week if the Texas Rangers were sold across the country, a windfall for Midland.

Kellogg had one other unique idea for the Rangers and had one of their representatives, Buckingham Gunn, discuss it with George Halley. They wondered if the band could record a number of one-minute spot announcements which would then be played on stations all over the nation, not just in Texas. Gunn and J. Walter Thompson's Chet Foust explained that they wanted to recommend to Kellogg that the company discontinue some newspaper advertisements and replace it with a series of radio ads for Rice Krispies and Corn Flakes. They envisioned three sets of 10, one-minute spots which feature the band playing or singing and then fading "to a hum or some sort of background for the commercial." The first set would be aired for two months, then the second set for two months, and finally the third set for another two-month span whereupon the sets could then be repeated. Kellogg emphasized that they considered the Texas Rangers "the *very best* in radio" for signing hymns and Western songs, the type of music proposed for the Corn Flakes ads.

Church had little interest in the concept, remarking that he "didn't wish to sell the Rangers for announcements to broadcast more than once each" nor did he want them to be tied up with short commercials for any significant length of time. He did not want to take the risk that the ads would cheapen the Rangers' brand value. Though not mentioned in his reply, Church must surely have been turned off by the fact that the boys would receive no on-air credit for the work, an issue which had cost them work on *Gene Autry's Melody Ranch*. Thus, the proposition was shot down with little discussion, though Church did relent and agree to work with Kellogg through 13-week renewal periods instead of the previously agreed upon 52-week period.

Dr. Pepper's 10-2-4 Ranch

During the summer of 1941, Midland Broadcasting Company was approached by the soft drink company, Dr. Pepper, about a partnership. Exploratory discussions began over the summer when Tom Revere, head of radio advertising for Benton & Bowles, advertising agency for Dr. Pepper, reviewed a Texas Rangers presentation left with him earlier by Bob Braun during a West Coast business trip by Revere. Braun followed up a few days later, and Revere asked him to go over the presentation in more detail with Revere's assistant, Bert Praeger. Praeger informed him afterward that Benton & Bowles did not have anything that seemed a good match for the band at that point, but he would keep his eyes open for a possible project.

Praeger was as good as his word, for a few weeks later in August Braun received a call from Betty Buckler of the Benton & Bowles' Los Angeles office requesting a price quote for five, quarter-hour transcriptions per week. She was not at liberty at the time, however, to divulge the potential sponsor. Braun agreed to get the quote as soon as possible and immediately wired Karl Koerper back in Kansas City for such a quote. Events then conspired against the Rangers and delayed Braun's response to Benton & Bowles. The wire happened to arrive in Kansas City just after a major storm hit the area destroying the radio station's broadcasting tower, a development which clearly occupied the attention of station officials for some time. By the time the head office got a response back to Braun, he had already left for Sacramento to oversee the California State Fair performances. By the time Koerper and Braun finally made contact with Benton and Bowles, it was simply to reply that without more information about the sponsor and broadcasting markets it would not be possible for them to provide the requested quote to the agency. Perhaps Church, himself, might give a quote if Braun could reach him in Portland where was he was currently traveling.

Before Braun had a chance to get input from Church, he was contacted by Joe Sameth, who had been asked by Benton & Bowles to put together a package deal with the Texas Rangers. Apparently, the agency was sold enough on the band to move ahead with a project even before receiving a definite asking price. Sameth was to produce the entire show, which included providing scripts and a producer, hiring the cast, and recording the episodes. With that in mind, what did KMBC want for the Rangers' performing services? Church instructed Braun to ask for a firm $1450 per week for 26 weeks, far surpassing the income for the ongoing Kellogg deal. Furthermore, Braun was to request an additional 25% fee increase with each 26-week renewal. The information was sent back to Sameth who, in the meantime, had lined up a tentative package which he submitted along with recordings of the *Circle G* show, allowing the agency a chance to hear both the Texas Rangers and vocalist Martha Mears.

Benton & Bowles was so intrigued by the *Circle G* recordings that they requested Sameth put together a new audition record for the agency to review. In response, Sameth suggested that KMBC's Fran Heyser serve as producer. Heyser had recently produced *Caroline's Golden Store*, a serial starring KMBC's Caroline Ellis that had been sponsored by Kellogg and aired first over NBC and then CBS from 1939 to 1940. Surprisingly, these qualifications were not sufficient and Benton & Bowles demurred, insisting Sameth find someone else for the job. He was successful, however, in convincing them to let Gomer Cool serve as scriptwriter, for which the station would receive $100 per week for five scripts, an amount on top of the compensation deal Sameth could negotiate for the use of the Texas Rangers as a group. Such a move would also serve to give Cool a desperately longed-for opportunity to produce some fresh broadcast writing.

The requested audition was recorded and copies were subsequently shipped to Dallas and New York. Sameth calculated his ongoing cost to put together such a daily program at $2,750, which included the musical talent, scriptwriter, producer and the hardware such as recordings, shipping supplies, and stenographic material. With this base cost, he quoted the advertising agency a price of $3,200 per week to allow for his margin of profit. Benton & Bowles did not take long to reject this proposal, and Sameth came back with a lower figure of $3,000. This, also, was rejected by the agency, so Sameth asked them to provide a firm offer with which he might be able to negotiate lower rates from the various participants. The offer from Benton & Bowles was $2,500, ten percent below Sameth's estimated cost for putting the show together in the first place, and not accounting for his income.

Joe Sameth fumed and accused the agency of trying to get him to do all the work of putting a show together for them and then paying him so little that "he would not make a dime." Conceding he might make a small amount off the recording of the episodes, he offered to back out of the negotiations and simply retain his part in the recording deal. Mann Hollinger, head of Benton & Bowles' Hollywood office, convinced Sameth to stay involved in the negotiations.

Swayed by Hollinger, Sameth attempted to shave down the various production costs in an effort to salvage the project and make it financially worth his time. One by one he approached the parties involved in the project and, in so doing, he offered Church $1,250 for the Rangers, $200 less than Church had originally quoted. The agent for actor Dick Foran had also been contacted about his participation in the program. Foran had been one of several singing actors the Hollywood studios tried to mold into Gene Autry's likeness, with middling results, though he continued to be a busy actor in 1941. He appeared in a variety of films and did not allow himself to be pigeonholed into only Western features. Sameth requested an option which would have given the agency priority use of the actor until December 15, 1941. Foran and his agent were cool to the idea, as it would limit their exploring other acting jobs. Foran insisted he would have to raise his overall price to agree to such an option, while his agent said the option would be signed without a raise but with an upfront $500 fee. Up to this time Foran actually had very little radio experience, spending several weeks in 1937 on the *Burns and Allen Show* billed as the Singing Cowboy.

Arthur Church capitulated on his firm $1,450 and agreed to the lesser $1,250 for 13 weeks if they began recording the programs immediately. With these negotiations now reaching into late September and very early October, 1941, he insisted that if the recording did not begin until December, then he had to insist on the original fee, since it would keep them from pursuing other projects.

During the first week of October, competition was introduced for the spot of series host. While Foran and his agent waffled and stalled in giving Sameth a firm answer, Tex Ritter's name was tossed into the ring as a potential replacement for Foran. Foran's option fee remained a non-starter for Benton & Bowles, even though he was ready to accept their salary offer of a $300 a week. Of more urgency to Church and the Rangers, however, was the entry of the Sons of the Pioneers into the picture, whom Tex Ritter was insisting were available for a mere $750 per week, nearly half the asking price of the Texas Rangers. Such was the price for Midland Broadcasting of maintaining the Rangers as an eight-piece act.

In a face-to-face meeting between Bob Braun and Joe Sameth with the agency's Mann Hollinger sitting in, but generally staying out of the conversation, Braun said KMBC would accept $1,250 for the first 13 weeks, $1,350 for the second 13 weeks, and $1,450 for the following 26 weeks. This was based on an initial 26-week minimum guarantee. Braun admitted to Church that he found this price "ridiculous" for what the Texas Rangers brought to the table. He was also a bit skeptical that the agency would agree to a 26-week deal upfront, but felt that perhaps they would be open to it in order to get the band at the lower rate.

Though it did not make a noticeable difference in discussions, Church and KMBC officials had discovered the sponsor for whom Benton and Bowles was working was Dr. Pepper. Another nationally recognized sponsor alongside Kellogg would have been a prized catch for the Texas Rangers. As much importance as he placed on partnering with a quality sponsor, however, Church was not going to waste his time with the project if the financial returns were not sufficient. Braun, for his part, was positive that Dr. Pepper was totally sold on the program based on the earlier audition. But he did not have any hard evidence to support his belief, and he was growing nervous with the continued mention of the Sons of the Pioneers. Surely, he tried to convince himself and others, the soda company was not interested at this point in redeveloping the concept with a new musical outfit that offered a very different sound. Bob Braun began to direct his frustration at the stalled deal toward Sameth, whom he now felt was more of a "stumbling block" than a help. It was Sameth's fee in putting the deal together which was causing much of the disagreement about costs and threatening the whole project. If Midland Broadcasting could just negotiate directly with Benton & Bowles, Braun was positive, fees could be agreed upon and the deal signed, but for whatever reason, the agency insisted on working through Sameth.

Kellogg, too, became an indirect player in the Dr. Pepper negotiations when, on October 9, George Halley approached J. Walter

Thompson's Chet Foust about releasing the Texas Rangers from Kellogg's exclusive contract to allow the band to appear on Texas stations for a second sponsor. Perhaps in a nod on Kellogg's part to Midland Broadcasting's willingness to restructure their contract from a 52-week deal to a renewing 13-week deal, George Halley could report to Arthur Church that "[i]t is absolutely all right with Kellogg and JWT so long as the name, Texas Rangers, is not used in any way in connection with the program." Both Kellogg and J. Walter Thompson were "fully cognizant of [KMBC's] investment in the boys and felt [they] had a perfect right to sell them elsewhere" so long as the Texas Rangers name was not used. The cereal producer did not think it would be appropriate for another sponsor "cashing in on [Kellogg's] nine months of advertising" in the state.

It appears that a deal with Dr. Pepper was finally reached, though the record is frustratingly spotty on this point. On November 3, 1941, a contract was submitted to Midland by Benton & Bowles on behalf of Dr. Pepper to enter into production of a series of transcribed fifteen-minute radio programs to feature the Texas Rangers and utilizing the writing talent of Gomer Cool. The terms outlined a whopping 104-week agreement, with rehearsals starting no later than January 15, 1942. Clauses were included allowing the parties to opt out of the contract after 13-week periods. The contract was non-exclusive, allowing the band and individuals within the band to take on other engagements. The proposed series was entitled *The 10-2-4 Ranch* and the words "Texas" and "Rangers" were specifically to be omitted from any title should Dr. Pepper decide to change it.

Although the new series looked like a done deal, a key memo dated February 25, 1942, sheds light on how the imminent deal fell apart. Sometime in early October, 1941, Chet Foust wrote to Church and informed him that since Benton & Bowles, the agency representing Dr. Pepper, also represented Kellogg's Post Toasties line of cereal, "[they] cannot acquiesce that another advertiser should be allowed to employ the name, Texas Rangers, even in publicity, in Texas." While not nixing the Dr. Pepper sponsorship, it was an ominous note.

A month later, November 5, Church met with Foust in New York at which point Foust "completely reversed himself from his statements of October 9," in which he indicated Kellogg was fine with Dr. Pepper's use of the Texas Rangers so long as the name was not used in any way in the show's title. Just two days after delivery of a preliminary contract, the deal between KMBC and Dr. Pepper was off. About three weeks later on November 25th George Halley managed to get to Battle Creek, MI, to meet with Kenneth Graham and J. A. Briggs with the hope of straightening out the entire issue and salvaging the sponsorship. Halley was stunned to hear that Graham and Briggs "were amazed to learn that the Dr. Pepper deal was off – that Kellogg had never told the agency [J. Walter Thompson] that we could not sell the Texas Rangers in Texas so long as the name, Texas Rangers, was not used."

Foust was irate when he found out that Halley had visited with Graham in Michigan and that KMBC was still trying to work out an agreement with Dr. Pepper. Foust ended the confrontational meeting declaring "he did not want to see me [Halley] again until they sent for me." It was months before the two spoke again.

While the reasons the contracts were never signed and the partnership between KMBC and Dr. Pepper never materialized are not completely clear, it appears that Chester Foust and the J. Walter Thompson advertising agency were not keen on the project. Evidence suggests they may have even deliberately sabotaged the deal, if not by outright misstatements, then at least by sharing communications between Kellogg and KMBC which were not entirely accurate. Just weeks after the proposed contract was submitted to Church, Benton & Bowles ended up inking the deal with the Rangers' old competitors, Sons of the Pioneers, the group which Bob Braun had confidently declared held little true interest to the soda company. Unfortunately for the Texas Rangers, Dr. Pepper and the Sons of the Pioneers agreed to terms on November 22, 1941. Similar monetary disagreements were overcome and Dick Foran agreed to serve as the initial MC for the series, a role Martha Mears took over in later years. *The 10-2-4 Ranch*, a series which Midland Broadcasting management thought was a done deal for the Rangers, ran through World War II, a bitter pill for all to swallow.

Despite this setback, and the devastating news of the Japanese attack on Pearl Harbor on December 7 that propelled the US into the war, the year ended positively for the Rangers, with more concentrated recording, including the group's first commercial recordings since their association with Decca in 1935. The Rangers waxed four songs for Columbia Records' Okeh subsidiary on December 4th, including several patriotic songs that reflected how close the country was edging towards a state-of-war mentality, even before the Pearl Harbor bombing. Among them were "The Air Corps Of Uncle Sam" and Bob Crawford's "I've Changed My Penthouse For A Pup-Tent." Crawford also wrote the session's other two songs, the ballad "I Wonder Why" and the novelty "Pull Out The Stopper," which featured one of the Rangers' trade-marks: several of the singers playing ocarinas. "I've Changed My Penthouse" got considerable jukebox action and was praised in the music press upon its release in early 1942. In addition to a fine performance by Crawford and the quartet, it boasted fine, jazzy solo work from Kratoska and Strand.

Some days later, perhaps Monday, December 8th, since Cool later recalled beginning session work for the music library session work on the day after Pearl Harbor, the group was back at World Broadcasting to begin adding to the more than 200 selections it had recorded in March and April. Only one recording sheet survives from this period (January 21, 1942), so the exact dates for some of the recording sessions are not certain, but fifty songs were waxed over several sessions in December, and a further fifty were added to the Rangers' growing music library in January. Of the 100 newly added tunes, almost a third were original compositions by band members, with Bob Crawford providing sixteen and Gomer Cool eleven. Fran Mahaney added a song, as well.

1942

The new music library sessions ended on January 22, 1942. As with the session for Columbia held prior to Pearl Harbor, a number of the new songs recorded reflected America's entry into the war and the fighting spirit sweeping the nation, including, from the January 21st recording date, two songs from Gomer Cool's pen, "Soldier Boy" and "Hymn to the Navy."

It was inevitable that the war would begin to intrude on both the personal and professional lives of the Rangers. Gomer Cool later recalled that soon after America entered the conflict, the wives of several band members became reluctant to remain on the West Coast. Beyond their understandable uneasiness with the wider situation and a desire to be near home and family, he recalled that the very real fear of Japanese attack along the country's Pacific Coast weighed heavily upon them.

Such fears, he hinted, lay behind several personnel changes in the band in the coming weeks. In early 1942, Fran "Irish" Mahaney told Bob Braun during a Friday night dinner that he intended to leave the Texas Rangers. His official reason for giving notice was apprehension about the band's future, fear that it would break up because of war-related pressures. Such a possibility had not been raised by Arthur Church, Braun or anyone else. Braun did not put much stock in Mahaney's story and laid most of the blame for his departure at the feet of his wife, Dorothy. Ostensibly, she claimed she was worried that that the group would disband or that Mahaney would be replaced, but her insistence on returning to Kansas City and subsequent refusal to return to the Coast, suggested there was more to it. At any rate, Mahaney had no intention of remaining in California without her, and when she wrote him from Kansas City on February 8, 1942, telling him in no uncertain terms that she would not rejoin him on the Coast, Mahaney told Braun he was leaving the band and returning to the Midwest. The situation was deeply disappointing to Church and to Braun, who told Church that he did "not believe that under normal conditions one could hope to find a better boy than Fran." His "unusual actions and statements" were "due to Dorothy's unreasonable attitude." Mahaney had been a key, as well as a consistent and dependable member of the Texas Rangers since 1935, and KMBC now had nearly seven years invested in his professional development. His departure was only the beginning of war-related problems, instability that would in the coming months escalate into a constant, and at times, critical concern.

On top of the turmoil within the band, Church found himself dealing with a suddenly deteriorating situation involving their prime sponsor, Kellogg, then still using the Rangers transcription library over Texas radio stations. Church was warned in a confidential letter sent February 3, 1942, that the Texas Rangers were in danger of losing the account. The sender, identified only as Sam, who was possibly Sam Bennett, a KMBC vice president and director of sales, said representatives at the J. Walter Thompson company, specifically Buck Gunn and Chet Foust, were being courted by Jerry Ellis, head of CBS recording and formerly of the World Broadcasting.

Foust, of course, was already disgruntled with Midland relating to the failed attempt by the company to sell a Texas Rangers program to Dr. Pepper. According to the letter, Ellis was pushing for Gunn and Foust to misrepresent certain facts to Thompson vice-president Henry T. Stanton in order to get Thompson and Kellogg to sponsor a night club orchestra instead of the Rangers. Ellis would have benefited from the new recording work, and the writer of the letter alleged that Gunn was getting a cut under the table of both recording fees and the talent fees that came in when a new act was signed to record transcription library material. "This type of orchestra for Kellogg … is ridiculous," the letter continued, but suggested that Church should get in touch personally with representatives at Thompson, including vice-president Stanton, to emphasize the value of the Texas Rangers and the band's availability for use in further markets outside Texas.

By the end of February, 1942, efforts to market the transcribed Texas Rangers music library beyond its current use for the Kellogg sponsored programs in Texas were underway. George Halley reported that, as of February 24, there had been 201 inquiries about the library, most importantly from WJZ, New York City's NBC Blue network outlet, which turned out to be the first sale. The station was also considering a series of live Texas Rangers broadcasts. While WJZ's interest in the Rangers might seem odd today, when New York–rightly or wrongly–has long been considered to epitomize a mindset that looks down its nose at such things as hillbilly and cowboy music, New York City and its environs had a lively country music scene during the pre-World War II years and beyond, with such stars as Elton Britt and Rosalie Allen basing there.

While the Texas Rangers transcription library could provide income for KMBC, it did not necessarily lead to any direct work for the band other than short spurts of recording. With little work coming the group's way beyond recording, keeping morale up, among other things, was proving a challenge. The Rangers continued to rehearse 2 ½ hours per day, three days a week, adequate time, Bob Braun assured Church, for them to stay "limber and … in good voice." It proved to be ample time to keep them tight on old tunes and arrangements, to introduce new songs to the repertoire, and to practice new arrangements. When an assignment did come along, they rehearsed six days per week. However, without a specific purpose like a concert or radio show, Braun warned, so much practice would likely lead to complaints and the rehearsals might turn into gripe sessions and ultimately be counter-productive.

Like that of the country as a whole, the Rangers' situation was far from stable and the future uncertain. Beyond worries about the paucity of jobs and of keeping the group intact in the face of possible wartime attrition, there were other concerns. During March, 1942, the contracts for Bob Crawford, Tookie Cronenbold, and Rod May were getting set to expire and Bob Braun found himself having difficulty convincing the trio to sign a new five-year deal, the standard length of a Midland Broadcasting contract. While Clarence Hartman and Joe Strand had no reservations about re-signing at $47.50 per week, Crawford, Cronenbold and May were holding out for $50 per week, roughly a five percent raise. Crawford told Braun he was set on $50, and if a contract could not be worked out at that rate, he was ready to strike out on his own, an idea he had been considering for a while. This explanation did not make any sense to Braun; how was an extra $2.50 a week enough money to induce a man interested in pursuing a solo career into signing an extended deal with a group act? The other two did not voice specific reasons for their requests other than they felt they could get it. Bob Braun had no doubt that Bob Crawford had talked them into holding out together for the raise.

Braun reminded the three Rangers of the benefits of their current situation and how good they had had it working for Arthur Church: a guaranteed weekly check over a decade that had been economically catastrophic for the nation. Even through the ups-and-downs of recent months, when the group had struggled for work at times, they had not had to fear for their jobs. Beyond the job security, Braun pointed out, the band members were given two weeks paid vacation a year, a $25 Christmas bonus, $25 in defense bonds, and earned a modest side income from recording.

Braun's pleas fell on deaf ears and he remained as baffled by their stance as he was frustrated by it: "Arthur, I am at a complete loss as to the reason for their attitude," he confessed. "I cannot understand their thinking. I have also believed that life (in business also) was give and take. I guess that the boys do not see it that way. They have a darn sweet deal, but I doubt if they realize it."

Whether or not they realized how "sweet" their situation really was in uncertain times, the trio did eventually re-sign at Church's original salary offer of $47.50 per week. Although his singers, Hartman and Strand, were safely under contract for the foreseeable future, Arthur Church would have been wrong to assume that the bumpy ride was over. Indeed, the next eighteen months would be the most difficult thus far faced by Church and his Texas Rangers.

Chapter 7: The Camel Caravan Tour

Kellogg Fallout

In early 1942 both guitarist Herb Kratoska and tenor Fran Mahaney took their leave from the Texas Rangers and returned to Kansas City. Kratoska's decision was not a total surprise; he had been hinting at such a move almost since the relocation to California in 1939. Braun's conversations with Mahaney, his wife, and family achieved nothing and they, too, headed back to Kansas City. Kratoska returned to KMBC, but effective February 23, 1942, Mahaney was off the KMBC payroll despite the friendly attitude he always had toward station officials.

If the Rangers were to continue as a unit – and particularly as a distinct and tightly rehearsed one – these gaping holes in the line-up needed to be filled immediately. It was far more a crisis than that created by Paul Sell's departure two years before. Replacing one key member in peacetime was one thing, but filling two, and potentially more, given the situation, key positions in wartime was another thing entirely. The remaining Rangers began rehearsing with Archie Berdahl on guitar in early March, 1942, to see if he would be a good fit for the group. After four days of practice, Braun confirmed to Church that Berdahl was "a very likeable boy" with "a good personality." Most importantly he was both a capable guitar player and a good singer. Before committing, Braun wanted to record a 15 minute acetate trial of Berdahl with the rest of the band to hear how they gelled. The results proved satisfactory, and on April 17, 1942, Archie Berdahl became the newest Texas Ranger.

Thirty-one years old when he joined the Texas Rangers, Berdahl came from a musical family and had an impressive resume which included radio, film, and records. Born in Dunn Center, North Dakota, Berdahl had formed his own dance band in high school before going professional. Proficient on guitar, the 7-string electric guitar, Spanish guitar, and ocarina, he had done some announcing, vocal and instrumental arranging, and had written some original songs.

Berdahl worked for eight years with the Tommy Tucker Orchestra and sang on some of Tucker's Vocalion records. Between October, 1937, and July, 1938, the Tommy Tucker Orchestra was featured on Mutual radio's *Thirty Minutes in Hollywood* which starred George Jessel and Norma Talmadge, and Berdahl was credited with all the vocal arrangements. Prior to joining the Rangers Berdahl had been playing with a novelty group called the Cracker Jacks. The Cracker Jacks had experienced moderate success, making a short musical film for Universal with the Jack Teagarden Orchestra, appearing on radio's *Hollywood Showcase* and *The Al Pearce Show*, some Warner Brothers Loony Tunes cartoons, and on several Standard Radio library transcription records.

Berdahl's tenure with the Rangers lasted only six months. He had been given a draft classification of 3A by the Army because his wife was in poor health and dependent upon his income. But on October 24, 1942, he gave his two weeks' notice to Bob Braun. He was certain he would be reclassified and wanted to return to North Dakota to train for railroad work, hoping that such experience would exempt him from military service. The timing was also important as he wanted to beat gas rationing scheduled to go into effect later in the year.

Berdahl's time with the Rangers did extend over the opening months of the next important phase in the group's history: its high profile but grueling work in the wartime Camel Caravan. Back in the spring, prior to Berdahl's hiring, Arthur Church renewed correspondence with J. Walter Thompson's Chester Foust in an attempt to thaw the icy relationship between Midland and Kellogg's advertising agency, which had grown frigid after Foust's meeting with George Halley on December 1, 1941. Church suggested that perhaps the group could record a further fifty selections for the music library, but Foust was sure Kellogg would not have any interest in increasing its investment with the group by footing the bill for another 50 recordings. Indeed, he informed Church in March, 1942, that Kellogg was considering a different direction.

"We have been considering what might be done to broaden the appeal of the Texas show," Foust wrote, "and have about decided that some kind of diversification is indicated. We have built a number of sample shows in which additional talent is employed," and they were looking very "promising." "Frankly," he added, seemingly attempting to deflate any hopes Church had of expanding the Kellogg sponsorship, "there is no reason for enthusiasm over the size of the audience or following that the Rangers are attracting. . . . The situation . . . provides no basis for thinking that Battle Creek is contemplating expansion of the show to points outside of the Texas area at this time."

Alarmed by the direction of Foust's communications, on April 8 Church sent along recent radio audience figures that he wanted to make sure Foust saw, to reassure the agency that the Texas Rangers were a great advertising match for the company. Over WOAI in San Antonio the Rangers were tuned in by 50% of listeners in their time slot, 25% beyond their nearest competition, while in Dallas, against stiff competition from the popular juvenile shows *Captain Midnight* and *Tom Mix*, they still held a ratings lead of 4%. Results from Houston, where they were scheduled against *Little Orphan Annie* and *Jack Armstrong, the All-American Boy*, were not as good. Yet up against *Jack Armstrong*'s impressive 44% audience share, the Rangers managed to pull in 29% of listeners in a less than ideal timeslot.

Church could see no validity in Foust's contention that these audience numbers might be strengthened by mixing other talent alongside the Rangers. He did not favor such a move ("at least not until we have had an opportunity to know what this talent is and give you our recommendation in connection therewith") and was clearly concerned it could open the door to Kellogg replacing the Rangers with another outfit.

"When you contracted with us for the Texas Rangers Library for Kellogg in Texas," Church told Foust, "it was my understanding this was to be a test of our Texas Rangers group with the idea the program would expand to other markets after thirteen, or twenty-six, or thirty-nine weeks, if the program was successful in building audience in Texas test areas.

"Last August when we gave you, at your request, quotations for other Kellogg sales areas, we were very hopeful at least some expansion would be made in the Fall or early Winter. To us, the excellent audience figures you so kindly passed on to us seem to bear this out. We are as eager as ever to serve Kellogg on an expanded basis and are keenly disappointed we seem not to have made the grade thus far.

"Since our Texas Rangers program is, so to speak, on trial, we are presently inclined to believe we would rather stand alone rather than have other talent brought into the program. <u>We are anxious for the Texas Rangers to make good for Kellogg.</u>"

Church asked Foust to reconsider his recent recommendations regarding the best broadcast times for the group. He was positive that a spot such as 7:30 to 7:45 in the morning, before or after an established news broadcast, would be prime. Similar timeslots had worked well when Kellogg sponsored the Rangers locally over KMBC in 1937, and the group's transcriptions were presently pulling in a 42.5% rating against six other stations in Kansas City for the Carey Salt Company. In addition, Church had little doubt that a noon spot would provide a significant return as well. He pointed out the noon hour had more radio sets turned on than any other part of the day, especially in rural areas such as those covered by the Texas stations carrying the Rangers. Ultimately, however, despite Church's entreaties, Foust was not interested, and neither was Kellogg. The company was not going to renew their sponsorship after the current deal expired.

On the Camel Caravan

When Arthur Church signed a contract with M. L. Tours, Inc., on May 2, 1942, to have the Texas Rangers appear on the Camel Caravan tour, sponsored by Camel's parent company R. J. Reynolds Tobacco Company, he surely did not envision that the move would contribute significantly to the dissolving of the band for the duration of the war and some months beyond. Not to be confused with the long-running radio program of the same name, the touring Camel Caravan was initiated by R. J. Reynolds during World War II to entertain troops. The company was so confident in the Caravan as a publicity effort and morale booster that it invested in multiple Caravans during the war years, each covering a different geographic area of the country. The Caravans toured military camps and bases throughout the West, Midwest, South, and East and featured a wide variety of entertainment in order to appeal to as many service personnel as possible.[1]

The Rangers actually began touring with one of the Caravans on April 27, 1942, before Church had signed the contract. A. B. C. Productions, another of Church's enterprises, received

---
1 *Billboard* July 18, 1942, p. 8

weekly payments of $857.50 (less a deduction of $17.50), via the William Morris Agency, Inc., which was the official employer of record for the tour. The eight musicians now playing as the Texas Rangers were veterans Clarence Hartman, Gomer Cool, Edward Cronenbold, Bob Crawford, Rod May, and Joe Strand, along with newcomers Archie Berdahl and Kenny Harpster. Harpster, identified by Bob Braun as "the additional man working with the boys," may not have been an official member of the band. He played saxophone, an instrument never before included in the Rangers' line-up but one that was not unheard of in Western bands of the era, and he may also have sung. The three singers (Cronenbold, Crawford, and May) received $47.50 per week while the musicians (except Hartman), were paid $73 weekly. Hartman, recognized as the band's leader on multiple documents, received 50% extra for this role, $109.50 every week. All, except Harpster, were given an additional three dollars per day, likely for travel expenses. Thus, the band's upkeep cost Church $691 per week, leaving a tidy $166.50 profit per week, some of which would have covered other expenses such as manager Braun's salary. To cover the $17.50 deducted by Morris, Inc., Braun pointed out that 2% of each Rangers' paycheck could be withheld which covered $10.88 of that amount.

Bob Braun wrote to Arthur Church in early May, 1942, and mentioned he had been meeting the group at Camp Elliot in San Diego. He would "see if everything is running smoothly & if all the boys are happy." But neither he nor Church had any idea of the toll the Camel Caravan would take on the Rangers.

The group was originally contracted to appear on the Caravan for five weeks beginning April 27, with the option of a four week extension through June 27. KMBC's Karl Koerper signed a letter on June 2 confirming another four week extension on top of the first nine weeks. By mid-June William Morris had already decided to run the Caravan at least through August 1, necessitating yet another contract update to cover the extra week on top of the four guaranteed by Koerper's contract. The contract provided for four additional one-week options which would start August 3.

With no new radio, recording, or film projects in the works, the Texas Rangers settled into a life on the road that would prove vastly different from their day-to-day existence since the move to California

The Texas Rangers playing on the Camel Caravan.
Courtesy of Ed Crawford.

three years earlier. Meanwhile, Arthur Church and George Halley wrapped up the remaining details of the band's soon-to-be completed run under the sponsorship of Kellogg. Church received official notice of cancellation from J. Walter Thompson's Chester Foust on May 12, 1942. Foust even noted Thompson's dubious intention to replace some of the Texas Rangers' numbers on the fifteen-minute transcribed series with those of other performers before the current agreement expired. A dismayed Church reiterated his opposition to this dilution of the Rangers' shows and said he would seek legal advice on the matter, a threat which made little impact on Foust and J. Walter Thompson. Clearly puzzled by Foust's seeming vindictiveness, Church wrote that he was "sorry you have not seen fit to consult with us so as to give us the opportunity of smoothing out problems concerning which we have never been advised."

A week later, Church informed Bob Braun in California of the loss of the Kellogg contract and also that Dr. Pepper was not interested in pursuing any sponsorship deal. Church was clearly frustrated by the situation, particularly with Foust, who deliberately deflected efforts to address any concerns Kellogg may have had with the Texas

Rangers. Midland Broadcasting was never given an official reason for the cancellation, but Church was in no doubt that "... Foust has undermined us at Kellogg ever since our request to him to give us a release on the Rangers for Dr. Pepper in Texas." Admitting he still did not have the entire story, Church found a bit of solace knowing that one of the Texas station owners had confided in him that his station would continue using the Texas Rangers library independent of the Kellogg sponsored broadcast, since they were drawing good audiences. Despite his best efforts, Church was disappointed in his inability to get Foust to share Kellogg's reasons for canceling the Rangers' show. The most he could get from Foust was a commitment for a complimentary letter detailing Kellogg's opinion of the "the Texas Rangers as a Western musical act and their audience-getting abilities."

With the Texas arrangement at an end, the participating stations began shipping their sets of the Texas Rangers transcription library back to Midland Broadcasting. George Halley undertook the tedious task of completing a full and careful inventory of all the records, many of which had gotten heavy use. Eight complete sets of the Texas Rangers library were returned, in varying condition, and Halley provided a detailed assessment to Church. The condition of the sets ranged from "excellent and usable condition" and "fair" to "absolutely worthless" and little more than "junk." Some individual records in the "fair" sets would need to be replaced before the library could be rented out again, though the condition seemed consistent with reasonable wear and tear. It was Halley's opinion that KMBC should seriously consider setting up a system of depreciation for the records so that, over time, the costs of pressing new sets could "be wiped out completely."

Even the sets that were in the best condition, George Halley observed, looked worn even though the sound was still fine; image counted for a lot. New subscribers would probably expect sets that looked better than what the station had on hand, even if the effect on sound quality was negligible. With the heavy use these discs saw, five times a week for 65 weeks, such wear and tear would be inevitable. This was a business cost that Midland "must foresee and plan to meet accordingly." There was little they would be able to do about the condition of returned records, he grudgingly wrote, but the depreciation would probably work out to around a measly $350 out of a total income from the Kellogg deal of $22,750.

Hard Times

When they signed new contracts earlier in the year, Braun and Church had convinced Crawford, May, and Cronenbold to continue to work for the same $47.50 weekly wage they were receiving on the previous contract. As non-playing singers who were apparently not members of the musician's union, they were making considerably less per week than the musicians, who had to be paid union scale, and less than half of what Clarence Hartman was making as leader of the group. Not surprisingly, they were not happy with this state of affairs and confronted Braun on July 19, just a few weeks into the Caravan tour. While Crawford informed Braun that he would finish out the current contract option, Cronenbold announced in, as Braun put it, "his usual hostile and dictitorial [sic] manner" (Braun's words) that he would not continue touring. Braun was not popular with Bob Crawford, and in light of his close friendship with Rod May and Ed Cronenbold, Braun was not popular with them, either. They were able to work together professionally, but the intensified touring of Camel Caravan, lack of any high-profile radio or film work, and the singers' frustration with the unequal pay scale placed a further burden on their already tense relationships.

Braun did all he could to assure the singers that he wanted a commercial program for the group just as badly as they wanted one. He would be more than happy to get the band off the road if that were possible, but there were simply no other profitable offers on the table at that point. There were several positives for hanging with the Camel tour, Braun assured them, involving not only income but "publicity, prestige and morale." Further, it looked much better for potential sponsors to be able to say the Rangers were touring with the Camel Caravan than to say they were currently not engaged anywhere. Despite Braun's entreaties, all three appeared determined to leave the Rangers as soon as contracts would allow.

The next week Braun met with the trio again, including Clarence Hartman in the conversation. Pleading with Crawford, Cronenbold, and May to reconsider about leaving the group, Braun announced that the Rangers' place on the tour was firm and that it might even last into early November. He hinted that a potential commercial program might be in the offing, as well. Tookie Cronenbold, who had steadily been insisting he would not continue on the tour, reiterated this stance but grudgingly agreed to run it by his wife after Crawford and May said they would do the same. But all three wanted more money – the same as the musicians received. Braun sympathized with their argument and agreed to look into but made no promises.

Within a week Braun could report to Church on August 2, 1942, that "everything [was] under control" and that the trio had agreed to continue the tour. Bob Crawford said "he could not help himself," perhaps referencing a deep devotion to the group with which he had spent the last decade, and to Church himself. Rod May also accepted Braun's terms, indicating that his wife Millie had agreed to his staying on the tour for the next seven weeks, though he would need to revisit the issue at the tour's conclusion. Cronenbold initially balked, which lead to a heated confrontation with Braun. When Braun informed him that he would need to find a replacement for him so that the band could meet its contractual obligations, Cronenbold threatened not to get on the bus three minutes before departure to the next show and told Braun he would not perform that night.

"I then had a quick 60 second conference with him which must have been successful," Braun recounted to Church. The next morning Cronenbold apologized and told Braun that he would like to continue touring with the group. The previous night's blow-up was the third time Cronenbold had threatened to skip a performance, Braun reminded him, and a shamefaced Cronenbold apologized again and signed a new contract. Cronenbold had a drinking problem, a fact that came up in discussions with management before he was finally terminated by KMBC in 1949, and his erratic behavior during this stressful period may have been a reflection of his increasing alcohol abuse.

Reflecting on the difficult contract negotiations of the recent weeks, Braun told Church that he felt "these boys are badly spoiled." Had Church given in to their salary demands "they would have become unmanageable in the future," he wrote, adding that "actions of this sort only tends [sic] to break down the morale of the group as a whole and encourages insubordination on the part of other members of the group."

Braun remained a company man who watched the pennies closely. Just how closely became apparent when, soon after he quelled the trio's mutiny, he informed the musicians that they had been overpaid for the year and would, therefore, not receive additional salary during their two week vacation. Ironically, after their humbling hold-out, the only exceptions to this were the three singers, who had been paid their contracted salary to date.

The Rangers continued to prove satisfactory to the Caravan organizers, and their services were requested for four more weeks as of August 17, with their primary responsibility being to "perform in a competent and artistic manner" as judged by William Morris management. Touring had been a regular part of the group's working life since its inception, but the Caravan was particularly grueling. The contract called for up to three performances per day, with no guaranteed days off, and most saw their families only when the tour passed through or near the Los Angeles area. The contractual week ran from Monday morning to Saturday night–the troupe was apparently given Sundays off–and continued to be paid $875 per week, with the right to pro-rate that payment for any concert missed by any one or more of the Rangers. All transportation was via bus, and the group members were responsible for room and board, likely the three dollar per diem noted above, as well as being expected to provide their own costumes and any other necessary props. Each week's tour began and ended in Los Angeles, but apparently, opportunities to see family came fewer and farther between as the tour dragged on.

Nor were there were many chances for relaxation and recreation on the tour. Birthdays, holidays, and anniversaries were celebrated on buses and in hotels. During a Caravan stopover in Oakland, California, on August 31, for example, Bob Crawford received a short, congratulatory telegram from Midland's Karl Koeper recognizing Crawford's twelve years of employment with the company. On the plus side, the Caravan offered the Rangers the chance to meet and mingle with several well-known celebrities, including Jimmy Stewart and a few up-and-comers who would make names for themselves, such as Marilyn Maxwell.

Gomer Cool had indicated as early as 1939 the he was not entirely satisfied with his role with the Rangers. The strain of months on the road was getting to everyone, but in September Cool became the first casualty. He informed Church that he wished to leave the band, return to Kansas City with his family, and settle into a local job with KMBC. Though he would, ironically, end up spending the rest of his long life there and enjoy a successful career in radio and television, he told Church at the time that after three years his family still did not feel at home in Southern California, and that the Rangers' lack of success had proven very disappointing to him.

Initially, Church and his executive staff gave Cool the choice to stay with the band or return to the Midwest–or even, if he chose, to "disassociate [himself] entirely from the organization." The latter hints of Cool's suggestion some months before, that perhaps he had outgrown the opportunities available to him at KMBC, had not fallen on deaf ears and that Church was reconciled to the possibility of bidding this longtime and faithful employee farewell.

If Cool decided to stay with KMBC in some capacity, Church insisted that he stay with the Rangers until a suitable replacement could be hired. Since finding professional musicians was proving more difficult as more men were drafted or moved out of music into defense related work, finding another musician who fit might prove difficult and take some weeks. Should he decide to return to the KMBC studios, Church would give Cool the chance to "sink or swim" as an Assistant Program Director. He could not, however, promise specific responsibilities or delineate his job duties. "With changing war conditions," Church explained, "it is difficult to say exactly what you can expect. My guess is that all of us will be doing a lot of 'doubling in brass' before this thing is over. And, to be clear, there would be no salary increase for the change in assignments."

Bob Braun joined the Rangers in Salt Lake City on September 11, 1942, and left them in Seattle on the 27th. He told Church that the Caravan had been "a grand trip as well as a wonderful experience." Whether naïve or overly optimistic, he felt that "there [was] a closer bond of friendship" among the Rangers due to their extensive hours together on the road. The earlier contract clause stipulating a return to Los Angeles every week had been discarded. Braun wrote that the group had an upcoming two-week stint around the San Diego territory before returning to Los Angeles for a five-day stand. From there they would be off to Santa Maria and San Luis Obispo. The commitment to the Caravan continued to be extended; the Rangers were now contracted through October 31. Though there were no definite plays for the group beyond that point, Braun was optimistic. All the R. J. Reynolds representatives on the tour "were unanimous in their praise for the Rangers, both as artists and regular fellows." Church and the Rangers, themselves, would likely have taken any such praise with a grain of salt, even with Braun's report that these Reynolds reps "would write in to their home office regarding the Rangers." The Rangers had heard similar assessments time and again since moving to the West Coast, but rarely had these led to substantive work.

Cool's situation was still up in the air at the end of September. He wanted to wait until he was back in Los Angeles and could discuss all options with his wife Margaret before coming to a decision. Communications indicate KMBC officials felt confident the Cool family would ultimately decide to return to Kansas City, and on September 30 he proved them right, wiring Church that "Margaret and I gratefully accept opportunity to return Kansas City and new job [sic]. I'm anxious to get back in the harness."

Church suggested Sam Leichter as Cool's possible replacement. He had played with the Rangers in their earliest years on KMBC, and Church considered him "an excellent violinist, a real showman, a good comedian." Leichter had apparently not been engaged as a musician recently and had taken a job working with his father dressing models and mannequins, a job that Church worried might be paying Leichter more than the Texas Rangers gig. At any rate, Church was positive Braun could find a new fiddler without too much trouble. Cool was a good violinist, though unarguably the least adventurous and assured of the instrumental quartet; however, his fiddling was only one of his contributions to the group, overshadowed in some ways by his songs, scripts, and his early framing of the group in his writing. If the group needed a serviceable fiddler and nothing more, Church could thus argue that "it should not be nearly as difficult to find a replacement for Gomer as it was for Herbie and Fran." But Cool had been much more than a fiddler, and the postwar Texas Rangers, unquestionably, felt his absence.

Braun and Church were not unaware of the implications that Cool's departure would have for the Rangers as a whole. He was not the only band member desperate to get off the road, and not the only one wishing to return to Kansas City. The other Rangers would certainly be asking why he was allowed to do so when no one else was. The vocal trio would jump at the chance to head back to Kansas City, and Joe Strand and Archie Berdahl were looking for any excuse to get off the Caravan. Although they were sympathetic to the members' plight, Braun and Church, nevertheless, could see no viable alternative for Rangers as a whole at this point but to continue to tour with the Caravan. Otherwise, the group's prospects were far from hopeful.

Braun made the decision to hire Sam Leichter on October 29, 1942. He traveled to Phoenix, AZ, to see Leichter perform and talked him into signing a regular five-year contract with KMBC. Leichter was not available until December 1, however, which meant that it would be necessary for Cool to stay on a few weeks longer than planned. Braun wanted to be fair to Cool, especially in light of his fifteen years loyal service to KMBC, but he was desperate to avoid further problems that would arise if it became necessary to find a temporary replacement until Leichter could start in December. Beyond logistical matters and the difficulties it would create for the remaining band members, it could also not only jeopardize the spot on the Camel Caravan, but affect the future prospects for sponsored radio work for Camel.

Archie Berdahl, who had given his two weeks notice on October 24, wrote a lengthy letter to Arthur Church to fully explain his decision to leave the Rangers after such a short stint. Contributing to his desire to leave and to the timing of it were family concerns (his wife had a chronic, debilitating illness), war-time travel restrictions and rationing, as well as his desire to avoid the expanding draft. This led to his plans to return to their native North Dakota to join his brother in railroad work, a "vital industry" that would almost certainly give him a deferment from military service.

Berdahl was also brutally honest about how much the grind of the Camel Caravan tours had contributed to his desire to leave the Rangers. Not only would such employments not lead to any deferment, but the tours were grueling, "too difficult for us to keep up indefinitely." Neither was the level of compensation commensurate to the work involved, and crucially for Berdahl, it was not enough for him to put away any savings to build up security for his family. "Had I known the Camel Caravan was coming up," Berdahl confessed, "I would never have joined the Rangers." In fact, he had left Tommy

Tucker's band after eight successful years with them for similar reasons: the non-stop road work was too much for a man in his position.

Berdahl tried to leave the door open for possible future employment with Midland Broadcasting. "I don't know exactly what my status with you is now as far as the contract is concerned. I hope when this is all over we can perhaps 'try it again' as I know I should surely like to continue working for you. I believe I could be a valuable man to you in a number of ways." Upon learning of Berdahl's two-weeks notice, Bob Crawford had even suggested that it might be possible to arrange a leave of absence instead. Whether Church was inclined to view Berdahl's predicament and untimely departure sympathetically is uncertain, but Berdahl was never to work again for Church, Midland, or KMBC.

While some band members were looking to get off the road at almost any cost, or to avoid being called up by Uncle Sam, others were finding their only hope of achieving the former in the foreseeable future was the latter. Church and his staff did what they could to get deferments for employees but successes were few. Even technical men, which Karl Koerper pointed out were increasingly difficult to replace, were receiving neither deferments nor reclassifications. Of all the petitions Arthur Church Productions staff had made, the best they had done was a six-month deferment for one person. When Rod May was called by the government, Koerper and Braun decided it would not even be worth filing a form 42-A. "I do not see how we could conscientiously make the statement that he cannot be replaced," admitted Koerper.

How close a relationship May had with Arthur Church is unclear. In the most in-depth personal communication written by May, one of the few letters by May extant in the historical record, he put his best foot forward in requesting a chance to return home to Kansas City. "I know that because of our long and enjoyable association together that you will give it full consideration," May wrote. Because he wanted to remain with the Rangers in the long run, he pointed out that, despite the fact that he had been one of the group who had hoped to return to Kansas City early in the year, he had remained with the band while others were bailing. He was frank with Church that he did not find the band to be as good as it had been in years past. For some reason, whether it was partly personal or purely musical, he cited Archie Berdahl as a major reason for this and felt that, with two more replacements coming on board soon to replace Berdahl and Cool, it would only "make the situation much worse."

May reminded Church that he would very likely be drafted soon and said he hoped to spend what time he could with his wife in Kansas City, adding that he was willing to do whatever he could around the KMBC studios should Church agree to his transfer. If this could not be arranged, May wished to give his two weeks notice, which would make November 15, 1942, his last day on the payroll. Bob Crawford and Edward Cronenbold, May's friends and singing partners since several years prior to the Rangers' inception, gave notice at the same time.

Usually calm and composed in his correspondence, Church was livid over this drastic development, and on November 3 he whipped out a telegram reminding the defecting Rangers about their contractual responsibilities, notably to the Camel Caravan. Irritated now with what he perceived as Cool's inflexibility–that he was leaving the Rangers and returning to Kansas City regardless of Church's wishes–the previously accommodating Church cited Cool's "arbitrary attitude" as evidence that "he would not properly represent management as assistant program director, so regretfully conclude we must withdraw proposal [sic] staff position." With that quick note Gomer Cool was released by Midland Broadcasting.

On November 7, 1942, Cool and Berdahl took their official leave of the Rangers during a stop at Monterey, CA. Bob Braun had worked feverishly to bring Sam Leichter back on board to replace Cool, but a temporary replacement would still have to be found in the meantime. Nor did Braun have any ready prospects to replace Berdahl, and any new member in that slot would be employed on a probationary basis.

Church's harsh reversal with Gomer Cool may have been intended as a message to the rest of the group; Church perhaps feeling that it might bring the rest of the group in line. He instructed Karl Koerper to inform those who had given two weeks' notice that they had "contractual responsibilities" and that Church "earnestly hope[d] they won't force us to resort to our legal rights under employment contract." Church described the developments from the West Coast as "almost unbelievable." He was positive that the Rangers had been "misguided by somebody . . . [that his] boys would not act so unreasonable."

Despite Church's threats and pleading, May and Cronenbold were apparently true to their word and left the tour after working out their two-weeks notice given November 1st, though what their status was within Church's organization remains uncertain. Morale continued to plummet, and on the 24th of the month Clarence Hartman wrote a desperate note to Karl Koerper to do something-anything-to turn things around. "This is the voice of the TWO TEXAS RANGERS shouting at you from the Camel Caravan," his plea began. "If Joe Strand should leave it will be Bob Braun representing THE LONE RANGER (Hartman)."

"Joe Wolverton, the guitar player, who arrived in Montery the same day that you made your departure has now gone the way of all flesh," Hartman continued. "His was somewhat of a record," added Hartman, underscoring the merry-go-round nature of the Rangers' recent history. "[He] gave me two week's notice before he ever played a note." Wolverton (1906 – 1989), who replaced Berdahl, is perhaps the best known performer to play with the Rangers after early associates Tex Owens and Ozie Waters. Wolverton was a talented multi-instrumentalist, though perhaps not as much a virtuoso as his predecessor, Herbie Kratoska, who played guitar, banjo, and fiddle. Wolverton has gained some fame as a mentor of the legendary guitarist Les Paul. He was also an electric guitar pioneer and later recorded for Columbia Records with his then-wife Polly Possum.

But there was more. As Hartman himself said, there was "never a dull moment on the Camel Caravan." Kenny Harpster, the saxophone player who had been with the outfit just a few months, also gave two week's notice. Fortunately, Hartman was able to find replacements for Wolverton and Harpster with minimal trouble. They were, he said, "okay" and "not tired musicians," which may have been the best they could hope for at this point.

It could have been even worse, however. Joe Strand, too, had given his two week's notice after a recent trip to San Francisco. Hartman reacted as Church would have by this point if gentle persuasion were not enough: resort to legal threats. Strand was, Hartman wrote, "persuaded to withdraw his notice," when told bluntly that due to the terms of his employment contract the notice could not be recognized or acknowledged. He worried that this was only a temporary solution. Strand's wife was now with him on the road and that, Hartman wrote, did "not help the situation."

Bob Crawford had been persuaded to stay for the time being, but the vocal trio was history and Hartman was having no luck finding replacements. In conversation with the Caravan's Ned Dobson, he discussed the possibility of using more musicians or even a female trio in their stead. Dobson held out hope a male trio could be put together and indicated a willingness to continue the Rangers' regular payments as long as quality did not suffer. Hartman was running out of ideas, though. "There are no trios available," he said flatly. "I have covered motion picture studios, radio stations, theatres, vocal coaches and nite clubs. All available trios are working in town and will not go on the road." Hartman's gut instinct was that if they could not find a new trio before the upcoming Christmas holiday, during which the Caravan would go off the road for a short break, Dobson would replace the Rangers in the New Year.

The reliance on legal recourse to enforce adherence to contractual obligations had proven useful as a last resort, but it had only dampened morale further. Crawford was far from happy about his situation and insisted on a raise for handling vocal duties that had previously been the domain of the trio, and before that, the quartet. He was, not surprisingly, turned down and then threatened to walk out again. Hartman told him he "did not think that it would be very smart on his part." Feelings were raw after six months on the road. "I hate quitters," Hartman closed, "and I am just stubborn enough to prove to them that their leaving will not break us up. All of them have been so certain that it was the end of the Texas Rangers and the Camel Caravan."

In December, because the Rangers had been performing as a six-man unit since May and Cronenbold had left in November, Church and company conceded the need to renegotiate the band's fee with the Morris Agency. There was disagreement on just what the appropriate rebate should be. Bob Braun wanted to press for $165 per week, equal to the percentage paid for the now-departed singers from the full amount paid to Church. The Morris Agency's Ned Dobson was pushing for a pro rata $250, one-fourth of the $1,000 paid to the band each week (to reflect the loss of one-fourth of the 8-man band). The money was to go to the William Esty Company, the R. J. Reynolds ad agency, though Braun was suspicious that the Morris agency would keep the difference of $85. He suggested Church agree to hand over up to $200 of the weekly pay. This would keep Church Productions' profit level at about the same level and, hopefully, keep the Rangers in the good graces of Dobson.

From December 21, 1942, the Camel Caravan took a two-week layoff, a hiatus that from the standpoint of the Texas Rangers, who had even spent Thanksgiving on the road, was sorely needed. The vacation would allow all the band members to enjoy time with their families over the festive period and also recharge their batteries after months of hard toil on the road. It would also give Bob Braun some time to shore up the Rangers' lineup and to solidify the group's slot on the Caravan, which had begun to look precarious with all the recent personnel turnover and turmoil.

On the same day Braun wrote an encouraging letter to Church about the benefits of the two week layoff, however, he received a note from Joe Strand requesting a six month leave of absence from the Rangers to coincide with the beginning of the break on December 21st. Strand claimed the tours were taking a toll on his marriage and that the time off was necessary to give him and his wife "a brighter look to the future." Strand had raised the issue of his departure with management in the past, but this was far more definitive. In a candid aside to Church, Braun indicated that the grind of touring was less a problem for the Strand marriage than Joe's reputation for playing the field while separated from his wife. "She does not trust him away from home," Bob confided, adding that he had had to straighten out a number of problems related to this since Strand had joined the band. Braun would try to smooth things out yet again. Still, he urged Church to reject the leave of absence; either Strand was in or out. Braun was ready to find a replacement if Strand walked.

Despite a long and difficult year, the Texas Rangers ended 1942 in the black. Most of the band's income was via subscriptions to their growing transcription library offered through Arthur Church Productions. The group's salaries and tour expenses were paid out of KMBC money, so the records kept by ABC Productions reflect only the recording library income. Over one-third of the library's 1942 receipts of $23,418 came from the Kellogg company which paid out $8,750 for 25 weeks of sponsored shows compiled from the transcriptions.

The single most profitable station was New York's WJZ which broadcast transcribed Rangers programs for 45 weeks that year at a cost of $2,437.50. The next biggest subscribers were Scranton, PA's WGBI and Los Angeles' KNX at $1,260 apiece and the remaining subscribing stations spanned the breadth of the country, from major urban areas like Chicago (WENR), Boston (WROL), and San Francisco (KSFO) to mid-size markets such as Chattanooga, TN (WDOD) and Richmond, VA (WRVA), and to smaller ones like Findlay, OH (WFIN) and Duluth, MN (KDAL). The group's appeal was clearly not limited to a single region, nor to rural and small town America. Though subscription fees to the smaller stations were far less substantial than those from WJZ or Kellogg, the $750 from WENR and $290 from WFIN, along with twenty other stations over the year, netted Church a profit of $7,263.42. The heaviest outlays were $3,000 for managerial salary and over $2,800 for advertising.

The 1942 annual report put together by the staff of Arthur B. Church Productions pointed out that marketing to individual stations was paying off much better than had their efforts to advertisers and agencies. The Rangers income was as dependent on the smaller, but more numerous, station accounts as it was the fewer, but more substantial, advertising agency accounts. It was, therefore, recommended that marketing efforts focus on these individual stations; "small one column four-inch adds [sic] in Broadcasting," the report noted, "seemed to have attracted more attention than any other individual ads." To build on the Rangers' growing transcription business, Church's staff laid out goals for the upcoming year to get success stories from various subscribers describing the sales benefits provided by the Rangers record library and focus on turning current subscribers into long-term subscribers.

Prairie Pioneers

When the Camel Caravan hit the road again in January, 1943, the Texas Rangers were not with it. Over the break, Church made the decision to put the Texas Rangers on hiatus. He had every intention, however, to reform the band after the war, an intention he confided to the Rangers' former and future tenor Fran Mahaney in a private note. After receiving word from William Morris that a replacement unit could continue on the Caravan in lieu of the Rangers, Clarence Hartman and Bob Braun assembled a new unit under the name the Prairie Pioneers.

The original Prairie Pioneers, formed around 1938, had been a group similar to the Rangers, but on a smaller scale. In addition to a core group of four musicians who also sang, the band featured Laura Lee Owens and, in the months after he and the Rangers came to a parting of the ways, her father Tex. The original Prairie Pioneers left KMBC in the early war years and were in Tulsa by 1944 as the Sons of the Range. It is unclear who comprised the new lineup for the Caravan beyond Hartman and Sam Leichter. Bob Crawford appears to have finally got his wish to head home to Missouri.

The Prairie Pioneers were teamed with young vocalist Ellen Sutton. Also billed as Ella Sutton, the nineteen year old, and reportedly 240 pounds, Sutton had relocated to the West Coast at age 17 in 1941 from her native Pittsburgh to appear on Gene Autry's radio show. She also recorded for Columbia's Okeh subsidiary that year, as did the Texas Rangers. The Pioneers were booked on the next Camel Caravan which toured the Western states. Others on the bill in early 1943 included Joe Rardin, Darlene Hutton, Jane Wright, and Jay and Paulette. An entirely separate Camel Caravan played Eastern dates and included such acts as Clyde Hager, Charlie Masters, the Three Debs, Bob and Maxine Clayton, and Michael Harmon and the Bobby Kuhn Orchestra.[1]

As a favor to Clarence Hartman, the backbone of the band throughout the Caravan tour and the most loyal of the Texas Rangers during a turbulent period, Bob Braun wrangled permission from R. J. Reynolds brass to let Hartman's wife accompany the group on the road. In the spring, new vocalist Bill Hall joined the group. He was an imposing six foot five baritone who made, according to Braun, "a terrific appearance in Western wardrobe," though he had originally been a New York stage singer. He was 39, and thus past draft age, but the $100 salary that Church could offer proved inadequate despite the exposure, and he was gone by the end of June.

Around the same time Hall gave notice, clarinetist Albie Berg left the band for an entirely different reason: he'd fallen in love with a fellow Caravan performer who jilted him. To make matters worse for

Braun and Hartman, Sam Leichter also gave notice that he wished to leave the tour when it returned to Los Angeles at the beginning of August. He had a history of appendix trouble and was, he said, worried about getting caught on the road during an appendix attack. But like Archie Berdahl the year before, he was also worried about the draft and wanted to get off the road and into a job in a defense-related industry, which might help him avoid being drafted.

A break in the late summer of 1943 allowed the musicians to recharge their batteries. In September, Braun announced to Church and Karl Koerper that the William Morris Agency had agreed to increase KMBC's pay for the Pioneers by $75, raising the station's total compensation for the band to $950 per week and Braun was still hoping for another $10. Out of this sum came the salaries for six musicians and one singer which allowed Midland to pull down $205 weekly.

Braun spend the Caravan's late summer break trying to find replacements for three departing players. He had to contact more than 100 musicians before finding three who could fill the positions. Braun's task was a difficult one; a vast majority of the musicians suitable for the job had either been inducted into the armed forces or, like Leichter and Berdahl, found work in defense-related industries and were, therefore, unable to travel. The three musicians he managed to find for the Pioneers all had received honorable discharges from the military, two for physical disabilities and the third because he was too old.

Up to this point the Prairie Pioneers had worn western or cowboy dress, as the Texas Rangers and the original Prairie Pioneers always had. But Braun decided to do away with the costumes, eliminating the need for continuous alterations as new members arrived and took over outfits worn by previous band members. Instead, they wore blue tweed sport coats and brown gabardine slacks for their shows.

With ever-increasing stress and responsibilities, Clarence Hartmann did a yeoman's job holding a coherent musical group together for the Caravan. He managed this monumental task seamlessly enough that there were numerous comments from military officials complimenting not only the overall quality of the Camel Caravan, but the Prairie Pioneers specifically. Originally booked only in Western states, during 1943 the Caravan made its way from

Los Angeles through Arizona, New Mexico, Texas, Louisiana, Mississippi, Alabama, Florida, Georgia, South Carolina, and North Carolina. The tour's return route snaked through New York and across the northern states.

The Camel Caravan ran through September 30, 1944, though it's unknown how long the Prairie Pioneers performed with the tour. Evidence suggests the group had been dissolved by Church before the Caravan was finally canceled by the Esty agency. Financial disagreements concerning payroll tax deductions and over which parties should be covering particular expenses ultimately brought an end to the long-running tour.[1]

---

1 *Billboard* September 23, 1944, p. 5

Chapter 8: The War Years and Beyond

Transcribed Across America

Though the Texas Rangers officially disbanded for approximately three years, from 1943 through 1945, Arthur Church continued to market the group's transcription library. Even before they broke up, the library had become the Rangers' most steady source of income for the duration of the war.

The Rangers may have been inactive, and band members may have been scattered throughout the States, but over the festive season in December, 1943, a makeshift lineup of the group gathered in Kansas City, probably in KMBC studios, to add over 80 songs to the transcription library. The original vocal quartet was reunited, though May was in the service and Crawford and Mahaney about to enter it. Whether Clarence Hartman returned to Kansas City for the sessions is uncertain, but unlikely, though the Camel Caravan would probably have been on hiatus for the two weeks over which the sessions were held. Gomer Cool had, of course, left KMBC's employ for good, as had Joe Strand. But Herby Kratoska, ineligible for the service because of his poor eyesight, was in town and still very much a KMBC staffer. His guitar was augmented by versatile fiddler Al "Slim" Phillips, a former member of another premier western group that had seen service in a Gene Autry western, Al Clauser and his Oklahoma Outlaws, and probably accordionist Gene Moore, who was working with Phillips at the station in a new group called the Tune Chasers. The bassist on the sessions remains unknown. KMBC's internal newsletter from March, 1944, indicated that it had been "quite a trick to match furloughs with vacations and leaves of absence" to pull off the sessions. In addition to those Rangers in the service or about to be, several, including Cronenbold, were employed in defense industries. But all the wrestling with logistics was worthwhile, as fresh material maintained interest in the transcription library.[1]

---

1 *KMBC Heartbeats* March 1, 1944, p. 1

Not surprisingly, the sessions had a looser feel than those cut in 1941-42 with the tight-knit unit of that period, but the standard remained high. While there had always been parallels in the Rangers' sound with the Western swing sounds that began to emerge in the Southwest around the time the group had formed, Western swing had also begun to blossom on the West Coast during their time there, and these sessions found the group adopting a more deliberate Western swing feel. The main impetus for this was probably the presence of Phillips, an excellent jazz violinist. The classic lineup had fine soloists in Kratoska and Sells or Strand. Gomer Cool had been a melody man, skilled, but not an improvising swing musician. The makeshift recording-only Rangers of December, 1943, took full advantage of the extra dimension that Phillips brought to the group.

Though the band was on a hiatus at least until the war was over, George Halley continued to line up new sponsors through the war years for local broadcasts of the Texas Rangers transcription library. Companies that used the band's music to promote their products in this period included Wildroot over WTAR, Norfolk, VA, the Standard Milling Company over KARK, Little Rock, AR, and Sears-Roebuck over WLAC, Nashville, TN. Refrig-O-Master sponsored the Rangers in their hometown over KMBC, a role that was taken over in 1944 by Purity Bakeries' Grennan Cakes.

While fresh material maintained interest in the Library, even far from fresh *Life on the Red Horse Ranch* was not absolutely buried. Church and company were wary of putting too much time and effort into marketing it further, particularly since the costs connected to the use of ASCAP-published songs in the series seemed prohibitive. For the time being, Midland Broadcasting decided that the 65-episode series was unsellable, except for isolated incidents.

In January, 1944, KFXJ in Grand Junction, Colorado, asked about running *Red Horse Ranch*. While acknowledging the fact that the series "had been shelved due to the fact, that it is composed largely of ASCAP music," Church agreed to look into the possibility of making it available to KFXJ, since the station's "prospective client is the one for whom the program was originally created" - Socony-Vacuum. After some investigation, however, ABC Productions had to turn down KFXJ. The ASCAP costs proved a moot point in the end. After checking with the New York offices of World Broadcasting, which had originally recorded the programs in Chicago in 1935, Church was informed that "the masters of the program ... have deteriorated beyond all possibility of using them to make new pressings." Thus, there was no way to rent them the discs.

Church must have been furious at the news. He had invested thousands of dollars in the *Red Horse* project and had only gotten about a year's worth of solid income from it. While some problems in later re-syndication efforts can be traced to the ASCAP problem, worthless master discs precluded *Red Horse Ranch* from ever being revived. Not surprisingly, staffers tried to make an alternative sale: maybe the station would be interested in the Rangers' musical transcription library at $15.00 per week, with a minimum contract of 13 weeks? It was important for the station to know, however, that another potential sponsor, Pueblo, Colorado's Walter Brewing Company, had approached ABC Productions about widening their use of the Texas Rangers library. Walter Brewing had been airing the program in Pueblo successfully for a year and had recently added Denver's KVOD to their advertising outlets. The company was now inquiring about using the library in further outlets, one of which was Grand Junction's KFXJ. Since the station's program director was not aware of such a prospect, this suggests the brewing company's plan was in the early stages. Nevertheless, Church advised Mildred Fuller of KFXJ to talk with Walter Brewing Company's ad agency, the W. B. Rodgers Advertising Agency in Pueblo, about the multiple sponsors interested in bring the Texas Rangers to the Grand Junction station.

Despite the fact that ABC Productions had indicated in January that *Red Horse Ranch* was not currently available for sale, the news apparently did not reach all relevant parties in in the Church organization. In March, 1944, J. Leslie Fox of the Paul H. Raymer Company in Los Angeles inquired about selling the series to the Smith & Drum Agency. The unknown KMBC staffer who responded was only too glad to send some episodes for audition. Either new pressings had been discovered since January or there was a lack of communication between Church's two businesses as to the status of the series. The responder also mentioned the original 65 scripts, though their location was unknown, perhaps with the goal of interesting Fox in purchasing rights to the scripts, from which broadcasts could be made with a new cast. There was also the chance Fox would be interested in the transcription library. Though L.A.'s KNX was currently subscribing to it, if the station should end its connection with the Rangers, then the Raymer company would be free to pick it up.

During March, 1944, the Texas Rangers made significant headway into the Canadian listening market. Under the sponsorship of Palm Dairies, Ltd., based in Calgary, twelve stations began airing the band's transcription library. Through the sales office of J. E. Baldwin of the All-Canada Radio Facilities in Vancouver, CKRC (Winnipeg), CKCK (Regina), CKBI (Prince Albert), CFAC (Calgary), CJCA (Edmonton), CJAT (Trail), CFQC (Saskatoon), CHAB (Moose Jaw), CJOC (Lethridge), CKOV (Kelowna), CJGX (Yorkton), and CFJC (Kansloops) joined the list of Rangers broadcasters.

The following list put together in April, 1944, gives an indication of the variety of markets in which the Texas Rangers were heard in the U.S.:

KMBC, Kansas City, MO	7:45 – 8:00 a.m. Mon thru Friday
	10:30 – 10:45 p.m. Mon, Tues, Fri
KOIN, Portland, OR	times unknown
WTOP, Washington, D.C.	5:00 – 5:30 p.m. Mon thru Friday
KNX, Los Angeles, CA	11:45 – 12:00 noon Mon thru Fri
WADC, Akron, OH	10:45 – 11:00 p.m. Mon thru Fri
WHLD, Niagara Falls, NY	6:15 – 6:30 p.m. Mon thru Fri
KRLD, Dallas, TX	12:30 – 1:00 p.m. Mon thru Fri
KSL, Salt Lake City, UT	6:45 – 7:00 a.m. Mon thru Fri
KFPY, Spokane, WA	5:15 – 5:30 p.m. Mon thru Fri
WEEI, Boston, MA	6:15 – 6:30 p.m. Mon, Wed, Fri
WBEN, Buffalo, NY	9:20 – 9:30 a.m. Tues, Thurs
	9:15 – 9:30 a.m. Fri
	12:30 – 12:45 p.m. Sat
WJDX, Jackson, MS	6:35 – 6:45 p.m. Mon thru Fri
WMC, Memphis, TN	12:30 – 12:45 p.m. Tues, Thurs, Sat.
WCCO, Minneapolis, MN	6:45 – 7:00 p.m. Wed, Thurs, Fri
KYW, Philadelphia, PA	6:45 – 7:00 p.m. Mon, Tues, Wed, Fri
KDKA, Pittsburgh, PA	12:15 – 12:30 p.m. Mon, Wed, Fri
WDBJ, Roanoke, VA	11:45 – 12:00 noon Mon, Wed, Fri
KOMO, Seattle, WA	10:15 – 10:30 p.m. Tues, Thurs
KWKH, Shreveport, LA	5:30 – 5:45 p.m. Mon thru Fri

The only region not well represented on the subscriber list is the Southwest, where one might reasonably expect a Western band like the Texas Rangers to attract a sizable following. George Halley recognized this gap in the Rangers' coverage and set about remedying it. In early 1944, he contacted a representative of the Atchison-Topeka-Santa Fe Railway's advertising agency in response to a notice the company had placed in a trade periodical. The railroad was in the process of purchasing a network show but, Halley wondered, perhaps there were some markets "important to you and your client which [could not] easily be reached by network." Possibly the Rangers library could be used by the agency to reach those markets, some of which were specifically in that Southwestern region where the band was so underrepresented, including Albuquerque and San Antonio.

In January, 1944, Ben Harkins, Acting Chief, Program Section of the Overseas Branch in the Pacific Bureau, approached Arthur B. Church Productions about playing selections from the Texas Rangers catalog in programs designed for the country's fighting troops. The rights were not for domestic use, he emphasized, but only for broadcasts in Australia, New Zealand, and possibly Hawaii and free China. George Halley, speaking for ABC Productions, responded to Harkins, who was working out of San Francisco's Office of War Information. "It is not known how it would be possible to release our Texas Rangers Library to you even though the cause is certainly a worthy one." A shortage of vinylite caused concern among Church's men about whether or not they'd even be able to press enough records for their own commercials needs, let alone for such non-commercial use. Halley's next excuse was a bit less convincing, though possibly a legitimate concern. "Furthermore," he continued, "our program has proven so popular wherever it is running, that were we to release some sets to you, in the regular course of events, we would receive additional requests from equally meritorious groups, until it would be a physical impossibility to furnish the service even if there were no shortage of vinylite from which the discs are pressed." Why the company could not just refuse further requests if they came is not adequately explained by Halley's responses.

On February 1, 1944, Bob Crawford, who had been inducted into the Army the previous month, departed for Fort Leavenworth, KS, where he was stationed temporarily. He was assigned to the Army's

Texas Rangers library advertisement.
Courtesy of Ryan Ellett.

Special Service, and hoped he would get to spend his time during World War II entertaining the fighting troops in uniform. However, by the end of 1944, Crawford was stationed in Camp Chaffee, AR, and he found himself on the other side of the mike, studying communication and receiving training on repairing infantry radio sets. On a brief return to Kansas City in November, 1944, he assured the

KMBC audience that when the war was over, he was not interested in the technical side of radio but would return to the airwaves as a performer. He later served in the Philippines before his honorable discharge in January, 1946. Fran Mahaney followed Crawford into the service in April. Second tenor May was stationed at Camp Luna in New Mexico where, in the summer of 1944, he received promotion to sergeant. May's official duties were that of an Administrative Clerk, but he kept his musical talent honed singing with the Post Chapel Quartet. Later, when May's time in the service was complete, he rejoined KMBC and sang with a quartet named the Camp Meeting Quartet, which focused on Western tunes and also included Don Sullivan, Ted Ross, and Bob Stevens.[1]

One Ranger who did not have to worry about the draft was Clarence Hartman, who, when the Prairie Pioneers left the Camel Caravan in 1944, was 54 years old. Initially, he returned to his home in California for a long vacation to recover from the toll the Caravan had taken on him both mentally and physically. He had proven very loyal to Church during a period of great upheaval, but his days as an employee of KMBC were about to come to an end. For the duration of the war he kept in contact with Church and, as a highly skilled, formally trained multi-instrumentalist, had little problem finding work. It may have been his old cohort Paul Sells who was responsible for Hartman's work with Gene Autry, in both the radio and recording studio, when the latter returned from war service and resumed his career. Hartman continued to work with Autry at least into 1950. Sam Leichter also worked with Autry, and worked and recorded, as well, with many other West Coast western stars, including Spade Cooley and Tex Williams. Though not working for Arthur Church during 1945, Hartman, who was now a grandfather and ready to slow his working pace, was pleasantly surprised to receive a small Christmas bonus, a sign of Church's fondness for this loyal musician.

Post-War Reunion

When the war ended with Japan's surrender on September 2, 1945, Arthur Church began mulling the possibility of reuniting his dormant Texas Rangers band. In January, 1946, Church identified the revamped lineup of the Rangers, only half of whom were with the band before the war. Returnees were Rod "Dave" May, Bob "Captain

Bob" Crawford, Edward "Tucson" Cronenbold, and Herb "Arizona" Kratoska. Fran Mahaney had received his discharge from the Army the previous summer, but appears to have tested the waters for a solo career in California rather than immediately returning to Kansas City. In early 1946, he was the featured vocalist on a set of transcriptions waxed under former Ranger Paul Sells' name for C.P. MacGregor's recording company, which may also have featured Clarence Hartman on bass. Mahaney's replacement as "Irish," temporarily, as it turned out, was veteran Don Sullivan. A Missouri native active on the music scene since the mid-1930s, Sullivan had worked as a radio cowboy in New York and had even traveled to Europe in that capacity; he was in France at the outbreak of World War II. He had been singing with May in the Camp Meeting Quartet.

The rest of the lineup was made up of KMBC staffers, including fiddler Emert Painter, who took on Gomer Cool's "Tenderfoot" sobriquet, accordionist Joe "Montana" Manning, and bassist Eddie "Idaho" Johnson. Within weeks of the group's reformation, Fran Mahaney returned to the group, replacing Sullivan. The new lineup would afterward remain intact until Manning's departure in 1947.

Arthur Church had his staff put together a list of sponsors who had demonstrated positive results using the band's transcription library. Included in the collection were some of the success stories shared by various businesses with ABC Productions:

Carey Salt Co. in Kansas City muscled its way onto the shelves of the region's dominant grocer, Safeway, by sponsoring the Texas Rangers tunes for eight months. That such a low-margin commodity like table salt could gain such clout with a radio show raised eyebrows.

Grennan Cakes reported that its sponsorship of the Rangers over KMBC had resulted in their highest product volume-to-advertising dollar ratio of all their markets.

Woodlawn Dairy, of Scranton, PA, used the library for a full year; this from a company that claimed never before to have sponsored a single program for more than thirteen weeks at a time. The Rangers were such a hit with Woodlawn's audience that, in fact, they bought the library for nearly two additional years beyond the first year.

Wildroot Toiletries for Men, through their advertising agency BBDO, was satisfied enough with the group to use them for two years in eight metropolitan markets.

The Henry H. Lohrey Packing Company in Pittsburgh continued the Texas Rangers' availability in the Steel City for two years after they had run in the city on KDKA for six months under the auspices of Grove Laboratories.

Grove Laboratories was impressed enough with the group to use them on fifteen stations outside of Pittsburgh for eighteen months over a three-year span.

Burkhart Brewing Co., based out of Akron, OH, claimed the largest growth of any Ohio brewery–to over 150,000 barrels–in the 3 ½ years they'd been using the Texas Rangers library in Akron, Lima, and Springfield.

The Walter Brewing Co., mentioned earlier and based in Pueblo, CO, considered the band "the most effective advertising they have ever done" in the three years they aired in Pueblo and the eighteen months they aired in Denver.

The Texas Rangers were heard regularly as far as Hawaii where Rico Ice Cream Co. had sponsored their show on Honolulu's KGU for three years.

Springfield, Missouri's, Purity Bakeries had been advertising their Taystee Bread via the band for two years.

Standard Milling's Eskimo Flour found the association with the Rangers profitable and used their program for over 2 ½ years in Little Rock, AR, on KARK and then KLRA.

Two national companies, Sears Roebuck and Kellogg, had eighteen month runs with the Texas Rangers. Sears Roebuck in the Nashville market and Kellogg on the six Texas stations discussed earlier.

The Texas Rangers, which had been on St. Louis' KMOX since 1943, were regularly tied for first place in their 8:15 a.m. time slot under Vicks' sponsorship.

In Kansas City, the band outperformed *The Kenny Baker Program* by a 4.1 rating to 7.5 rating despite costing the same to advertisers.

Representatives of Binghamton, New York's WMBF, on behalf of Hamlin's Red Cross Drug Store, claimed "the first show (13 weeks) we advertised but one product, a private label toothpaste. The results were so good that we had to revert to institutional advertising in order to let manufacturing catch up with sales."

As of February 12, 1946, the Texas Rangers had a notable coast-to-coast air presence as demonstrated by this list of subscribers as of that time:

KMBC (Kansas City) KOIN (Portland, OR) KGU (Honlulu)
KGHF (Pueblo, CO) WKBH (La Crosse) KARM (Fresno, CA)
WTAR (Norfolk, VA) KQV (Pittsburgh) WCSC (Charleston, SC)
KMOX (St. Louis) WQAM (Miami, FL) WGBI (Scranton, PA)
KWTO (Springfield, MO) WADC (Akron, OH) WAKR (Akron, OH)
WHKK (Akron, OH) WLOK (Lima, OH) WIZE (Springfield, OH)
WNBF (Binghamton, NY) WNEX (Macon, GA) KTUL (Tulsa, OK)
WAOV (Vincennes, IN) WDZ (Tuscola, IL) KBIX (Muskogee, OK)
KSTP (Minneapolis-St. Paul) KDYL (Salt Lake City)

Still, the band had failed to make much progress in the Southwestern markets, though they had had opportunities as evidenced by records indicating the Rangers had formerly been on the air in Phoenix, Amarillo, San Antonio, and Corpus Christi. Additionally, their West Coast presence was noticeably diminished from earlier years including the loss of stations in Los Angeles, San Francisco, Seattle, and Spokane, WA. They also no longer had a foothold on Canadian radio, having lost their spots on CKRC (Winnipeg), CFQC (Saskatoon), CFAC (Calgary), CKOV (Kelowna), CKCK (Regina), CHAB (Moose Jaw), CJOC (Lethbridge), CJGX (Yorkton), CKBI (Prince Albert), CJCA (Edmonton), CFJC (Kamloops), and CJAT (Trail).

In February, 1946, KMBC's Rhythm Riders debuted a program on CBS called *Night Time on the Trail*, a series title formerly used by the Texas Rangers. One of several Western bands developed in the KMBC stable, their popularity never approached that of the Rangers. They were featured on KMBC throughout the late 1940s on their own 5:30 show called *Western Echoes*, as well as the station's *Brush Creek Follies* broadcast over the Columbia network. The band also made appearances on the legendary *National Barn Dance* broadcast over Chicago's WLS. The Rhythm Riders quartet consisted of Ray Hudgens, Andy Anderson (accordion), Howard Smith (bass fiddle), and Val Tatham (guitar), two of whom would later join the Texas Rangers. *Night Time on the Trail* would also be the broadcast vehicle through which the reformed Rangers were introduced to a national audience.

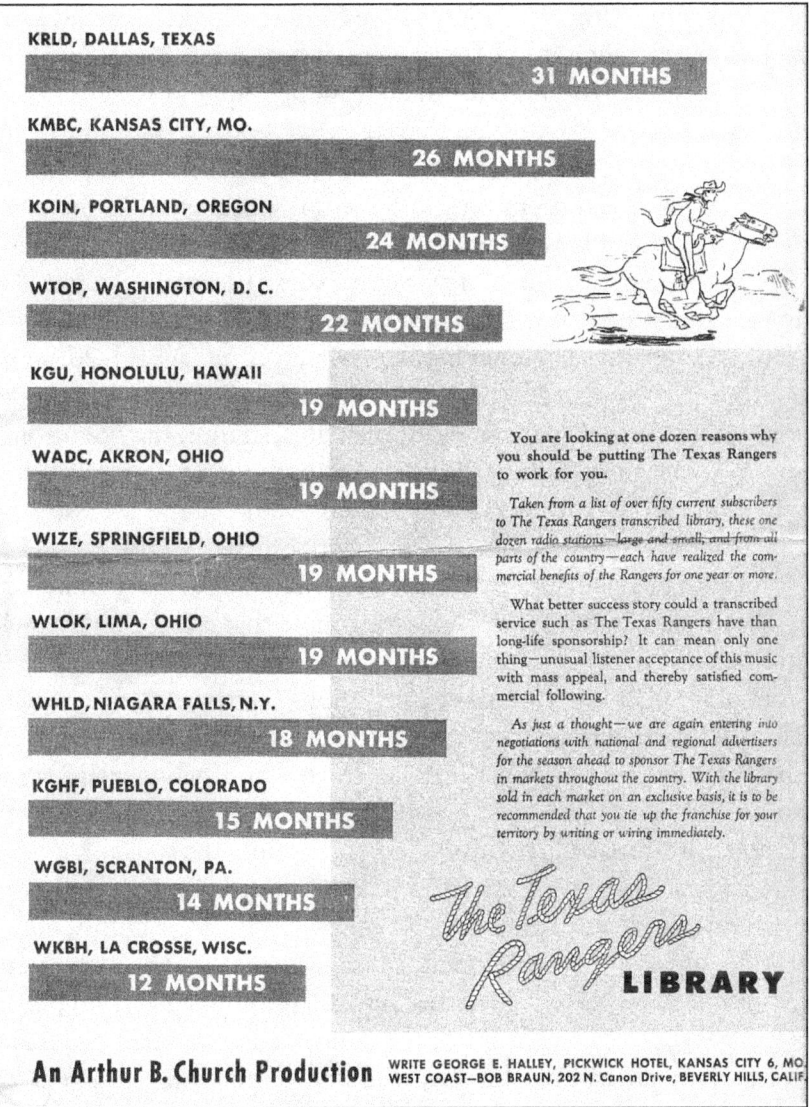

Transcription library advertisement.
Courtesy of Ryan Ellett.

Church's management staff set about creating new buzz for a band which had been out of the public's eye for a couple years. Their efforts focused on national radio publications and promotional appearances in New York City. The group was reintroduced gradually to radio listeners with one song on the February 18, 1946, episode of *Night Time on the Trail* and two songs on the February 25 episode.

Jim McConnell, the band's long-time Midwest booker, secured a full week's engagement at the Tower Theater beginning March 1.

When the Tower engagement wrapped up, the Rangers took the train to New York where they appeared on the March 11 *Night Time on the Trail* broadcast from the CBS studios in the Big Apple. McConnell joined them on the coast for appearances in the city's "showcase" theaters and for a blitz of advertising and network agencies to earn support for a new radio series. The group would also make its first post-war library recordings for World while in New York, adding over sixty tunes between March 12 and March 20. Some sources give the dates as March 28-April 1, but these appear to be mastering dates rather than recording dates. In three days of recording in Chicago beginning June 19, 1946, the new Rangers would add a further fifty titles. All this activity would culminate with the opening of Arthur B. Church's New York office.

Announcements in *Broadcasting*, *Variety*, *Tide*, *Radio Daily* and *Billboard* set Church Productions back more than $1,400 above their normal advertising budget. Over 3,000 cards announcing the New York office opening were mailed to stations, advertisers, and agencies along with telegrams to selected recipients inviting them to attend the Texas Rangers' New York arrival. There were also hopes that some sort of publicity stunt could be worked up involving President Harry Truman, a Kansas City native.

Things did not go off entirely as expected. The band's initial performance at the Tower Theater raised red flags for both Church and Halley, and they recommended that a professional director with vaudeville and theater experience be brought in to create and polish a "proper routine" for the band. The band's immense talent would be wasted otherwise. Fran Heyser, who had prepared the Rangers for their first post-reunion concerts, simply did not have the requisite experience, being primarily a radio man. It was suggested that someone of the caliber of Radio City Music Hall's Gus Eysell or William Morris' Bill Murray would be a good choice.

The new incarnation of *Night Time on the Trail* left the CBS schedule in early June, 1946. Davidson Taylor, vice Vice President Director of Programs at CBS, wrote a kind, but not overly convincing, letter to Arthur Church about the show's demise. "I felt great regret," Taylor assured Church, "that the program is being discontinued and great gratitude to you and your colleagues who have made the series possible. It gave me as a listener a lot of pleasure, and I think that the standard of performances was very high indeed."[1]

Despite, and surely because of, the time and effort being put into the revival of the Texas Rangers band, Church continued to be quick in going after any perceived infringements on his intellectual property. In the summer of 1946 this included the Valley Amusement Company, a California company that had recently booked a tour by Bob Wills and his Texas Playboys, among other ventures. Its representative, William Wagnon, Jr., of the William B. Wagnon, Jr., & Associates, Public Relations Counselors, who was later the producer of the famed L.A.-area country music showcase, *Town Hall Party*, assured Church in a July 2 letter that the Valley Amusement Company had stopped using the Texas Rangers name, not realizing it had been copyrighted by Church.

Six months later, Church focused his attention on the Continental Record Company based in New York. In a January 31, 1947, communique he noted that they had recently released several recordings by Texan Red River Dave McEnery with backing by Sula's Texas Rangers. Sula was Sula Levitch, and Sula's Texas Rangers was merely a name used for the group of studio musicians he used to back McEnery. Pointing out that the Kansas City band had been "distributed nationally and internationally both as phonograph records and as electrical transcriptions" and had "appeared on coast-to-coast network programs," it seemed to Church that "there appears to be a conflict." The situations with both Valley Amusement and Continental Records were taken care of to Arthur's satisfaction in a timely manner.

ABC Productions ramped up the Rangers' promotions throughout the summer of 1946, getting interest from New York and Chicago promoters. After testing the waters in their March trip to the city, New York seemed a promising market. There were negotiations for a network program, as well as a possible run at the Radio City Music Hall, but both fell through after negotiations with the local American Federation of Musicians about the logistics "proved insurmountable." In Chicago, the act got interest from the Wade Advertising Agency,

---

1 Information on the Rhythm Riders comes from a variety of sources including *Billboard*, February 2, 1946, p. 87, the Arthur B. Church archive (Iowa State University), and http://www.hillbilly-music.com.

which was convenient, since they had just completed their second post-war recording session.

Though *Night Time on the Trail* had been canceled by CBS, evidence suggests the group continued to appear on the program locally over KMBC on Friday nights. However, this live broadcast was removed from the station's schedule in March, 1947, to make way for *Jean Sablon Sings*. Formerly aired at 5:45 early Saturday afternoons, *Sablon Sings* moved into the Rangers' 7:30 Friday night spot.

Jean Sablon Sings' old Saturday timeslot was filled by another musical program, *Bandstand*, which did not feature the Rangers. At the time, no new broadcast time was given to the band in exchange for the loss of the Friday spot.

Further transcription library recordings were planned for the end of 1946 at World's studios in Chicago, but the sessions were delayed. Fran Heyser had created a hectic, packed agenda for the occasion, which called for the Rangers to leave Kansas City December 28 on a train bound for Chicago as soon as *Brush Creek Follies* went off the air. After a day allotted for travel, the band was to record December 30 and 31. New Year's Day, 1947, a Wednesday, was a day off, but on January 2 and 3 they were back to work. The entire following week, January 6–10, was to be spent in the studios as well.

The band was expected to travel overnight on January 10 to arrive in Denver the next day for a weekend stand at the Western Livestock Show under the sponsorship of Sears Roebuck.

The Denver shows were followed by another overnight trip back to Chicago. They were then expected to finish the week cutting more records. As soon as they left the World studios on the 17th, they faced yet another overnight trip back to Kansas City in order to be available for the *Brush Creek Follies* on Saturday, January 18.

It appears that this brutal schedule was relaxed and that the recording sessions were postponed until later in January. The Rangers recorded over 80 songs for the music library at World's studios in the Windy City from January 21 to 24. There were two, two-hour sessions each day, from 10:00 a.m. to noon and from 1:00 to 3:00, with twenty songs, or four sides of sixteen inch transcription discs, completed each day. The Rangers' stay in the studios was followed by four days of recordings by KMBC pianist Harry Jenks.

Unfortunately, the music publishing royalty costs and complications that had hampered further sales of *Life on the Red Horse Ranch* in previous years also appear to have begun to affect the music library. The Harry Fox Agency, a company founded in 1927 and still very much active at this writing, deals with the granting of "mechanical" licenses for performances of songs held by various music publishers, and deals with the collection of fees and royalties for the use of these properties. Money was surely the issue and an inner office memo from 1948 appears to limit or negate the future use of discs in the music library that contained copyrights that were under Fox's jurisdiction. In addition, some of the transcriptions cut at these sessions appear not to have been pressed by World at all (and to survive only through the metal masters and test pressings that were part of Arthur Church's estate). There would be a handful of tracks cut in the fall of 1947 in California, ostensibly for use in the library. It is unclear if they were ever issued, and the money issues relating to copyrights and royalties that arose not long after the January, 1947, Chicago sessions, appear to have somewhat dampened Church's enthusiasm for the entire endeavor.

Back to California

Though efforts to reestablish the band beyond its home base of Kansas City had been slow, and despite the highly publicized New York visit and recording sessions that added over 200 songs to the band's transcription library, word was, nevertheless, getting around that the Rangers were back. On March 19, 1947, Arthur Church received an unexpected telephone call from Mitchell J. Hamilburg, of the Mitchell Hamilburg Agency located in Los Angeles.

Aware of the Rangers and their transcription library, Hamilburg inquired if Church would be willing to consider some sort of deal to distribute a Hoosier Hotshot radio program. Always a realist, Church did not feel that his ABC Productions was up to producing another band's program at this time and said so. In fact, he was not even satisfied with the production and sales of their own musicians, including the Texas Rangers, to warrant taking on an outside act.

Trying to stroke Church's ego, Hamilburg continued: "Perhaps I have heard exaggerated stories, and I thought you were doing so well on the Texas Rangers series." Church did not bite and came back with a zinger, though it may have been unintentional, a reflection of his unfamiliarity with Hamilburg's agency.

"Are you of Hammel & Hammel?" Church asked him. "Are you listed as advertising agencies?" "No, Hamilburg... Under theatrical agency – motion picture agency." The typed transcript of this phone conversation consistently refers to Hamilburg as Hammelberg indicating he really was not a familiar figure to those in Church's employ. Only later did a staffer go back and hand write in the correct spelling, Hamilburg.

While Church and his aides may have been unfamiliar with him, Hamilburg represented some leading Western entertainers, including the aforementioned Hoosier Hotshots, which was not so much a western act as a novelty act. They were famous for their long stint on the *National Barn Dance* out of Chicago, and they appeared in a number of westerns in the same sort of capacity as the Rangers had after relocating to the coast in the mid-40s. Hamilburg also represented Smiley Burnette and Gene Autry; so, some sort of relationship between Church and Hamilburg offered potential benefits for both, and Church turned the conversation to his Rangers.

Hamilburg was happy to talk about their prospects as well. Would Church "be interested in another picture deal?" Church demurred, indicating that William Morris' Bob Braun had been handling the band's California representation before the war. Nevertheless, Hamilburg persuaded Church to agree to send some promotional materials and the band's songbook, which was being sold at music stores. Further, Church was willing to let Hamilburg do some scouting work on spec, with the assurance that "if I [Hamilburg] produced some pictures for you that you would accept, you could send me the legitimate commission."

One interesting note to come out of the conversation was Church's equivocal attitude about the permanent make-up of the Rangers. They had traditionally been an eight-man outfit, though during the war years on the Camel Caravan six, or sometimes fewer performers, were in the ranks. When Hamilburg asked how many men were in the band, Church replied, "There are four singers – the Texas Rangers singing group consists of four men, and we back them up with four musicians." It appears that in Church's mind the Rangers were not a single cohesive unit but rather two sub-units, the singers and the backing musicians. Apparently, the quartet took more precedence in his mind; after all, they were to him, in essence, the Texas Rangers, because he noted that he was undecided as to whether or not he would be sending the musicians if the group, again, relocated to California. Hamilburg even discouraged sending all eight, "I don't think that [sending the musicians] would be necessary if we knew what you wanted out here."

Hawk Larabee

The full group did, as it turned out, leave Kansas City again for California just a few weeks after that phone conversation, but Church and Hamilburg's discussions regarding the need for the full group also proved somewhat prophetic. The Rangers' quartet of Crawford, Cronenbold, Mahaney, and May, sans the backing musicians, was hired by CBS's West Coast Division for a western radio show called *Hawk Larabee*. Described by old time radio historian John Dunning as "radio's first half-hearted attempt at an adult western drama," *Hawk Larabee* premiered on July 5, 1946, as *Hawk Durango*, the title changing to *Hawk Larabee* after six weeks. It starred radio veterans Elliott Lewis and Barton Yarborough in the two main roles and was produced and directed by William N. Robson, who is remembered for his work on such popular series as *Big Town*, *Escape*, and *Suspense*.

The quartet was hired in early May, 1947, to provide the show's musical bridges. Their first broadcast was May 10, 1947, for which they received AFRA scale wages plus 5%. The original contract stipulated that the singers' duties were to include "theme, bridge and background music, and three one-minute arrangements of songs during the three one-minute periods provided in this type for cooperative network program for local announcements by network stations when and if desired."

Hawk Larabee was unsponsored when the Rangers were cast, and it was understood that compensation would increase if a sponsor signed on. Terms would also be renegotiated if the backing musicians were added to the program, which Church hoped would happen. Exact future terms were not spelled out, but Church expressed his satisfaction with the Old Gold contract used with CBS years before and indicated comparable terms would be ideal. He did not want to tie his Rangers down with a long-term deal that could limit other commercial possibilities, especially those that might utilize all eight performers. The agreement with CBS thus stipulated that either side could terminate the deal with a mere two week's notice.

Both Church and John Gordon, the Rangers' newest manager, were pleased to hear from Robson two weeks later that the program was moving from Saturdays to Fridays. Such a move would open up Saturday nights for live performance bookings. Robson also indicated to Gordon that there was a good chance the four musicians would be added to the radio line-up, which would allow them to finally receive billing in the credits as the Texas Rangers. In fact, it was not until June 20 that the program moved to Fridays, but the new time, 4:00 Pacific Standard Time, meant early evening show times in the Midwest and East Coast, a positive development in Church's view. This new time slot was scheduled to last through July 25. Unfortunately for the musicians, they never were added to the *Hawk Larabee* productions.

The Last Roundup

Though the backing musicians were never added to *Hawk Larabee*, the show was fortunately not the only avenue open to the full group. Hamilburg had begun working on the Rangers behalf almost immediately after his conversation with Church, and he quickly secured work for the full group in Gene Autry's upcoming movie, *The Last Roundup*. Pre-recording and filming coincided with the beginning of *Hawk Larabee*. As before, the group was hired primarily as a musical added attraction, a practice that remained common in musical B-westerns until shortly before the genre's demise in the early 1950s.

A memo from John Gordon outlined financial terms of the film. For two days of pre-recording on May 13 and 14, 1947, each member of the quartet received $25 and $35, or $60 total. The musicians made more, as usual. Herb Kratoska, the only remaining musician from the pre-war years, was now the group's "leader" so far as the AFM was concerned, and he was paid accordingly. Fiddler Emert Painter and bassist Eddie Johnson had both come to the Coast with the group, as well, but for unknown reasons the accordionist Joe Manning had not. He was replaced by the veteran Art Wenzel, a former member of the *National Barn Dance* cast, who had been in California since 1939 and had been leading his own groups in recent years. However, Wenzel did not appear on screen with the group, his place being taken by Bob Weir. It is clear, however, that Wenzel did join the band for a while at this time, since it was reported in at least one Western music trade publication.

The pre-recording sessions brought the Rangers $632.50, though just two days before the budget for the recording was set at $499.20. They were then in line to receive an additional $1,200 for the actual shooting. Hamilburg, for his part, asked for a commission of $150, which was ten percent of the original total of $1,500. The payment system was a bit complicated: the Rangers signed statements which allowed Hamilburg to get and endorse their checks. He would then mail a single check to Church, minus his commission. This seemed the best choice to John Gordon who was under the impression that Church did not want the musicians handling their own checks.

After the shooting was all completed on June 6, Church sent a note to Gene Autry Productions confirming the following total payments made to each Texas Ranger:

Herbert Kratoska	$363.08
Emert L. Painter	214.79
Edwin B. Johnson	228.09
Edward L. Cronenbald	217.83
Robert G. Crawford	217.83
Roderick May	217.83
Francis Mahaney, Jr.	217.83
Bob Weir	134.99
Arthur A. Wenzel	126.35

Church additionally signed away all rights to the Rangers' work in the *The Last Round-Up*. Autry Productions could "reproduce all or any part of [Texas Ranger] performances, acts, poses, plays or appearances" as they saw fit in perpetuity.

Hamilburg continued to seek other film work for the group, but it would not, for the time being at least, be with Autry, who would use the Cass County Boys in his next film. Hamilburg was under the impression, likely correct, that Autry did not want to use the same band in each movie and was looking to alternate between proven performers, though the Cass County Boys would often work with him in this period, both on and off screen. More jobs with Autry would be nice but could not be counted on for any regular employment.

Instead, Hamilburg focused his attention on the Hoosier Hotshots, who were planning two more films for 1947. Speaking with the Hotshots' producer at Columbia, Hamilburg offered the services of the Texas Rangers for $2,500. Open to the idea, Columbia studios accepted the band's publicity stills and some sample recordings of their work. Besides Columbia, Hamilburg felt Republic Pictures, one of the biggest producers of western films, might be able to fit the Rangers into as many as eight movies a year.

Hamilburg's high hopes would ultimately prove unrealistic. Not only was the heyday of musical westerns beginning to pass, but the eight-man Rangers unit was perhaps too expensive for the budget-minded studios producing B-westerns. John Gordon in a June 16, 1947, letter to Arthur Church brought up another obstacle to more gainful film employment: a lack of developed acting ability. In a candid discussion with film producer Mandy Schaeffer, Gordon shared Schaeffer's comments that "if the boys could only act as well as they sing and play they would be terrific." The Rangers, Schaeffer continued, "show very little animation in the pictures." While he blamed this largely on the film's director, Schaeffer also admitted that B-western directors did not have the luxury of much time to coax performances out of performers and needed seasoned, assured performers who could step in and do the job. Gordon talked with the band about the issue and was assured that "it will be remedied." However, the Texas Rangers were singers and musicians, not actors, despite a few of the band members equipping themselves more than adequately in the past when the opportunity arose, as in *Life on the Red Horse Ranch*. At any rate, there's no indication that the Rangers actually did anything to "remedy" their mediocre acting skills and bland stage presence.

Other Work

In addition to radio and film jobs, the Rangers continued to pursue live performance bookings, though the paucity of surviving documentation makes it difficult to know how successful they were in this. An American Guild of Variety Artists contract signed June 19, 1947, provides some insight to the types of live shows they played during the time. This particular contract was for a concert at the U.S. Naval Station located at Terminal Island, San Pedro, CA, on June 24, 1947. Booked by the Al Wager Theatrical Agency through the

Mitchell Hamilburg Agency, one rehearsal and one performance netted the Rangers $150.

Beyond the vocal quartet's work on *Hawk Larabee*, the full group made occasional radio broadcasts during this period. On Friday, June 27, 1947, the Rangers served as the inaugural guests on a new program over Los Angeles' KFWB called *Preview Theatre of the Air*. The brainchild of station manager Harry Maizlish, the show's focus was to spotlight new talent over the air. That the Rangers had been broadcasting since 1932, and in Southern California beginning in 1939, did not seem to matter. The station had a broad idea of "new talent," so under the guidance of program director Bill Ray, Midland Broadcasting's not-so-new Texas Rangers appeared with old pal Lou Crosby serving as MC.

The station's original plan for the series was to air a mix of recorded and live programs on the *Preview Theatre of the Air*. Maizlish put together enough material for 26 broadcasts with the thought that more could be made if quality acts could be found. KFWB hoped that by sending out preview cards and soliciting feedback from listeners, it might be able to develop some future stars out of the sustained series.[1] Bad news about the *Hawk Larabee* job at CBS came late in June, delivered to KMBC staff via John Gordon. He informed Karl Koerper and others that the upcoming July 4 show would not feature the Texas Rangers but, instead, a 12 piece orchestra "so as to see just what difference it would make." Gordon was certain that the network would consider the Rangers a superior musical accompaniment after the experiment. His prediction proved accurate and the orchestral background was used just that one time. The boys were back on the show, but not for long as it turned out.

Arthur Church was informed by Gordon on July 17, 1947, that *Hawk Larbee* was going "co-op" as of August 1.[2] While director

---

1 *Variety* June 27, 1947, p. 8.
2 In private correspondence old time radio historian Martin Grams, Jr., explained what "co-op" meant in the radio industry. This arrangement was used when "the sole (primary) sponsor agreed to allow the radio program to be heard over other stations across the country under a different sponsorship. The reasons varied considerably from one show to another. The primary reason would be that the producers of the program (or the advertising agency) owned the show and the sponsor had no say over it unless dictated by the terms of the contract. Many times it was because the sponsor didn't have distribution in other parts of the country, and hence, they had no interest in pitching their product elsewhere, but the advertising agency had a client interested." In the case of Hawk Larabee, it's not exactly clear what might have been meant by a show "going co-op" when it was not sponsored.

William Robson wanted to continue using the Rangers, a network executive named Ernie Martin insisted the quartet was too expensive and told Robson to find replacements. Robson "felt very badly as he knew that he wouldn't get anyone as good as the Texas Rangers," but what could he do? He might, however, be able to sell Martin on the band if they were willing to drop their talent fee to sustaining scale wages plus 5% for a 26-week test period. Then, if the show "went commercial" and was picked up by a sponsor, the terms could be renegotiated.

It was a bitter pill to swallow for all involved. Gordon knew the band would take it hard, not only losing the job, but being replaced by another group, which they would surely think inferior in quality. Job assignments on the West Coast were few for the Rangers, and *Hawk Larabee* had given them all a focus around which they could channel their energies. "I would like to tell CBS what to do," Gordon wrote in frustration, but at the same time, he would like to see the Texas Rangers making some money rather than no money at all, even if it was at sustaining scale rather than the higher co-op scale.

Contrary to John Gordon's advice to take the deal and see what came of it, KMBC executive Karl Koerper replied that Church was not interested in such a deal with CBS at this time.

Exactly when the Texas Rangers were replaced is not certain, but communications on August 10, 1947, confirm that the Plainsmen had taken over background musical responsibilities for the show. Whatever Gordon, or the Rangers themselves, may have thought, far from being inferior to the Rangers musically or technically, Andy Parker & the Plainsmen were among the cream of Western vocal and instrumental groups of this, or any other, era. Ironically, writing credits for many of the later episodes of *Hawk Larabee* included former Ranger Gomer Cool, whose post-Rangers career as a writer, and eventually producer, in California was kicking into high gear, though it's uncertain whether Cool was involved in *Larabee* prior to the Rangers' departure. Whatever the case, John Gordon tried to make the best of the situation when he commented "inasmuch as the musicians were not to be used at all that it was the best thing." It was a strained note of consolation as he turned around and admitted in the same communication, that the band had little chance of getting any new assignments from CBS.

Never one to let previous professional disappointments interfere with future prospects, two months after the Rangers were dismissed from *Hawk Larabee*, Arthur Church made one more attempt to win over CBS' Ernest Martin, Director of Network Programs in Los Angeles, the man who had decided to use the Plainsmen instead of the Rangers. Church recounted the summer events that led to the Rangers being dropped from the radio show and apologized for not getting out to California until October to broach the topic. He had been listening to *Hawk Larabee* since the musical change and could not help but think that, despite the Plainsmen's lower performance fee, "the outstanding work of the Texas Rangers justifies their cost." Ever the shrewd businessman, he avoided any hint that his Rangers would accept a lesser fee in return for work on the program. Martin did not bite. Ultimately, it was a decision based on costs and neither side was willing to budge. But Church's overture proved a moot point, anyway: *Hawk Larabee* left the air for good on February 7, 1948.

By the end of summer, 1947, except for the occasional live show, the Rangers were exasperatingly idle. There were no film prospects on the immediate horizon, nor were there any regular broadcasting opportunities following their replacement on *Hawk Larabee*. Those associated with the band played up every positive angle they could. Gordon wrote to Karl Koerper in Kansas City on August 3, for example, to highlight a concert the band gave at a private party hosted by Smiley Burnette. The Rangers were the primary entertainers that evening, performing alone and also behind such singers as Roy Rogers and Ozie Waters.

Since leaving Kansas City after working with the Rangers at KMBC as the "Colorado Ranger," temporarily stepping into Tex Owens' shoes early in the band's existence, Waters had continued to perform as a solo act. He worked in Colorado and elsewhere before hitting the L.A.-area during the war years, where he remained until returning to Colorado in 1948. He signed to Coast Records in 1944 and began working in western films with his Colorado Rangers the following year, including entries in Columbia's *Durango Kid* series and some *Hopalong Cassidy* features.

At the Burnette get-together, Waters expressed interest in hiring the Rangers for one of his upcoming films and wanted to know their fee. Gordon avoided the question until more details of the project could be explored but was enthusiastic about the potential, nevertheless. He also hoped for more publicity from a *Look* magazine spread which covered the party.

Church was interested in any legitimate offer, but he was not desperate and had no indication of accepting minimal fees in return for the Rangers' services. A telegram on September 5, 1947, berated Gordon for the terms he had tentatively accepted for a Texas Rangers engagement in Phoenix. Gordon and Hamilburg had responded positively to an offer of $900 for a weekly series of shows in the city, an amount which Church sternly advised should receive "serious discussion" before being accepted. In Church's judgment, it would set a precedent for a figure that was too low. Church had two serious reservations about the Phoenix engagement. First, the compensation was less than desirable and "without a definite and liberal expense allowance" would not be financially feasible. Second, he found the proposed sponsorship by a local dentist highly objectionable. "Very definitely we would not approve such sponsorship in this part of the country," he reprimanded his agents, "and [we] have turned down many similar borderline radio accounts." Even with higher payments, Church needed convincing that such sponsorship would not have any ill effects on the band's efforts to land a national sponsor.

This episode illustrates curious thinking toward advertisements by many radio executives. Seemingly an uncontroversial sponsor, dentists and opticians were common sponsors of locally aired country or Western music programs in many markets in the country. Church's reluctance to accept a dentist's account perhaps reflected a somewhat outdated level of modesty for the air. Advertisements for deodorants, laxatives, and other products involving various bodily functions had not been allowed on the CBS network fifteen years before in the early 1930s by the dictate of president William Paley. On the other hand, tobacco firms were some of the most prolific advertisers on radio.

Further film deals continued to elude the Rangers. They received confirmation they would not be appearing in the Hoosier Hotshots new film. Colbert Clark, the picture's producer, did not want to pony up for an eight-piece backing band, instead opting for a quartet, the Sunshine Boys. The Sunshine Boys were an established group, originally from Georgia, that had appeared in a number of westerns with Eddie Dean and others. Later known primarily as a gospel group but also adept at western swing, they were a versatile group that had, as did the Plainsmen who replaced the Rangers on *Hawk Larabee*, an edge on the Rangers. The singers were also instrumentalists and required no backing musicians, thus making them a far more appealing prospect for a film producer worried about his bottom line. Was the Texas Rangers quartet, sans the backing group, considered by Clark or even offered by Church? Even if they were, was hiring them without any built-in musical accompaniment a false economy? While the quartet was more than capable of performing a cappella, as numerous World transcriptions prove, it seems unlikely that such a sound is what was sought for the film.[1]

While the notification letter does not name the film, it is presumed to be *Song of Idaho* which was released on March 20, 1948. Interestingly, despite Clark's claim that the Sunshine Boys would save money, the movie also featured a female trio, the Sunshine Girls, and a male quintet, the Starlighters. The movie's songs were recorded in mid-November, a month after the Rangers received word they would not be in the film.

---

1 Additional information about *Song of Idaho* comes from the Internet Movie Database and *Billboard*, November 15, 1947, p. 102. The Sunshine Boys are profiled in the *Encyclopedia of American Gospel Music* and www.b-westerns.com. Members of the band performed into the 21st century.

Chapter 9: The Texas Rangers on Television

Decline of Radio, Rise of Television

It may have begun to dawn on Arthur Church and the Texas Rangers themselves as the 1940s wound down, that there was little likelihood that the group might regain its pre-war momentum. Tastes and entertainment technology were both changing, and the Rangers position as part of a larger entertainment business rather than a free-standing band, arguably, and crucially, made them less able to respond to these changes in a timely fashion.

After a string of ten films between 1939 and 1941 after moving to Hollywood, and gaining a spot in Autry's *The Last Round-Up* upon their return to the coast in the spring of 1947, they would appear in only one more, *The Arkansas Swing* with the Hoosier Hotshots in the summer of 1948. The number of radio stations subscribing to their transcription catalog was declining as well. To a considerable extent, they were victims of that changing cultural landscape. Radio would cede to television as the dominant form of home electronic entertainment, an evolution that would also have devastating effect on other areas important to a group like the Rangers, live performances and musical western movies.

While it may have extended the band's life, perhaps artificially so, with Church effectively propping the group up during periods in which its earnings were far below its overhead, the Rangers' unique status as Arthur Church's property was also a major factor in their downfall. Had they existed as a free-standing organization, forced to sink or swim, not only on artistic merit, but through the many intangibles that determine such a band's fortunes, they might have been compelled by circumstance to adapt more radically to challenges and changing tastes and times. In the end, with the Rangers themselves lacking any real autonomy, it was Church who eventually had to take radical action, but this occurred as a last ditch effort to salvage anything from what, to Church, had become a crumbling mess. Ironically, the post-Rangers career of Bob Crawford, though it was not on a national scale, gave some glimpse of the possibilities that might have existed for a free-standing Rangers removed from both the protection and control of Arthur Church's radio and production companies.

The Rangers' demise may have been written on the wall by 1948, but that was not yet something that either group members or Church were willing to cede. One avenue open to the, admittedly, struggling group was, as mentioned above, television.

Even though television's popularity grew rapidly after World War II, the roots of the technology actually go back decades before that, and in theory, it was just one step beyond radio. Throughout the 1920s, countless radio writers spoke of the inevitable coming of radio-with-pictures, and by 1928 General Electric was broadcasting television programming on a regular, if very limited, schedule. CBS station W2XAB had the first daily broadcast schedule in 1931 and the radio network experimented the following year in creating a television network. Arthur Church, incidentally, was a part of that project which, in Kansas City had included the Tex Owens television show mentioned earlier.

CBS' efforts were unsuccessful at the time, and it was not until the 1939 World's Fair in New York that television was demonstrated to large numbers of visitors, and sets started to become more widely available to the general public. Few were yet ready to accept the new technology, however. RCA had sets available for between $200 and $600, a substantial sum at the time, and the entertainment provided for the outlay was sparse. The medium's promoters quickly found television faced the same primary challenge as had radio two decades before: providing enough quality programming to justify the public's investment in television sets. Before the challenge could be adequately addressed, the United States entered World War II, and the technology's further development was put on hold so the nation's more pressing military needs could be met.

In 1948, Church's staff turned their attention to the now ever-expanding medium, though still experimental, and began to seek outlets there for the Rangers' talent. It was an historic year for television, most notable because it was the first year for formal operations by television networks ABC, CBS, NBC, and DuMont. On January 22, KMBC executive John Gordon sent Church a letter outlining his thoughts on the group's potential future in television. Recognizing the rapid expansion of the industry, he clearly hoped the Rangers could get in on the ground floor. At least two other Western music shows were already under consideration, *Village Barn* in New York and *Hayloft Hoedown* in Philadelphia. Other companies which were providing recorded libraries and transcription services to radio stations, notably Cincinnati's Frederick W. Ziv, were even then moving into television where they were selling filmed programs. "A half-hour program on film with the Texas Rangers and other prominent Western Stars would be a very colorful picture for Television, and also a very listenable one," Gordon predicted. Because stations could not fill all their broadcasting time with live programs, such a Rangers production "would be a very saleable item to individual stations and to advertising agencies." He was sure that a video version of the Rangers' music library could be immensely profitable over the long run once it recouped initial start-up costs.

Church shared Gordon's enthusiasm but did not believe such a series could be undertaken any time in the near future. Just as the members' lack of acting and basic cowboy skills had limited their effectiveness in motion pictures, so Church acknowledged these deficiencies stood in the way of a quality television product. Replying to Gordon, he was forced to admit that "it [was] likely to be quite a long time before The Texas Rangers are doing ... television" whether on film or the soon-to-be completed television networks. Still, the idea of a filmed song series intrigued Church, and he encouraged Gordon to pursue that avenue and make contact with men such as Jerry Fairbanks, the film veteran who had opened his own television production company. Well aware of Ziv's success in radio, he pushed Gordon to make informal contact with Ziv's production men to get a feel for their future video forays.

Through the spring of 1948, as Church and his men slowly investigated television possibilities, they also continued pushing the Rangers' radio library, hoping interest would revive. By March the number of subscribing stations was less than two dozen: WGBI (Scranton, PA), KARM (Fresno, CA), KTUC (Tucson, AZ), KGNC (Amarillo, TX), WBOC (Salisbury, MD), KFVS (Cape Girardeau, MO), KHMO (Hannibal, MO), WDOD (Chattanooga, TN), KADA (Ada, OK), KPHO (Phoenix, AZ), KPRO, (Riverside and San Bernardino,

CA), KROP (Brawley and El Centro, CA), KREO, (Indio and Palm Springs, CA), KUBC, (Blythe, CA), KPOR (Riverside and San Bernardino, CA), WXGI (Richmond, VA), WTRC (Elkhart, IN), KTUL (Tulsa, OK), WIRE (Indianapolis, IN), and WABI (Bangor, ME). Weekly cash flow from these rentals was just over $300 per week.

Ziv Radio Productions, whom Church had sought out in the past to form a commercial partnership, resisted another approach from representatives of the Texas Rangers. Ziv personally rebuffed Church's attempts to get the successful syndicator to sell The Texas Rangers' library. He had two new series coming out, Ziv insisted, and he "would not be playing fair with [Church] if [he] took on the Texas Rangers and did not do a job."

Network radio spots, which had so often proven elusive for Church and the Rangers, continued to be just out of reach. Hubbell Robinson, vice-president and director of programs at CBS, was clearly disappointed in the group's latest audition effort for the chain. On March 25th he wrote to Church and expressed his dismay at the most recent Rangers script. "I am sorry to say," Robinson began his letter, "that it does not at all fit my conception of how the musical show we discussed should be set up." In fact, the entire effort was looking like "a mistake." He conceded that Church had a very skilled ensemble, but the proposed script was "uninspired" and "second-rate;" it only got in the way of the boys' natural talent. Robinson urged Church to get back to the basics and create a music-driven vehicle for the Rangers. "If people tune into this program, it is because they want to hear 'The Rangers,'" Robinson explained in his reply. He conceded that using Lou Crosby as announcer and creating a cowboy setting would be appropriate, but there should be just enough copy to move from song to song. The band's days of musical dramas were over.

Church quickly had an unknown KMBC staffer crank out an audition script reusing the title "Under Western Skies" which was delivered April 1. Following Robinson's advice, the script incorporated Lou Crosby (as Cactus Lou Crosby) and Martha Mears as well as Smiley Burnette, all three of whom had played alongside the Rangers on radio and in motion pictures. After an introductory tune with Mears on vocals, Crosby opened the show: "Yes, welcome to Under Western Skies, folks - - a good old western get-together starring the

Texas Rangers - - with yours truly Cactus Lou Crosby, and featuring that lovable star of stage, screen and radio, Smiley Burnette, and that sweet singing little cowgal from Columbia Pictures Martha Mears - - -." As Robinson prescribed, the show was a string of numbers with bare bones dialog in between.

Bob [Crawford]: Martha's right here with her hair in a braid, Cactus Lou - - but where is Smiley?

Crosby: (LAUGH) Here now, Bob - - don't you worry about ol' Froggy - - just start that music and he'll come a-runnin' - -

Bob: What, Smiley, . . Runnin'? . . That I *gotta* see

Crosby: (LAUGH) OKAY - - but here's a ditty that ought to start A LOT OF FOLKS a-runnin' our way - - The Texas Rangers and "When The Bloom Is on the Sage."

Whether Church went ahead and okayed the recording of the script, or if CBS' Robinson weighed in positively and approved, within a week an audition recording was cut. The record was subsequently sent to the Rangers' Hollywood representative Mitchell Hamilburg.

Back on the Road

Church and Gordon, however, were quickly growing impatient with Hamilburg's efforts. Gordon was convinced that Hamilburg was not invested in representing the Rangers, and they might do better seeking out a new agent. He blamed Hamilburg for The Riders of the Purple Sage getting selected to appear in Monty Hale's Republic pictures, and he resented that Hamilburg had not even advocated for the Rangers until Gordon pushed him to do so. Hamilburg was hopelessly focused on Columbia because of Autry's connections there, Gordon argued, and he overlooked considerable other options for the ensemble.

The band needed an agent who would "daily [make] the rounds of the picture companies." In addition to the loss of the Hale pictures, Gordon was irked that Hamilburg had not made any effort to engage the Texas Rangers in a series of six shorts being produced by Will Cowan at Universal-International. The set of 24-minute films was not even a hush-hush project; Gordon had read about them in *Variety*! In later correspondence, Gordon added that he felt the Cowan project was more than a simple six-short project; it might actually be an experiment to shoot television films at the same time, a situation

The Texas Rangers on the road ca. 1948.
Courtesy of Ed Crawford.

Gordon foresaw all the movie studios undertaking. However valid Gordon's and Church's criticisms of Hamilburg's efforts may have been, it is again perhaps equally arguable that neither Church nor Gordon were fully acknowledging two major factors that greatly handicapped Hamilburg's efforts. One, which Hamilburg had raised from the beginning, was the size of the Rangers ensemble and its implications in financial negotiations. Two, the musical B-western was on its way out.

While Church and John Gordon attempted to position the Rangers for more television, film, and radio work, the group itself hit the touring circuit. On the morning of Saturday, April 10, 1948, the group left Hollywood for an extended series of personal appearances, which would not bring them back to Los Angeles until early May. With the eight-man line-up, it was no small expense to send the Rangers out on the road. The band members' weekly pay during this road trip was $95 apiece, which included their regular salary plus an advance amount. To cover room, board, and other touring costs, each performer received an additional seven dollars per day.

John Gordon made sure the Texas Rangers made a memorable impression on passersby. The octet traveled by car, pulling a trailer, painted in matching shades, with their equipment. Added on the rear of the trailer were the words "The Texas Rangers, Hollywood, Calif," while "The Texas Rangers" was emblazoned across the car doors. KMBC invested $342.11 to make sure the car and trailer were road-worthy and safe.

The itinerary of the Rangers' first week on the road trip has been preserved. It records their travels through Kansas, in the heart of their early stomping grounds, and provides a glimpse into the details – both financial and logistical – of the tour.

April 14, 1948 - Garden City, KS, Garden City Army Air Field, 8:00 p.m.

Sponsor: Junior Chamber of Commerce, Vincent Beckett contact person

KMBC received the first $400 of gross receipts and the Chamber the next $300. Any take beyond this was split evenly. Admittance was one dollar.

April 15, 1948 - Great Bend, KS, City Auditorium, 8:00 p.m.

Sponsor: Masonic Drill Team, Joe McMullen contact person

KMBC received a flat $350 and was to provide advertisements over sister station KRM, 50 window cards, mats, special stories and promotional pictures.

April 16, 1948 Emporia, KS, City Auditorium, 8:00 p.m.

Sponsor: Junior Chamber of Commerce, Bob Patterson contact person.

KMBC received a flat $350 and was to provide additional musicians for the dance.

April 19, 1948 Hays, KS, City Auditorium, 8:00 p.m.

Sponsor: Veterans of Foreign Wars, R. A. (Bob) Mermis contact person.

KMBC received the first $400 of gross receipts and the Chamber the next $300. Any take beyond this was split evenly. Admittance was one dollar.

April 20, 1948 Beloit, KS, Municipal Building, 8:00 p.m.

Sponsor: Mitchell County Rural Life, Joanne Murray contact person.

KMBC received the first $400 of gross receipts and the Chamber the next $300. Any take beyond this was split evenly. Admittance was one dollar.

April 21, 1948 McPherson, KS City Auditorium, 8:00 p.m.

Sponsor: Junior Chamber of Commerce, Merwin Hapgood contact person.

KMBC received the first $400 of gross receipts and the Chamber the next $300. Any take beyond this was split evenly. Admittance was one dollar. On this date there was also a matinee show at 4:30 for children with a $0.25 admission price. These proceeds were split fifty-fifty.

April 22, 1948 Junction City, KS, Municipal Auditorium, 8:00 p.m.

Sponsor: Junior Chamber of Commerce, C. E. (Jack) Rosenquist contact person.

KMBC received the first $400 of gross receipts and the Chamber the next $300. Any take beyond this was split evenly. Admittance for adults was one dollar and $0.40 for children.

The preparations required to pull off such a tour were extensive and complex, even more so than might at first be expected. At the Rangers' Garden City, KS, engagement, John McDermott, who acted as KMBC's point man on this particular date, was responsible, not only for such mundane tasks as finding hotel accommodations, but primarily for ensuring the performance was adequately publicized. On April 10, four days before the show, he arranged for an interview with local newscaster Max Bicknell to talk about the Texas Rangers over KIUL. Then on April 14, the day of the show, he arranged for the Texas Rangers to appear in person on the same station between 4:30 and 4:45. He also convinced the Junior Chamber of Commerce to pay for twenty promotional spots on both KIUL and KGAR.

The owner of Garden city's two movie theaters was enthusiastic to help the band, too, having been impressed with their appearance in Autry's *The Last Roundup*. He agreed to show some promotional slides in the theaters on the three days preceding the performance of the 14th. McDermott and members of the Junior Chamber blanketed Garden City's main businesses with posters and also made arrangements for a sound truck to make the rounds through town the day of the show. McDermott was less successful getting some free ink through the local newspaper. The sponsor of the show, the city's Junior Chamber of Commerce, was able to get a small 4-inch story placed in the April 9 edition, but beyond that, the group had to purchase print ads for the paper.

While the Texas Rangers hit the road throughout Kansas, Arthur Church hit the meeting rooms trying to earn new assignments for his group. He approached Hollywood-based promoter Martin Wagner in early April, 1948, about setting up a tour for the group after they returned to California. Wagner had an impressive resume of booking tours with big name talent such as Paul Whiteman and Fred Waring through his association with the William Morris Agency. Wagner had also served as the personal manager for famous pianist Jose Iturbi, managed the coast-to-coast production of *Porgy and Bess*, and managed the Sigmund Romberg Orchestra. His experience booking western tours, which encompassed some of the biggest names around, such as Tom Mix, Ken Maynard, Gene Autry, Roy Rogers, Tex Ritter, the Sons of the Pioneers, and Smiley Burnette, was second to none.

Even with Wagner's extensive skills and connections, regretfully, such a job was too great for the short notice given by Church. Wagner would need at least 60 days to put together a tour with back-to-back dates, which could be profitable for everyone involved. If Midland Broadcasting could quickly confirm that the Rangers would be available during the summer months, he told Church he could put together a worthwhile itinerary. To be successful, he told Church, it would be necessary for Midland to relent on some of their booking requirements, two of which posed considerable obstacles to his efforts. First, it would not realistically feasible for Wagner to clear every single venue with Church before arranging the booking. It might be possible to run the final list of venues by Midland staff before the bookings were confirmed, but to give Church notice of every possible theater under consideration would take too much time, and create unnecessary delays, when speed was frequently of the essence. Second, Church's demand that Wagner not consider booking into any sites where liquor was served was a huge handicap that would make it "too confining to possibly obtain a good route." Whatever aversion he and Church may personally have to alcohol, he stressed, "the majority of good commercial dates do not exclude liquor from the premises." Those that did prohibit alcohol were too few to put together a profitable tour.

If Church was willing to proceed under these revised conditions, Wagner's terms were fairly standard. He received a flat ten percent commission, and out of this amount he paid for phone calls, telegrams, and book correspondence. Wagner did not pay for any "exploitation" or advertising materials, a not inconsiderable cost which would fall to Midland Broadcasting.

Television and touring plans occupied most of the attention of those involved with the Rangers, but May saw the release of the group's first commercial recordings since its 1941 session for Okeh. Probably recorded in late 1947, before the American Federation of Musician's recording strike that lasted almost all of 1948, the recordings were released on the independent Bibletone label, which as the name implies, was devoted to gospel music. The six recordings were released as an album set, which in the days before the introduction of 12-inch long-play (LP) sets, soon to be introduced, meant a set of ten-inch, 78 rpm records packaged together with a connecting theme or artist. There were three records in the case of this set of "Cowboy Hymns" by the Rangers. The collection consisted of six Western-flavored hymns: "The Touch of God's Hand," "Jubilation," "Cowboy Camp Meetin'," "Gallopin' to Glory," "Golden Wings and Silver Spurs," and "Trail to Our Salvation," Western standards written by the veteran Fleming Allan, and the peerless Tim Spencer and Bob Nolan of the Rangers' rivals, the Sons of the Pioneers. Perhaps not surprisingly, the collection received little attention and sales were tepid at best; only $660 worth of units was sold by the end of the year. The Bibletone set did have one benefit in that it attracted the attention of the still-new MGM label, which signed the Rangers within a month of its release, much to John Gordon's excitement. But, because of the union strike, the group would not enter the studios for MGM until early in 1949.

Gordan still had not received any promising television leads for the Rangers by June of 1948. Discussions with L.A.'s Don Lee at station W6XAO and Hal Hudson at KNX led nowhere. One prospect that had Gordon's attention was working with Gene Autry's production company, which, given the Rangers' history with Autry, seemed to have real potential. Just as Jerry Fairbanks, whom Church had earlier encouraged Gordon to contact, was developing films for NBC, Les Atlas was doing the same at CBS, the network with which Church, the Midland Broadcasting Company, and the Texas Rangers had been affiliated for so long. Though everything was still in the talking stage, Gordon felt the discussions were worthy of Church's attention. If they were going to make a splash on television, their CBS network contacts were stronger than those with any other organization.

If the lack of real progress in the television negotiations was frustrating, then the final numbers for the Texas Rangers' Kansas tour between April 10 and May 1, 1948, were a bitter disappointment. Financially, the tour was an absolute disaster for Church and Midland. The tables below outline the income via ticket and songbook sales compared to the costs involved in putting the eight-piece band on the road.

Location	Tickets	Songbooks
Garden City, KS	$214.20	$6.30
Great Bend, KS	$350.00	$27.90
Emporia, KS	$350.00	$6.75
Hayes, KS	$180.40	$8.70
Beloit, KS	$272.70	0
McPherson, KS	$405.59	$11.70
Junction City, KS	$201.01	$3.60
St. Joseph, MO	$199.59	$11.91
Brush Creek Follies (KMBC)	$600.00	0
	$2,773.49	$76.86
Total Income: $2,850.35		

The next table itemizes the tour expenses:

Expenses		
Texas Rangers Travel	$1,225.00	
John Gordon Travel	$124.21	
Car Expense	$275.37	
Musicians Scale	$1,658.00	
American Federation of Musicians Dues	$26.40	
Telephone & Telegraph	$195.78	
Hall Rental – St. Joseph	$134.50	
McConnell Travel	$300.00	
Enslow Travel	$150.00	
McDermott Travel	$180.00	
Advertising	$360.48	
Ticket Sellers – St. Joseph	$8.00	$4,637.76
Net Loss		$1,787.41

The net loss of nearly $2,000 was more than just a financial letdown. It appeared to underscore what was becoming more and more apparent: that even in the heart of KMBC/Texas Rangers territory, the group could not be counted on to generate enough income via live performance to justify its payroll and ancillary expenses. Church and his staff can only have looked grimly at such figures and their implications for the Rangers' future.

KTTV

Out on the West Coast, somewhat removed from the bitter disappointment of the money-losing Midwestern tour, John Gordon continued to follow up on leads no matter how slim and without the level of discouragement felt by his Kansas City colleagues. One discussion, which did not pan out, involved Bud Barry, a program manager with the American Broadcasting Company. During the summer of 1948, the two had a series of meetings about creating a half-hour series featuring the Texas Rangers for the network. Barry informed Gordon that ABC was interested in developing a western program which might be a good fit for the Rangers.

Miscommunication about the potential broadcast time of the series led to confusion which slowed momentum on the series. Gordon thought ABC was looking for ideas for an evening show, while Barry thought he had been clear in stating the network was working to fill a daytime slot. This was no small misunderstanding, because those stations that still used the band's transcription library frequently used it to fill air space during the day. Generally, rental contracts specified that the sponsored party, the Texas Rangers in this case, would not be used elsewhere in a potentially competitive spot. Thus, some markets would automatically be out of consideration from the start to avoid just such schedule conflicts. Arthur Church was not overly keen on a daytime broadcast simply because he was most interested in selling the band for a full half hour evening program. These prime time broadcasts were where the real money and publicity were, not shows aired during work hours.

To give Gordon room to negotiate, Church relented and indicated he would support a short term daytime sale if both parties went into the project with the understanding that it would be used to build support for a full thirty minute evening program starting in the fall.

Having received Church's parameters for terms he would find acceptable in a deal, Gordon went to work on Barry, reminding him what good profit-makers westerns had proven to be for the film studios. They were cheap to make and brought in steady audiences, a winning formula. Gordon had no doubt that the continued popularity of movie westerns was indicative that there existed a healthy potential for radio westerns as well. To facilitate a deal, Gordon offered "to cooperate and give [them] a very inexpensive show" and even suggested ABC look at Sunday afternoons if he truly could not find an evening slot.

Barry's reply was slow in coming, a bad sign, and it became clear to Gordon, who conveyed as much to Church, that there was little hope the American Broadcasting Company would be using the Texas Rangers that fall. Ironically, Gordon's arguments in his communications with Barry were not too far off base. Westerns, in fact, would enjoy a renewed popularity on radio in the next decade, especially those aimed at adult audiences, like *Gunsmoke*, *Fort Laramie*, *The Six Shooter*, *Frontier Gentleman*, and *Tales of the Texas Rangers*. But, while Gordon may have been right in general, he also surely knew it was action, not music, which was the main impetus repeatedly drawing fans back to the theaters and drawing them to the radio westerns.

Gordon thought the Rangers still had some life left on radio, but, at the same time, he was not going to back off on his push to get the Rangers a television deal. He, again, suggested that Church invest in a half-hour audition film, and he even took the liberty of lining up a quality writer and producer who were ready to shoot the demo. Church was a visionary, a quality he had demonstrated over and over since getting into radio broadcasting more than three decades before. Television was the next logical step, and Gordon implored Church to look long-term, as he had so many times before at KMBC, to recognize that if the Texas Rangers were to have a real future they had to become a presence on the small screen.

No one argued that the initial costs were insignificant; they were prohibitive but could be overcome. The Texas Rangers *needed* to be one of the first Western bands in the television film business, Gordon argued. Being first did not guarantee success, but it surely would not hurt. Waiting too long could jeopardize any future the group might have on the new media. Paramount and Don Lee were, even then, airing programming in the fertile Southern California market, and CBS and NBC would soon have operable outlets there. Each and every one of them would need quality programming to stay competitive, and the Rangers had proven their quality to nationwide audiences and sponsors.

For perhaps the first time in his career, however, Arthur Church seemed to vacillate. He knew full well the financial risk such a move entailed, which was especially relevant considering the band's meager income over the past year. Yet, he also instinctively knew Gordon's arguments were on the money. Television was going to make or break the Rangers' chance to climb to the top of what remained of the Western music market.

The production company run by Jerry Fairbanks seemed to offer Church exactly the compromise proposal necessary to dip his toe in the television water. A representative from Jerry Fairbanks, Inc., which produced several short subject series including *Popular Science*, *Unusual Occupations*, and *Speaking of Animals*, suggested in July, 1948, that Church consider a series of films which paired the proven Texas Rangers transcription library with photographic stills. The cost of such a venture was not clear yet, but it seemed likely to be considerably less than filmed performance. It was a compromise that might give Church the confidence to take even bigger steps if it proved successful. Fairbanks was ready to provide the film production services if Church agreed to provide the Texas Rangers, their records, and the necessary musical rights. Fairbanks was interested in creating a test reel to determine the overall costs of such an endeavor and to explore what kind of profitable partnership could be created with the resulting films. Church still could not bring himself to commit to such a television project, however, and nothing ultimately came of the potential partnership with Fairbanks.

Arthur B. Church Productions' contacts with Hal Hudson paid off just a few short months later. After spending considerable time investigating the television scene in New York, and getting a better feel for the industry as a whole, Hudson came back with a potential deal. KTTV in Los Angeles, CBS' new outlet, was preparing to go on the air January 1, 1949, and might be interested in a Texas Rangers production. From his offices in Hollywood's Beekman Storage Building, Hudson warned Church and Gordon that there was no money in television yet, at least at the upstart KTTV. Even with Gordon's assurances that the Rangers would work for scale, Hudson insisted the station could not afford to pay the entire eight-man outfit. Instead, he offered to pay the four musicians, to whom he would probably be bound because of union rules, but not the singing quartet.

Control of television actors contracts had not yet been decided among the American Federation of Radio Artists, the Screen Actors Guild, and the American Guild of Variety Artists, but scale pay for musicians had been set at $12 per half-hour plus an additional $3.33 per rehearsal. This was not an excessive cost, Gordon insisted, and it did not seem fair to pay the musicians but not the singers. He, nevertheless, acknowledged that the quartet was willing to do the show for free with the expectation that the publicity and experience would pay off later, a strategy which the band had first employed on radio in 1939. Gordon was also positive that once the public caught the Rangers' performances on television, a sponsor would soon follow, after which, the group could demand higher compensation.

As Gordon predicted, the members of the Rangers agreed to such an arrangement. The musicians would be compensated at the scale established by the union; the singers would receive no payment until a scale for their work was established when the proper union jurisdiction had been decided. On December 16, 1948, the Texas Rangers signed a contract with Arthur B. Church Productions that would bring them into the world of television via KTTV.

In addition to the quartet of Bob Crawford, Rod May, Fran Mahaney and Edward Cronenbold, the group now included Emert (Mert) "Tenderfoot" Painter (fiddle) and Edwin "Idaho" Johnson (bass fiddle), both of whom had been with the Rangers since the postwar reincarnation two and a half years previous, and William "Monty" Lorentz (accordion), who had come aboard in the latter half of 1947. However, the group's musical lynchpin, plectrist Herbie Kratoska, had left the group and returned to Kansas City to work again as a staff musician at KMBC. He was replaced by Mert Painter's brother Ted, former guitarist with KMBC's Tune Chasers band. As the other musicians had adopted the monikers of their predecessors on their respective instruments, Ted took on Kratoska's nickname "Arizona."

It certainly felt like Christmas to the Texas Rangers family. Not only was a television show now in the works, but Gordon had gotten assurances from Bob Simon, attorney for Weber's Bread, which sponsored the *All-Star Western Theatre* radio program on the West Coast, that if the program directors decided to replace their musical accompanists, The Kings Men, the Rangers would be contacted. They also had new access with Republic Pictures via a casting director named Jack Grant. Republic had two singing cowboy stars, Roy Rogers and Monty Hale, who regularly used Western backing bands and who might be persuaded to give the Rangers a shot. Additionally, Rangers' film agent Mitchell Hamilburg reported that he was close to signing the group to a six-picture deal. There was even a possibility of an overseas trip with a tentative offer to tour and broadcast for six weeks in Australia with Carolina Cotton and Shug Fisher. As 1948 wound down, the band suddenly found themselves with more projects developing than they had the entire time since reforming after the war. Gordon assured Church that things were about to "break for the group."

As further details of the upcoming Texas Rangers' 1949 broadcast series emerged, however, it remained unclear whether these many promising potential projects would come to fruition. KTTV was planning to begin broadcasting on January 1 with coverage of the Rose Bowl while the Rangers would go on January 3rd or 4th around 9 o'clock in the evening. The station's sales team was busy trying to find a commercial sponsor for the outfit to cover the cost of union scale for all eight members. Station officials also were feverishly trying to figure out how to film the shows, a prospect discussed by Church, Gordon, and others from the outset of their conversations and correspondence about the Rangers' possible future in television. The expense of creating the musical films could be passed on by Church to KTTV's affiliated network CBS, which felt these films would appeal to other affiliates, especially in the larger Eastern markets. If the show's growth matched everyone's rising expectations, all involved could look forward to higher payment rates.

Producers originally considered adding a comedian to the program but ultimately decided against such a move. They agreed that a guest artist would add sufficient variety and star power to each show but not overshadow the Rangers. John Gordon knew he had his work cut out for him finding performers who would commit to the broadcasts, since guests on sustaining television shows were generally not paid. On sponsored shows, a guest could look forward to a $30 paycheck. A further challenge was that the shoestring budget of a sustaining show would not permit the hiring of any sort of professional writer, leaving it up to Gordon and Bob Crawford to hammer out the weekly outline and any dialogue. As a small gesture to the performers, the station assured them the use of a blackboard on which they could scribble any notes and cues necessary during filming.

Excited by the new broadcasting venture, Gordon, nevertheless, recognized its inherent risk and was not willing to let the group become chained to the sustaining feature at the cost of other paying work. KTTV agreed to let him substitute another band for the Texas Rangers if they were booked to out-of-town performances which prevented their appearing on their weekly slot. In return, the station sought some sort of assurance that the Rangers would not bail on the station after they invested the initial resources in getting the group on the air. As their television premier approached, the band was forced to begin their show without a contract because Church was not yet willing to sign one.

KTTV scheduled the Rangers' first appearance for January 3, 1949, at the prime evening time of 8 o'clock. The station's Hal Hudson and his artistic director agreed to create a bunk house setting for the group and add props which would distinguish the act from other similar programs on the air, which came across as stilted and static. The format was shaping up to be similar to that of their earlier radio series *Under Western Skies*, which featured the Rangers' music with a minimum of patter and plot. On December 27, 1948, one week before air time, the band held a grueling two-hour rehearsal claimed to be the first ever held at CBS' Los Angeles television studios. The edges were still rough but spirits were high. The Rangers found themselves programmed between *Make Mine Music* which aired from 7:45 to 8:00 and *Western Film Theatre* (airing *Gentlemen With Guns* that week) which started at 8:30.

1949

A lot was riding on the KTTV program for the Texas Rangers. Year-end financial statements for 1948 show that Arthur B. Church

Productions was hemorrhaging cash, with the Rangers losing close to $12,000 that year, not an insignificant sum. Everyone involved with the Rangers knew business had to improve or Church would be forced to disband the group once again, this time for economic reasons rather than war challenges.

The year got off to a promising start, not only with the new television show, but with word from Hubbell Robinson and Bill Fineschriber at CBS, that CBS Radio was giving the Rangers a sustaining spot, to be called simply *The Texas Rangers*. The series of thirty minute episodes was to begin Saturday, January 22, and air weekly at 4 o'clock in the afternoon. Former Texas Ranger and KNX (CBS' Los Angeles affiliate) writer Gomer Cool was contracted to write the scripts and John Gordon, the band's manager, acted as co-producer. That Church did not require payment for the use of the Rangers for the first six to eight weeks dampened the enthusiasm a bit, but the point had been reached when regular unpaid radio and television gigs were better than no gigs at all.

The radio series posed a notable risk for Church. Not only was he fronting all the talent costs, but he was also giving up control over the writing, producing, and directing, something he would have considered only very reluctantly in years past. But he and the Rangers had their backs against the wall, and everyone knew it. The film and touring prospects that Gordon had gushed about just a month before had fizzled. CBS practically dictated the terms for *The Texas Rangers*, claiming the right of cancellation with two weeks' notice, which was also given to the Rangers, though it was highly unlikely to be used, and insisting that Church deliver terms and conditions under which the network could pick up the Rangers on a commercial basis for five years. Though those terms have not survived in the documentary record, they surely favored CBS over the floundering musical act.

The group was nearly two months into the television series before Arthur Church could get away from Kansas City for a Hollywood visit to finally see his Rangers in action on the small screen. As gloomy as the future looked, Church put on a brave face and emphasized to Harry Witt that he was optimistic about the Rangers' prospects, something the always pragmatic Church could not have meant with all sincerity. Looking for ways, as ever, that his product could be improved, Church noted some production values he felt could be bettered. He had particular complaints with the camera work which he described as "mediocre." Despite the explanation that two of the three cameras were not functioning, he insisted that it was critical that the band be "produced under conditions which will utilize fully their potentialities." He ended his visit to KTTV by telling Witt that he was doing "a swell job," but immediately began to make plans to meet with network higher-ups to find out the next step for the Rangers.

Church Productions remained bullish on the television prospects of the Texas Rangers as February turned to March, even though production problems continued to plague the fledgling KTTV. John Gordon bluntly told the station's Hal Hudson that he was not satisfied with the show's production values and that he hoped for better. Gordon was subsequently pleased to learn from Hudson that a new producer would be taking over at the beginning of March. After the February 28, 1949, broadcast Gordon met with the new producer and the program's head cameraman to discuss ideas, including enlarging the set and adding some props. They also proposed inserting action shots from western movies to keep things lively and interesting for the viewers. All of these new ideas left Gordon confident in the show's future.

Reporting back to Kansas City two weeks later, Gordon confirmed that the changes had significantly improved the program, and that he could honestly say he thought the band had the best show on KTTV, an opinion shared by many station staff. At the same time, working to the Texas Rangers' disadvantage, in his opinion, was the overall weakness of the KTTV schedule. They did not have any stand-out shows, and even their top program, *Pantomime Quiz*, lacked a sponsor despite the fact that it won an award as television's top show while earlier airing on KTLA. Gordon was encouraged that KTTV had lined up two potential sponsors, McMahon Furniture Stores and Dr. Ross Dog Food, for the band's program. In addition, two representatives of the Santa Fe Railroad, Owen Smith and Leo Burnett, had promised to be in attendance at an upcoming show.

Kinescope

By mid-March, Gordon was satisfied with the direction of the KTTV effort, and again turned his attention to film recordings, which he had pushed to Church so strongly a few months before. A short meeting with Frank Pittman, radio director for Needham, Louis & Brorby, prompted him to revisit the prospect. Pittman's company had hired Rockett Pictures, an investment interest of *Fibber McGee & Molly* announcer Harlow Wilcox, to produce a series of one minute 16mm films for Johnson's Wax. Later, talking with Wilcox himself, Gordon learned that Rockett Pictures had filmed in both 35mm and 16mm, and many of the new television film production companies had little experience with the work and were putting out a poor product. Quality broadcast film could not be done well on the cheap, at least not yet; it was expensive and required a certain expertise.

Wilcox invited Gordon to talk more in-depth with Rockett producers to get a feel for what they could do and what the costs might be. He also suggested looking into the Grant-Realm company and Jerry Fairbanks' outfit, with whom the Rangers' had dealt before. He advised Gordon and Church to keep their eye on motion picture companies who would likely be forming their own television units, as they had the necessary experience in film that newcomers to the field lacked. In the end it all came back to money, and there was no getting around the expense involved in putting together a quality package of Texas Rangers television films.

To nudge Arthur Church in the right direction, Gordon subtly suggested that it might be worth having a Rangers program kinescoped to get an idea of what a half hour film would look like. The process was relatively cheap and nearby station KTLA had the equipment and experience necessary to set up recorders at KTTV. The idea proved intriguing to Church, and he authorized Gordon to move ahead with the project. Gomer Cool, who had written the continuity for the television show so far, was engaged to create the script for the episode chosen for kinescoping. Ginny Jackson, recently the featured thrush with Spade Cooley's big Western swing band, agreed to provide vocals in a deal which would pay her union scale for all further shows and ensure her $75 per episode if CBS picked up the series on kinescope. Payments were subject to further negotiation if a sponsor signed on. The group was glad to get Jackson because her former boss, Spade Cooley, who had gone on the air on another station and had the sponsorship of Hoffman Radio, was vying for her services as well. This may have been a long shot as when she had left Cooley to tour with Autry, the hot-headed Cooley had tried to throw her off the Santa Monica pier! Represented by the Rangers' former agent Mitch Hamilburg, Jackson had proven to be a valuable asset to Gene Autry's road show and the members of the Rangers felt she would benefit not only from their broadcasts, but also any potential personal appearances.

To keep costs at a minimum, Gordon wrangled with Hal Hudson to get free use of additional engineering staff and rehearsal time before the cameras. A company called Consolidated took care of printing the kinescope on 16mm film from the original 35mm print at a cost of $40.50. The date for kinescoping was set for April 11, 1949, with the hope that Church and his associates could screen the demo for CBS executives at a meeting to be scheduled sometime after the Midland Broadcasting Company contingent arrived in New York on April 18. What the Rangers' team ended up doing, in actuality, was to create a quasi-kinescope film. Their program of April 11 was microwaved to KTLA, where a 35 mm camera recorded it off a ten-inch picture tube. The 35mm film was then reduced to 16mm. It is possible such a complicated process was used because of difficulties with the American Federation of Musicians and their stand on recording members' television performances.

Beginning of the End

As promising as things may initially have looked, the Texas Rangers and KTTV soon came to a parting of the ways. It's not clear exactly when the Rangers' show on KTTV left the air, but it had occurred by the beginning of May, 1949. It's also not clear what became of Gordon's efforts to interest CBS in a Rangers program based on the half-hour kinescoped audition film. Considering he was actively meeting with NBC TV and AM radio staff by the middle of May, however, it seems likely that a deal with CBS had already proven to be a dead end.

Gordon's meetings in early May with NBC Television Program Manager Bob Brown and AM Program Director Homer Canfield were discouraging. Brown informed him that NBC had already committed to the *Tex Williams Show* and was expending considerable effort to get it sold to a sponsor. The Texas Rangers were an entirely different type of program, Gordon protested, and had proven very popular on KTTV. The only drawback, Gordon explained, and the primary reason they had dropped their KTTV spot, was that without an AM broadcast to complement the television broadcast, the project had not proven to be worth the expense and work. Despite Gordon's arguments, Brown demurred and insisted he did not have the budget for another western. However, if the Rangers could get interest from his counterpart Canfield in an AM program, then he would reconsider and entertain the idea of a simultaneous broadcast.

Unfortunately, meetings with Homer Canfield were no more fruitful. While waiting to see Canfield, Gordon overheard an audition that had been recorded only the night before, featuring Andy Devine, Bob Nolan, and the Sons of the Pioneers. Even though the recording was a variety show format and different from the Rangers' songs and banter pattern, his heart sank. Gordon suspected his timing was wretched, a suspicion confirmed during his conversation with Canfield who revealed that he just finished auditioning two western-themed programs, the *Andy Devine Show* and one featuring Tex Williams, the latter likely connected to Williams' television show. Both had already been approved by NBC executives in New York, and Canfield had no money to invest in yet another western show. While it was possible either Devine or Williams would ultimately be rejected by NBC, which would give the Rangers an opening, Gordon did not hold out much hope for such a development.

Gordon had slim hopes that the other major network, ABC, might offer an opportunity. By July, 1949, it seemed his only hope was now to eat a little crow and return to Hal Hudson at KTTV to see if a new deal could be arranged with them. Fate intervened to make the reconciliation process a bit less humbling. On July 6, Arthur Church was informed that Hudson, the Rangers' primary contact at KTTV, had left the station for a position under Harry Ackerman at CBS TV. Fortunately, the reasons for the Rangers' leaving the station in May were of no consequence to his replacement, Bob Forward, KTTV's new program director. Forward was immediately interested in having the Texas Rangers back on the Los Angeles airwaves and even offered the group what he considered a plum spot, Saturday evenings from 7:00 to 7:30, right before Bozo the Clown's live broadcast. Bozo was a successful show for the station and could be expected to draw a healthy audience to the Rangers' lead-in spot. Without a sponsor, compensation would continue to be scale, but it would get the group back on the air and receiving public exposure. Gordon was further encouraged when Ginny Jackson again agreed to sing with the band.

The next week, while following up on his earlier communications with Church, Gordon was dismayed to find that his boss was nixing the new KTTV arrangement. Church bluntly advised Gordon that it was probably best at that time to shelve any discussions of future television opportunities. The future of the Texas Rangers, shaky at best for the last two years despite some brief high points, was up in the air, and it did not seem prudent to expend any more time or resources pursuing a TV deal. Church brought himself to utter what many associated with the Texas Rangers had probably realized by this time but kept to themselves: Maybe it was time to disband the group for good.

Chapter 10: Fade Away

Dismissals

During the summer of 1949, Arthur Church, John Gordon, and even the members of the Texas Rangers, themselves, recognized that efforts to make the group at least self-sustaining had not been successful despite hard work from everyone. The opportunities for wider success that television promised had been thoroughly explored over the last eighteen months but had fizzled.

Hitting the road, which, alongside radio, had been the original outlet for the group, was not looking like a viable alternative. A tour in June 1949, organized as the Rangers prepared to leave California to resettle in Kansas City, represented the last tour of the full eight-man line-up Texas Rangers. The short two-week tour bounced back and forth between Missouri and Kansas:

June 5 – Star Theater, Warrensburg, MO
June 7 – Plaza Theater, Trenton, MO
June 8 – Macon Theater, Macon, MO
June 9 – Granada Theater, Lawrence, KS
June 10 – Wareham Theater, Manhattan, KS
June 11 – *Brush Creek Follies*
June 12 – Lee Theater, Harrisonville, MO
June 13 – Lee Theater, Clinton, MO
June 14 – Arcada Theater, Holton, KS
June 15 – Davis Theater, Higginsville, MO
June 16 – Auditorium, St. Joseph, MO
June 17 – City Auditorium, McPherson, KS
June 18 – *Brush Creek Follies*

In a lengthy letter written June 21, 1949, Gordon outlined some possible performing venues for the band. They had picked up some short-term gigs, such as one at Los Angeles' Zephyr Cocktail Lounge where patrons could find lunch for $0.85 or dinner for $1.25, and where the group's one-night stand found them billed just above the

Lounge's regular "Lady of Melody" Jane Jones. Such gigs would not even come close to paying for the band's expenses, but Gordon continued to plug away on the Rangers' behalf, trying to make something out of very little. A man named Joe Daniels had put Gordon in touch with Spokane-based businessman Denny Spellacy, business manager of the Spokane Indians minor league baseball club, with the thought that Spokane might have immediate openings for live bookings. Daniels also offered to book the group into a Vancouver venue called The Cave with a seating capacity of 800. The club was currently hosting the Delta Rhythm Boys, to be followed by *The Great Gildersleeve* actress Lillian "Birdie" Randolph, who was scheduled for a week with an option for a second week. Come July, said Daniels, there might be room to book the Rangers for a limited engagement.

A few gigs on the horizon, however, could not disguise the fact that the Rangers were hemorrhaging money. One cost-cutting measure under consideration by Church was downsizing the band from eight-pieces to five, with the possible addition of singer Ginny Jackson as an unofficial sixth member. Promoter response was positive to such a consideration. It would allow for appearances in a wider array of venues and a five-person group pulling in $1,000 per week could prove profitable, whereas such a sum was not sufficient for an octet. Going to a smaller lineup was even more attractive when factoring in Jackson, who would not only improve audience draw, but pull in another $250 compensation. Gordon knew Jackson was not fond of touring, but he was hopeful that if the Rangers could get an extended series of bookings in a single area, she might be more open to their offer.

On July 19, 1949, after considering all the information Gordon and others had provided, Arthur Church weighed in with a six-point memo in which he summed up the dim future for the Rangers as they currently, and traditionally, operated. First and foremost, and Church was chillingly clear on this, the Texas Rangers must become self-sustaining, or very close to it. Since the band members were already settled in Hollywood, Church's preference was to find sufficient radio and television engagements there to produce satisfactory revenue. He could not, however, continue to subsidize them in California were they to continue to produce the small amount of income they were currently generating. While he understood the members were not

The Texas Rangers back on *Brush Creek Follies* ca. 1949.
Courtesy of Ed Crawford.

excited about the prospects of heading back out on the road, with their families and homes in Los Angeles, it would be a necessity if no further, or more lucrative, bookings were found beyond their current run at the Zephyr Room in Chapman Park, which ended August 2.

Church told Gordon that he was cool to the idea of expending too much energy in negotiations with Jim McConnell, a regional booker of fairs, though he did not dismiss the idea entirely. Still, the fees had to warrant keeping the Rangers together. Similarly, he was not interested in pushing for television deals, especially on unsponsored programs, if the band's income would not allow for them to permanently remain on the coast. Television alone would not pay the bills, and other chances for employment in the Los Angles area seemed to be drying up. KTTV, which had continued to express interest in bringing them back to the station, would have to be put on hold indefinitely. So, too, would their work on acquiring a network radio show based out of L.A. Gordon had been working hard for a deal on KFWB radio with Harry Maizlish that would give the band a daily program. Church did not see how the spot would provide appropriate payment and would additionally cause problems in getting the boys out of town to tour. One gig or the other, or even both, would likely not be sufficient and, by tying the group down in the area, would prevent exploration of other more lucrative avenues.

Downsizing

After a hard look at finances, Church and Gordon were forced to conclude that such a large ensemble could no longer be supported; the Rangers' long history as a singing quartet backed by four instrumentalists, sadly, had to come to an end. In Gordon's opinion, there was no feasible future in live performances if they continued with eight men; the money earned simply would never cover the expenses of so many musicians. The favored option of both Church and Gordon was to keep Bob Crawford as the master of ceremonies and baritone for a reconfigured trio, which would also include Edwin Johnson and Mert Painter, two of the four musicians. The other musicians, Ted Painter and Bill Lorentz, would be retained as well while Crawford could also pick up duties on rhythm guitar, though he would need to join the musicians union. Left out of the reconfiguration entirely would be long-time singers Fran Mahaney, Rod May, and Ed Cronenbold.

The decision was not taken lightly, but the "favored option" soon became a reality, and Mahaney, May and Cronenbold were given notice. In the end, however, May and Cronenbold had made the decision easier for Church. Both men had developed drinking problems in their years with the Rangers. One account claims that on one occasion, when both were drinking during a road trip at some point in 1949, they had, apparently and deliberately, done a considerable amount of damage with hammers to the trailer the group used to transport their equipment and instruments. Church was livid when he found out. The writing may have already been on the wall, but this may have been the final straw.

Cronenbold was devastated when he found out he was being let go. He wasted no time firing off a letter to station executives pleading for continued employment in some capacity. Feeling "let down," to say the least, after devoting nearly a decade and a half to Church, KMBC, and the Texas Rangers, he met with KMBC manager Rod Cupp, to whom he offered several suggestions which might allow him to stay in the KMBC family. These included picking the tunes for the Rangers' two daily KMBC broadcasts and serving as MC as well. Perhaps extending the band's show from a quarter-hour to a half-hour would be good, too. If given the chance, Cronenbold argued, he was sure he could sell local commercials to make the effort profitable.

Cronenbold also mentioned the possibility that he could work with fellow KMBC staffer Hiram Higsby, who produced a local show called *Lucky Corner*. Higsby had worked with the Texas Rangers during their years on *Brush Creek Follies* and apparently was open to using Cronenbold. As a third possibility, Cronenbold proposed a weekly disc jockey show with a late night one hour slot using KMBC's extensive library of transcriptions made over the years with station talent. He suggested taking requests during the first last ten minutes with a forty minute "hillbilly hit parade" in the middle. Cronenbold was also willing to perform as a solo artist on the *Brush Creek Follies* as well as on personal appearances, or to act as manager and booker for a road show of station talent.

The talent and versatility Cronenbold brought to the band were not really at issue, however. The real concern was his drinking, a problem which had been hinted at over the years but repeatedly overlooked. Cronenbold insisted that he only drank "because his time wasn't occupied," and that if he were busier it would not be an issue. His drinking was only natural, he said, "not a sickness or weakness," nor something that KMBC needed to be worried about in the future.

Cronenbold's entreaties were in vain. Effective July 22, 1949, he was released from employment by the Midland Broadcasting Company. His termination letter recognized his 15 ½ years of service to the company, interrupted only by a stint with the armed forces during World War II from November 12, 1942, until February 1, 1946. It confirmed that he worked primarily as a singer with the Midwesterners quartet, which was later subsumed into the eight-man Texas Rangers. His singing, both a capella and with accompaniment, had extended to transcription records, radio broadcasts, personal appearances, film, commercial records, and television. It did not end as Cronenbold had envisioned, but his career with KMBC, which took him from Kansas City to Chicago and finally California, was one in duration and achievement that few of his performing peers could match.

That same day Samuel R. May, who had performed as Rod "Dave" May for so many years, received via certified mail his official termination notice from KMBC. His official term in the station's employ was 14 ½ years, one less than Cronenbold, but the unofficial primary reason for dismissal was the same as his long time singing buddy: excessive drinking. Joining the Midwesterners in June of 1931, he also asked for leave to join the armed forces, a request which was granted November 4, 1942. He worked the same 3 ½ year post-war stint that Cronenbold did before being fired as of July 22, 1949.

Surviving KMBC/Midland Broadcasting correspondence is mum about the details of Fran Mahaney's departure. The group's star tenor since he replaced Duane Swalley in 1935, Mahaney seems to have been as unceremoniously dismissed as were Cronenbold and May. Without the underlying alcohol problems as a contributing factor, he appears simply to have been collateral damage in Church's decision to downsize the Texas Rangers, which now consisted of founding member Bob Crawford and the much newer musical quartet of Ed Johnson, Bill Lorentz, and the Painter brothers, Mert and Ted.

On July 25, Gordon checked in with Church and admitted that after the Zephyr Room booking ended on August 1st, he did not see any way the band could earn enough to break even. The offers were simply not coming in. Joe Daniels, on whom he had laid considerable hope of a tour of the Northwest, never came through. Aggravating the situation was the decision by Local 47 in Los Angeles to raise the required per diem for its traveling members to $9.50 per day, $1 for breakfast, $1.50 for lunch, $2.00 for dinner, and $5.00 for room. Added to their weekly salary of $85, the $66.50 necessary for daily room and board brought the total road coasts for the five men to just over $750 per week, not counting any other incidental touring costs. The only opening that might open up was the fair circuit, if Jim McConnell could arrange it, and the compensation offered by McConnell of $1,250 per week would make a small sum for Midland Broadcasting.

The Mayfair Transcription Negotiations

A handful of offers trickled in while Church debated the future of the Texas Rangers. In August he was approached by the Mayfair Transcription company, which was interested in making an open-ended transcription series pairing the Rangers with Pappy Cheshire. Pappy was a one-time radio staple in the Midwest, based out of St. Louis, who had successfully relocated to the West Coast a few years previous. It was a proposition Mayfair's Bob Reichenbach had mentioned numerous times to Gordon as well as some other KMBC salesmen. Reichenbach wanted to take Texas Rangers transcription tracks, of which the station had hundreds in its library, and piece them together into a program interspersed with patter between Cheshire and the band members. No new musical performances would be required, which hopefully would save hassles with the musicians' union. Only spoken lines were necessary to create the between-song banter. Reichenbach noted that the Sons of the Pioneers had done just such a show via dubbing and had experienced no problems with the union. At this point, what did Church and company have to lose? Creating at least a few audition shows would cost virtually nothing and could be done with the four musicians currently on staff. He did not need to hurry and find a replacement for Crawford to start the project.

Gordon thought highly of Mayfair's sales team, which included six men located in New York, St. Louis, Columbus, OH, Atlanta, and two on the West Coast, who handled the entire territory west of Kansas City. The team had proven itself while selling the Alan Ladd-led syndicated radio series *Box 13*. Ladd, in fact, owned Mayfair Transcriptions, and he made every effort to ensure the 52-episode *Box 13* was of the highest quality. Similarly, Gordon held Reichenbach in high esteem, having successfully handled various western properties as the sales promotion manager for St. Louis' KMOX. He had also worked closely with Pappy Cheshire for some time on various ventures, including broadcasts at KMOX and Cheshire's *Old Corral* program produced by Ziv. His contract with Ziv was set to expire in September, and Cheshire was excited at the chance to work with the Texas Rangers.

It did not cost Church anything to at least entertain a full proposal, so he told Mayfair to go ahead and put together an in-depth presentation which would be reviewed by Arthur B. Church Productions. Mayfair reviewed the recent success of an open-ended transcription series entitled *Chuck Wagon Jamboree*, which featured Western singer and actor Ken Curtis and the vocal group the Novelty Aces, as well as the older series *Old Corral* with Cheshire and confidently predicted there was a steady market for such fare. Further, the pairing of the Texas Rangers' musical talents with that of Cheshire's "stylized" western character would result in "a most attractive and salable" fifteen-minute program. Cheshire would handle the duties of MC and story-teller. He would introduce each broadcast and the members of the Rangers. After some tunes by the group, Cheshire would tell a short three-minute story with some sort of Western theme, potentially supported by a Rangers instrumental.

To proceed, Mayfair would need any and all rights associated with the Texas Rangers, including their names and all music, to ensure the most professional production. The company saw the production as most potentially attractive to regional sponsors as opposed to a single national sponsor. Citing the example of a current client, Montag Stove Company based in Portland, OR, Mayfield's executives suggested the business might be interested in the Texas Rangers in the near future. They were currently sponsoring a program of music by The Riders of the Purple Sage and would have given more consideration to the Rangers if they'd had the freedom to manipulate the band's name to create a closer association between product and program. If Montag, which was advertising in twenty Northwestern markets, could brand the musicians, The Montag Rangers, for instance, the company could be a strong candidate for sponsorship.

The Frederic Ziv Company had sold Pappy Cheshire's series to New Orleans' Riley Coffee Co. which used the spots to advertise Louisiana Coffee. It was so successful that Louisiana Coffee was advertised in sixty Southern markets from Texas to Virginia. Cheshire appealed to a wide slice of the listening public and, most importantly, he sold goods. Riley Coffee Company might be persuaded to move their account to Mayfield if Cheshire was teamed with the Rangers, and if they had the freedom to rechristen the quintet The Southern Gentlemen or The Louisiana Rangers. Other regional sales might more readily be made if the Texas Rangers moniker was open to modification, an allowance made years before when the band sang for Kellogg as the Box K Ranch Boys.

Church's response to Mayfair's request for exclusive rights to the Rangers' name and the transcription library is unknown. That no reply exists among surviving documentation may indicate he very likely did not think highly of the idea. This would not be surprising since Church was very proud of the reputation the Texas Rangers had built over the years and was very careful to protect it. Allowing them to be marketed under other names would almost certainly have made him bristle. Church expressed little or no interest in breaking up KMBC's creative properties, which he felt were too valuable to parcel out for an easy dollar, as when Kellogg had wanted to use the band in a series of short commercials. Further, giving such exclusive rights would surely have limited any further projects with which he might engage the Texas Rangers, even if no such projects were on the horizon.

The Final Lineup

The Texas Rangers entered the 1950s as a quintet. This final incarnation of the band would have been unrecognizable to any fans who remembered their debut in 1932; not a single original performer remained. At some point during the fall of 1949, Bob Crawford finally decided he could not see himself going on at KMBC without his close friends, Cronenbold and May, who had been fired months earlier. The three had been performing together for half their lives, since college days, and there seemed no alternative to Crawford other than to make a clean break with Church and KMBC. Church understood, though Crawford's decision torpedoed his plans to build the new smaller group around him. Instead, Crawford struck out on his own to start a new phase of his career apart from the Texas Rangers.

Thus, the membership was now entirely composed of musicians who had been added since 1946. Eddie Johnson, who, having joined the Rangers when they reformed in early 1946, was now the member of longest standing, played bass. Two others, with one to two years of experience with the Rangers, were Ted Painter on guitar and banjo, who had replaced Herb Kratoska in 1948, and accordion player Bill Lorentz, who joined the group in the second half of 1947. The two newest recruits were Val Tatham and Ray Hudgens. Tatham, on the fiddle, replaced Ted Painter's brother Mert as "Tucson" and Hudgens, referred to as "Captain Ray," took Crawford's place as the Rangers' front man singing lead and playing rhythm guitar. Tatham and Hudgens had been long-time members of the Rhythm Riders, a KMBC musical group formed during the war years. Despite the changes, the Texas Rangers remained popular with Kansas City area audiences and the group had no problem landing local sponsorship. BC Remedy Powder paid for their time on Mondays, Wednesdays, and Fridays at 7:00 a.m. while Hy-Power Chili and Meatballs sponsored them on Tuesdays, Thursdays, and Saturdays at 7:00 a.m. In the early evenings Grennan Cakes sponsored them every weekday at 5:00, while Taystee Bread sponsored the group thirty minutes later at 5:30 p.m. on *Western Echoes*.

Defending the Texas Rangers Brand

In 1950, with the group now firmly reestablished as a strictly regional presence on KMBC, Church spent as much energy defending the Texas Rangers name as he did working on new projects for his musical franchise. In April, Donald Davis, president of Kansas City station WHB informed Church that NBC was planning a new program starring Joel McCrea to be titled *The Texas Rangers*. Never one to overlook a perceived commercial threat to his properties, Church was buoyed by a federal court case in Ohio, which had earlier upheld their claim to the Texas Rangers title against a traveling circus which billed an act as the Texas Rangers. He immediately entered into discussions with NBC which, in short order, agreed that the network would come up with a new title which would "result in no conflict."

For a few weeks in May and June the new working title became *Pearson, Texas Ranger*, and Church was assured that the network had agreed not to use another proposed name, *Tales of the Texas Rangers*. Therefore, Church and associates must have been surprised when the series premiered July 8, 1950, as *Tales of the Texas Rangers*. Soon after, Church informed NBC that he planned to begin legal proceedings to force changes.

Not everyone agreed with Church's zeal. Long-time associate George Halley attempted to reassure him that the series could not reasonably be mistaken for the KMBC franchise. According to Halley, the show was "just another 'Gangbusters' with the Texas Rangers being used instead of FBI or local police. There was no singing or anything even remotely competitive with our show. The show was well done but exactly like the rest of that type." Halley conceded, however, that the *Kansas City Star* newspaper listed the show as *Texas Rangers*. Whether Church decided to let the matter lie or whether he could not find traction in court, NBC did not alter the show's name and *Tales of the Texas Rangers* ran for just over two years.

Even small infringements did not escape the notice of Church and his associates. In August 1950, Karl Koerper sent Church a clipping from *Country Song Round-Up* which profiled well-known Dallas-based singer and western bandleader Bill Boyd. By this time Boyd had been a regular on WRR for two decades, had been recording for RCA Victor and its subsidiaries since 1934, and had appeared in a number of B-westerns in the early '40s. The blurb identified Boyd's backing band as the Texas Rangers. Whether this was an error, a one-off or something else is not clear, but Boyd had called his band the Cowboy Ramblers since the first half of the 1930s. Though Church's response to this perceived infringement does not survive, there is little doubt Boyd was promptly informed of the "problems" with using the Texas Rangers name.

Later that year in August, Church was apprised by a letter from the Free & Peters, Inc. television agency that a program under development would not use the title *Steve Donovan – Texas Ranger* per Midland Broadcasting's request. General Artists Corporation, the company behind the series, had no interest in the "legal complications which would inevitably arise out of its use." It appears that General Artists had potential sponsors lined up with Tasty Bread and Marigold Butter and did not want to lose momentum. Church was assured that Free & Peters would disassociate itself from the production if the Texas Ranger moniker was used in any way with the program. The television series eventually hit the airwaves a few years later as *Steve Donovan, Western Marshall*.

Apart from policing possible trademark infringements, Church and his staff also put some effort into reviving the Rangers' vast transcription library. In May, two of the very few stations still airing the Rangers, WARM in Scranton and WBRE in Wilkes Barre, both in Pennsylvania, canceled their subscriptions to the transcription service. An ad man at the Leo Burnett Company, which had been working with Arthur B. Church Productions on selling the Texas Rangers, admitted that they had no further prospects, but offered his assurance that "the name of the 'Texas Rangers' will remain quite firmly implanted in my mind." This assurance was likely of little consolation to Church, Halley, and others who were watching the final trickle of revenue dry up from the transcription service. In one final burst of activity George Halley took it upon himself to attempt to convince Arthur Church to approve the development of a Texas Rangers film library, a goal John Gordon had failed to achieve during 1948-49. In October, 1950, Halley received a detailed letter from Miller Robertson, vice-president in charge of sales at KSTP AM-TV-FM in St. Paul-Minneapolis, MN. He was of the opinion that Church's best option at that point was to create a film library which could be used by television stations much as his transcription library had been used by dozens of radio stations for nearly a decade.

Robertson did not see much promise with the networks but insisted that individual stations would likely find value in such a service, as they frequently had short spots of airtime to fill. With so many sixty second ad buyers, television stations were having trouble acquiring "disc jockey material" around which they could build broadcasts for small, local sponsors. Unlike the Rangers' audio transcription service, which was just one of many such radio libraries, a video version would have far fewer competitors. One such competitor, Ike Leavy out of Philadelphia, had a library of over 1,000 3/12 minute films, but broadcast executives found fault with them, including "astronomical" pricing, uneven quality, and a number of individual films, such as those with singers and dancers dressed inappropriately, considered unfit for the television market.

Another, Louis Snader Telescriptions, produced musical shorts more palatable to station tastes and had a formula which Church might emulate to his advantage. Cost, Robertson admitted, was the big hang-up. Any viable film series had to be cheap enough to allow stations to use it profitably. KSTP was not going to use such productions as mere filler or some sort of loss-leader, nor were many other stations likely to do so, either. In addition to the price of the films, stations had to keep in mind the cost of an MC which would still be necessary to host a program built around the musical shorts. There would be additional incidental production costs as well.

Robertson was convinced the idea had merit and could turn a nice profit if smartly produced. Church was also advised that if he went forward with the films, they had to include action of some sort, be it square dancing, lively performing by the band, or even interviews with the performers. It was imperative that the pieces not be Texas Rangers music set against a single, still picture.

It is difficult to ascertain the extent to which Arthur Church concerned himself with these television development explorations. George Halley seems to have sent and received most of the surviving documents pertaining to the subject. In October, 1950, Halley received a lengthy outline of the nuts-and-bolts costs of creating a film library. Although he sought cost projections for a six-film order, perhaps with the idea of using it to gauge interest in a larger order, the details for a 65-film purchase and a 260-film purchase were more realistic for pursuing a profitable business venture.

Basore Longmoor Studio's Clarence Gerber indicated that 65 films would run $29,500, or $450 per 3 ½ minute film and 260 films would cost $110,500, or $425 per 3 ½ minute film. These figures must have been mind-boggling for Halley and Church. Their biggest gamble had been *Phenomenon*, the cost of which was not too much less than that proposed for 65 Texas Rangers music films, but just a fraction of the cost of 260 films, and it was difficult for either of them to convincingly argue that *Phenomenon* had paid off.

The Longmoor proposal stipulated that all filming would be done on 16mm Kodachrome commercial stock, and Arthur B. Church Productions would receive one print of each film. The studio provided the necessary cameramen, assistants, gaffers, sound engineer, and editors. They also supplied all the required equipment, from lights, cables, and meters, to microphones and amplifiers. Further, Longmoor offered a sound stage which could be used for filming and synchronous sound recording. Any montage sequences beyond what would be included in the base proposal would run fifty cents per foot of film with a minimum of $250 required. Church's only responsibility was to supply the talent, along with a liaison and any desired directions and sets.

Rod Cupp weighed in on the renewed conversations about entering the realm of television. He felt the idea of a syndicated series of films had merit and strongly urged the consideration of a six-film package, which would cost $2,900 through Basore Longmoor Studio that could be shopped to prospective stations. With enough interest, Church could feel safer investing in a larger library. Cupp outlined a five-minute film broken down as follows:

Commercial announcement	1:00
The Texas Rangers	2:45
Station Identification	:15
Commercial announcement	1:00

The Rangers' portion could consist of a song, a medley of songs, or an action sequence.

In contrast to Halley's enthusiasm for a larger project, Cupp was not unduly optimistic. He encouraged investing in a short run for two primary reasons, both prudent. First and foremost came earning a worthwhile profit from the cost of a larger library; next came the accompanying uncertainty of recouping that cost. Second, but nearly as important to Cupp, was the lack of experience by production companies at making such film libraries. The field was brand new and everyone, not just KMBC's staff, was still learning how best to create quality television entertainment. He felt it was just as important to build experience in the medium among the Kansas City personnel as it was to watch cash outlays.

In November, Church asked Halley to collect and summarize all the information gathered about the Texas Rangers' TV prospects so he could make a final decision. The requested report was submitted on November 15, 1950. Halley's presentation reviewed the numerous inquiries that had come to KMBC about Texas Rangers television material and reminded Church of the notable enthusiasm Miller Robertson had expressed in a film library. Members of the KMBC Program and Continuity Departments created proposals for a Texas Rangers production, as well as a series of films featuring a magician, Claude Enslow, and another KMBC musical outfit, Harry Jenks and the Tune Chasers. Halley also included the detailed costs provided by the Basore Longmoor Studios. In the end, however, as much as Halley supported the project, he admitted one major question remained, both for himself and John Gordon, still a solid backer of a television project: "Will TV stations react like radio stations have done in the matter of a library type program" or "will the station be too lazy to put the show together?"

Church, a radio visionary who could never reconcile himself to the higher costs and risks of television, had the same reservations as Halley and Gordon and ultimately answered "no" to Halley's question. After reviewing the reports from Cupp and Halley, he dictated a short letter which essentially put the matter to rest. It is also one of the last known statements he made concerning his beloved Texas Rangers. On December 20, 1950, he wrote, "I don't see any possibility of my working on this soon – physically impossible, and financially, too, I'm afraid ... Our stock in trade for a long time will be our present transcriptions as you know."

Riding Into the Sunset

On that note, the future of the Texas Rangers, which arguably may have been invigorated by a concerted move into television, was decided. The group would play out the rest of its existence on radio and on stage and not make the transition to the visual medium for a major syndicated series. The final years of the Texas Rangers were quiet ones. There were no further films, no coast-to-coast radio or television series with big-name entertainers, just local Kansas City radio and television and regional live appearances. In 1952, the band's 20th anniversary went unobserved by everyone connected with the Texas Rangers. Perhaps Herb Kratoska, one of the first Rangers and the only member of the classic line-up still on the KMBC payroll, or Bob Crawford, forging a solo career on radio and television in Texas, spent a moment or two reflecting on the amazing longevity of a hillbilly act put together to fill some air time in the depths of the Great Depression.

That year, Church and Halley briefly looked into the feasibility of transferring the Texas Rangers' vast transcription library to tape, a recording medium growing quickly in popularity throughout the industry. The two were especially interested in the ability to do high-speed dubbing of multiple copies at a time. Recognizing that the

American Federation of Musicians had regulations regarding tape dubbing, Church proposed utilizing Frank Lott, a man who was close to AFM president Jim Petrillo and very knowledgeable about Midland Broadcasting. He was confident a deal could be worked out with the union to go forward with the idea. Not only could it add new income for Church Productions, but it would allow them to dispose of the hundreds of transcriptions which were becoming a storage problem as the company looked to minimize office space. If the dubbing was done, no evidence of the project has been discovered either in written or recorded form.

In February or March, 1953, the Texas Rangers and other KMBC staff met with Missouri Governor Phil M. Donnelly. That same year, the group made its final recordings, the only known recordings made by the smaller, post-Bob Crawford group. Recording in Kansas City for MGM, the label with whom the old Rangers had made their final recordings in 1949, the group backed singer Bobby Lee, a recent arrival to KMBC from Coffeyville, Kansas. Accordionist Bill Lorenz recalled the Rangers playing over television's channel 9 in Kansas City and performing at state and county fairs in Missouri. This was likely in 1954, since Church and his staff were at the time, again, discussing the logistics of getting the Rangers on the small screen. The biggest obstacle was getting the American Federation of Musicians' approval, which seemed likely to happen, since the group would be acting within the range of its normal staff duties.

Due to health issues, in 1953 Arthur Church began to consider selling his beloved KMBC, the station he had spent nearly thirty years building. He had given his life to radio and now it was time to move on to other ventures. The sale to Cook Paint and Varnish Co. was announced on April 20, 1954, and finalized on June 9. With the change of ownership, the talent pool Church had so painstakingly assembled and nurtured over many years was dispersed. Some were retained by the new owners, but others were forced to pursue other opportunities. Kratoska stayed on staff with the Tune Chasers until 1955 when he became a full-time teacher. The fate of the Texas Rangers is less clear, but Bill Lorenz told historian Glenn White that the band remained together to the end of the 1950s.

The 1950s were tough for radio, and the industry would sound fundamentally different at the end of the decade than when it began.

Radio drama and A-list comedians still dominated the broadcasting hours, but that would soon change as television set ownership soared from less than 200,000 in 1948 to over 32 million in 1955 when revenue reached more than $370 million. Bob Hope and Jack Benny, radio icons, entered television in 1949 and 1950, respectively, though they continued simultaneously on radio for a time. Edgar Bergen and his wooden companion Charlie McCarthy left the air in 1956, the same year as *Fibber McGee & Molly*, all radio stalwarts.

Radio stations increasingly found the expense of keeping musicians on staff too onerous, so there was less live music with every passing year, though it was not for lack of effort. In the mid-1950s the networks debuted at least 59 musical programs, none of which survived for a second year. Even the king of the singing cowboys, Gene Autry, was canceled in 1956. If he could not continue on radio as a live feature, then what other Western artists could? Somewhere during this period, when live music on radio was becoming rarer and rarer, the Texas Rangers, like countless other performers who graced the airwaves during radio's early years, disappeared from the air without fanfare or pomp, even less auspiciously than they debuted way back on November 1, 1932. Live bookings, too, finally dried up, and one day the Texas Rangers quietly dispersed.

Afterward

* The man responsible for creating the Texas Rangers, Arthur Church (b. August 5, 1896), sold his radio businesses in 1954, as outlined earlier, and left his long-time home in Missouri. The rest of his years were spent in Colorado where he continued to be very active in his community but never again worked professionally in radio. Church passed away September 22, 1978.

* Wartime Ranger Archie Berdahl (b. November 9, 1910) died at 70 in June, 1981.

* After leaving the Texas Rangers and Midland Broadcasting Company in 1942, Gomer Cool (b. April 20, 1908) went to work as a writer for CBS. In 1947 he wrote some episodes of *Hawk Larabee*, a series on which his former band, the Texas Rangers, provided music for a few weeks. Cool's most notable writing assignment was the series *Rocky Jordan*, which he wrote from 1948 to 1950. He is also credited with penning a 1952 series *Armchair Adventures* and, the

same year, an episode of *The Whistler*. While still involved in radio, Cool was elected president of the Radio Writers Guild and, in 1956, second vice-president of the Writers Guild of America, West. He was an active writer through the 1950s. He also wrote, produced, and directed for television. Upon retiring, Gomer and his wife Margaret moved to Santa Barbara and opened a candy store called Cool's Candies. This new career, a dramatic change from that of Los Angeles writer, lasted fifteen years. Cool who claimed he never picked up his violin again after leaving the Rangers, except shortly afterward for a handful of gigs with Spade Cooley, passed away during the writing of this book at his home in California on March 4, 2012. At 103, he was the last known living member of the Texas Rangers.

*"Captain" Bob Crawford (b. May 13, 1910) stayed active in radio after his departure from KMBC, going first to WBAP in Fort Worth, TX. There he put together a band called the Southwesterners which were briefly billed as the Texas Rangers, to the chagrin of Arthur Church. Crawford also worked briefly at a small station in Nebraska. The job was not satisfying, and Bob and his wife soon returned to Ft. Worth. The talented and adaptable Crawford taught himself bass and formed a club trio, playing for many years in the Fort Worth area. One December night in 1986 he was murdered during a robbery attempt. No one was ever charged for his death.

Bob Crawford Publicity Still.
Courtesy of Jim Crawford.

* Nothing is known of Edward Cronenbold's (b. September 15, 1909) activities after he was dismissed from the Rangers in 1949. He died outside of Kansas City on December 20, 1981, at the age of 72.

* Blackface character "Cookie" in the Rangers early years, George Herman "Eddie" Edwards (b. November 28, 1908) died at 72 in July 1981.

* "Alabam" Marion Fonville (b. August 7, 1889), one of the most important figures in the Rangers' formative years (1932-35) died at 74 in California on July 21, 1964.

* The death of wartime replacement Kenneth Harpster (b. July 26, 1907) was the earliest known among former Texas Rangers. He was 46 or 47, there are discrepancies surrounding the year of his birth, when he died on August 15, 1954.

* Clarence Hartman (b. September 24, 1890) remained in California after leaving the Rangers and KMBC following the end of the group's run on the Camel Caravan in 1944. After the war, he worked at times and recorded alongside fellow ex-Ranger Paul Sells, in Gene Autry's organization until at least 1950. He died at 78 on February 18, 1969.

* Karl (or Carl) Hays. Little is known about the Rangers' original bassist, including his birth and death dates.

* Bob Crawford's replacement as the Rangers' Captain, Ray Hudgens (b. 1914), appears to have died in 1975, aged 61.

* The band's postwar bassist Eddie Johnson (b. 1910) died at 56 in 1966.

* Herbie (Herbert) Kratoska (b. January 16, 1913) was 62 when he died in Kansas City in February, 1975. After leaving the Rangers in 1948, he continued to work at KMBC as a staff musician before leaving to teach guitar full time in 1955.

* A fiddler in the band's early days and then again during the war, Sam Leichter (b. November 3, 1902) remained in California after leaving KMBC's employ. He worked with Spade Cooley, Tex Williams, and others after the war. He lived to age 95, dying on April 22, 1998.

* After the Rangers dissolved, the group's final accordionist Bill Lorentz (b. 1917) eventually moved to Mountain Home, Arkansas, where he remained musically active into the 1990s. He died at 83 in 2000.

* Briefly, the band's bassist before the Massey Family left Kansas City for Chicago, Milt Mabie (b. June 27, 1900), Louise Massey's husband, retired with his wife to New Mexico in the mid-1940s. He died at 73 on October 1, 1973.

* Little is known of Fran Mahaney's (b. March 5, 1914) life after he left the Rangers in 1949. He subsequently moved to Louisiana, where he died at 76, the last of the classic vocal quartet of the 1930s-40s, on May 14, 1990.

* Little is known about early postwar accordionist Joe Manning, including his birth and death dates and his activities beyond the Rangers.

* Rangers for a brief time before heading to Chicago, and national fame, in 1933, brothers Allen Massey (b. December 12, 1907) and Dott "Curt" Massey (b. May 3, 1910) died in California on March 3, 1983 and October 20, 1991, respectively.

* Nothing is known of Rod May's (b. October 1, 1909) life after he was let go by Arthur Church in 1949. The earliest of the classic Rangers line-up to pass away, he died on August 9, 1956, aged only 46.

* Doie Hensley "Tex" Owens (b. June 15, 1892) died in his native Texas on September 9, 1962, aged 70.

* The younger of the Painter brothers, Cyril Eugene "Ted" Painter (b. November 7, 1915) died in 1970 at 54. Looking back on a musician's career, Painter once mused, "there's really no great future in music unless you are on top and that only lasts for a short time."[1]

* Emert Painter (b. September 22, 1913) was 63 when he died in California on May 19, 1977.

* Like fellow Texas Ranger Gomer Cool, Paul Sells (b. January 20, 1907) stayed in California after parting with the band. He worked with Gene Autry's organization from 1940 until at least 1950 and was very active as a musician and arranger thereafter. He died at 63 on October 21, 1970.

*Paul Sell's replacement as accordionist and arranger, active with the Rangers from 1940-43, the Swede, Joe Strand (b. March 26, 1902) died in California at 80 on October 2, 1982.

* Briefly, a Ranger in early 1946 before the return of Fran Mahaney, Don Sullivan (b. July 5, 1917) had a career in country

---

1 1 *The Kansas City Times*, September 15, 1967, p. 7A.

music that stretched from the 1930s into the new millennium. He died at 88 on February 12, 2006.

* Original vocal quartet member Duane Swalley (b. December 5, 1910) left KMBC and followed his wife to Chicago where he worked for a number of years as a staff musician at WLS. He lived there until 1962 when he moved to Phoenix, AZ because of his very poor health. Swalley died on May 7, 1963, of a self-inflicted gunshot wound at the age of 53.

* A part of the Rangers broadcasts during 1933, "Colorado Ranger" Ozie Waters (b. December 8, 1903) went on to a long career in country music, including a number of appearance in 1940s B-westerns. He died at 74 on March 10, 1978.

* Arthur Wenzel (b. May 5, 1907), the Rangers accordionist in 1947 between Joe Manning and Bill Lorentz, had a long career that stretched from the late 1920s through the 1950s. He was only 53 when he died on February 10, 1961.

* Ralph E. "Joe" Wolverton (b. July 8, 1906), Herb Kratoska's replacement, who gave his two-weeks' notice the day he joined the band in 1942, enjoyed a long career as a respected multi-instrumentalist. Best known for mentoring future musical legend Les Paul, he died at 88 on August 27, 1994.

Appendix A: The Texas Rangers Recording Sessions, 1934-1953

This compilation includes all commercial recordings for Decca, Okeh, Bibletone, and MGM, as well as transcribed 16-inch disc sessions for World Broadcasting System. Not included are any live airchecks, program audition recordings, or dramatic radio series. Details on *Life on the Red Horse Ranch* may be found elsewhere.

Generally, with a large portion of the recordings listed below unavailable at the time for audition, we have made little attempt to identify vocal features unless that information has been given on surviving discs or in other extant paperwork. Nor have we always been able to note those recordings that are a capella or that feature all eight members of the group on vocals. Instrument listings are also generally not specific to a performance. That is, we have made no broad attempt, for example, to identify which recordings feature Herb Kratoska on banjo rather than guitar. Composer is listed in parentheses.

August 27, 1934. Decca Studios, Furniture Mart, Chicago, Illinois. Marion "Alabam" Fonville, leader/speech; Robert "Bob" Crawford, Edward "Tucson" Cronenbold, Roderick "Dave" May, Duane Swalley, vocal quartet; Doie "Tex" Owens, guitar/vocal; Gomer "Tenderfoot" Cool, fiddle; Herb "Arizona" Kratoska, guitar/banjo; Paul "Monty" Sells, accordion; Clarence "Idaho" Hartman, bass/jug. All band members take part in spoken interludes.

C-9353 Dude Ranch Party – Part I   Decca 5022
C-9354 Dude Ranch Party – Part II   "   "   "   "

April 5, 1935. Chicago, Illinois. World Broadcasting Studio. As above, except omit Marion Fonville.

C-2244 Lay Down Dogies (Cowboy's Night Song) World
        Prairie Dream Boat (Osborne-Sanford)
        We're All Goin' Down To Santa Fe Town (Massey)
        Let The Rest Of The World Go By (Ball-Brennan)

C-2245 Cattle Call (Owens) (featuring Tex Owens)
Press Along To The Big Corral
Bury Me Not On The Lone Prairie
Texas Cowboy (Maniloff) (featuring Bob Crawford)
C-2246 I'm Popeye The Sailor Man (Sammy Lerner)
(featuring Herb "Arizona" Kratoska)
Lonesome Valley Sally (Kennedy-Sanford-McConnell)
(featuring Roderick "Dave" May, tenor; Robert
"Bob" Crawford, baritone)
They Cut Down The Old Pine Tree (Raskin-Brown-Eliscu)
New River Train

NOTE: Evidence indicates that the above session occurred after the Rangers finished waxing the final show (number 26) of the first recording sessions for the series *Life on the Red Horse Ranch* on April 5, 1935, but the exact date is not definitely confirmed.

April 6, 1935. Chicago, Illinois.

Details as above. Decca Studios, Furniture Mart, Chicago.

C-9896-B Goin' Down To Santa Fe Town (Massey) Decca 5107
C-9897-B Prairie Dream-Boat (Osborne-Sanford) Decca 5107
C-9898-A Careless Love Decca 5139
C-9899-A Let The Rest Of The World Go By Decca 5217
          (Ball-Brennan)
C-9900-A New River Train Decca 5139
C-9901-A Lonesome Valley Sally Decca 5217
          (Kennedy-Sanford-McConnell)
C-9902-A The Big Corral Decca 5183
C-9903-A The Trail To Mexico Decca 5183

April 6, 1935. Chicago, Illinois. As the HAPPY HOLLOW HOODLUMS. Gomer Cool, fiddle-1; Herb Kratoska, guitar; Paul Sells, accordion; Clarence Hartman, bass.

C-9904-A Down Home Rag-1 (Sweatman) Decca 5098
C-9905-A Panama (Tyers) " " " "

Note: During 1936, the Rangers recorded two hundred songs in Chicago for World Broadcasting System for radio play. The exact dates and many details are uncertain, since it has so far proven impossible to audition any of these recordings, which are all extant. What is known follows below.

1936. Chicago, Illinois. World Broadcasting Studio.
Bob Crawford, Edward Cronenbold, Fran Mahaney, Rod May, vocal quartet; Tex Owens, guitar/vocal; Gomer Cool, fiddle; Herb Kratoska, guitar/banjo; Paul Sells, accordion; Clarence Hartman, bass/jug. Instrumentalists almost certainly also sing on some performances and some or all of the musicians and vocalists may at times play ocarina on certain novelty tunes.

		Texas Rangers Music Catalog Number
C-3417	That Little Boy Of Mine (Meroff-King-Hirsch)	1
	When You And I Were Young (J. A. Butterfield)	2
	Good-Bye My Lover, Good-Bye	3
	Levee Song (Stephen Fay)	4
	I'll Take You Home Again Kathleen (T.P. Westendorf) (feat. Francis "Irish" Mahaney, tenor)	5
C-3420	Ride Beneath That Texas Moon	11
	By The Rushing Waterfall	12
	While The Happy Years Roll By	13
	Night Herding Lullaby	14
	My Missouri Home In The Hills (Tex Owens)	15
C-3421	Sweet Genevieve (Henry Tucker)	6
	Sylvia (Speaks)	7
	Cornfield Melodies (B. Cecil Gates)	8
	Drink To Me Only With Thine Eyes (Ben Jonson)	9
	Juanita (Norton)	10
C-3424	Stars Of The Summer Night (Heinriche)	16
	Old Mill Stream (Taylor)	17
	In The Gloaming (Harrison)	18
	Long, Long Ago (Bayly)	19
	Pale In The Amber West (J.A. Parks)	20
C-3425	Po' Lil' Lamb (J.A. Parks)	21
	End Of A Perfect Day (Bond)	22
	Standin' In The Need Of Prayer	23

	Shoutin' All Over God's Heaven	24
	Steal Away	25
C-3428	Red Roses Bring Memories Of You	26
	Cattle Call	27
	Lover's Quarrel (Tex Owens)	28
	Susan Van Duzan	29
	Dancing Sweethearts (Tex Owens)	30
C-3429	Have Thine Own Way (Stebbins	31
	Remember Me (Kinkel)	32
	Let The Lower Lights Be Burning (Bliss)	33
	(featuring Francis "Irish" Mahaney, tenor)	
	Now The Day Is Over (Barnby)	34
	(featuring Francis "Irish" Mahaney, tenor)	
	In The Garden (Miles)	35
C-3430	Faith Of Our Fathers (Hemy)	36
	(featuring Francis "Irish" Mahaney, tenor)	
	Wandering Child Come Home (Botterf)	37
	Old Rugged Cross (Bennard)	38
	No Night There (Davis)	39
	More Love To Thee (Doane)	40
C-3432	Jesus Saviour, Pilot Me (J.E. Gould)	41
	Rock Of Ages (Hastings)	42
	Shall We Meet (Rice	43
	God Will Take Care Of You (March)	44
C-3433	La Rosita (Dupont)	45
	Sharpshooters March	46
	La Golondrina (La Forge)	47
	Arpeggio (Sells)	48
C-3437	Cowboy's Last Ride (Al Crocker)	49
	(featuring Francis "Irish" Mahaney, tenor)	
	Cowboy's Heaven (Marvin-Autry)	50
	(featuring Francis "Irish" Mahaney, tenor)	
	Dear Old Western Skies (Autry)	51
	(featuring Francis "Irish" Mahaney, tenor)	
	Home On The Range (Guion)	52

C-3438	In An Old Fashioned Garden (Crocker-Sharratt)	53
	(featuring Francis "Irish" Mahaney, tenor; Robert "Bob" Crawford, baritone)	
	In That Utah Valley (Al Crocker)	54
	(featuring Roderick "Dave" May; Francis "Irish" Mahaney, tenor)	
	Little Mother Of The Hills (The Vagabonds)	55
	Empty Saddles (Billy Hill)	56
C-3439	Ride, Ride, Ride (Osborne- Sanford)	57
	(featuring Francis "Irish" Mahaney, tenor)	
	Prairie Home In Old New Mexico (Bob Crawford)	58
	(featuring Robert "Bob" Crawford, baritone)	
	Old Nevada Home (Oudeans-Livernash)	59
	Wagon Wheels (Billy Hill)	60
C-3440	My Pretty Quadroon (Howard-Vincent)	61
	(featuring Robert "Bob" Crawford, baritone; Francis "Irish" Mahaney, tenor)	
	Pals Of The Prairie	62
	(featuring Robert "Bob" Crawford, baritone)	
	White Azaleas (Bob Miller)	63
	Dogies Lullaby (Bob Crawford)	64
	(featuring Francis "Irish" Mahaney, tenor)	
	Lonesome Road	65
C-3442	Mama Don't Allow (Davenport)	66
	Craw-Dad Song	67
	I Had A Gal And Her Name Was Sue	68
	Great Grandad	69
	Sourwood Mountain	70
C-3443	Lilly Lucy Lane (Hedges)	71
	Old White's Whiskers (Butler-Box-Cox)	72
	On Account Of The Mother-In-Law (Osbourne-Sanford)	73
	Swallow Tail Coat (Bob Miller)	74
	I'm An Old Cowhand (Mercer)	75
C-3444	Twenty-one Years Ago (Hedges)	76
	Down In Arkansas (Evans)	77
	True-Blue Bill (Autry-Raney-Marvin)	78

	(featuring Herby Kratoska, yodels)	
	Go Long Mule (Creamer-King)	79
	Clementine (Sherwin-Katzman)	80
C-3445	April Kisses (Eddie Lang)	81
	Dinah (Akst)	82
	Honeysuckle Rose (Waller)	83
	Farewell Blues (Rappolo-Mares-Schoebel)	84
	Blue Guitar Stomp	85
C-3446	Sweet Prairie Rose (Miller)	86
	When It's Night Time In Nevada (Pascoe-Dulmage-Clint)	87
	When The Bloom Is On The Sage (Howard-Vincent)	88
	Prairie Dreamboat (Osborne-Sanford)	89
	Mexicali Rose (Stone-Tenney)	90
C-3447	It's Heck To Bum In Texas (Sanford-McConnell)	91
	I Wish I Was Single Again	92
	11 More Months And 10 More Days (Hall)	93
	Great Grandma	94
	Take Me Back To Colorado (Moran-Moore)	95
C-3448	Sleepy Rio Grande (Miller)	96
	Silvery Prairie Moon (Miller)	97
	Roll Along Covered Wagon (Kennedy)	98
	Dying Cowboy	99
	Yippey Ti Yio	100
C-3449	Red River Valley (Body)	101
	I Know There's Somebody Waiting (Carson Robison)	102
	Cowboy's Lament	103
	Moonlight On The Colorado (Moll-King)	104
	Roll On	105
C-3450	Cowboy's Meditation	106
	I'd Like To Be In Texas	107
	Little Old Sod Shanty	108
	Wandering Cowboy	109
	Return To The Prairie (Luther-Gayne)	110
C-3455	I'm Going Back To Old Texas	111
	Soldier's Farewell (Tex Owens)	112
	I've Got The Freight Train Blues (Foley-Lair)	113
	Pals Of The Prairie	114

	Sing Brothers And Sisters Sing (Tex Owens)	115
C-3456	Goofus (Kahn-King-Harold)	116
	Jennie Lynn Polka	117
	Kingdom Come	118
	Mama Inez (Grenet)	119
	Down Home Rag	120
C-3457	Will The Circle Be Unbroken (Gabriel)	121
	Royal Telephone (F.M. Lehman)	122
	Where We Never Grow Old (Mare)	123
	My Last Moving Day (Oatman)	124
	The Last Mile Of The Way (Marks)	125
C-3458	Medley. Old Gray Mare; The Gal I Left Behind Me; Dixie	126
	Nobody's Sweetheart Now (Schoebel-Meyers)	127
	Oh Susanna (Foster)	128
	Dark Town Strutters ball (Brooks)	129
	Chicken Reel (Daly)	130
C-3463	Life's Evening Sun Is Sinking Low (Tex Owens)	131
	I Dreamed I Searched Heaven For You	132
	How Beautiful Heaven Must Be (Sizemore)	133
	When I Take My Vacation In Heaven (Buffum)	134
C-3464	Tumbling Tumble Weeds (Bob Nolan)	135
	Ridin' Down The Canyon (Autry-Burnette	136
	(featuring Robert "Bob" Crawford, baritone)	
	We'll Rest At The End Of The Trail (Poulton-Rose)	137
	When I Was A Boy From The Mountains (Young)	138
C-3465	When I Rock Our Babies To Sleep	139
	(featuring Robert "Bob" Crawford, yodels)	
	The Martins And The Coys (Weems-Cameron)	140
	Pony Boy (O'Connell)	141
	Pride Of The Prairie (medley) (Botsford)	142
	Goin' Back To Texas (Robison)	143
C-3466	Left My Gal In The Mountains (Robison)	144
	Little Girl Dressed In Blue (Vinard)	145
	(featuring Robert "Bob" Crawford, baritone)	
	Open Up Them Pearly Gates (Robison)	146
	Ride, Cowboy, Ride (Bob Crawford)	147
	(featuring Francis "Irish" Mahaney, tenor	

	Riding Down That Old Texas Trail (Massey-Mabie)	148
C-3467	Utah Trail (Palmer)	149
	There's A Home In Wyoming (DeRose)	150
	They Cut Down The Old Pine Tree (Hill)	151
	Big Corral	152
	Old Chisholm Trail	153
C-3472	Jack O'Diamonds	154
	Ridin' Old Paint	155
	Careless Love	156
	Jesse James (E.V. Body)	158
C-3473	China Boy (Winfree-Boutelje)	159
	Hold That Tiger	160
	12th Street Rag (Bowman)	161
	San (Mitchell)	162
	St. Louis Blues (Handy)	163
C-3474	New River Train	164
	Goodbye Old Paint	165
	The Oregon Trail (Hill-DeRose)	166
	Texas Cowboy (Tex Owens)	167
	I Want A Girl (Dillon-Von Tilzer)	168
C-3475	Trail To Mexico	169
	Ain't Ya Comin' Out Tonight	170
	Big Ball In Texas (Miller)	171
	His Trade Marks	172
	Wait Till The Sun Shines, Nellie (Von Tilzer)	173
C-3476	Blarney In The Chicken Coop (Tex Owens)	174
	Arkansas Traveler (Guion)	175
	Irish Washerwoman	176
	Soldier's Joy	177
	Pop Goes The Weasel	178
	Some Of These Days (Brooks)	179
C-3480	Mother's Smiling Face	180
	My Daddy And Mother	181
	Out In The Golden West	182
	Can You Love Another?	183
	My Mother's Call	184
	Riding On The Western Trail (Tex Owens) (featuring Tex Owens)	185

C-3481	Little Green Valley	186
	Memory That Time Cannot Erase	187
	Carry Me Back To The Mountains (Robison)	188
	Mellow Mountain Moon (Howard-Vincent)	189
	Carry Me Back To The Lone Prairie (Robison)	190
C-3482	Kentucky Babe (Geibel)	191
	Hush Yo' Honey, Hush (Greggs)	192
	Abide With Me (Monk)	193
	By The Bend O' The River (Demond)	194
	Spend One Hour With Jesus (Grimes)	195
C-3483	Broom Tails (Demond)	196
	Southern Moon (Kerr-Zamecnik)	197
	Silver Moon Waltz (Frosini)	198
	Feelin' My Way	199
	Gay Cabellero	200

March 17, 1941. World Broadcasting Studios, Hollywood.
Bob Crawford, Edward Cronenbold, Fran Mahaney and Rod May, vocal quartet; Gomer Cool, fiddle; Joe Stand, accordion; Herb Kratoska, guitar/banjo; Clarence Hartman, bass/jug. Vocal quartet sometimes becomes an octet and some vocal performances are unaccompanied. These are detailed below when known, but as noted in the introductory section, because we have been unable to audition many recordings, some recordings that feature the vocal octet or feature no instrumental accompaniment may not be indicated here. On a few occasions, several band members play ocarinas.

		Unit Number
HH-2553	Wait For The Wagon (Hall-McCreary)	1
	Sing Cowboy Sing (Vern Spencer)	2
	It Ain't So Rosy On The Range (Fleming Allen)	3
	Sky Ball Paint (Bob Nolan)	4
	Covered Wagon Rolled Right Along (Wood-Heath)	5
HH-2554	I'm a Bronco That Won't Be Broken (Leeds-Shirl-Manners)	6
	Happy Cowboy (Bob Nolan)	7
	Song Of The Pioneers (Vern Spencer)	8

	When The Bloom Is On The Sage (Howard-Vincent)	9
	I'm Gonna Round Up My Love (Stanley)	10
HH-2555	No One to Call Me Darling (Gene Autry)	11
	Trail Of Memory (Maness-Livernasy)	12
	Ride On (Blackmore-Cortez)	13
	Over The Santa Fe Trail (Vern Spencer)	14
	Goodbye To Old Mexico (Dwight Butcher)	15
HH-2556	Chopo, My Pony (Howard Thorpe)	16
	A Home On The Range (Hall-McCreary)	17
	Ridin' Down The Canyon (Autry-Burnette)	18
	Hold On Little Doggie (Gene Autry)	19

March 18, 1941, 10:00 am–12:00 pm. As above. Instrumentalists only*

HH-2557	Kingdom Coming (Appleton)*	20
	Poinciana (Simon)*	21
	Climbing Up The Golden Stairs (Cole)*	22
	Ciribiribin *	23
	Listen To The Mocking Bird *	24
HH-2558	Down At The Old Red Barn	25
	Buffalo Gals	26
	Corn Cob Willie	27
	She'll Be Coming Round The Mountain	28
	True Blue Bill	29
	Oh! Susannah	30

March 18, 1941, 1:00 pm–2:40 pm. As above. Vocal quartet only.

HH-2559	Jesus Saviour Pilot Me	31
	Shall We Meet	32
	Jesus Lover Of My Soul	33
	How Gentle God's Command	34
	Abide With Me	35
	The Church In The Wildwood	36
HH-2560	My Faith Looks Up To Thee	37
	He Leadeth Me	38
	Just As I Am	39
	Sweet Hour Of Prayer	40
	Pass Me Not, O Gentle Saviour	41

My Jesus I Love Thee	42

March 19, 1941, 10:00 am-12:30 pm. Details as March 17.
HH-2561 Little Girl Dressed In Blue	43
Mexicali Rose	44
Take Me Back To Renfro Valley	45
Dear Old Western Skies	46
Yellow Rose Of Texas	47
HH-2562 Way Out West In Texas	48
Sweet Kitty Wells	49
The Strawberry Roan	50
Me And My Burro	51
Where The Mountains Meet The Moon	52

March 19, 1941, 1:00 pm-3:30 pm. As above.
HH-2563 Cowboy's Heaven	53
There's An Empty Cot In The Bunkhouse Tonight	54
Wonder Valley	55
When It's Prayer Meeting Time In The Hollow	56
Sagebrush Serenade	57
HH-2564 Mellow Mountain Moon	58
My Dear Old Arizona Home	59
End Of The Trail	60
Blanket Me With Western Skies	61
Sweet Allalee (Cole)	62

March 21, 1941, 10:00 am-12:00 pm. Details as March 17.
HH-2565 The Texas Cowboy (Manaloff)	63
Guns And Guitars (Autry)	64
Dreaming Of The Western Plains (Ulen)	65
My Pinto Pony And I (Burnette)	66
Pretty Quadroon (Howard-Vincent)	67
HH-2566 I Only Want A Buddy Not A Sweetheart (Jones)	68
Little Old Sod Shanty (Public domain)	69
Camptown Races (Public domain)	70
Shy Little Ann From Cheyenne (Butcher)	71
Lonely Valley (Carlisle)	72

March 21, 1941, 1:00 pm-3:00 pm. As above.
HH-2567 As The Old Chuck Wagon Rolls Along (Allen) 73
 Steal Away (Public domain) 74
 Levee Song (Public domain) 75
 The Dude At The Crescent Star (Randolph-Jones) 76
 The Cowboy's Meditation (Public domain) 77
HH-2568 The Old Round-Up In Cheyenne (Autry-Burnette) 78
 When The Prairie Camp Fires Burn (Ulen) 79
 Careless Love (Public domain) 80
 Cowboy Jack (Public domain) 81
 We're Brandin' Today (Fleming Allen) 82

March 25, 1941, 11:00 am-1:00 pm. As March 17, except vocal quartet only is present.
HH-2577 God Be With You Till We Meet Again (Public domain) 83
 Rock Of Ages (Public domain) 84
 I Would Be True (Public domain) 85
 Day Is Dying In The West (Public domain) 86
 What A Friend (Public domain) 87
 Let The Lower Lights be Burning (Public domain) 88
HH-2578 More Love To Thee (Public domain) 89
 Softly Now The Light Of Day (Public domain) 90
 Faith Of Our Fathers (Public domain) 91
 Shall We Gather At The River (Public domain) 92
 Where He Leads Me (Public domain) 93
 In The Sweet Bye And Bye (Public domain) 94

March 25, 1941, 2:00 pm-4:00 pm. Details as March 17.
HH-2579 Old Chisholm Trail (Public domain) 95
 In An Old Fashioned Garden (Al Crocker) 96
 Songs I Heard At Mother's Knee (Al Crocker) 97
 Cowboy's Last Ride (Al Crocker) 98
While Those Chapel Bells Are Ringing (Al Crocker) 99
HH-2580 I Ride An Old Paint (Public domain) 100
 In That Utah Valley (Al Crocker) 101
 In The Foothills Of Old Wyoming (Al Crocker) 102
 Cielito Lindo (Arr. Glenn H. Woods) 103

The Quilting Party (Public domain)   104

March 26, 1941. Details as March 17, except only vocal quartet is present.
HH-2581 In The Gloaming (Arr. J. A. Parks)   105
Sweet and Low (Arr. J. A. Parks)   106
Juanita (Arr. J. A. Parks)   107
Drink To Me Only With Thine Eyes (Arr. J. A. Parks) 108
Long, Long Ago (Arr. J. A. Parks)   109
I Cannot Sing The Old Songs (Arr. J. A. Parks)   110
HH-2582 Last Night (Arr. J. A. Parks)   111
Stars Of The Summer Night (Arr. J. A. Parks)   112
How Can I Leave Thee (Public domain)   113
Massa's In The Cold Cold Ground (Arr. J. A. Parks) 114
My Old Kentucky Home (Arr. J. A. Parks)   115
Old Black Joe (Arr. J. A. Parks)   116
HH-2583 Po' Little Lamb (Arr. J. A. Parks)   117
The Soldier's Farewell (Arr. J. A. Parks)   118
Dear Evalina (Public domain)   119
Grandfather's Clock (Public domain)   120
Annie Laurie (Arr. J. A. Parks)   121
Sweet Genevieve (Public domain)   122

March 26, 1941. As above, except Crawford, May and Cronenbold are absent, and instrumentalists return: Fran Mahaney, vocal; Gomer Cool, fiddle; Joe Strand, accordion; Herb Kratoska, guitar; Clarence Hartman, bass.
HH-2584 I Love To Tell The Story (Public domain)   123
O Worship The King (Public domain)   124
I Need Thee Every Hour (Public domain)   125
Blest Be The Tie That Binds (Public domain)   126
Awake My Soul (Public domain)   127

April 1, 1941. Details as March 17.
HH-2585 Puttin' On The Style (Public domain)   128
Rootin' Tootin' Two Gun Shootin' Cowman (Collins-Wade)   129
Friendship Hall (Gomer Cool)   130

	West Wind (Gomer Cool)	131
	Dream With Me (Gomer Cool)	132
HH-2586	Polly Wolly Doodle (Public domain)	133
	Cowboy's Dream (O'Malley)	134
	Ride, Cowboy, Ride (Bob Crawford)	135
	Me and My Old Paint Hoss (Bob Crawford)	136
	Headin' Home (Bob Crawford)	137
HH-2587	It's Heck To Bum In Texas (Sanford-McConnell)	138
	Two Gun Bill (Sanford-McConnell)	139
	Yo Ho The Rodeo (Sloate-Schneider-Boyd)	140
	Old Dan Tucker (Emmett)	141
	Bicycle Built For Two (Dacre?)	142
HH-2588	Whoopee Ti-Yi-Yo (Public domain)	143
	Billy Boy (Public domain)	144
	We Buried Her Beneath The Willow (Cumberland Ridge Runners)	145
	Take Me Back To Peaceful Valley (Sanford-McConnell)	146
	There's A Mountain Boy Who's Longing (Sanford-McConnell)	147

April 2, 1941. Details as above. Vocal quartet absent.
Gomer Cool, fiddle; Joe Strand, accordion; Herb Kratoska, guitar/banjo; Clarence Hartman, bass.

HH-2589	La Cucuracha (Public domain)	148
	Over The Waves (Rosas)	149
	La Paloma (Yradier)	150
	Lorita (Fleming Allen)	151
	Merry Widow Waltz (Lehar)	152
HH-2590	The Old Gray Mare (Public domain)	153
	The Old Oaken Bucket (Kiallmark)	154
	The Last Rose Of Summer (Public domain)	155
	The Spanish Cavalier (Hendrickson)	156
	Under the Double Eagle (Wagner)	157
HH-2591	Dark Eyes (Public domain)	158
	Vilia (Lehar)	159
	La Golondrina (Serradell)	160

        Liebestraum (Liszt)   161
        Veremeland (Public domain)   162
April 3, 1941. Details as March 17.
HH-2592 Hard Times Come Again No More (Stephen Foster) 163
        Uncle Ned (Stephen Foster)   164
        Gentle Annie (Stephen Foster)   165
        Fairy Belle (Stephen Foster)   166
        Old Dog Tray (Stephen Foster)   167
HH-2593 I Wish I Were Single Again (Public domain)   168
        Skip To My Lou (Public domain)   169
        Swing Low Sweet Chariot (Public domain)   170
        Sing Me a Song of the Saddle (Hartford-Autry)   171
        America the Beautiful (Bates-Ward)   172
HH-2594 The Fiddle Doesn't Fit His Chin   173
        (Kennedy-Sanford-McConnell)
        Old Bill Smith (Kennedy-Sanford-McConnell)   174
        Lonesome Valley Sally   175
        (Kennedy-Sanford-McConnell)
        Ridin' The Trails (Gomer Cool)   176
        The Plains Of Old Wyoming (Gomer Cool)   177

April 3, 1941. As above, except vocal quartet is absent.
HH-2595 Darling Nellie Gray (Hanby)   178
        Irish Washerwoman (Public domain)   179
        Flight of the Bumblebee (Rimsky Korsakoff)   180
        Comin' Through the Rye (Public domain)   181
        Pop Goes the Weasel and Gal I Left Behind Me   182
        (Public domain)
        Golden Slippers (Bland)   183

April 4, 1941. Details as March 17.
HH-2596 Dry And Dusty (Fleming Allen)   184
        That Silver Haired Daddy (Autry)   185
        Man On The Flying Trapeze (Leybourne)   186
        Bury Me Out On The Prairie (Public domain)   187
        Give Me The Life Of A Cowboy (Fleming Allen)   188

April 4, 1941. As above, except Crawford, Cronenbold, and May do not participate.

HH-2597 Come Back To Erin (Claribel)   189
         The Rose Of Tralee (Glover)   190
         Shortnin' Bread (Public domain)   191
         I'll Take You Back Again Kathleen (Westendorf)   192
See April 8   193*

April 4, 1941. Details as March 17.

HH-2598 Red River Valley (Public domain)   194
         Hand Me Down My Walking Cane (Public domain) 195
         While I Rock Our Babies To Sleep (Public domain) 196
         Trail To Mexico (Public domain)   197
         Where The Hilltops Kiss The Skies (Canter)   198

April 8, 1941. Details as March 17.

HH-2599 Loch Lomond (Public domain)   199
         Silver Threads Among The Gold (Danks)   200
         Birmingham Jail (Public domain)   201
         Jeanie With The Light Brown Hair (Foster)   202
         When You And I Were Young Maggie (Butterfield) 203
HH-2600 Song Of The Trail Drive (Bob Crawford)   204
         My Prairie Home In Old New Mexico   205
            (Bob Crawford)
         Six Gun Dan (Bob Crawford)   206
         Little Pal (Bob Crawford)   207
         Pull Out the Stopper (Bob Crawford)   208
HH-2640 Little Pony (Gomer Cool)   209
         My Wyoming Home (Bob Crawford)   210
         Ridin' Along (Gomer Cool)   211
         Pals Of The Prairie (Bob Crawford)   212
         Powder River (Gomer Cool)   213
HH-2641 Joseph de Renaldo (Gomer Cool)   214
         When the Sun Goes Down on the Desert   215
            (Bob Crawford)
         We Wanna Sing (Gomer Cool)   216
         Dogie's Lullaby (Bob Crawford)   217

A final track was recorded this day but added as fifth track to
master HH-2597 (see April 4 session):
Believe Me if All Those Endearing Young Charms   193

December 4, 1941, Hollywood.
Bob Crawford, Edward Cronenbold, Fran Mahaney and Rod May,
vocal quartet; Gomer Cool, fiddle; Joe Stand, accordion;
Herb Kratoska, guitar/banjo; Clarence Hartman, bass/
jug.* Several band members play ocarinas on H-592.

H-590-1	The Air Corps Of Uncle Sam	Okeh 06543
	(Behmer-Behmer-White)	
H-591-1	I've Changed My Penthouse For A Pup-Tent	Okeh 06543
	(Bob Crawford)	
H-592-1	Pull Out The Stopper (Bob Crawford)*	Okeh 06629
H-593-1	I Wonder Why (Bob Crawford)	Okeh 06629

c. December 8-9, 1941. Details as March 17, 1941.

HH-2700	Move Along Dogie (Fran Mahaney)	218
	My Prairie Song (Gomer Cool)	219
	Beans 'n Muddy Coffee (Gomer Cool)	220
	Old Timer Of The Trails (Bob Crawford)	221
	We'll Go Ridin' On To Glory (Bob Crawford)	222
HH-2701	Down At The Rodeo (Bob Crawford)	223
	I Wonder Why (Bob Crawford)	224
	The Stars Ride High (Gomer Cool)	225
	Let's Sing Like They Do In The Mountains (Gomer Cool)	226
	When the Bugle is Sounding Taps (Bob Crawford)	227
HH-2702	Hang Out Another Star (Don Rich- Batty Jackson-Fanny Carroll)	228
	On That Lonesome Desert Trail (Rusty Campbell-Scott Seeley)	229
	It's A Ranger's Life (Gomer Cool)	230
	Cool Water (Bob Nolan)	231
	At The Rainbow's End (Bob Nolan)	232
HH-2703	Ridin' High (Gomer Cool)	233
	The Touch Of God's Hand (Bob Nolan)	234
	In San Clemente (Gomer Cool)	235

         Prairie Night (Arsa Hitt- Dick Guttmann)   236
         A Cowboy Has To Sing (Bob Nolan)   237

c. December 9-10, 1941. Details as above.
HH-2704 Bringing in the Sheaves Hymn (Public domain)   238
         Safe In The Arms Of Jesus (Public domain)   239
         Were You There (Public domain)   240
         Nobody Knows De Trouble I've Seen (Public domain) 241
         Softly And Tenderly (Public domain)   242
         Work For The Night Is Coming (Public domain)   243
HH-2705 Moonlight On The Painted Desert   244
            (Fleming Allen-Oliver Drake)
         I've Changed My Penthouse For A Pup Tent   245
            (Bob Crawford)
         At the Old Bar X Tonight   246
            (Rusty Campbell-Scott Seely)
         Down An Old Spanish Trail   247
            (Walker-Buntin-Franklin McCormich)
         Ridin' In The Saddle (Len Slye)   248
HH-2706 I've Sold My Saddle For An Old Guitar (Fleming 249
            Allen)
         Song Of The Prairie (Bob Crawford)   250
         Dreamin' Of The Girl I Left Behind (Bob Crawford) 251
         Ride Vigilantes Ride (Bob Crawford)   252
         Sweet Rosalie (Gomer Cool)   253
HH-2707 Singin' A Carefree Song (Bob Crawford)   254
         If You'll Only Come Back to Me (Bob Crawford) 255
         When I Get Back On The Range   256
            (Rusty Campbell-Scott Seely)
         I Need America   257
            (Sylvester Cross-Fleming Allen-Myrtle Miller)
         L'il Liza Jane (Public domain)   258

c. December 10-12, 1941.
HH-2708 I'm At Home In The City (Hal Raynor)   259
         Termite's Love Song (Hal Raynor)   260
         Volga Boatmen (Public domain)   261
         Horse's Love Song (Hal Raynor)   262

	Etiquette (Hal Raynor-Joe Penner)	263

Vocal quartet is absent on remaining songs from this session:

HH-2709	Turkey In The Straw (Public domain)	264
	Funiculi, Funicula (Denza)	265
	Rakes of Mallow (Public domain)	266
	Yankee Doodle (Public domain)	267

c. January 18-20, 1942. Details as March 17, 1941.

29603	No Good Son-of-a-Gun (Nolan)	268
	Falls On The Prairie (Nolan-Perryman)	269
	Song Of The Bandit (Nolan)	270
	When The Prairie Sun Says Good Mornin' (Nolan)	271
	Stars Of The West (Spencer)	272
29604	Saddle Your Worries To The Wind (Nolan)	273
	This Old White Mule Of Mine (Nolan)	274
	Echoes From The Hills (Nolan)	275
	Sunset On The Trail (Cooper-Van Fossen-Clay)	276
	The Life Of A Cowboy For Me (Mitchell-Male-Obney)	277
29614	Singin' In The Saddle (Obney-Schell-Scales)	278
	Back In My Old Ranch Home (Houston-Barlow-Faithful)	279
	Water Hole (Berg-Bundy-Carroll)	280
	Lullaby Of The Prairie (Smith-Sprowls Taylor)	281
	There Are More Cowboys On Broadway (Passineau-Lorraine-Pidcook)	282
29615	Over The Blue Horizon (Holst-Barton-Harris)	283
	Climbin' That Stairway To The Sky (Earl)	284
	Old Silver (Schumaker-Sharp-Singletary)	285
	Strummin' My Old Guitar (Meredith)	286
	Then We Go Ridin' (Gomer Cool)	287

January 21, 1942. Details as March 17, 1941.

29656	Soldier Boy (Gomer Cool)	288
	Hymn To The Navy (Gomer Cool)	289
	Then I'll Come Back To You (Bob Crawford)	290
	There's An Old Rail Fence (Bob Crawford)	291
	We'll Fight For Uncle Sam (Bob Crawford)	292

29657	Broken Hearted (Bob Crawford)	293
	Don't Tell Me That You Love Me (Bob Crawford)	294
	My Little Prairie Rose (Campbell-Seely)	295
	Rollin' Driftin' Sand (Clauser-Hoepner)	296
	Hillbilly Bill (Walker)	297

January 22, 1942. As above.

29658	Fairest Lord Jesus (Public domain)	298
	Jesus Is Calling (Public domain)	299
	Jesus Loves Me (Public domain)	300
	Now The Day Is Over (Public domain)	301
	The Haven Of Rest (Public domain)	302
29659	Fort Worth Jail (Reinhart)	303
	A Pumpkin Has No Pump (McConnell-Kennedy-Sanford)	304
	She Works Third Tub At The Laundry (Burnette)	305
	Corinna (Hubbert)	306
	I'll Never Let You Go Little Darlin' (Wakely)	307
29665	On the Banks Of The Sunny San Juan (Dean-Strange)	308
	Hoof Beats On The Prairie (Spencer)	309
	Hold That Critter Down (Nolan)	310
	Blue Prairie (Spencer-Nolan)	311
	I Wonder Where You Are Tonight (Bond)	312

Vocal quartet is absent for remaining tracks:

29670	Killarney (Balfe-Appleton)	313
	Monday Morning Blues (Herb Kratoska)	314
	Arkansas Traveler (Public domain)	315
	Annie Laurie (Scott-Douglas)	316
	Polly Wolly Doodle (Public domain)	317

December 17, 1943. Kansas City.
Bob Crawford, Edward Cronenbold, Fran Mahaney, Rod May, vocal quartet; Al Phillips, fiddle; possibly Gene Moore, accordion; Herb Kratoska, guitar; Unidentified, bass.

| A-15218 | Carry Me Back To The Mountains (Carson J. Robison) | 329 |
| | Goin' Back To Texas (Carson J. Robison) | 330 |

	Left My Gal In The Mountains (Carson J. Robison)	331
	Open Up Them Pearly Gates (Carson J. Robison)	332
	The Big Corral (Public domain)	333
A-15219	Serenade Of The Cowboy (Cindy Walker)	340
	Old Pioneer (Glenn & Tim Spencer)	341
	Keep A Light In Your Window Tonight (Lester McFarland- Roberta Gardner-Jack Turner)	342
	Hitch Old Dobbin To The Shay Again (J. R. Lewis, Jr.-Jud Conlon)	343
	Trail Of The Mountain Rose (Al Clauser-Tex Hoepner)	344
A-15220	If I Had A Girl Like You (Bob Crawford- Rod May)	350
	I Wonder What Became Of That Old Quartette (Bob Crawford-Rod May)	351
	Did You Mean It (Bob Crawford)	352
	One More Kiss (Bob Crawford)	353
	Every Step Of The Way (Bob Crawford)	354

December 18, 1943. Details as above.

A-15217	A Charge To Keep (Chas. Wesley- Dr. Lowell Mason)	392
	Am I A Soldier Of The Cross (Isaac Watts-Thos. Arne)	393
	Oh! Master Let Me Walk With Thee (Washington Gladden-H. Percy Smith)	394
	Soldiers Of Christ Arise (Charles Wesley-George J. Elvey)	395
	Stand Up For Jesus (George Duffield- George J. Webb)	396
	There's An Old, Old Path (Vida E. Smith-M. A. Anderson)	397

December 19, 1943. Details as December 17.

A-15230	Open Range Ahead (Bob Nolan)	370
	The Man In The Moon Is A Cowhand (Roy Rogers)	371
	West Of The Waste Land (Milton Leeds-Fred Wise-Fred Stryker)	372
	Trail Herdin' Cowboy (Bob Nolan)	373

   Singing A Song Of The Trails   374
   (Charles Dant-Jimmie Davis)

Possibly December 19, 1943. Details as above.
B-15231 All Hail The Power Of Jesus Name 334
   (Edward D. Perronet-John Rippon-Oliver Holden)
   How Firm A Foundation (George Keith) 335
   Saviour Like A Shepard Lead Us 336
   (Wm. B. Bradbury-Dorothy Ann Thrupp)
   Yield Not To Temptation (H. R. Palmer) 337
   Tell Me The Old, Old Story 338
   (Catherine Hankey-W. H. Doane)
   From Greenland's Icy Mountains 339
   (Reginald Heber- Dr. Lowell Mason)

December 19, 1941. Details as above.
B-15232 Precious Name (M. H. Forscutt, W. H. Doane) 375
   Holy Is The Lord (Fanny J. Crosby-Wm. B. Bradbury)376
   Saviour Teach Me Day By Day 377
   (Jane E. Leeson-Powell G. Fithian)
   Be With Me Lord Where Ere I Go 378
   (J. P. Holdbrook)
   Jesus I My Cross Have Taken 379
   (Henry F. Lyte-Charles C. Converse)
   There's No Love Like His Love (John L. Newkirk) 380

December 20, 1943. Details as December 17.
B-15235 My Bonnie Lies Over The Ocean (H. J. Fuller) 323
   Boogie Woogie (Herb Kratoska) 324
   O Solo Mio (Di Capua) 325
   In The Little Red School House 326
   (Al Wilson-Jack Brennan)
   You Tell Me Your Dreams And I'll Tell You Mine 327
   (Rice-Brown-Daniels)
   Nightingale (Rosner-Wise-Cugat) 328
Vocal quartet is absent on 381-386:
A-15236 The Arkansas Traveler (Public domain) 381
   The Kerry Dance (J. L. Molloy) 382

	Frenesi (Dominquez)	383
	El Manisero (Moises Simon)	384
	Cross Bow (Al Phillips)	385
	La Cinquintaine (Gabriel-Marie)	386
B-15237	Don't You Believe It (Carson J. Robison)	355
	In The Little Shirt Mother Made For Me (Bradley Kincaid)	356
	Nellie Bly (Stephen Foster)	357
	Camptown Races (Stephen Foster)	358
	Carry Me Back To Old Virginny (James Bland)	359
B-15238	I'm Thinking Tonight Of My Blue Eyes (A. P. Carter)	387
	The Utah Trail (Robert Palmer)	388
	Cactus Blossoms (Floyd Holmes)	389
	Will I Ride The Range In Heaven (Chick Hurt-Jack Taylor)	390
	Don't Say Goodbye Little Darling (Randall Atcher)	391

December 27, 1943. Details as December 17.

A-15225	You Don't Love Me But I'll Always Care (Lou Wayne)	360
	Rose Of Santa Fe (Foy Willingham)	361
	This Little Rosary (Cindy Walker)	362
	He's Gone, He's Gone Up The Trail (Tim Spencer)	363
	Wyoming (Eddie Dean-Bradford Browne)	364
A-15226	You're From Texas (Cindy Walker)	318
	My Adobe Hacienda (Louise Massey-Lee Penny)	319
	Granny Ain't A Rockin' In Her Old Rockin' Chair (Russ Hull-Gordon Dow)	320
	The Gals Don't Mean A Thing (Arbie Gibson-Curt Massey)	321
	The Little Guy That Looks Like You (Tim Spencer)	322
B-15227	I Don't Know What To Say (Bob Crawford-Rod May)	365
	Alone And Lonely (Jimmy Wakely)	366
	Old Pinto (Curt, Allen & Louise Massey-Larry Wellington)	367
	She's The Lily Of Hillbilly Valley (Tim Spencer)	368
	Sugar Hill (Alan Crockett)	369

December 31, 1943. Details as December 17.

B-15228	That Pioneer Mother of Mine (Vern Spencer)	398
	Just Rollin' On (Ernest Tubb)	399
	Down On The Old Plantation (Carson J. Robison)	400
	Dude Cowboy	401
	(Allen & Curt Massey-Larry Wellington)	
	Song Of The Lariat (Milt Mabie-Larry Wellington)	402
B-15229	There's An Old Enchanted Mesa	345
	(Bill Watters-Jerry Campbell)	
	Love Song of the Prairie (Al Crocker)	346
	I'll Ride a Dream Land Pinto	347
	(Mark Delaney-Claude Heriter-Russ Hull)	
	Smile A While (Chick Hurt-Gladys Hurt)	348
	Low Down Blues (Floyd Holmes)	349

March 28, 1946. World Broadcasting Studios. New York.
Bob Crawford, Edward Cronenbold, Fran Mahaney, Rod May, vocal quartet; Emert Painter, fiddle; Joe Manning, accordion; Herb Kratoska, guitar; Eddie Johnson, bass.
Note: The dates listed her March 28-April 1 as recording dates for the following 60+ recordings below might, instead, indicate mastering dates, and the sessions may have occurred earlier in March.

45537	Ridin' Home	403
	Round Up In The Sky (Nolan)	404
	(featuring Francis "Irish" Mahaney, tenor)	
	When The Golden Train Comes Down (Nolan)	405
	(featuring Robert "Bob" Crawford, baritone)	
	Westward Ho (Spencer)	406
	I Still Do (Nolan)	407
	(featuring Francis "Irish" Mahaney, tenor)	
45538	Whisperin' Wind (Spencer)	408
	(featuring Francis "Irish" Mahaney, tenor)	
	Come On Home (Spencer)	409
	Roll Along Jordan (Spencer)	410
	(featuring Francis "Irish" Mahaney, tenor)	
	When Pay Day Rolls Around	411

	Following The Sun All Day (Nolan)	412
	(featuring Francis "Irish" Mahaney, tenor)]	
45355	The Boss Is Hanging Out A Rainbow (Nolan)	413
	(featuring Francis "Irish" Mahaney, tenor)	
	Down Along The Sleepy Rio Grande (Rogers)	414
	(featuring Francis "Irish" Mahaney, tenor)	
	Wind (Nolan)	415
	(featuring Robert "Bob" Crawford, baritone; Francis "Irish" Mahaney, tenor)	
	There's A Rainbow Over The Range	416
	(featuring Francis "Irish" Mahaney, tenor)	
	Cowtown Hoe Down (Foran-Allen)	417
45356	Give Me A Home On The Plains (Foran-Allen)	418
	(featuring Francis "Irish" Mahaney)	
	Great Guns Are Silent Tonight (Foran-Allen)	419
	Night Herder's Song (Foran-Allen)	420
	(featuring Francis "Irish" Mahaney, tenor)	
	Rose Of Laredo	421
	Hifalutin' Cowboy (Foran-Allen)	422
45374	Every Day Will Be Sunday Bye And Bye (Foran-Allen)	423
	(feat. Francis "Irish" Mahaney, tenor)	
	Columbus Stockade Blues (Davis-Sargent)	424
	Rock Me To Sleep In My Saddle (Marion)	425
	Tomorrow Never Comes (Tubb-Bond)	426
	(feat. Francis "Irish" Mahaney, tenor)	
	Springtime In Texas (Wakely)	427
	(feat. Herb "Arizona" Kratoska, guitar**)	
45375	Palomino Pal Of Mine	428
	The Road To Santa Fe (Foran-Nolan)	429
	(feat. Francis "Irish" Mahaney, tenor)	
	Night Time On The Trail	430
	(featuring Francis "Irish" Mahaney, tenor)	
	My Yodel Song (Bob Crawford)	431
	(feat. Robert "Bob" Crawford, yodels)	
	Poor Old Bill (Foran-Allen)	432
	(feat. Robert "Bob" Crawford, baritone)	

45363	I Dreamed Of An Old Love Affair (Dodd-Davis-Mitchell) (featuring Francis "Irish" Mahaney, tenor)	433
	Over The Hill To Heaven (Krenz-Gallop) (feat. Francis "Irish" Mahaney, tenor)	434
	When Red Leaves Are Falling (Prosen-Carlisle)	435
	Roll On Your Weary Way (Carlisle) (feat. Francis "Irish" Mahaney, tenor)	436
	Blue Guitar (Fortner-Peyton) (feat. Herb "Arizona" Kratoska, guitar)	437
45364	Rise An' Shine (feat. Francis "Irish" Mahaney, tenor; Robert "Bob" Crawford, baritone)	438
	On The Rhythm Range (feat. Robert "Bob" Crawford, baritone)	439
	Chant Of The Wanderer (Nolan) (feat. Robert "Bob" Crawford, yodels)	440
	The New Frontier (Spencer) (featuring Francis "Irish" Mahaney, tenor)	441
	A Sandman Lullaby (Nolan) (featuring Francis "Irish" Mahaney, tenor)	442

April 1, 1946. Details as above.

45394	Tico Tico (Abreu)	443
	Serenade (Schubert)	444
	Mexican Hat Dance (Partichela)	445
	Andalucia (Lecuona)	446
	Chiapanecas (DeCampo) (featuring Herb "Arizona" Kratoska, guitar)	447
45395	El Choclo (Villoldo)	448
	Barbara Polka (Kovarik)	449
	La Cumparsita (Rodriguez)	450
	A Media Luz (Donato)	451
	My Shawl (Cugat-Adams)	452
45396	Almost Persuaded (Bliss) (featuring. Francis "Irish" Mahaney, tenor)	453
Art Thou Weary (Neale-Baker) (featuring. Francis "Irish" Mahaney, tenor)		454

	Angry Words (Oh Let Them Never) (Palmer) (featuring Francis "Irish" Mahaney, tenor; Robert "Bob" Crawford, baritone)	455
	Angel Voices Ever Singing (Pott-Sullivan) (featuring Francis "Irish" Mahaney, tenor)	456
	Angels From The Realms Of Glory (Montgomery-Smart)	457
	Ashamed Of Jesus (featuring Francis "Irish" Mahaney, tenor)	458
45457	Behold A Stranger At The Door (Grigg-Oliver)	459
	Beautiful Valley Of Eden (Cushing-Sherwin) (featuring Francis "Irish" Mahaney, tenor)	460
	Blessed Assurance (Crosby-Knapp) (featuring Francis "Irish" Mahaney, tenor)	461
	Begin My Tongue Some Heavenly Theme (Watts) (featuring Francis "Irish" Mahaney, tenor)	462
	Beneath The Cross Of Jesus (Clephane-Maker)	463
	Christ Receiveth Sinful Men (Neumeister-McGranahan)	464

June 19, 1946, World Broadcasting Studios, Chicago.
Personnel as March 28, 1946 session.

C-19242	Arizona Bill (featuring Francis "Irish" Mahaney, tenor)	465
	Whoa, Mule, Whoa (Clauser-Hoepner) (featuring Robert "Bob" Crawford, baritone)	466
	She's The Sweetest Girl (Polden)	467
	Swing Those Gates (Clauser-Hoepner)	468
	I'm Headin' For Old New Mexico (Wilkerson-Dzurus-Marlin) (featuring Francis "Irish" Mahaney, tenor)	469
C-19243	Cherokee Strip (featuring Robert "Bob" Crawford, baritone)	470
	Don Juan (featuring Francis "Irish" Mahaney, tenor)	471
	Springtime On The Range (featuring Robert "Bob" Crawford, baritone)	472
	Where The Rio Rolls Along (featuring Robert "Bob" Crawford, baritone)	473
	Come And Get It (Spencer)	474

	(feat. Francis "Irish" Mahaney, tenor)	
C-19244	Ridin' On The Rocky Ranger	475
	(featuring Francis "Irish" Mahaney, tenor)	
	We're Headin' For The Home Corral (Spencer)	476
	Linda May Polka (Starzyk-Rice-Van Ness)	477
	Grandma Drives Us Crazy (Hickey-Van Ness)	478
	(featuring Herb "Arizona" Kratoska, vocals)	
	Just Hand Me A Pair Of Silver Spurs	479
	(Cross-Scales-Wright)	
C-19245	Old Denver Dan ([Hamilton-Mays)	480
	featuring Francis "Irish" Mahaney, tenor)	
	Honey, Be My Honey Bee (Shepard-Foley)	481
	(featuring Francis "Irish" Mahaney, tenor)	
	I Ain't Gonna Worry No More (Carver-Rollins)	482
	(featuring Robert "Bob" Crawford, baritone)	
	How Can You Hate Me (Prosen-Carlisle)	483
	(featuring Francis "Irish" Mahaney, tenor)	
	I'm Headin' East (Williams-Deckard, Jr.)	484
	(featuring Francis "Irish" Mahaney, tenor; Edward "Tucson" Cronenbold, bass)	

June 20, 1946. Details as above.

C-19250	Cimmaron (Roll On) ([Bond)	485
	Detour (Westmoreland)	486
	(featuring Francis "Irish" Mahaney, tenor)	
	Silver Spurs (On The Golden Stairs) (Autry-Walker)	487
	(featuring Edward "Tucson" Cronenbold, bass; Robert "Bob" Crawford, baritone)	
	Night Train To Memphis (Smith-Hughes-Bradley)	488
	(featuring Francis "Irish" Mahaney, tenor)	
	Goodbye Liza Jane (Duncan)	489
	(featuring Francis "Irish" Mahaney, tenor)	
C-19251	A Cornstalk Fiddle And A Shoestring Bow	490
	(King's Jesters-Foy-Lampman)	
	He's A Hillbilly Gaucho (Gallop-Litman)	491
	(featuring Francis "Irish" Mahaney, tenor; Robert "Bob" Crawford, baritone)	

	Boogie Woogie Cowboy	492
	(Dean-Blair-Snow-Statham)	
	(featuring Francis "Irish" Mahaney, tenor)	
	I Don't Give A Hang Anymore (Hull-Heriter)	493
	(featuring Francis "Irish" Mahaney, tenor)	
	Melody Of The Plains (Berlau-Sives)	494
	(featuring Francis "Irish" Mahaney, tenor; Robert "Bob" Crawford, baritone)	
C-19252	A New Ten Gallon Hat (Penny-Wills)	495
	(featuring Francis "Irish" Mahaney, tenor)	
	Old Buck-a-roo (Allen)	496
	You Broke My Heart, Little Darlin' (Spencer)	497
	(featuring Robert "Bob" Crawford, baritone)	
	Over And Over Again (Autry-Walker)	498
	I'm A Lone Cowboy (Fletcher)	499
	(featuring Francis "Irish" Mahaney, tenor)	
C-19253	Sweet Potato Polka (Reade-Taylor)	500
	South (Moten-Charles-Hayes)	501
	Perfidia (Dominguez)	502
	Ida (Sweet As Apple Cider) (Leonard)	503
	Song Of India (Rimsky-Korsakov)	504

June 21, 1946. Details as above.

C-19254	Blue Prairie Moon (Sargent)	505
	(featuring Robert "Bob" Crawford, baritone)	
	Garden In The Sky	506
	Homesick For The Prairie (Sargent)	507
	(featuring Francis "Irish" Mahaney, tenor)	
	A Gay Ranchero (Las Altenitas)	508
	(Espinosa-Tuvim-Luban)	
	Terrible Terry The Termite (Hickey-Van Ness)	509
	(featuring Herb "Arizona" Kratoska, vocal)	
C-19255	Holka Polka (Leopoldi-Friedlander)	510
	Yours (Quiereme Mucho) (Roig)	511
	Georgia On My Mind (Carmichael-Gorrell)	512
	Jazz Me Blues (Delaney)	513
	Fly A Kite (Zattas)	514

January 20, 1947. World Broadcasting Studios, Chicago.
Personnel as March 28, 1946.

UB 544	Blue Bonnet Trail (Briggs-Cooper-McCollum) (Mahaney, solo)	515
	Kicking the Dust In The Face Of The Wind (Jarrel-Dickens-Jackson)	516
	Land Of The Golden West (Turcanik-Ross-Walker)	517
	When The Stars Shine Over the Prairie (Weltner-Ross) (Crawford, solo)	518
	I'm Gonna Go Back To Arizona (Priestley-Barton-Jones) (Mahaney, solo)	519
UB 545	Bed Down, Bed Down, Little Doggies (Johns-Hale-Webb) (Mahaney, solo)	520
	My Beautiful Wild Desert Flower (Mulhair-Yarwood-Hutson) (Mahaney, solo)	521
	I'm Just A Ramblin' Cowboy (Barton-Rich-Walters) (Crawford, solo)	522
	I'm Lonely Tonite For The Prairie (Dyer-Heard-Gretschmann) (Mahaney, solo)	523
	Dream Little Cowgirl (Sharp)	524
UB 546	The Outlaw Trail (Johnson-Yarwood-Freund) (Mahaney, solo)	525
	Texas Is My Home (Ripps-Olsen-Fossen) (Mahaney, solo)	526
	Lonely Cowboy's Lament (Johnson-Cain) (Crawford, solo)	527
	Moonlight Trail (O'Reiley-Helle-Hathaway) (Mahaney)	528
	My Arizona Mountain Home (Jarrel-Balch-Russell) (Mahaney, solo)	529
UB 547	The End Of The Trail	530
	There's A New Moon Over My Shoulder	531
	Baby, You've Gotta Quit That Noise	532
	Day After Day	533
	You Only Want Me When You're Lonely	534

Note: Evidence seems to indicate that UB 547 above and some other masters that follow – those that have no vocal or composer credits listed beside titles -- may never have been pressed for broadcast use by World.

January 21, 1947. Details as above.

UB 552	Colorado Memories (Baker-Wright-Vestal) (Mahaney, solo)	535
	When It's Twilight On The Mesa (Ring-Brown-Langenfeld) (Mahaney, solo)	536
	A Cowboy Played A Serenade (Sammy-Cooper-McCollum) (Mahaney, solo)	537
	Texas Oh Texas, Where's My Baby Gone (Vestal-Jarrel-Anderson)	538
	Old Winding Trail (Baker-Rupert-Albright)	539
UB 555	The Cabin Of My Dreams (Knappenberger-Schneider-Mobley) (Crawford, lead; Mahaney, solo)	540
	Just Tune Into Heaven When You're Blue (Platt-Heywood-Carsley) (Mahaney, solo)	541
	You're Always Welcome Back Home (Bell-Rich-Peterson) (Mahaney, vocal)	542
	A Lone Cattle Puncher (White-Stone-Reader) (Crawford, solo)	543
	My Texas Rose (Voss) (Crawford, solo)	544
UB 556	I See Through You (Liddell) (Crawford, solo)	545
	Gee, I Don't Know Why (Wayne-Shelton) (Mahaney, solo)	546
	Marinita (Wade-Hull) (Mahaney, solo)	547
	Where The Mountains Meet The Sky (Williams) (Crawford, solo)	548
	Too Little, Too Late (Tuttle) (Mahaney, solo)	549
UB 557	Divorce Me, C.O.D.	550
	Trouble Keeps Hangin' Round My Door	551
	I Was Wrong	552
	Someday	553

	Make Room In Your Heart For A Friend	554

January 22, 1947. Details as above.

UB 558	Have I Told You Lately That I Love You	555
	A Petal From A Faded Rose	556
	Old Timer's Last Ride	557
	If It's Wrong To Love You	558
	Though I've Tried	559
UB 565	You Two-Timed Me One Time Too Often	560
	Heart-Break Trail	561
	Tears And Kisses	562
	Some Other World	563
	Have You Got Someone Else On The String	564
UB 566	You Can't Break My Heart (Cooley-Rogers) (Mahaney, solo)	565
	Missouri (Duncan-Penny) (Mahaney, solo)	566
	Old Shep (Foley) (Crawford, solo)	567
	Monongehala Valley (Smith) (Mahaney, solo)	568
	Trail To San Antone (Spriggens) (Mahaney, solo)	569
UB 567	A Cowboy And His Horse	570
	These Tears Are Not For You	571
	You Were Only Teasing Me	572
	Don't Break Your Heart For My Sake	573
	Please Don't Turn Your Back On Me	574

January 23, 1947. Details as January 21.

UB 572	I'm Always Blue For You (Wakely-Smith) (Mahaney, solo)	575
	Just For Me (Murray) (Mahaney, solo)	576
	Heading Back To Old Wyoming (Fleming Allen) (Mahaney, solo)	577
	Lonesome Trail (Wakely-Baxley) (Mahaney, solo)	578

	Moon Over Montana (Wakely-Drake)	579
	(Mahaney, solo)	
UB 573	A Wanderer Wandering Home	580
	Sincerely Yours	581
	Good-bye, Good Luck, My Darling	582
	Worried Mind	583
	Time Changes Everything	584
UB 574	You're My Darling	585
	Sweethearts Or Strangers	586
	There's An Old Fashioned House On A Hillside	587
	Over The River	588
	I Wish I Had Never Met Sunshine	589
UB 575	There's A Little Bit of Everything In Texas (Tubb)	590
	(Mahaney, solo)	
	My Darlin' Tell Me True (Davis-Horton)	591
	(Mahaney, solo)	
	My Madonna Of The Trail (Spencer)	592
	(Mahaney, solo)	
	Under The Western Sky (Burney-Lindal)	593
	I'm Looking For The Man Who Sings Those	594
	Hillbilly Songs (Wiley-Wilz-Henry) (Crawford, yodels)	

January 24, 1947. Details as January 21.

UB 580	It Makes No Difference Now	595
	You Are My Sunshine	596
	I'll Keep On Loving You	597
	In The Cumberland Mountains	598
	Sleepy Rio Grande	599
UB 581	Two More Years	600
	I Got To See Texas	601
	Out On The Trail	602
	Alla En El Rancho Grande	603
	Pass The Biscuits, Mirandy	604
UB 582	How Can I Say Goodbye To The Prairie	605
	Singing A Song To The Sky	606
	This Is My Lazy Day	607
	Oh, Why Did I Get Married	608
	No, I Don't Wanna Be Rich	609

UB 583	Wabash Cannonball (traditional)	610
	(Crawford, solo)	
	Ridin' Old Paint In The Sky (Vale)	611
	(Mahaney, solo)	
	Some Must Win, Some Must Lose (Davis-Wayne)	612
	(Mahaney, solo)	
	An Old Claim Shanty On The Prairie	613
	(Cole-Olsen-Collom)	
	He's A Radio Cowboy (Symonds-Clyde)	614
	(Mahaney, solo)	

November 17, 1947. Probably Los Angeles.
Bob Crawford, Edward Cronenbold, Fran Mahaney & Rod May, vocal quartet; Emmert Painter, fiddle; Bill Lorentz, accordion; Herb Kratoska, guitar; Eddie Johnson, bass.

52271   I'm Riding On To Far Horizons (West-O'Neill)
        (Mahaney, solo)
52272   Smoke, Smoke, Smoke (That Cigarette)
        (Travis-Williams)
        (Crawford, solo)
52273   Am I To Blame? (Dexter-Paris)
        (Mahaney, solo)
52274   Chained To A Memory Of You (Carson)
        (Mahaney, solo)
52275   Dangerous Ground (Nelson-Leeds-Nelson)
        (Mahaney, solo)
52275 [sic] I'll Step Aside ((Johnny Bond)
        (Crawford, solo)
52276   Crazy 'Cause I Love You (Spade Cooley)
52277   I'd Trade All Of My Tomorrows (Carson)
52278   Don't Look Now (But Your Broken Heart Is Showing)
        (Tubb)
52279   Shame On You (Spade Cooley)(Mahaney, solo)

c. late 1947. Location unknown.
Personnel as November 17, 1947.

Jubilation	Bibletone TR 9001
The Touch Of God's Hand	
Cowboy Camp Meeting	Bibletone TR 9002
Golden Wings And Silver Spurs	
Gallopin' To Glory	Bibletone TR 9003
Trail To Our Salvation	

Note: Released as a 3-record set as "Bibletone Presents Cowboy Hymns" in May 1948

The remaining studio transcriptions listed below seem to date from 1948-49 and are, apparently, unconnected to the World Library recordings, though they may have originally been intended for use in that series.

Personnel is the same as that for the late 1947 recordings with one exception: Ted Painter replaces Herb Kratoska on guitar

48996	There's An Old Rail Fence (Crawford)
	Cowboy's Serenade
	The Girl I Left Behind Me
	Never Trust A Woman (Carson)
	My Wyoming Home (Crawford)
48997	When The White Azaleas Start Blooming (Massey)
	Take Me Home (Miller)
	Tumbling Tumbleweeds (Nolan)
	Wagon Wheels (Hill-De Rose)
	The Last Roundup (Hill)
49000	Gallopin' To Glory
	The Trail To Our Salvation
	Golden Wings And Silver Spurs (Fleming Allen)
	Cowboy Camp Meeting (Tim Spencer)
	Bow Down Brother
49001	I Want Somebody Just Like You
	A Broken Promise Means A Broken Heart
	Why Do I Love You, Oh Why (Smokey Rogers-Wally Prichard)
	A Penny For Your Thoughts (Jenny Lou Carson)
	Gonna Give You Back To The Indians

49002   Ridin' Herd Along The Rio Grande
           My Heart Went Thataway (Roy Rogers-Dale Evans)
           Baby Doll (Bob Newman)
           Under Stars Over Texas
           Mollie Darlin' (Eddy Arnold)
49003   Five instrumental selections featuring Emmert Painter, fiddle.
           Titles not known.

March 8, 1949 (15:30-18:30). Radio Recorders, Hollywood.
Bob Crawford, Edward Cronenbold, Fran Mahaney & Rod May,
           vocal quartet; Emmert Painter, fiddle; Bill Lorentz, accordion; Ted Painter, guitar; Eddie Johnson, bass

49-S-3049-3 (51-XY-910)	Make Believe Cowboy	MGM 11148
49-S-3050-3	There's An Old Rail Fence (Bob Crawford)	MGM 10416
49-S-3051-3 (51-XY-911)	The Sun Beats Down	MGM 11148
49-S-3052-2	Frettin' And A-Poutin'	MGM 10416

Bobby Lee with the Texas Rangers.
1953. Kansas City, Mo.
Robert L. Altendorf (Bobby Lee), vocal; with probably: Ray
           Hudgens, fiddle/clarinet; Bill Lorentz, accordion; Val Tatham and/or Ted Painter, guitar; Eddie Johnson, bass.

53-S-6028	Always Sorry	MGM 11478
53-S-6029	Lightning Bug Blues (Sweat)	MGM 11478
53-S-6030	The Last Desire Of A Broken Heart	MGM 11597
53-S-6031	I Found The End Of The Rainbow (English-Lee)	MGM 11597

Appendix B:
Life on the Red Horse Ranch
Guide to Episodes 1 - 65

Episode 1
Writer: Gomer Cool
Script checked March 27, 1935 by KMR (presumably Karel Rickerson, J. Stirling Getchell's Kansas City branch manager)
The patriarch and owner of the Red Horse Ranch, Sam Carter, learns that he may lose his ranch. The ranch hands Bob, Tenderfoot, Idaho, Arizona, Cheyenne, Alabam, Tex, and Cookie won't allow that to happen if they can help it.
Songs:
Press Along to the Big Corral
Buffalo Gal – fiddle, banjo, harmonica
Cattle Call
Hand Me Down my Walkin' Cane
Note: The identity of "KMR," the person who checked each script in the series, is unknown. It may have been a KMBC employee or a staff member of the sponsor Socony-Vacuum Oil. The scripts for the first 26 episodes are all titled Flying Horse Ranch. "Flying" has been crossed out on all the scripts and replaced with "Red." Scripts 27 – 65 do not have these edits and should be considered later versions.

Episode 2
Writer: Gomer Cool
Script checked March 27, 1935 by KMR
Rose Carter, the daughter of Sam Carter, is returning to the Red Horse Ranch after completing her studies back East. The boys have entered a horse race and the winner gets the privilege of picking Rose up at the train station and escorting her back to the ranch. Idaho is the winner and he sets of on the buck board to get Rose.
Songs:
Ridin' Old Paint and Leadin' Old Dan – Texas Rangers
Rustler's Warning – Tex Owens
Jenny Lind – Harmonic Choir

Pony Boys – Texas Rangers
Episode 3
Writer: Gomer Cool
Script checked March 27, 1935 by KMR
While Idaho is gone to town where Rose Carter waits, the boys of the Red Horse Ranch have gathered on the main porch. They've kicked off work for the day and are preparing their trademark music for the upcoming festivities.
Songs:
Oh Suzannah – Fiddle, Banjo Harmonica
New River Train – Texas Rangers
Blue Yodel – Tex Owens
Pride of the Prairie – Texas Rangers

Episode 4
Writer: Gomer Cool
Script checked March 27, 1935 by KMR
Night has come! Time for the barn dance at Sam Carter's. The Red Ranch cowboys are ready to entertain the folks that have ridden in from all around the countryside. The evening is full of great cowboy tunes.
Songs:
His Trademarks – Texas Rangers
Bugle Call Rag – banjo
Roses Bring Memories of You – Tex Owens
Roll On – Texas Rangers

Episode 5
Writer: Gomer Cool
Script checked March 27, 1935 by KMR
In celebration of Rose Carter's return from boarding school in the East, Sam Carter throws the biggest barn-dance the countryside has seen in quite some time. The Red Horse Ranch boys happen to be accomplished musicians and make the dance one that will be remembered for some time.
Songs:
Devil's Dream – Orchestra
Down the Rocky Mountain Trail

Comin Round the Mountain – Texas Rangers
Sweet Bunch of Daisies – Orchestra

Episode 6
Writer: Gomer Cool
Script checked March 27, 1935 by KMR
A stranger has moved in the area, Steve Bradford. He's purchased the nearby Bar D Ranch and has his sights set on the Red Horse.
Songs:
Jack o' Diamonds – Quartet
Strawberry Roan – Quartet
Lonesome Valley Sally – Texas Rangers
Cut Down the Old Pine Tree – all

Episode 7
Writer: Gomer Cool
Script checked March 27, 1935 by KMR
Ranch hand Alabam has his eyes set on breaking Rex his sleek roan horse. Everyone else, including ace horseman Idaho, failed to tame this stallion but Alabam is successful.
Songs:
Old Paint – Texas Rangers
Old Gray Mare – Tex Owens
Tiger rag – banjo solo – Arizona
Notes: Rex, Alabam's horse, was originally named Pegasus.

Episode 8
Writer: Gomer Cool
Script checked March 27, 1935 by KMR
After Cookie dishes up a good meal, Arizona decides to take his chances with Alabam's horse, Rex. Unfortunately for Arizona, Rex throws him over the corral fence, injuring his body and his pride.
Songs:
Lone Driftin' Riders – Texas Rangers
Yodelin' Ranger – Tex Owens
Dark Town Strutter's Ball – Idaho and Orchestra
Buckin' Bronco – Texas Rangers

Episode 9
Writer: Gomer Cool
Script checked March 27, 1935 by KMR
Arizona is still taking jabs from the other hands about his being thrown by Rex. In the meantime, Steve Bradford's offer for the Red Horse Ranch is weighing heavily on Sam Carter's mind. Alabam, Carter's ranch foreman, takes it on himself to investigate Bradford's reasons for wanting to buy the Red Horse.
Songs:
Strawberry Roan – Tex Owens
Good Old Turnip Greens – Tex Owens
Sally Goodin – French Harp Choir
Poor Married Man – Texas Rangers
Cowboy's Dream – all

Episode 10
Writer: Gomer Cool
Script checked March 27, 1935 by KMR
While the ranch hands ponder the possible sale of the Red Horse Ranch to Steve Bradford, things get fishy. While Rose is out riding her horse, Blackie, a mysterious shot is fired, causing Blackie to bolt. Before Rose is injured on the runaway horse Steve Bradford appears and pulls her from the frightened Blackie.
Songs:
I Had a Gal and Her Name was Sue – Texas Rangers
Dinah – Guitar
Great Granddad – Texas Rangers

Episode 11
Writer: Gomer Cool
Script checked March 27, 1935 by KMR
Sam Carter, owner of the Red Horse Ranch, has fallen on hard times and desperately needs the money that would come from selling the ranch. The boys continue to investigate the reasons for Bradford's sudden interest in the Red Horse and surrounding ranches.
Songs:

Dill Pickle Rag – banjo
Rockin' Alone in the Old Rockin' Chair – Tex Owens
Jesse James – Texas Rangers
Cowboy Jack – Texas Rangers

Episode 12
Writer: Gomer Cool
Script checked March 27, 1935 by KMR
The Red Horse is safe for now, Sam Carter has declined Steve Bradford's offer. The boys celebrate by riding wild horses, bull dogging some steers, and, of course, singing.
Songs:
Red River Valley
La Golondrina – Accordion
Beautiful Life – Tex Owens
Wait Till the Sun Shines Nellie – Texas Rangers

Episode 13
Writer: Gomer Cool
Script checked March 27, 1935 by KMR
While celebrating the good news that the Red Horse Ranch will not be sold, Alabam's horse, Rex, disappears without a trace.
Songs:
Little Brown Jug – Texas Rangers and Jug
Dixie Melody
Git Along Cincy – Tex Owens
Man on the Flying Trapeze – Arizona and Texas Rangers with Yodel Chorus

Episode 14
Writer: Gomer Cool
Script checked March 27, 1935 by KMR
Ever since Steve Bradford was rebuffed in his efforts to buy the Red Horse, foreman Alabam has told the boys to be on the lookout for any shenanigans. Meanwhile, Alabam heads over to Bradford's Bar D to investigate some rumored rustling of Red Horse cattle.
Songs

Little Green Valley – Texas Rangers
Blarney in the Chicken Coop – Orchestra
Cattle Call – Tex Owens
San Anton – Texas Rangers

Episode 15
Writer: Gomer Cool
Script checked March 27, 1935 by KMR
While Alabam is investigating the neighboring Bar D Ranch for rustled cattle, he falls from his mount, Rex. Sensing trouble, Rex races to the Red Horse and brings back Sam Carter and the other ranch hands who take him to the bunkhouse to recover
Songs:
Chicken Reel
Old Wishing Well – Texas Rangers
Banks of a Lonely River – Tex Owens
Little Old Sod Shanty – Texas Rangers

Episode 16
Writer: Gomer Cool
Script checked March 27, 1935 by KMR
Alabam reveals to Tenderfoot that he was injured as a result of a run-in with Steve Bradford; as far as the rest of the boys know he simply became dizzy and fell from his mount. Because Alabam is still confined to his cot his bunkmates play some music to lift his spirits.
Songs:
Lonely Valley – Texas Rangers
Empty Cot in the Bunkhouse – Tex Owens
Sourwood Mountain – Texas Rangers
Lonesome Valley Sally – Texas Rangers

Episode 17
Writer: Gomer Cool
Script checked March 27, 1935 by KMR
The day of the big round-up has arrived but the ranch hands have some misgivings. Alabam, still injured, must stay behind and in his place Steve Bradford is being sent to lead the round-up efforts.

Sam Carter, the Red Horse owner, is still not aware of Bradford's part in Alabam's injured leg.
Songs:
Down in Arkansas – Texas Rangers
I'll Remember You in My Prayer – Tex Owens
Prairie Home in Old New Mexico – Texas Rangers

Episode 18
Writer: Gomer Cool
Script checked March 27, 1935 by KMR
Rose, Sam Carter, and the injured Alabam are left to watch over the Red Horse Ranch while the rest of the boys, led by Steve Bradford, go out to round up the Red Horse herd. Carter reveals that he must sell all his cattle in order to raise enough money to pay off the ranch's obligations.
Songs:
Press Along to the Big Corral – Texas Rangers
Clock and the Banjo – banjo
Blue Yodel – Tex Owens

Episode 19
Writer: Gomer Cool
Script checked March 27, 1935 by KMR
Suspicious of Steve Bradford, Alabam cannot stay on the Red Horse while everyone else rounds up the herd of cattle. Despite a bum leg he mounts up and rides to find the ranch boys who are being led by Bradford.
Songs:
Gal I Left Behind – harmonica
I've Got No Use For the Women – Arizona
Doggie's Lullaby – Tex Owens
Cowboy's Meditation – Texas Rangers
Buffalo Gal – Texas Rangers

Episode 20
Writer: Gomer Cool
Script checked March 27, 1935 by KMR

Alabam has joined his companions on the round-up trail and they spend time around the campfire singing. The mood has lightened since Alabam arrived

Songs:
Original Cattle Call – Tex Owens
Cowboy's Heaven – Texas Rangers
Turkey in the Straw – French Harp
Roll on Silver Moon – Tex Owens
Doggies Lullaby – Texas Rangers

Episode 21
Writer: Gomer Cool
Script checked March 27, 1935 by KMR
On the last night of the round-up disaster strikes and much of the herd is rustled! While the Red Horse Ranch boys want to pursue the thieves, Steve Bradford, who was put in charge of the round-up by ranch owner Sam Carter, insists they stay with the remaining cattle and let the rustlers go. This leaves a bad taste in their mouth and puts Carter in trouble; he was counting on the proceeds from selling the herd to help steady the ranch's perilous finances.

Songs:
Ridin' Down That Old Western Trail – Tex Owens
Trouble for the Range Cook – Texas Rangers
Twenty One Years Ago – Texas Rangers

Episode 22
Writer: Gomer Cool
Script checked March 27, 1935 by KMR
The Red Horse Ranch hands guide the remnants of Sam Carter's herd back to the ranch. Round-up leader Steve Bradford has trouble explaining to Carter why he refused to allow the boys to pursue the rustlers. Meanwhile, it has started to rain so the remaining cattle cannot be driven into town for sale. The Red Horse boys pass the rainy day with songs.

Songs:
Little Joe the Wrangler – Texas Rangers
Lone Cowboy – Tex Owens
Old Chisholm Trail – Texas Rangers

Episode 23
Writer: Gomer Cool
Script checked March 27, 1935 by KMR
Sam Carter, owner of the Red Horse Ranch, is about ready to give up hope for saving the ranch after a good number of his cattle were stolen during the round-up. He sees no other choice than to finally sell out to Steve Bradford but Carter's foreman, Alabam, talks him into holding out just a little longer. Alabam has a plan to save the Red Horse but needs the help of his ranch hand buddies.
Songs:
Great Grandma – Texas Rangers
Down Home Rag – French Harp Choir
Old Wishing Well – Texas Rangers

Episode 24
Writer: Gomer Cool
Script checked March 27, 1935 by KMR
Sheriff Simpkins attempts to serve an attachment to Carter's cattle head, a move that would have spelled certain doom for the Red Horse Ranch. However, the threat of rattlesnakes deterred the sheriff, buying the boys more time in devising a way to avert a sale.
Songs:
Texas Maiden – Tex Rangers
A Slice of Bacon – Tex Owens
Bingo Farm – Texas Rangers
Jenny Lind – Tater Bug Band

Episode 25
Writer: Gomer Cool
Script checked March 27, 1935 by KMR
This episode takes a break from the ongoing story line and simply offers a quarter-hour of western songs by the Rangers who are relaxing in the bunk house. Arizona, however, enjoys the moon on the clear night.
Songs:
Mountain Music – Texas Rangers
West, a Nest and You – Texas Rangers
Johnny Much Ado – Tex Owens

Episode 26
Writer: Gomer Cool
Script checked March 27, 1935 by KMR
Alabam makes the shocking revelation to the ranch hands that he believes oil exists on the Red Horse Ranch. He swears the boys to secrecy, insistent that Rose and Sam Carter should not yet know this information. The mystery deepens when Alabam refuses to explain what has led him to make this remarkable claim.
Songs:
Pretty Quadroon – Texas Rangers
Prairie Dream Boat – Texas Rangers
Down That Rocky Mountain Trail – Tex Owens
Better Times are Comin' – Texas Rangers

Episode 27
Writer: Gomer Cool
Script checked March 27, 1935 by KMR
Alabam is expecting a letter which may reveal the true identify of Steve Bradford, the mysterious stranger trying to buy the Red Horse Ranch. He enlists Tenderfoot to travel with him to Danville to pick up the letter at the post office. To no avail Sam Carter tries to convince the two to postpone the trip, leaving the rest of ranch boys to keep tabs on the herd.
Songs:
Farewell Blues - guitar
Cheyenne Round-Up - Slim and Quartet
Dear Old Western Sky – Quartet

Episode 28
Writer: Gomer Cool
Script checked March 27, 1935 by KMR
In Danville Alabam finds himself in a scuffle with none other than Steve Bradford. The odds are against him and one of Bradford's men knocks Alabam out from behind in a saloon fight. There is trouble at the Red Horse Ranch, too, as rustlers make off with the remaining cattle.
Songs:
Polly Wolly Doodle

Red River Valley - Quartet
Cheyenne - Quartet
Frankie and Johnnie – Piano

Episode 29
Writer: Gomer Cool
Script checked March 27, 1935 by KMR
With no word from Alabam, Sam Carter receives word from Bradford that the night before – at the time Carter's last cattle were stolen – Alabam was drunk in a Danville saloon. The boys want nothing more than to search out their friend but Carter insists they stay put on the ranch while he takes care of some business.
Songs:
Swanee River - banjo
Lonely Valley – Texas Rangers
In the Land Where We Never Grow Old

Episode 30
Writer: Gomer Cool
Script checked March 27, 1935 by KMR
Alabam finally makes his way back to Red Horse Ranch where Carter admits he has no reason not to believe Bradford's story of Alabam's drunkenness. Disheartened at letting down their boss, Alabam and the boys set out, determined to recover the Ranch's rustled cattle.
Songs:
Honeysuckle Rose - Guitar
Birmingham Jail - Quartet
Bring Back My Buddy to Me – Tex Owens

Episode 31
Writer: Gomer Cool
Script checked March 27, 1935 by KMR
The boys of the Red Horse Ranch are on a single-minded mission; to retrieve the ranch's stolen cattle. Sam Carter and Rose are on hand to see the herd being led home by Alabam and the others.
Songs:

Blues ain't Nothin' - Cookie
Lay Down Doggies - Cookie, Rose

Episode 32
Writer: Gomer Cool
Script checked March 27, 1935 by KMR
Alabam reveals to the other ranch hands that he is sure that oil will be found on the Red Horse Ranch. However, he has not shared this with Sam or Rose Carter. In the meantime, Sam has left for Danville to sell the herd and raise money for the ranch.
Songs:
Crawdad Song
Yodelin' Ranger - Tex Owens
Mom-Inez - instrumental
Little Girl Dressed In Blue – Texas Rangers
Sweet Bunch of Daisies - Background instrumental

Episode 33
Writer: Gomer Cool
Script checked March 27, 1935 by KMR
Upon returning from Danville Sam Carter shares the good news with his ranch men; the herd's sale will provide enough money to pull the operation through for another year. Alabam continues to keep his suspicions about an oil find a secret and has started keeping a close eye on his horse Red, much to the confusion of the others.
Songs:
Cowboy's Heaven – Quartet
Soldier's Joy - instrumental
Dying Cowgirl - quartet

Episode 34
Writer: Gomer Cool
Script checked March 27, 1935 by KMR
Alabam's horse Red, escapes his pen at night by jumping the corral fence. Alabam and Tenderfoot trail the horse where they make an exciting discovery. They don't share this with Rose but Alabam is excited to tell her about his midnight ride.

Songs:
Old Covered Bridge
Broken Engagement - Tex Owens
Bugle Call Rage - background banjo
Arkansas Mule - Alabam and Rangers

Episode 35
Writer: Gomer Cool
Script checked March 27, 1935 by KMR
The mood on the ranch is much lighter now that financial disaster has been averted for at least another year. To celebrate, Sam Carter decides to hold a barn dance and invite neighbors from the surrounding ranches and farms.
Songs:
Prairie Dream Boat - background Rangers
Pop Goes the Weasel - Jug - Rangers
Two Lovers - Tex Owens
Roy Bean - Rangers

Episode 36
Writer: Gomer Cool
Script checked March 27, 1935 by KMR
A stranger shows up at the barn dance and speaks privately with Alabam who later declines to tell his friends what the conversation was about. Tenderfoot, meanwhile, is falling for Rose Carter, daughter of his boss, Sam "Dad" Carter.
Songs:
Santa Fe Town
Blue Eyes – Tex Owens
Little Brown Jug - Rangers
Rye Waltz

Episode 37
Writer: Gomer Cool
Script checked March 27, 1935 by KMR
It's revealed that an Eastern oil company has requested an oil lease for the Red Horse Ranch land after conducting some tests. Mr.

Niles, of the oil company, has entered into negotiations with Sam and Rose Carter.
Songs:
Wandering Cowboy – Texas Rangers
Turkey in the Straw - banjo, all
Bury Me Not - all
Loveless Love - Rangers

Episode 38
Writer: Gomer Cool
Script checked March 27, 1935 by KMR
The storyline of *Life on the Red Horse Ranch* takes a turn from Carter's troubles with Steve Bradford to the introduction of a new character, the young son of "Trigger" Dawson, an outlaw who was fatally wounded by a sheriff's posse. Alabam instructs Tenderfoot to travel to Roaring River and bring the orphaned boy back to Red Horse Ranch, against the wishes of the other ranch hands.
Songs:
Down South - banjo
Strawberry Roan - Rangers
Train Whistlin' Blues
Old Gray Bonnet - Rangers

Episode 39
Writer: Gomer Cool
Script checked March 27, 1935 by KMR
Dewey Dawson, son of deceased outlaw "Trigger" Dawson, is brought back to the Red Horse Ranch where he fails to make a good first impression. Sam Carter is adamant that the boy must go but the ranch boys have other plans.
Songs:
Down in Arkansas
Jack's Letter From Home - Tex Owens
Swanee River - all
Pony boy - Rangers

Episode 40
Writer: Gomer Cool
Script checked March 27, 1935 by KMR
Reluctantly Sam Carter has been talked into letting young Dewey Dawson stay at the Red Horse Ranch. Having the son of slain outlaw "Trigger" Dawson around makes the boys a bit nervous and Sam Carter has told Cookie, the cook, to get rid of Dewey's dog.
Songs:
Little Joe the Wrangler – Texas Rangers
Irish Washer Woman - orchestra
I've got no use fer the women - Arizona
Fornortaling Town - Tex Owens
Billy Boy – Texas Rangers

Episode 41
Writer: Gomer Cool
Script checked March 27, 1935 by KMR
Taking both Dewey Dawson and the boy's dog under his wing, Alabam ensures the dog can stay at Red Horse Ranch. Coming up soon is a big rodeo at Danville and the boys are excited to attend. Tenderfoot, however, can't stop thinking of Rose Carter
Songs:
Ridin' Old Paint – Texas Rangers
A Slice of Bacon - Tex Owens
Dill Pickle Rag - banjo solo
Jack O' Diamonds – Texas Rangers

Episode 42
Writer: Gomer Cool
Script checked March 27, 1935 by KMR
Tenderfoot's heart is broken when he finds that Rose has eyes for Alabam, not for him. Alabam, however, remains unaware of the conversation between his friend and Rose.
Songs:
Roll on Silver Moon – Tex Owens
Lonesome Valley Sally – Texas Rangers
Nevada Moon – Texas Rangers
Estrellita – accordion

Episode 43
Writer: Gomer Cool
Script checked March 27, 1935 by KMR
After some soul-searching Tenderfoot decides to get away from Red Horse Ranch for a time so he will no longer come between Alabam and Rose Carter. Alabam, hearing of his friend's departure, goes searching for him.
Songs:
Cut Down the Old Pine Tree – Texas Rangers
Cattle Call - Tex Owens
Jenny Lind Polka – Tater Bug Band (Arizona, Tex, Idaho, Monty on makeshift instruments)
New River Train – Texas Rangers

Episode 44
Writer: Gomer Cool
Script checked March 27, 1935 by KMR
The big Danville rodeo has arrived and, as usual, Sam Carter is taking his entire crew, many of whom want to compete in the scheduled events. Steve Bradford, former nemesis of the Red Horse ranch hands, is rumored to be entering his horse in one of the races. To prove the merit of his own horse, Red, Alabam is eager to get to the rodeo.
Songs:
Puttin' on the Style
Limehouse Blues - Guitar
I know there is somebody waiting - Quartet
Comin' Round the Mountain – all

Episode 45
Writer: Gomer Cool
Script checked March 27, 1935 by KMR
The boys of Red Horse Ranch have high expectations for the Danville rodeo, both in competitions and entertaining the audiences with their tunes.
Songs:
Oh Mona
Utah Carl - Quartet

Sorgum Molasses - Tex Owens
Oh Suzannah – Rangers

Episode 46
Writer: Gomer Cool
Script checked March 27, 1935 by KMR
The first big event for the Red Horse Ranch boys is a horse race including Alabam and Steve Bradford, the winner earning a place in the finals. While waiting for the race to begin they take the opportunity to perform for the crowd.
Songs:
Old Grey Bonnet – banjo
Ridin' Down that Old Texas Trail - quartet
Yodelin' Ranger - Tex Owens
Jesse James – Texas Rangers

Episode 47
Writer: Gomer Cool
Script checked March 27, 1935 by KMR
The anticipated horse race involving Alabam and Steve Bradford is underway but disaster strikes when Alabam is thrown by his horse, Red. Upon investigation Alabam finds cactus under Red's saddle blanket, surely the cause of Red's unexpected behavior.
Songs:
His Trademarks – Quartet
Chicken Reel - harmonicas
Lone Driftin' Riders - Quartet
Down Home Rag – instrumental

Episode 48
Writer: Gomer Cool
Script checked March 27, 1935 by KMR
Steve Bradford's win at the horse race is suspect to all the Red Horse Ranch boys when they discover cactus under the saddle blanket of Red, Alabam's horse. Nevertheless, they still find success in several other rodeo events.
Songs:
Buckin' Bronco - Quartet

Doggies Lullaby – Quartet
La Rosita - accordion
I Want a Girl – Quartet

Episode 49
Writer: Gomer Cool
Script checked March 27, 1935 by KMR
While Alabam did not make the finals of the rodeo's horse race, Idaho and his horse did. However, as the final race approaches Idaho discovers his mount has bum foot and can't compete. He makes every attempt to get Alabam and Red to take his place in the final race against Steve Bradford.
Songs:
San Antonio - quartet
Nickety Nackety now…with yodeling - Tex
Panama - instrumental
Two Gun Bill

Episode 50
Writer: Gomer Cool
Script checked March 27, 1935 by KMR
The Danville rodeo ends on a high note for all the Red Horse Ranch gang when Alabam and his trusty horse, Red, win a rematch with Steve Bradford at the rodeo's final horse race.
Songs:
Spanish Cavalier – Instrumental
Goodbye Old Paint - Quartet
Hold that Tiger – banjo

Episode 51
Writer: Gomer Cool
Script checked March 27, 1935 by KMR
It's been tough going for Dewey Dawson, the young boy brought to the Red Horse Ranch under the guiding eye of Alabam. With persistence, however, he has won over the ranch's crew along with Sam and Rose Carter who were skeptical of the lad's place at the ranch. Alabam's victory in the Danville rodeo horse race has put all in highest spirits.

Songs:
Let the Rest of the World Go By – Ensemble
Mother the Queen of My Heart – Tex Owens
Dreamy Moon - violin and guitar
I had a gal and her name was Sue - Quartet

Episode 52
Writer: Gomer Cool
Script checked March 27, 1935 by KMR
The Red Horse Ranch Boys hear that two members of the "Trigger" Dawson gang have escaped from jail in Roaring River. In the dead of night an attempt is made by some mysterious riders to make off with Dewey Dawson, son of "Trigger."
Songs:
Pride of the Prairie – vocal and instruments
Little Mother of the Hills
My Prairie Home in Old New Mexico - quartet
Shine on Harvest Moon – accordion

Episode 53
Writer: Gomer Cool
Script checked March 27, 1935 by KMR
Dewey Dawson was almost kidnapped and the Red Horse Ranch boys are positive it was the work of two escaped members of "Trigger" Dawson's gang.
Songs:
Home in Wyoming – Quartet
Wonder Valley
Dark Town Strutter's Ball – jug, instrumental

Episode 54
Writer: Gomer Cool
Script checked March 27, 1935 by KMR
After a previous kidnapping attempt by members of "Trigger" Dawson's gang, Dewey Dawson is now missing . The Red Horse Ranch gang take off to find the boy.
Songs:
Little Old Sod Shanty - Quartet

We Got a Cow Down on our Farm - Quartet
The Answer to Twenty One Years – Quartet

Episode 55
Writer: Gomer Cool
Script checked March 27, 1935 by KMR
Young Dewey Dawson was given a locket by his father, "Trigger" Dawson before he was killed. Dewey was warned by his father to never open or share the locket. Two of "Trigger" Dawson's old gang members have escaped from jail and want Dewey's locket.
Songs:
Banjo solo
Broken Hearted Cowboy – Tex Owens
Take me back to peaceful Valley - Quartet
Texas Cowboy – quartet

Episode 56
Writer: Gomer Cool
Script checked March 27, 1935 by KMR
Dewey's locket is opened to reveal a mysterious map. Alabam and his Red Horse Ranch companions think the map may show the way to some loot hidden by "Trigger" Dawson before he was murdered. If only they could figure out how to read the map.
Songs:
Loveless Love - vocal and instrumental
True Blue Hill - Arizona and boys
Yellow Rose of Texas - Quartet

Episode 57
Writer: Gomer Cool
Script checked March 27, 1935 by KMR
The boys stumble on a clue which may help them decipher the mysterious map found in Dewey Dawson's locket. There is invisible writing on the map which can only be seen when a match is held under it. Alabam thinks the discovery is so important he shares it with Sam and Rose Carter.
Songs:
Trail to Mexico - Quartet

No One to Call Me Darling - Quartet
Way Out West in Texas – Quartet

Episode 58
Writer: Gomer Cool
Script checked March 27, 1935 by KMR
After considerable effort Alabam and the others discover the invisible writing on Dewey Dawson's map reveals that the other part of the map is hidden on Lookout Point along Roaring River. If they can uncover the rest of the map the Red Horse Ranch boys will surely find "Trigger" Dawson's lost treasure from his criminal career.
Songs:
Wishing Well – Quartet
La Golondrina - accordion
Ride Cowboy Ride - Quartet
Ridin' Down That Old Texas Trail - Quartet

Episode 59
Writer: Gomer Cool
Script checked March 27, 1935 by KMR
Alabam goes to search Lookout Point for the missing half of "Trigger" Dawson's map but finds that someone has beat him to the old Native American mound along the Roaring River.
Songs:
Missouri Waltz – Harmonica Choir
Ghost of the banjo - Arizona
Beautiful Colorado – Tex Owens
Cowboy Jack - Quartet

Episode 60
Writer: Gomer Cool
Script checked March 27, 1935 by KMR
Alabam and his friends from the Red Horse Ranch are determined to find the loot hidden somewhere in the mountains along Roaring River.
Songs:
It's Heck to Bum in Texas - Quartet

Old Circle B - Tex Owens
Me and my burro - Quartet

Episode 61
Writer: Gomer Cool
Script checked March 27, 1935 by KMR
The search for Dawson's treasure continues on a trail along Roaring River.
Songs:
The Old Covered Wagon – Background quartet
April Kisses - Guitar
When It's Roundup Time in heaven – Tex Owens
White Azaleas - Quartet

Episode 62
Writer: Gomer Cool
Script checked March 27, 1935 by KMR
The search for "Trigger" Dawson's loot continues. The Red Horse Ranch boys are sure they're getting close on a trail overlooking Roaring River. Alabam takes a few of the ranch hands down into the canyon to investigate while the others maintain watch along the ridge.
Songs:
When Uncle Joe Plays the Rag on His Old Banjo – Banjo
Two Gun Bill - Quartet
The Gal I Left Behind Me – French harps

Episode 63
Writer: Gomer Cool
Script checked March 27, 1935 by KMR
Alabam takes Bob, Idaho, and young Dewey with him to descend into the canyon along Roaring River in search of the loot hidden by Dewey's slain outlaw father, "Trigger" Dawson.
Songs:
Turkey in Straw – Banjo Solo
Lonely Mountaineers - Quartet
Blues Ain't Nothin' - Cookie
Blue Yodel Number – Tex Owens

Episode 64
Writer: Gomer Cool
Script checked March 27, 1935 by KMR
Alabam and the others find "Trigger" Dawson's loot hidden beneath a water fall on Roaring River. The boys safely return with the treasure to Red Horse Ranch.
Songs:
Take me Home - quartet

Episode 65
Writer: Gomer Cool
Script checked March 27, 1935 by KMR
In the safety of Red Horse Ranch Alabam insists that the reward they receive for recovering Dawson's stolen goods should be set aside in a bank for Dawson's son, Dewey. Meanwhile, the oil company which took out a lease on the Red Horse land has moved their drilling equipment onto the ranch. The series concludes with the announcer's statement: "We found a happy gang on Red Horse Ranch today, didn't we? We wonder if he [San Carter] feels that everything will go so smooth when the oil company begins its drilling operations?" No further episode were produced so this new storyline was never developed further.
Songs:
Nobody's Sweetheart - accordion, bass, fiddle, guitar
Little Girl Dressed in Blue - Quartet
Swaller Tail Coat - Quartet
Wait Till the Sun Shines Nellie – Quartet

Appendix C:
Under Western Skies
Station List

WABC – New York City
WCAO – Baltimore
WGAR – Cleveland
WDRC – Hartford
KFAB – Lincoln
WJSV – Washington, D.C.
WORC – Worcester
WNBF – Binghamton
WHP – Harrisburg
WGAN – Portland
WMAS – Springfield, MA
WWNC – Asheville
WSJS – Winston-Salem
KLRA – Little Rock
WMBR – Jacksonville
WDAE – Tampa
KRLD – Dallas City
KTSA – San Antonio
WKBH – La Crosse
KSL – Salt Lake City
KROY – Sacramento
KOIN – Portland
KVI - Tacoma

WADC – Akron
WGR – Buffalo
KRNT – Des Moines
WFBM – Indianapolis
WHAS – Louisville
WBNS – Columbus
WPG – Atlantic City
WCHS – Charleston
WBRY – New Haven
WGBI – Scranton
WIBX – Utica
WRVA – Richmond
WGST – Atlanta
WLAC – Nashville
WQAM – Miami
WJNO – West Palm Beach
KTRH – Houston

KWFT – Wichita Falls
WCCO – Minneapolis
KFBB – Great Falls
KTUC – Tucson
KIRO – Seattle

WOKO - Albany
WKRC – Cincinnati
WJR – Detroit
KMBC – Kansas City
WPRO – Providence
WHEC – Rochester
WABI – Bangor
WMMN – Fairmont
WPAR – Parkersburg
WFAM – South Bend
KFH – Wichita
WDBJ – Roanoke
WAPI – Birmingham
WWL – New Orleans
WDBO – Orlando
CFRB – Toronto
KOMA – Oklahoma

KDAL – Duluth
WNAX – Yankton
KOY – Phoenix
KARM – Fresno
KFPY – Spokane

Appendix D:
Filmography

Colorado Sunset
Republic Pictures
Released July 31, 1939
William Berke: Producer
George Sherman: Director
Luci Ward and Jack Natteford: Authors
Betty Burbridge and Stanley Roberts: Screenplay
William Nobles: Camera
Lester Orlebeck: Editor
Featuring:
Gene Autry
Smiley Burnette
June Storey
Barbara Pepper
Larry "Buster" Crabbe
Robert Barret
Patsy Montana
Purnell Pratt
William Farnum
Kermit Maynard
Jack Ingram
Elmo Lincoln
Frankie Marvin
The Texas Rangers (as the CBS-KMBC Texas Rangers)
Songs:
"On the Merry Old Way Back Home" (with Gene Autry and Smiley Burnette)
"Cowboys Don't Milk Cows" (with Smiley Burnette)
"I Want to be a Cowboy's Sweethearts" (with Patsy Montana)
"Beautiful Isle of Somewhere" (with Gene Autry and the townsfolk)
"Autry's the Man – Vote for Autry" (with Smiley Burnette)

Autry and pal Burnette are tricked into buying a dairy ranch, unbeknownst to them landing the pair in the middle of a dairy feud. Local dairymen are being forced into a combine and a local radio station is being used to abet the schemers. Autry and his boys bring down the plot after a notable fistfight.

Oklahoma Frontier
Universal Pictures
Released October 10, 1939
Albert Ray: Associate Producer
Ford Beebe: Director
Ford Beebe: Screenplay
Jerome Ash: Camera
Featuring:
Johnny Mack Brown
Bob Baker
Fuzzy Knight
Anne Gwynne
James Blaine
Robert Kortman
Charles King
Harry Tenbrook
The Texas Rangers (as The CBS-Texas Rangers)
Songs:
"Buffalo Gal"
"My Cincinnati" (with Fuzzy Knight)
"Get Along Little Pony"
"In Old Oklahoma" (with Bob Baker)
"Push Along to the Big Corral"
"Get Along Little Dogies"

Refusing to kill his friends who have broken the law, Brown quits his job as Western marshal. Deciding what to do next, he makes his way to the Cherokee Strip which is about to be opened to settlers. He joins up with his old friend, played by Baker, and Baker's sister, played by Gwynne. In their efforts to claim a prime piece of land Baker is killed and Brown just narrowly takes care of a gang of murderous land grabbers.

Chip of the Flying U
Universal Pictures
Released January 24, 1940

Ralph Staub: Director
Larry Rhine and Andrew Bennison: Screenplay
William Sickner: Camera
Featuring:
Johnny Mack Brown
Bob Baker
Fuzzy Knight
Doris Weston
Karl Hackett
Forrest Taylor
Anthony Warde
Henry Hall
Claire Whitney
Cecil Kellogg
The Texas Rangers (As the CBS-Texas Rangers)
Songs:
"Ride On" (with Bob Baker)
"Git Along" (with Bob Baker)
"Mr. Moon" (sung by Bob Baker)
"Aches and Pains" (sung by Fuzzy Knight)
"A Gal Named Sue" (sung by Fuzzy Knight)

    Brown escapes a holdup with Weston, daughter of his employer. The villains, lead by Hackett, are trying to force Brown's boss off his ranch so they can get to some munitions that were previously stored on the land. The bad guys are delivered to the law but not before a bank robbery and kidnapping.

Scatterbrain
Republic Pictures
Released July 20, 1940
Gus Meins: Associate Producer and Director
Jack Townley and Val Burton: Screenplay
Paul Conlan: Additional Dialog
Camera: Ernest Miller
Supervising Editor: Murray Seldeen
Film Editor: Ernest Nims
Art Director: John Victor Mackay
Musical Director: Cy Feuer

Featuring:
Judy Canova
Alan Mowbray
Ruth Donnelly
Eddie Foy, Jr.
Joseph Cawthorn
Wallace Ford
Isabel Jewell
Luis Alberni
Billy Gilbert
Emmett Lynn
Jimmy Starr
Cal Shrum's Gang
Matty Malneck and Orchestra
The Texas Rangers (as The KCBS-Texas Rangers)
Songs:
"Scatter-Brain" (sung by Judy Canova)
"Benny the Beaver" (sung by Judy Canova)

 Canova, playing a loud, hog-calling hillbilly singer gets a contract by mistake with a talent agent (Foy, Jr.). This leads to a string of complications which inadvertently cause Canova to rise to stardom.

Son of Roaring Dan
Released July 26, 1940
Universal Pictures
Josephy G. Sanford: Associate Producer
Ford Beebe: Director
Clarence Upson Young: Screenplay
William Sickner: Camera
Featuring:
Johnny Mack Brown
Fuzzy Knight
Nell O'Day
Jeanne Kelly
Lafe McKee
Robert Homans
Tom Chatterton

John Eldredge
Ethan Laidlaw
Eddie Polo
Dick Alexander
The Texas Rangers
Songs:
"Sing Yippi Ki Yi"
"And Then I Got Married"
"Let 'Er Buck Powder River" (written by Gomer Cool)

    Brown stars as a vengeful son seeking his father's killer. He discovers the head of a gang of rustlers, played by Eldredge, is the murderer. An Eastern girl, played by Kelly, witnesses an outlaw killing and her kidnapping is ordered by Eldredge. His men carry out the deed but Brown and his sidekick, played by Knight, rescue Kelly and she serves as the star witness in bringing the evil-doers to justice.

Ragtime Cowboy Joe
Universal Pictures
Released September 20, 1940 (New York: September 25, 1940)
Ray Taylor: Director
Sherman Lowe: Screenplay
Jerome Ash: Camera
Featuring:
Johnny Mack Brown
Fuzzy Knight
Nell O'Day
Dick Curtis
Marilyn Merrick
Walter Soderling
Roy Barcroft
Harry Tenbrook
George Plues
Ed Cassidy
Buck Moulton
Harold Goodwin
Wilfred Lucas
The Texas Rangers (as the KCBS Texas Rangers)

Songs:
"Cross-Eyed Kate" (with Fuzzy Knight)
"Do the Ooh La La" (sung by Fuzzy Knight)
"Song of the Trail Drive" (written by Bob Crawford)

    A gang of cattle rustlers is on the loose and Brown, a cattle association detective, is charged with tracking them down. Brown himself is suspected of murdering an esteemed rancher before proving his innocence to the sheriff and delivering the rustlers into his hands.

Law of the Range
Universal Pictures
Released June 20, 1941, (New York: July 7, 1941)
Ray Taylor: Director
Will Cowan: Producer
Charles Van Enger: Camera
Featuring:
Johnny Mack Brown
Fuzzy Knight
Nell O'Day
Riley Hill
Roy Harris
Hal Taliaferro
Pat O'Malley
Elaine Morey
Ethan Laidlaw
Al Bridges
Lucile Walker
The Texas Rangers (as the KCBS-Texas Rangers)
Songs:
"Pals of the Prairie" (written by Bob Crawford)
"Six Gun Dan" (with Lucile Walker, written by Bob Crawford)
"Moving on Little Pony"
"I Plumb Forgot" (with Fuzzy Knight)

    Rancher Brown is accused of killing one of his neighbor's men by the bad guy (Harris). A mistaken feud erupts and Brown's neighbor (Taliaferro) is also murdered by Harris. Brown clears and his name and prevents Harris and his gang from taking over the cattle ranches for their own sheep herds.

Rawhide Rangers
Universal Pictures
In production May, 1941
Released June 18, 1941 (New York: August 18, 1941)
Ray Taylor: Director
Featuring:
Johnny Mack Brown
Fuzzy Knight
Kathryn Adams
Nell O'Day
The Texas Rangers
Songs:
"Huckleberry Pie (sung by Fuzzy Knight)
"A Cowboy is Happy"
"Oh, Susanna" (sung by Riley Hill)
"It's a Wrangler's Life" (written by Gomer Cool)
"Then We Go Riding" (written by Gomer Cool)

Brown pretends to go outlaw when his brother is killed by an outlaw named Blackie. When he is conscripted into Blackie's gang, Brown exposes the murderer and redeems himself.

The Last Round-Up
Columbia Pictures
Released November 5, 1947
Harold MacArthur: Art Director
Earle Snell and Jack Townley: Screenplay
Featuring:
Gene Autry
Trevor Bardette
Lee Bennett
Bobby Blake
John L. "Bob" Cason
George C. Fisher
John Halloran
Jean Heather

Ralph Morgan
Carol Thurston
The Texas Rangers
Songs:
"Last Round-Up" (Gene Autry and studio singers)
"She'll Be Comin' Round the Mountain" (Gene Autry and children)
"You Can't See the Sun When You're Crying" (Gene Autry and the Texas Rangers)
"One Hundred Sixty Acres" (Gene Autry and the Texas Rangers)
"An Apple for the Teacher" (Gene Autry)
"Last Round-Up" (Gene Autry)

    An aqueduct is planned for Mesa City, driving some ranchers and Native Americans from their land. Autry is targeted for trouble when he tries to ensure that both parties benefit from the project.

Arkansas Swing (Also referred to as *Texas Sandman*)
Columbia Pictures
Barry Shipman: Story and Screenplay
In production March, 1948
Released July 29, 1948
Gloria Henry
The Hoosier Hotshots (Ken Trietsch, Paul Trietsch, Gil Taylor, Charles Ward)
Stuart Hart
The Texas Rangers
Songs:
"Texas Sandman" (The Hoosier Hotshots)
"Bread and Butter Woman" (The Hoosier Hotshots)
"What I Do"
"Sweetheart of the Blues"
"Not Today"
"That Lucky Feeling"
"Happy Birthday Polka"
"It Ain't Nobody's Business What I Do"
"The Whoopee Hat Brigade"

Members of the Hoosier Hotshots discover trouble at a local racetrack. A horse with championship potential only performs his best when a certain tune is played.

Appendix E:
Early Radio Appearances of the Texas Rangers and Associated Musicians

Week of December 5, 1931
6:45 a.m. (M, T, W, H, F, Sa) Ozie and George (15m)
7:15 a.m. (M) Ozie and George (15m) to network
7:30 a.m. (T, H, Sa) Texas Ranger – Old Time Songs (15m)
12:30 p.m. (T, H, Sa) Ozie and George (15m)
12:35 p.m. (M, W, F), Ozie and George (17m)
5:00 p.m. (M, T, W, H, F, Sa) Big Brother Club (25m)
5:25 p.m. (M, T, F, Sa) Happy Hollow (20m)
8:00 p.m. (Sa) Happy Hollow Columbia Barn Dance (30m) also to CBS

Week of December 12, 1931
6:45 a.m. (M, T, W, H, F, Sa) Ozie and George (15m)
7:15 a.m. (M) Ozie and George (15m) to network
7:30 a.m. (T, H, Sa) Texas Ranger – Old Time Songs (15m)
12:30 p.m. (T, H, Sa) Ozie and George (17m)
12:35 p.m. (M, W, F), Ozie and George (12m)
5:00 p.m. (M, T, W, H, F, Sa) Big Brother Club (25m)
5:25 p.m. (M, T, W, H, F, Sa) Happy Hollow (20m)
8:00 p.m. (Sa) Happy Hollow Columbia Barn Dance (30m) also to CBS

Week of January 2, 1932
6:45 a.m. (M, T, W, H, F, Sa) Ozie and George (15m)
7:00 a.m. (M) Ozie and George (30m) network only
7:30 a.m. (T, H, Sa) Texas Ranger – Old Time Songs (15m)
12:30 p.m. (T, W, H, Sa) Ozie and George (15m)
12:35 p.m. (M, F) Ozie and George (15m)
5:00 p.m. (M, T, W, H, F, Sa) Big Brother Club (25m)
5:25 p.m. (M, T, W, H, F, Sa) Happy Hollow (20m)
8:00 p.m. (Sa) Happy Hollow Barn Dance (30m) also to CBS

Week of January 9, 1932
6:45 a.m. (M, T, W, H, F, Sa) Ozie and George (15m)

7:30 a.m. (T, H, Sa) Texas Ranger – Old Time Songs (15m)
7:30 a.m. (M) Ozie and George (15m) Network
12:30 a.m. (M, T, W, H, F, Sa) Ozie and George (17m)
5:00 a.m. (M, T, W, H, F, Sa) Big Brother Club (25m)
5:25 a.m. (M, T, W, H, F, Sa) Happy Hollow (20m)

February, 1932
7:15 a.m. (W) Ozie and George (20m)
7:30 a.m. (M, F) Ozie and George (15m) also to CBS on Mon
12:10 p.m. (W, H) Ozie and George (15m)
12:15 p.m. (F) Ozie and George (10m)
12:45 p.m. (M) Ozie and George (15m)
5:00 p.m. (M, T, W, H, F, Sa) Big Brother Club (25m)
5:25 p.m. (M, T, W, H, F, Sa) Happy Hollow (20m)
8:00 p.m. (Sa) Happy Hollow Columbia Barn Dance Varieties (30m) also to CBS

March, 1932
9:00 a.m. (Su) Big Brother Club (15m)
5:00 p.m. (M, T, W, H, F, Sa) Big Brother Club (25m)
5:25 p.m. (M, T, W, H, F, Sa) Happy Hollow (20m)
8:00 p.m. (Sa) Happy Hollow Columbia Barn Dance Varieties (30m) also to CBS

April, 1932
9:00 a.m. (Su) Big Brother Club (45m)
5:00 p.m. (M, T, W, H, F, Sa) Big Brother Club (25m)
5:25 p.m. (M, T, W, H, F, Sa) Happy Hollow (20m)
8:00 p.m. (Sa) Happy Hollow Columbia Barn Dance Varieties (30m) Network

May, 1932
8:45 a.m. (Su) Big Brother Club (45m)
12:15 p.m. (M, T, W, H, F, Sa) Happy Hollow (25m)
4:45 p.m. (M, T, W, H, F, Sa) Big Brother Club (30m)

June, 1932
8:45 a.m. (Su) Big Brother Club (45m)

12:35 p.m. (M, T, W, H, F, Sa) Happy Hollow (25m)
4:45 p.m. (M, T, W, H, F, Sa) Big Brother Club (30m)

July 1932
8:45 a.m. (Su) Big Brother Club (45m)
12:35 p.m. (M, T, W, H, F, Sa) Happy Hollow (25m)
2:00 p.m. (Sa) KMBC Orchestra with Midwesterners Quartet
4:45 p.m. (M, T, W, H, F, Sa) Big Brother Club with Brother Bob and Willie (30m)

August , 1932
8:45 a.m. (Su) Big Brother Club (45m)
12:35 p.m. (M, T, W, H, F, Sa) Happy Hollow (25m)
4:45 p.m. (M, T, W, H, F, Sa) Big Brother Club with Brother Bob and Willie (30m)

September, 1932
9:00 a.m. (Su) Big Brother Club (30m)
12:35 p.m. (M, T, W, H, F, Sa) Happy Hollow (25m)
5:00 p.m. (M, T, W, H, F, Sa) Big Brother Club with Brother Bob and Willie (30m)

October, 1932
7:45 a.m. (M, T, W, H, F, Sa) The Texas Ranger – Tex Owens (15m)
12:00 p.m. (F) Aladdin Neighbors with Tex Owens (15m)
12:10 p.m. (M, T, W, H) Aladdin Neighbors – Tex Owens (20 m)
6:00 p.m. (M, T, W, H, F, Sa) Happy Hollow (15m)

January, 1933
7:45 am (T,W,H,F,Sa) The Texas Ranger – Tex Owens (15m)
9:00 am (Su) Big Brother Club (30m)
12:10 (M,T,W,H,F) Aladdin Neighbors with Tex Owens (20m)
1:00 (H) Texas Rangers (15m)
4:45 (M,T,W,H,F,Sa) Big Brother Club (30m)
6:00 (M,T,W,H,F) Happy Hollow (15m)
6:00 (Sa) Happy Hollow Barn Dance (30m)

February, 1933
7:45 a.m. (M,T,H,F,Sa) The Texas Ranger – Tex Owens (15m)
12:10 p.m. (T,W,H,F) Howdy Neighbors - Tex Owens (20m)
12:15 p.m. (Sa) Howdy Neighbors – Tex Owens (15m)
1:00 p.m. (T,H) Texas Rangers (15m) to CBS
5:00 p.m. (M,T,W,H,F,Sa) Big Brother Club (30m)
6:00 p.m. (M,T,W,H,F,Sa) Happy Hollow (15m)

March, 1933
9:00 a.m. (Su) Big Brother Club (30m)
7:45 a.m. (M,T,W,H,F,Sa) The Texas Ranger – Tex Owens (15m)
12:15 p.m. (M,T,W,H,F,Sa) Tex Owens (15m) also television
5:00 p.m. (M,T,W,H,F,Sa) Big Brother Club (15m)
6:15 p.m. (M,T,W,H,F,Sa) Happy Hollow (15m)

April, 1933
7:45 a.m. (M,T,W,H,F,Sa) The Texas Ranger – Tex Owens (15m)
9:00 a.m. (Su) Big Brother Club (30m)
12:15 p.m. (M,T,W,H,F,Sa) Tex Owens (15m) also television
4:45 p.m. (M,T,W,H,F,Sa) Big Brother Club (15m)
6:15 p.m. (M,T,W,H,F,Sa) Happy Hollow (15m)

May, 1933
12:10 p.m. (M) The Texas Rangers and Velma Massey (20m)
12:10 p.m. (T) The Texas Rangers and the Midwesterners Quartet (20m)
12:10 p.m. (W) The Texas Rangers and Jerry Barrett (20m)
12:10 p.m. (H) The Texas Rangers (20m)
12:10 p.m. (F) The Texas Rangers and the Songssmiths (20m)
12:10 p.m. (F) Texas Rangers and the McCarty Girls (20m)
4:30 p.m. (T) The Midwesterners Quartet (15m)
5:15 p.m. (T) Danny and Doug and Uncle Ezry (15m)
5:15 p.m. (H) Danny and Doug (15m)
6:00 p.m. (M,W) Texas Rangers (15m) to CBS
6:15 p.m. (M,W,H,F) Happy Hollow (15m)
6:45 p.m. (W) Ruth Royal and the Midwesterners Quartet (15m) to CBS
8:00 p.m. (T) Happy Hollow Varieties (30m) to CBS

June, 1933
12:30 p.m. (M) The Texas Rangers and Those McCarty Girls (15m)
12:30 p.m. (T) Texas Rangers and the Midwesterners Quartet (15m)
12:30 p.m. (W,H) The Texas Rangers (15m)
12:30 p.m. (F) The Texas Rangers and George Washington White (15m)
12:30 p.m. (Sa) The Texas Rangers and Velma Massey (15m)
12:45 p.m. (M,T,W,H,F,Sa) Happy Hollow (15m)
5:15 p.m. (M,T,W,H,F,Sa) Big Brother Club (15m)
5:45 p.m. (W) Midwesterners and Ruth Royal (15m) also to CBS
5:45 p.m. (H) The Texas Rangers (15m) also to CBS

July, 1933
8:15 a.m. (M,W,F) Uncle Ezry and the Midwesterners (15m)
12:30 p.m. (M) Texas Rangers and Those McCarty Girls (15m)
12:45 p.m. p.m. (M,T,W,H,F) Happy Hollow (15m)
5:15 p.m. (M,W,H,F) Big Brother Club (15m)
5:45 p.m. (T) Midwesterners and Ruth Royal (15m) also to CBS
12:30 p.m. (W) The Texas Rangers (15m)
12:30 p.m. (H) The Texas Rangers and Velma Massey (15m)
5:45 p.m. (Th) The Texas Rangers (15m) also to CBS
12:30 p.m. (F) The Texas Rangers and George Washington White (15m)
12:30 p.m. (Sa) Happy Hollow Barn Dance (30m)

August, 1933
8:15 a.m. (M,W,F) Uncle Ezry and the Midwesterners (15m)
12:35 p.m. (M,W,F) The Texas Rangers (10m)
12:45 p.m. (M,T,W,H,F) Happy Hollow (15m)
1:00 p.m. (T,H) The Texas Rangers (15m)
4:45 p.m. (M,T,W,H,F,Sa) Big Brother Club (15m)
5:45 p.m. (T) Midwesterners and Ruth Royal (15m) also to CBS
5:45 p.m. (H) The Texas Rangers (15m) also to CBS
12:30 p.m. (Sa) Happy Hollow Barn Dance (30m)

September, 1933
12:35 p.m. (M,F) The Texas Rangers (10m)
3:00 p.m. (W) The Midwesterners (15m)
4:45 p.m. (M,T, W,H,F,Sa) Big Brother Club (15m)
5:00 p.m. (M,T, W,H,F) The Texas Rangers (15m)
6:00 p.m. (M,T, W,H,F,Sa) Happy Hollow (15m)
7:30 p.m. (F) The Midwesterners (15m) to CBS

October, 1933
4:45 p.m. (M,T,W,H,F,Sa) Big Brother Club (15m)
6:00 p.m. (M,T,W,H,F,Sa) Happy Hollow (15m)
6:15 p.m. (M,T,W,H,F) The Texas Rangers (15m) to CBS

November, 1933
6:45 a.m. (M,W,F) The Ozark Rambler (15m)
6:45 a.m. (T,H,Sa) Tex Owens (15m)
12:00 p.m. (Sa) Tex Owens – The Aladdin Lamplighter (25m)
12:15 p.m. (M,T,W,H,F) Tex Owens – The Aladdin Lamplighter (10m)
12:45 p.m. (T,W,H,F) The Ozark Rambler (15m)
4:45 p.m. (M,T,W,H,F,Sa) The Big Brother Club (15m)
6:00 p.m. (M,T,W,H,F) Happy Hollow (15m)
6:00 p.m. (Sa) Happy Hollow Barn Dance (30m)
6:15 p.m. (M,T,W,H,F) The Texas Rangers (15m) also to CBS
6:30 p.m. (Sa) The Texas Rangers (15m)

December, 1933
6:45 a.m. (M,W,F) The Ozark Rambler (15m)
6:45 a.m. (T,H,Sa) Tex Owens (15m)
9:15 p.m. (M,W,F) Midwesterners Quartet (15m)
12:00 p.m. (Sa) Tex Owens – Aladdin Lamplighter (25m)
12:15 p.m. (M,T,W,H,F) Tex Owens – Aladdin Lamplighter (10m)
12:45 p.m. (T,W,H,F) Ozark Rambler (15m)
5:15 p.m. (M,T,W,H,F,Sa) Big Brother Club (15m)
6:00 p.m. (M,T,W,H,F) Happy Hollow (15m)
6:00 p.m. (Sa) Happy Hollow Barn Dance (30m)
6:15 p.m. (M,T,W,H,F) The Texas Rangers (15m) also to CBS

January, 1934
6:45 a.m. (M,T,W,H,F,Sa) Tex Owens – songs (15m)
12:00 p.m. (Sa) Tex Owens – The Aladdin Lamplighter (25m)
12:15 p.m. (M,T,W,H,F) Tex Owens – The Aladdn lamplighter (15m)
12:45 p.m. (T,W,H,F) The Ozark Rambler (15m)
5:15 p.m. (M,T,W,H,F,Sa) Big Brother Club (15m)
6:00 p.m. (M,T,W,H,F,Sa) Happy Hollow (15m)
6:15 p.m. (M,T,W,H,F) The Texas Rangers (15m) also to CBS

February, 1934
6:45 a.m. (M,T,W,H,F,Sa) Tex Owens – songs (15m)
12:15 p.m. (M,T,W,H,F,Sa) Tex Owens – The Aladdn lamplighter (10m)
12:45 p.m. (T,W,H,F) The Ozark Rambler (15m)
5:15 p.m. (M,T,W,H,F,Sa) Big Brother Club (15m)
6:00 p.m. (M,T,W,H,F) Happy Hollow (15m)
6:15 p.m. (M,T,W,F) The Texas Rangers (15m) also to CBS

Bibliography

The vast majority of this book is based on historical documents located in the Arthur B. Church collections at Iowa State University and the University of Missouri-Kansas City. The other sources noted below were used to supplement the Church material.

Archival Material

Arthur B. Church Papers, 1885-1980, Special Collections Department, Parks Library, Iowa State University.

Arthur B. Church KMBC Radio Collection, LaBudde Special Collections, Miller Nichols Library, University of Missouri-Kansas City.

Gene Autry Archive, Autry National Center.

Jerome Lawrence and Robert E. Lee Theatre Research Institute, The Ohio State University.

Books

Allen, Jules Verne. *Cowboy Lore*. San Antonio, TX: Naylor Co., 1971.

Balk, Alfred. *The Rise of Radio, from Marconi through the Golden Age*. Jefferson, NC: McFarland & Company, Inc., 2006.

Barnouw, Erik. *A Tower in Babel: A History of Broadcasting in the United States* to 1933. NY: Oxford University Press, 1966.

Barnouw, Erik. *The Golden Web: A History of Broadcasting in the United States* 1933-1953. NY: Oxford university Press, 1968.

Berry, Chad. *The Hayloft Gang: The Story of the National Barn Dance*. Urbana, IL: University of Illinois Press, 2008.

Birkby, Robert. *KMA Radio: The First Sixty Years*. Shenandoah, IA: May Broadcasting Company, 1985.

Bronson, Edgar. *Reminiscences of a Ranchman*. Chicago, IL: A. C. McClurg, 1910.

Cox, Jim. *American Radio Networks: A History*. Jefferson, NC: McFarland & Company, Inc. 2009.

-----. *Frank and Anne Hummert's Radio Factory*. Jefferson, NC: McFarland & Company, Inc., 2003.

-----. *Say Goodnight, Gracie: The Last Years of Network Radio.* Jefferson, NC: McFarland & Company, Inc., 2002.

-----. *Sold on Radio: Advertisers in the Golden Age of Broadcasting.* Jefferson, NC: McFarland & Company, Inc., 2008.

Cusic, Don. *The Cowboy in Country Music: An Historical Survey with Artist Profiles.* Jefferson, NC: McFarland & Company, Inc., 2011.

Dempsey, John Mark. *The Light Crust Doughboys Are on the Air: Celebrating Seventy Years of Texas Music.* Denton, TX: University of North Texas Press, 2002.

Dunning, John. *On the Air: The Encyclopedia of Old-Time Radio.* New York: Oxford University Press, 1998.

Fox, Stephen R. *The Mirror Makers: A History of American Advertising & Its Creators.* Illini Books, 1997.

George-Warren, Holly. *Public Cowboy No. 1: The Life and Times of Gene Autry.* New York, NY: Oxford University Press, 2007.

Grant, Lee. *Everybody on the Truck! The Story of the Dillards.* Nashville, TN: Eggman Publishing, 1995.

Green, Douglas B. *Singing in the Saddle: The History of the Singing Cowboy.* Nashville, TN: Vanderbilt University Press, 2002.

Hall, Randal L. *Lum & Anber: Rural American and the Golden Age of Radio.* Lexington, KY: The University Press of Kentucky, 2007.

Hawes, William. *Live Television Drama, 1946-1951.* Jefferson, NC: McFarland & Co., 2001.

Hester, Charley. *The True Life Wild West Memoir of a Bush-Popping Cow Waddy.* Lincoln, NE: University of Nebraska Press, 2004.

Hollis, Tim. *Ain't That a Knee Slapper: Rural Comedy in the Twentieth Century.* Jackson, MS: The University Press of Mississippi, 2008.

Hollywood Reporter, The. *Production Encyclopedia 1952.*

Jaker, Bill, Frank Sulek, & Peter Kanze. *The Airwaves of New York: Illustrated Histories of 156 AM Stations in the Metropolitan Area, 1921-1996.* Jefferson, NC: McFarland & Company, Inc., 1998.

Keegan, John. *The Second World War.* New York, NY: Penguin Books, 1989.

Lewis, Tom. *Empire of the Air: The Men Who Made Radio.* New York, NY: HarperCollins, 1991.

Loy, R. Philip. *Westerns and American Culture, 1930 – 1955.* Jefferson, NC: McFarland & Company, Inc., 2001.

Malone, Bill C. & Jocelyn R. Neal. *Country Music, U.S.A. 3rd Edition.* Austin, TX: University of Texas Press, 2010.

McNeil, W. K. (Ed.) *Encyclopedia of American Gospel Music.* New York, NY: Routledge, 2005.

Millard, Andre. *America on Record: A History of Recorded Sound, 2nd Edition.* New York, NY: Cambridge University Press, 2005.

Moore, Barbara, Marvin R. Bensman, & Jim Van Dyke. *Prime-Time Television: A Concise History.* Westport, CT: Praeger, 2006.

Rogers, Roy & Dale Evans with Jane and Michael Stern. *Happy Trails: Our Life Story.* New York, NY: Simon & Schuster, 1994.

Ruppli, Michel. *The Decca Labels: A Discography, Volume 2: The Eastern & Southern Sessions, 1934 – 1942.* Westport, CT: Greenwood Press, 1996.

Siringo, Charles A. *A Texas Cowboy: or, Fifteen Years on the Hurricane Deck of a Spanish Pony.* Lincoln, NE: University of Nebraska Press, 2966.

Smith, Packy & Ed Hulse. *Don Miller's Hollywood Corral: A Comprehensive B-Western Roundup.* Burbank, CA: Riverwood Press, 1993.

Stanfield, Peter. *Horse Opera: The Strange History of the 1930s Singing Cowboy.* Urbana, IL: University of Illinois Press, 2002.

Stumpf, Charles & Tom Price. *Heavenly Days: The Story of Fibber McGee and Molly.* Waynesville, NC: The World of Yesterday, 1987.

Watson, Mary Ann. *Defining Visions: Television and the American Experience Since 1945.* New York, NY: Harcourt Brace College Publishers, 1998.

Wolff, Kurt. *Country Music: The Rough Guide.* London: Rough Guides, 2000.

Young, William H. & Nancy K. Young. *Music of the World War II Era.* Westport, CT: Greenwood Press, 2008.

Articles

Maxwell, Jim. "Amateur Radio: 100 Years of Discovery." *QST* (January, 2000).

Newspapers

Chicago Tribune
Kansas City Journal-Post
Kansas City Star
Kansas City Times
Los Angeles Times
New York Times
Ocala Star Banner

Magazines

Billboard
The Film Daily
KMBC Heartbeats
The Screenwriter
Stand By!
Variety

Websites

www.b-westerns.com
www.hialaddin.com/aladdin-history.html
www.hillbilly-music.com
www.imdb.com
www.mokangoodwill.org
www.otrr.org
www.worldcat.org

Personal Correspondence

Church, Jr., Arthur
Cool, Gomer
Crawford, Jim
Crawford, Bob
Kratoska, Herbie (interview conducted by Glenn White)
Lorentz, Bill (interview conducted by Glenn White)
Waters, Melody

Other Sources

Coffey, Kevin. Liner notes, *The Texas Rangers, Vol. 1: The Early Years. British Archive of Country Music*, Kent, UK: British Archive of Country Music, 2009.

About the Authors

Ryan Ellett is a school teacher with his M.S. and Ph.D. from the University of Kansas. He is the recipient of the 2008 award for Outstanding Contributions to the Preservation of Old Time Radio and author of over thirty articles on radio history. Ellett's first book was *Encyclopedia of Black Radio in the United States, 1921-1955* (McFarland, 2012). He lives near Lawrence, KS.

Kevin Coffey has been documenting American Roots music for almost a quarter of a century, with a particular emphasis on western swing. Along with Cary Ginell, he is the author of *Discography of Western Swing & Hot String Bands, 1928-1942* (Greenwood Press, 2001). He has written numerous articles, compiled and/or annotatedmany reissues of historical recording. His work has been cited by the Association for Recorded Sound Collections. He was born and reared in Texas and lives in the Orkney Islands in Scotland.

As new information about the Texas Rangers is uncovered, the authors will make these discoveries available on Ryan Ellett's website www.ryanellett.com.

Index

10-2-4 Ranch 148-154
20th Century Fox 99
8MK 6
8ZZ 6
9AVK 5
9AXJ 5
9MK
9WU 2
9XM 6
9YO 2, 5
9ZH 6
A Day at Circle G 112-114, 122, 125-136, 133, 137, 138, 141
A Day at Circle J, see *A Day at Circle G*
A Song is Born 77
A.B.C. Productions 162, 176, 177, 182-183, 185, 192, 222, 224-225, 238, 242, 243
A. H. Grebe & Co. 5
Ace, Goodman 13
Across the Breakfast Table 122
Addams, Jane 20
Adult Educational Round Table 84
Adventures in Adversity 71
Adventures of Dari Dan 63
A-G Musical Grocers 33
Air Adventures of Jimmy Allen 45
Al Clauser and his Oklahoma Outlaws 181
Al Pearce and His Gang 104
Al Pearce Show, The 104, 160
Al Wager Theatrical Agency 200
Aladdin Hotel 9
Aladdin Lamps 21, 79
Allan, Fleming 217
All-Canada Radio Facilities 184
Allen, Fred 61
Allen, Gracie 19, 49, 61
Allen, Jules Verne v, viii
Allen, Rosalie 156
Allison, Chick 69
Allred, James 80, 81
All-Star Western Theatre 223
Amateur Radio Relay League 1
American Broadcasting Company 219-220
American Federation of Musicians 113, 135-136, 145, 193, 216, 222, 228, 246

American Guild of Variety Artists 200, 222
American Museum of Natural History 21
American Society of Composers, Authors and Publishers (ASCAP) 135, 136, 142, 182, 183
American Tribute to Music 110
Amos 'n' Andy 11, 12, 45, 55, 61, 139
Anderson, Andy 190
Andy Devine Show 229
Andy Parker & the Plainsmen 202-203, 205
Aristos Flour 33
Arkansas Swing, The 207
Arkansas Woodchopper, see Ossenbrink, Luther
Armchair Jaunts 17
Armstrong, Edwin 4
Artists Bureau, Inc., The 90
AT&T 7
Atchson-Topeka-Sante Fe Railway 185
Atlas, Les 217
Atwater Kent Hour, The 12
Autry, Gene vii, 35, 36, 60, 83, 87-94, 101-102, 105, 107-111, 120, 178, 187, 196, 198, 215, 227, 247, 249, 250
Baker, Bob 97
Balk, Alfred 1
Bandstand 194
Barrett, Curt 22
Barrett, Jerry (see Barrett, Curt)
Barth, Ruth 47
Basore Longmoor Studio 243-245
Batcher, Ralph 3
BC Remedy Powder 240
Benny, Jack 11, 61, 102, 120, 139, 247
Benton & Bowles 148-154
Berdahl, Archie 159, 171-172, 247; pre-KMBC years 159-160
Berg, Albie 178
Bergen, Edgar 61, 247
Bernie, Ben 19
Between the Bookends 17, 33
Beverly Hill Billies viii, 21, 35, 88
Beverly Hillbillies, The 49
Bibletone 216-217
Big Brother Club, The 21, 25, 31, 32
Big Town 197

Bingham, Harry 69
Blackett, Sample, Hummert 68-69
Blondie 120
Blue Monday Jamboree 104
BMI 135, 136, 142
Bobby Benson and the H-Bar-O Rangers 39
Bobby Kuhn Orchestra 178
Bond, Johnny 111
Box 13 237
Box K Ranch Boys 61-64, 239
Boyd, Bill 241
Boyland, Johnny 97
Bozo the Clown 229
Bradley, Joe "Curly" 53
Braun, Robert 113-114, 116
Breakfast Serenade 62
Briggs, J. A. 122, 145, 153
British Archive of Country Music 43
Britt, Elton 156
Bronson, Edgar vi
Brophy, Murry 92-93
Brown, Bob 228-229
Brown, Johnny Mack 88, 94-98, 96, 105, 107, 121, 132, 137, 144
Brown, Milton and his Musical Brownies 35, 59
Brunswick Records 35, 42
Brush Creek Follies 66-67, 79, 190, 194, 231, 235
Buckler, Betty 148
Buffalo Bill Cody's Wild West show v
Buffalo Bill v
Burkhart Brewing Co. 189
Burnette, Smiley 91, 93, 196, 203, 210-211, 215
Burns & Allen Show, The 49
Burns, George 19, 49, 61
Butcher, Blayne 125, 126
C. P. MacGregor Service 45, 188
Cabot, Bruce 92
California State Fair 114, 120, 126, 145, 148
Calloway, Cab 19
Camel Caravan 160, 162-166, 196
Camel cigarettes 104, 105, 111
Camp Chaffee 186
Camp Dodge, Iowa 5
Camp Meade, Maryland 5
Camp Meeting Quartet 187, 188
Canfield, Homer 228-229
Canova, Judy 121, 137
Cantor, Eddie 11, 19

Captain Jack and His Jolly Crew 57
Captain Midnight 161
Carey Salt Co. 188
Carrolls, Earl 100-101, 102, 107, 120
Carson, Ken "Shorty" 53
Carter's Birthday Party 21
Casablanca 50
Case, Cicely Ida 4
Cass County Boys 199
CBS Artists Bureau 92, 98
Cecil and Sally 45
Central Radio Company 6
Central Radio School 5, 6
CFAC 184, 190
CFJC 184, 190
CFQC 184, 190
CHAB 184, 190
Chandu the Magician 19, 45
Chautauqua circuit 14
Cheshire, Pappy 237-239
Chip of the Flying U 97, 105
Chuck Wagon Jamboree 238
Church, Arthur viii, 35, 42, 46, 55-56, 81, 89, 95, 98-99, 173, 215, 216, 225-226, 232-234, 247; copyright infringements 59, 193, 240-241; early years 2-3; in World War I 4-5; negotiations 65, 90, 105, 110, 125-126, 134-135, 141-142, 146-147, 149-150, 204; on the air 6-7; radio sales 5; sale of KMBC 246; radio training 5
Church, Charles F. 2
CJAT 184, 190
CJCA 184, 190
CJGX 184, 190
CJOC 184, 190
CKBI 184, 190
CKCK 184, 190
CKOV 184, 190
CKRC 190
Clark, Colbert, 204
Clayton, Bob and Maxine 178
Coast Records 203
Cocktail Hour 63
Colorado Pete 67
Colorado Sunset 90-92, 94, 95, 105
Columbia Broadcasting System 9, 11, 20, 34, 68, 94-95, 127, 135, 225
Columbia Management, Inc. 112, 113, 114, 120
Columbia Pacific Network 128

Columbia Phonograph Association 9
Columbia Phonograph Broadcasting System, Inc. 9
Columbia Records 44, 136, 174
Columbia Studios 200
Continental Record Company 193
Cook Paint and Varnish Co. 246
Cool, Gomer ix, 17, 32, 69-70, 168-169, 170-171, 173, 247, 250; on Happy Hollow 13; pre-KMBC years 29; writing 28, 33, 40, 45, 46, 51, 55, 66, 68, 70-71, 76, 89, 96-97, 112, 116, 126, 138, 202, 225, 227
Cooley, Spade 187, 227, 248, 249
Cool's Candies 248
Corn Flakes 147
Corn Kix 69
Correll, Charles 45
Cotner, Carl 108
Cotton, Carolina 223
Country Song Round-Up 241
Courage of the North 49
Cowboy Lore v
Cowboy Ramblers 241
Cowen, Will 211
Cox, James M. 6
Cox, Jim 12
Coy, Jimmy 74
Cracker Jacks 160
Craig, Paul 28
Crawford, Bob ix, 71, 74, 101, 103-104, 157, 185-187, 239, 248; member of the Midwesterners 26, 28
Crazy Water Hotel 48
CRKC 184
Crocker, Alvin 56
Cronenbold, Edward ix, 27, 103, 174, 234-236, 249; member of the Midwesterners 28, 236; drinking problem 167, 234-235
Crookes, William 1
Crosby, Lou 112-113, 126, 201, 210-211
Curtis, Ken 238
Davy Crockett ix
De Forest, Lee 4, 5
Deadey Dick v
Dean, Eddie 204
Death Valley Days 39
Decca Records 24, 42-44, 52, 53, 153
Delta Rhythm Boys 232
Devine, Andy 229

Dodge's Institute of Wireless 2, 3,
Dole Pineapple 104
Donnelly, Phil M. 246
Dr. Pepper 148, 164-165
Dr. Ross Dog Food 226
Dream Boat 17
Dunbar, Ralph 24
Dunning, John 127, 197
Durango Kid 203
Eason, Bill 91
Eb and Zeb 104-105, 107, 111, 119-120
Eddie Cantor Show, The 12
Eddy, Nelson 19
Edison Manufacturing Company vii
Edwards, Eddie 13, 16, 18, 50, 67, 131, 249
Eggleston, Stu 76
Ellis, Caroline Crockett 70
Enslow, Claude 244
Erwin, Wasey & Co. 134
Escape 197
Eskimo Flour 189
Fairbanks, Jerry 217, 221, 227
Fanchon & Marco vaudeville act 16
Farm Crop Insurance 70-71
Farr, Hugh 36
Farr, Karl 36
Ferguson, George 90, 92
Fessenden, Reginald 1
Fibber McGee & Molly 49, 61, 89, 110, 227, 247
Fighting Fury 144
Filming of the West, The vii
Fisher, Shug 223
Fleischmann's Yeast Hour 12
Flying Horse Ranch, The, see *Life on the Red Horse Ranch*
Foley, Red 50
Fonville, Marion 18, 24, 32, 34, 44, 50, 54, 74, 249; early years 24-25
Fonville, W. D. 24
Foran, Dick 87, 153
Fort Laramie 220
Fort Leavenworth, Kansas 4, 185
Forward, Bob 229
Foust, Chester 122, 160-162, 164
Fox, J. Leslie 183
Frederic Ziv Company 238
Free & Peters, Inc. 241
Frontier Gentleman 220
Gateway to Hollywood 108

Gayle, Leta 94, 95
Gene Autry's Melody Ranch Radio Show 108-111, 112, 115, 137, 147
General Artists Corporation 241
General Electric 4, 7, 208
Gentlemen With Guns 224
George-Warren, Holly 107
Gershwin, George 77
Gosden, Freeman 45
Graceland College 2, 4, 5, 28
Grahm, Kenneth 114, 153
Grande Ole Opry vii, 59, 66
Great Gildersleeve, The 110, 232
Great Train Robbery vii
Green Acres 49
Green, Douglas v, vii, ix
Green, Johnny 76
Griffis, Ken 26
Grove Laboratories 189
Gunfighter, The 87
Gunn, Buckingham 147
Gunsmoke 220
Hager, Clyde 178
Hale, Monty 211, 223
Hall Johnson Choir 120
Hall, Bill 178
Hall, Randal 13
Halley, George 45, 46, 121, 242-244
Halloway, Ruth 94, 95
Hamilburg, Mitchell J. 195-197, 199-200, 211-212, 223, 228
Hamlin's Red Cross Drug Store 189
Happy Hollow 13, 16, 17, 21, 26, 29, 31, 39, 52
Happy Hollow Barber Shop Quartet 28, 29
Happy Hollow Barn Dance 31
Happy Hollow Bugle, The 15, 17
Happy Hollow Hoodlums 52
Harding, Warren G. 6
Harmon, Michael 178
Harpster, Kenny 163, 174, 249
Harry Fox Agency 195
Hartman, Clarence ix, 29, 57, 71, 90, 103, 112, 113, 174-175, 178-179, 187, 249; background 48
Haskins, Jenny 67
Hawk Durango 197
Hawk Larabee 197-198, 201-203, 205
Hawkeye Bulletin 3
Hayloft Hoedown 209

Hays, Carl 27, 29, 48, 249
Helping Hand Farm 71
Helping Hand Institute 71
Helping Hand of Goodwill Industries, The 71
Henning, Paul 33, 49, 89, 91
Henry H. Lohrey Packing Company 189
Hertz, Heinrich 1
Hester, Charley vi
Heyser, Fran 34, 54, 192
High Noon 87
Higsby, Hiram 67, 235
Hill, Billy 30
Hill, Rich 128
Hits from Hollywood 62
Hoffman Radio 227
Hollywood Showcase 160
Hoosier Hotshots 195, 196, 200, 204, 207
Hopalong Cassidy 203
Hope, Bob 247
Horlick's Malted Milk 134, 138
Hudgens, Ray 190, 240, 249
Hudson, Hal 217, 221-222, 226, 228, 229
Hummert, Anne 69
Hummert, Frank 69
Hunt's Tomato Sauce 127
Hutton, Darlene 178
Hy-Power Chili and Meatballs 240
I Was There 126, 127
In Old Santa Fe 87
Iowa State College of Agricultural and Mechanic Arts, see Iowa State University
Iowa State University 3, 4, 40
Iturbi, Jose 215
Ivanhoe Temple (Kansas City) 67
J. Stirling Getchell, Inc. 47, 51
J. Walter Thompson company 107, 108, 110, 122, 142, 145
Jack Armstrong 61, 69, 161
Jack Teagarden Orchestra 160
Jackson County Stump Jumpers 67
Jackson, Ginny 227, 232
Jean Sablon Sings 194
Jenks, Harry 194, 244
Jessel, George 160
Jimmy Wakely Trio 110
Jimmy Wakely's Rough Riders 132
Joanne Taylor Show, The 70
Joanne Taylor's Fashion Flashes 70
Johnson, Bea 70

Johnson, Eddie 188, 239, 249
Johnson, Russ 114, 126, 141
Jolson, Al 11
Jones, Buck 87, 88
Jones, Jane 232
Jordan, Jim 61
Julian Kohange Company 52
Just Plain Bill 69
KABN 53
KADA 209
Kaltenborn, H. V. 61
Kansas City Star 6, 7, 241
Kansas City Symphony 48
Kapp, Jack 42
KARK 182, 189
KARM 190, 209
KBIX 190
KDAL 177
KDFN 53
KDKA 6, 184, 189
KDYL 190
KECA 21
Kellogg Company 62, 114, 121-122, 137, 139, 142-148, 155-156, 161-162, 164-165, 189, 239
Kemp, Arthur 138, 142
Kemp, Everett 13
Kenny Baker Program, The 189
KFBB 53
KFH 34, 53
KFI 21
KFIX 6
KFOR 53
KFPY 184
KFRC 25, 104
KFRU 53
KFVS 209
KFWB viii, 21, 100, 201, 234
KFXJ 53, 182, 183
KGAR 215
KGCX 53
KGFX 53
KGHF 190
KGIR 53
KGIW 53
KGKY 53
KGNC 209
KGNO 53
KGU 189, 190

KHJ viii, 20
KHMO 209
Kid Brother 45
KIDW 53
Kings Men, The 223
KIUL 215
KLDS 7, 9
KLPM 53
KLRA 189
KLZ 53
KMBC Artists Bureau 25
KMBC Orchestra 26
KMBC viii, 5, 6, 32, 44, 50-51, 64, 94, 135, 184, 187, 190; CBS affiliate 9, 21, 35; originating broadcasts 12-13, 15
KMMJ 53
KMOX 53, 189, 190, 237
KMPC
Knight, Fuzzy 97
KNX 21, 102, 109, 114, 126, 130, 141, 177, 184, 217
Koeper, Karl 94, 148, 163
KOIN 184, 190
KOMO 184
KPHO 209
KPO 25
KPOR 210
KPRO 209
KQV 190
Krahl, Kenneth 5
Kratoska, Herb ix, 17, 22, 27, 33, 34, 57, 71, 101, 103, 115, 117, 119, 222, 249, 251; pre-KMBC years 30
KREO 210
KRLD 184
KROP 210
KSFO 177
KSL 184
KSOO 25
KSTP 190, 242
KTAB 25
KTLA 226, 227, 228
KTM 21
KTTV 221-230, 234
KTUC 209
KTUL 190, 210
KUBC 210
KVOD 183
KWKH 184

KWTO 190
KWYO 53
KXBY 62
KYW 184
Labor Union issues 66, 90, 93-94, 99, 135-136
Lackawanna Railroad 3
Ladd, Alan 237
Lake, Arthur 120
Lamoni Gin-Seal Gardens 2
Lamp Post Four 29
Lane, Wade 74
Larson, Larry 62
Last Roundup, The 198-200, 207, 215
Law of the Range 144
Lawrence, Jerome 96-97
Leavy, Ike 242
Lee, Bobby 246
Lee, Don 217
Leichter, Sam 17, 20, 24, 170-171, 178, 179, 187, 249
Lennen & Mitchell 126-128, 131
Leo Burnett Company 242
Levitch, Sula 193
Lewis, Elliott 197
Liberty Theatre (Oklahoma City) 34
Life on the Red Horse Ranch 16, 24, 39, 43, 44, 46-58, 66, 69, 74, 76, 79, 87, 131, 134, 135, 13, 182-184; broadcast stations 53; cast 47, 48, 49; sequel 55-56
Light Crust Doughboys 35, 88
Little Orphan Annie 19, 61, 161
Lomax, John vi
Lombardo, Guy 19
Lone Ranger 39
Lone Wolf Tribe 39
Lopez, Vincent 7, 19
Lorentz, William 222, 240, 249, 251
Los Angeles Colisum 120
Louis Snader Telescriptions 242
Louise Massey & the Westerners 14
Louisiana Coffee 238
Lubrite 47, 51
Lucky Corner 235
Lulling's City Laundry and Dry Cleaners 59
Lum & Abner 13, 61, 104, 112
M. L. Tours, Inc. 162
Ma Perkins 61, 69
Mabie, Milt 14, 18, 25, 250
MacKaye, Frederick 7

Madison Ensemble 20
Magazine of the Air 21
Magic Key of RCA 83
Mahaney, Dorothy 155
Mahaney, Fran ix, 50, 99, 103, 187, 188, 234, 236, 250; departs 155, 159; Perry Sargeant audition 76-77
Mahaney, Melissa Anne, 99
Maizlish, Harry 201
Make Mine Music 224
Malone, Ted 13, 17, 29, 33, 44, 59
Malt-O-Meal 57
Manning, Joe 188, 250, 251
Marcell, Lou 50, 91
Marconi, Guglielmo 1, 4
Marvin, Dick 111
Marvin, Frankie 101, 108
Marvin, Johnny 101-102, 110
Marx, Groucho 110
Massey Family viii, 26, 250; join KMBC 14; on *Happy Hollow* 14
Massey, Allen 14, 15, 18, 25, 26, 250
Massey, Curt 14, 18, 250
Massey, Louise 14, 250
Massey, Velma 22
Masters, Charlie 178
Maxwell, Marilyn 168
May, Rod ix, 98-99, 103, 172-173, 174, 187, 234-236, 250; member of the Midwesterners 28, 236
Mayfair Transcription Company 237-239
Maynard, Ken 87, 215
McCarthy, Charlie 61, 247
McCarty Girls, The 22
McCrea, Joel 240
McCune, Vance 25
McGinty, Billy viii
McGuillin, R. E. 4
McMahon Furniture Stores 226
Mears, Martha 112-113, 125, 128, 135, 139, 149, 153, 210-211
Memorial Hall (Kansas City) 67
Merriman, Dana 143
MGM Records 44, 217, 246
MGM Studios 99
Michigan Radio Network 128, 132
Midland Broadcasting Company viii, 47, 50, 121, 125, 128, 131, 142; incorporation 7, 9

Midwesterners (quartet) 17, 22, 23, 26, 29, 30, 54
Mignon Wireless Corporation 3
Miller Theatre (Wichita, KS) 34
Missouri Military Academy 24
Mitchell Hamilburg Agency 195-196
Mix, Tom 26, 32, 87, 161, 215
MJB Coffee 33
Mobil Oil 127
Moler, Ray 5
Montag Stove Company 238
Montgomery Wards 70
Moore, Gene 181
Mr. Keen, Tracer of Lost Persons 69
Mrs. Wagner's Pies 53
Municipal Auditorium (Kansas City) 67
Murrow, Edward R. 61
Music Corporation of America (MCA) 145
Music in the Air 62
Musical Clock 62, 84
Musical Masseys 14, 15
Musical Revue 20
Mystery Mountain 87
N. W. Ayer & Son 62
National Association of Broadcasters 95
National Barn Dance vii, 35, 59, 66, 190, 196, 198
National Broadcasting Company (NBC) 7, 11, 61, 135, 240-241
National Register of Historic Places 9
Nebraska Wesleyan University 5
Needham, Louis & Brorby 227
Negime, Job 67
Nelson, Adele 21
New York Symphony 7
New York World's Fair (1939) 208
News of the Churches 62
Night Time on the Trail 44, 46, 56, 70, 74-76, 190, 191, 192, 194; audience feedback 75
Nolan, Bob 31, 217, 229
Novelty Aces 238
Oakley, Arthur 28
Office of War Information 185
Okeh Records 178
Oklahoma Frontier 95, 97, 105
Old Corral 237, 238
Old Gold Cigarettes 121, 125, 128, 130-133
Olympic Preview 83
One Man's Family 110
Ossenbrink, Luther viii, 14

Otto Gray's Oklahoma Cowboys viii
Owens, Laura Lee 22, 101, 115, 119, 178
Owens, Tex 43, 54, 250; 1938 tour 78-79; conflicts with Texas Rangers 21-22, 79-81; early years 22; solo broadcasts 21, 31; solo career 67, 77-79, 80; Texas Rangers member 16, 18, 19, 26, 27
P. Lorillard Company 125-128, 131
Painter, Emert 188, 240, 250
Painter, Ted 222, 239, 240, 250
Paley, William S. 9, 204
Palm Dairies, Ltd. 184
Pantomime Quiz 226
Paramount Studios 99
Parker, Jean 92
Partington, Jack 104, 120
Paul H. Raymer Company 183-184
Paul, Les 174, 251
Pearce, Al 104, 105, 111
Pearl, Jack 19
Pearson, Texas Ranger 240
Perdee, William 5
Perry Sargeant (men's clothing store) 76
Petticoat Junction 49
Phantom Empire 87
Phenomenon 17, 49, 76, 135, 243
Phillips, Al "Slim" 181, 182
Pierce, Sam 129-130
Pinto Pete & His Ranch Boys 74
Plainsmen, The 36
Pla-Mor Ballroom 30
Pla-Mor Orchestra 26, 30
Plantation Grill Orchestra 20
Pomona County Fair 114
Popular Science 221
Porgy & Bess 77, 215
Possum, Polly 174
Post Chapel Quartet 187
Post Toasties 152
Praeger, Bert 148
Prairie Pioneers 67, 178-180
Prairie Ramblers 35
Preston, John (film actor) 49
Preston, John 47, 49-50, 54
Preview Theatre of the Air 201
Purity Bakeries' Grennan Cakes 182, 188, 240
R. J. Reynolds 105, 120, 162
Radio Act of 1912 1, 4
Radio City Music Hall 193

Radio Corporation of America (RCA) 7, 208
Radio Writers Guild 248
Ragtime Cowboy Joe 121
Ranch Boys, The viii, 35, 53, 74
Randolph, Lillian 232
Rardin, Joe 178
Rawhide Rangers 144
RCA Victor 241
RCA/NBC Thesaurus Library 45
Reagan, Phil 92
Real Folks of Thompkins Corners, The 13
Red River Dave McEnery 193
Redman, Don 19
Redpath Lyceum Bureau 14
Refrig-O-Master 182
Reichenbach, Bob 237
Reorganized Church of Jesus Christ of Latter Day Saints 4, 5, 7, 9, 28
Republic Studios 89, 93, 94, 200, 211, 223
Revere, Tom 148
Rex Cole Mountaineers 35
Rhythm Riders 190, 240
Rhythmaires 20
Rice Krispies 147
Rickenbacker, Paul 108
Rickerson, Karel 47
Rico Ice Cream Co. 189
Riders of the Purple Sage, The 36, 211
Riley Coffee Co. 238
Rise of the Goldbergs 12
Ritter, Tex 87, 215
Robbins, Marty ix
Robinson, Bill 120
Robinson, Hubbell 210, 225
Robison, Carson vii, 35
Robson, William N. 197, 202
Rockett Pictures 227
Rodgers, Jimmie 88
Rogers, Roy ix, 87, 203, 215, 223
Rogers, Will 7, 108
Romance of Helen Trent, The 61, 69
Rooney, Mickey 120
Rose Bowl (1949) 223
Rose, Billy 59
Ross, Jack viii, 53
Ross, Ted 187
Roy, Manny 67
Royal, Ruth 22
Rylee, Andrew Jackson 49

Salvation Army Benefit program 102
Sameth, Joe 148-149
Santa Fe Railroad 226
Santa Fe Slim 67
Satherley, Art 35
Scatterbrain 121, 137
Schaeffer, Mandy 200
Scott, Fred 87
Screen Actors Guild 93, 222
Sea Island Sugar Cane 127
Sears-Roebuck 182, 189
Sells, Paul ix, 27, 33, 90, 95, 103, 109, 114, 115-116, 249, 250; departs KMBC 117-119, 121; post-KMBC years 121, 188; pre-KMBC years 29-30
Shadow, The 61
Shane 87
Shields, Fred 97
Si and Elmer 21
Sigmund Rombert Orchestra 215
Silver King 33
Singer, Harry 100, 109-109, 111-112
Singleton, Penny 120
Siringo, Charles v
Six Shooter, The 220
Sixth Annual Police Show 120
Skelton, Red 61
Smilin' Valley Dude Ranch 62, 66, 68-70, 76; audition scripts 71-72; interest by Blackett, Sample, Hummert 68-69
Smith & Drum Agency 183
Smith, Frederick M. 5
Smith, Glad 67
Smith, Howard 190
Smith, Woody, 76, 143
Socony-Vacuum Oil Company 47, 51, 182
Somerville, Bob 125
Son of Roaring Dan 121
Song of Idaho 205
Songsmiths 20, 22
Sons of the Pioneers viii, ix, 31, 36, 42, 53, 59, 88, 153, 215, 217, 229, 237
Sons of the Range 178
Southwesterners 248
Speaking of Animals 221
Spellacy, Denny 232
Spencer, Tim 31, 217
Spitalny, Phil 50
Spokane Indians 232

Standard Milling Company 182
Standard Radio Library 45, 160
Standard Theatres Corporation 33
Stanfield, Peter vi
Starrett, Charles 88
Steve Donovan - Texas Ranger 241
Steve Donovan, Western Marshall 241
Stevens, Bob 187
Stewart, Jimmy 168
Strand, Joe 130, 171, 174-175, 176, 250
Strand, Manny 130
Strollin' Tom 74
Strucik, Jack 67
Stuart Hamblin's Covered Wagon Jubilee 53
Studebaker, Hugh 13, 16-17, 19-20
Sula's Texas Rangers 193
Sullivan, Don 187, 188, 250-251
Sunshine Boys 204
Sunshine Girls 205
Suspense 139, 197
Sutton, Ellen 178
Swalley, Duane ix, 251; member of the Midwesterners 28; post-KMBC work 50
Swayze, John Cameron 25
Swiss Yodelers 20
Tales of the Texas Rangers 220, 240-241
Talmadge, Norma 160
Tarzan 45
Tatham, Val 190, 240
Taystee Bread 189, 240
Tennessee Ramblers 88
Terrace Café Orchestra 20
Tesla, Nicola 1
Tex Williams Show 228
Texas Cowboy v
Texas Outlaws 21
Texas Rangers, audience ratings 62, 63, 83-84, 161, 162; classic line-up ix, 28 61-62; early drama broadcasts 39-42; formation 15; honorary members of the Texas Rangers law enforcement 79, 81-83, *82*; impact of World War II 154-155; live performances 33-34, 58-59, 200-201, 213-219, 231; original lineup 15-18; radio debut viii, 18, 19; recording library 44, 52, 136-138, 165-166; recording sessions 42-44, 52, 143-144, 153-154, 181-182, 192, 194-195; relocation to California 87-89, 91; television 209, 217, 219-224; television film shorts 227-228,
242-245; transcriptions 45-46, 58; War years break up 177-178, 181-182; tape 245-246
Thirty Minutes in Hollywood 160
This Way Please 89
Thomas, Norman 63
Thorpe, Jack vi
Three Debs, The 178
Thunder in the West 138
Timber Terrors 49
Tin Pan Alley vi, 36
Tomlinson, Tommy 126, 130, 138
Tommy Tucker Orchestra 160, 171-172
Town Hall Party 193
Trail Blazers 84-85, 89
Travels of Mary Ward, The 70
Tudor, Eddie 108
Tune Chasers 222, 244
Tuska, Jon vii
Twilight on the Trail 74
U.S. Navy 4
U.S. Signal Corp. 4, 5
Under Western Skies 94-100, 107, 224
Union Oil 95
United Independent Broadcasters Association 9
Universal Pictures 95, 97, 132, 144, 160
Universal Radio Manufacturing Company 3
Universal-International 211
University of Missouri 24
Unusual Occupations 221
Vallee, Rudy 12
Valley Amusement Company 193
Vanda, Charles 94-95
Variety 13, 34, 53, 59, 96, 107, 134
Vic and Sade 19
Village Barn 209
W.B. Rodgers Advertising Agency 183
W2XAB 208
W6XAO 217
W9XAL 21
WABI 210
WADC 184, 190
Wade Advertising Agency 193
Wagner, Martin 215-216
Wakely, Jimmy 111
WAKR 190
Walter Brewing Company 183, 189
WAOV 190
Waring, Fred 215
WARM 242

Waters, Melody 16
Waters, Ozie 13, 16, 20, 31, 31, 203, 251; Texas Rangers member 18, 27, 79
WBAP 248
WBEN 184
WBOC 209
WBOW 53
WBRE 242
WCCO 53, 184
WCSC 190
WDAF viii, 6, 7, 9, 62, 63
WDAY 53
WDBJ 184
WDOD 63-66, 177, 209
WDZ 53, 190
Webb, Chick 19
WEBQ 53
WEEI 184
Weir, Bob 198
Wellington, Larry 14, 18, 26
WENR 177
Wenzel, Art 198, 251
Western Echoes 190, 240
Western Electric 4, 45
Western Film Theatre 224
Western Livestock Show (Denver) 194
Westerners, The 14, 26
Westinghouse 4
WFBM 53
WFIN 177
WGBI 177, 190, 209
WGN 53
WHB 6, 62, 240
WHBU 53
White Eagle 47, 51
White, Glenn 17, 26, 27, 246
Whiteman, Paul 215
WHK 51, 53
WHKK 190
WHLD 184
WHO 53
WIBW 14, 53
Wilcox, Harlow 227
Wildroot Toiletries 182, 188
Will, G. F. vi
William B. Wagnon, Jr., & Associates 193
William Morris Agency 163, 175-176, 179
Williams, Tex 187, 229, 249
Wills, Bob 35, 59, 193

Wilson, Woodrow 4
WIRE 210
Wireless Age 5
Wireless Telegraph and Signal Company, Ltd. 1
WIZE 190
WJBL 53
WJDX 184
WJZ 177
WKBH 190
WKVB 53
WLAC 182
WLBC 53
WLOK 190
WLS vii, 14, 26, 35, 50, 87, 190, 251
WMAQ 20
WMBF 189
WMC 184
WNBF 190
WNEX 190
WOAI 161
WOC 53
Wolverton, Joe 174, 251
Woodlawn Dairy 188
WOR 20
Words and Music 21
World Broadcasting Service 45, 52, 76, 137, 154, 182-183
World Transcription Company 43-44, 143
WOW 53
WPE 6
WQAM 190
WREN 62
Wright, Bill 104, 111
Wright, Jane 178
Wright, Will 139
Wrigley Gum 107, 109, 110
Wrigley, Philip K. 107
Writers Guild of America, West 248
WROL 177
WRR 241
WRVA 177
WSM vii, 59
WTAD 53
WTAR 182, 190
WTOP 184
WTRC 210
WWJ 6, 51, 53
WXGI 210
WXYZ 53

Wynn, Ed 19
Yarborough, Barton 197
You Bet Your Life 110
Zephyr Cocktail Lounge (L.A.) 231
Ziv Radio Productions 210, 238
Ziv, Frederick W. 209, 210

www.ingramcontent.com/pod-product-compliance
Lightning Source LLC
Chambersburg PA
CBHW070905170426
43202CB00012B/2195